Dear Reader:  P9-CME-132

The book you are about to read is the latest bestseller from the St. Martin's True Crime Library, the imprint the New York Times calls "the leader in true crime!" Each month, we offer you a fascinating account of the latest, most sensational crime that has captured the national attention. St. Martin's is the publisher of bestselling true crime author and crime journalist Kieran Crowley, who explores the dark, deadly links between a prominent Manhattan surgeon and the disappearance of his wife fifteen years earlier in THE SURGEON'S WIFE. Suzy Spencer's BREAKING POINT guides readers through the tortuous twists and turns in the case of Andrea Yates, the Houston mother who drowned her five young children in the family's bathtub. In Edgar Award-nominated DARK DREAMS, legendary FBI profiler Roy Hazelwood and bestselling crime author Stephen G. Michaud shine light on the inner workings of America's most violent and depraved murderers. In the book you now hold, IN BROAD DAYLIGHT, Harry N. MacLean looks at a crime that shook a small community to its core.

St. Martin's True Crime Library gives you the stories behind the headlines. Our authors take you right to the scene of the crime and into the minds of the most notorious murderers to show you what really makes them tick. St. Martin's True Crime Library paperbacks are better than the most terrifying thriller, because it's all true! The next time you want a crackling good read, make sure it's got the St. Martin's True Crime Library logo on the spine—you'll be up all night!

Charles E. Spicer

Charles E. Spicer, Jr.
Executive Editor, St. Martin's True Crime Library

IN BROAD
DAYLIGHT

Harry N. MacLean

St. Martin's Paperbacks

IN BROAD DAYLIGHT

Copyright © 1988 by Harry N. MacLean.
Epilogue: 2006 copyright © 2006 by Harry N. MacLean.

Cover photo of eyes courtesy Bettmann/Corbis. Cover photo of street courtesy Robert Warren/Getty Images.

ISBN: 0-312-94236-2
EAN: 9780312-94236-6

Printed in the United States of America

Previously published by Harper & Row
Dell edition / February 1990
St. Martin's Paperbacks edition / December 2006

St. Martin's Paperbacks are published by St. Martin's Press, 175 Fifth Avenue, New York, NY 10010.

10 9 8 7 6 5 4 3 2 1

*For
Mom and Dad
and
my sister
Sharon*

ACKNOWLEDGMENTS

Over the years of researching and writing this book, I came to know well many people in the Skidmore community and northwest Missouri. More than a few of them opened their homes and spent hours, in some cases days, sharing their recollections and perceptions of what happened between Ken McElroy and the town of Skidmore. Foremost among those were Q and Margaret Goslee, who farm outside Skidmore. By the time the book was completed, they had become my second family, and their kindness and generosity, as well as that of their sons Kermit and Kirby, provided the environment which allowed me to persevere in my search to understand the course of events described herein.

Kriss Goslee, the youngest son of Q and Margaret, conducted a series of interviews soon after the killing which were used extensively in the preparation of the manuscript. Kriss also provided ongoing research assistance which was extremely valuable.

The contribution of Anne Meadows to the book is immeasurable. Ms. Meadows, a friend and free-lance editor in Washington, D.C., edited the book from an initial rough draft through three versions to its final form. With extraordinary skill and dedication, she reorganized sentences, paragraphs, scenes, and chapters, pushing mercilessly and relentlessly for clarity and simplicity. Her mark is everywhere present. Any awkward sentences remain only over her protest.

I would like to express my profound gratitude to Jules Roth.

Acknowledgments

Without his caring support and his unflagging faith in me, the idea would never have become reality.

The heart of the book was written at the home of Tom Austin and Jean Obert (and son Gabe) in Kealakekua, Hawaii. From the deck of the guest quarters of their home, I looked out over the bay and began putting to paper what I had learned of the killing in Skidmore, Missouri. I relied immensely on their love.

Mike and Pat MacLean, my brother and sister-in-law, and brothers Jim and Jack believed absolutely in the book from the beginning. Their affection and encouragement were a constant source of support.

I am grateful for the generosity of Mary and George Leyland, at whose summer home on Fishers Island, New York, the final pieces of this book fell into place.

Others I would like to thank for their assistance in various ways: Charles Cortese, associate professor of sociology at the University of Denver; Thomas Carneal, associate professor of history, Northwest Missouri State University; Tom Watkins, attorney, St. Joseph; Charles Lepley, chief deputy district attorney, Denver, Colorado; and typists Janet Lange and Laurie Brasel.

Thanks to Glenna Kelly for her invaluable assistance in fine-tuning the final draft.

Lastly, I acknowledge a lasting debt to Lawrence University, where my study of the art of learning continues to shape the course of my life.

SKIDMORE, MISSOURI

1 CHRISTIAN CHURCH   7 BANK
2 PARSONAGE   8 B&B GROCERY
3 SUMY OIL   9 POST OFFICE
4 OIL STATION   10 D&G
5 LEGION BLDG   11 RESTAURANT
6 PARK   X PICKUP

NEBRA

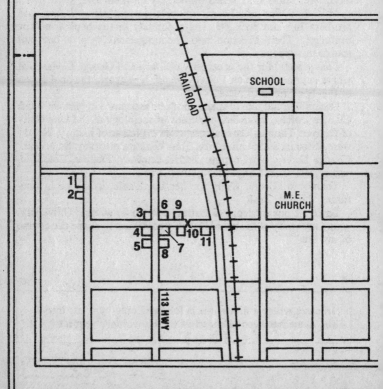

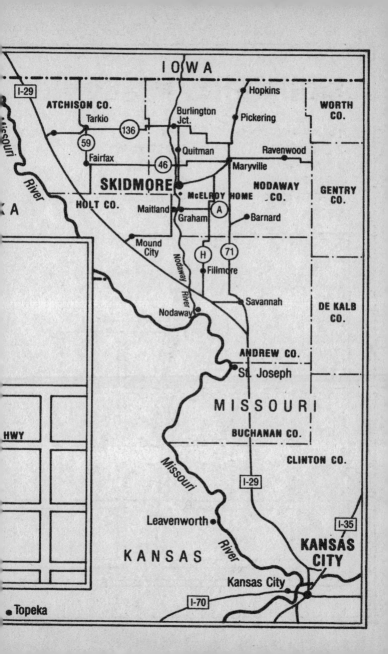

PART
ONE

1

On the morning of July 10, 1981, Cheryl Brown stood by the small window at the rear of her parents' grocery store and looked out at the pickups lining both sides of the main street. All but a few of them she recognized as belonging to farmers or merchants from the surrounding area. Cheryl folded her arms, glanced around the store to locate her parents, and looked back out the window—there wasn't a person in view. It was a strange sight, particularly for midmorning on a Friday, but she understood it; the town had finally been pushed too hard, or perhaps the wrong people had finally been pushed too hard.

Cheryl lived on a farm a few miles west of town with her husband and two children. An attractive woman in her early twenties, Cheryl had curly brown hair, hazel eyes, and an engaging smile. She loved to talk, and spent much of her boundless energy participating in community activities. In the past fifteen months, before her family's problem had become the town's problem, her spirited resiliency had been vital in keeping herself and her family together.

The B & B Grocery sits on Route 113 just as the road completes its climb to the top of the hill from the Nodaway River bottoms. A few yards further on is the main intersection where 113 turns right and proceeds down the hill as Elm Street, the main street of Skidmore. The front of the grocery store faces the American Legion building across 113 and the back looks out across a gravel drive at the side of the D & G Tavern, which is around the corner facing on Elm Street.

The small window at which Cheryl stood was behind the freezer and a few feet from the two large doors opening onto the loading dock. Had she been standing on the loading dock itself, or even looking through the windows in the doors, she would have been easily visible to anyone entering or leaving the tavern across the drive. But even if someone had glanced in the direction of her small window, Cheryl's face would probably have been hidden by the sun's reflected glare. From here she could see most of the street and sidewalk area in front of the tavern.

Since January, when she had begun working at the store, and particularly in the past few months, Cheryl had spent a lot of time at this place by the window. She believed, along with her mother, that if violence were to erupt again at the store, it would come from the back. Last summer her dad, Ernest "Bo" Bowenkamp, had been standing just inside the rear door when he was shot in the neck at close range with 00 buck, shotgun pellets the size of .32 caliber bullets. Bo spent most of his time at the meat counter, which was only a few feet inside the loading-dock doors. The rear of the store, although not blocked from public view, was less visible than the front. If McElroy intended to carry out his most recent threats, he would either hit Bo at home or come in the back of the store, like he had before.

Word usually came to the store by phone when McElroy was in town or when one of his trucks had been spotted in the area. If Cheryl was there, she would bolt the back door, pile 100-pound bags of potatoes on the trapdoor to the cellar and take up her post at the window. She knew all four McElroy trucks by both sight and sound, the way one might know a neighbor's sons. Last summer, after the candy incident in the store, she began to automatically scan every street and alley for the trucks whenever she came to town. If McElroy was in town, he would, sooner or later, pull up and park in front of the tavern. If Trena was with him, as she often was, she would stay out in the truck for however long he was inside, sometimes sitting by herself for hours in the bitter cold or the sweltering heat. If he was alone, Cheryl would scan the streets for the backup—the other McElroy truck—almost always driven by a woman, always with rifles visible in the rear window rack. Cheryl usually found the truck in front of the post office across the street, or on one of the Four Corners, or at the bottom of the hill, with a clear view of the front of the tavern. In either case, she would stay by the window until she saw McElroy leave the tavern, get in his truck, and drive out of town.

This morning, as she stood and looked out the window at the gleaming Silverado parked in front of the tavern, and mentally linked the other pickups with their owners, she understood that everything was finally coming to a head. The nature of the struggle had been irretrievably altered by the events of the past few weeks. The affidavits, the pickups lining the streets, the meeting in the Legion Hall, the absolute stillness of the town itself, all meant to her that the community, however belatedly, was finally responding to the threat that she and her family had faced virtually alone for so many months. Whatever happened, her family's long ordeal, their tormented isolation, would soon be over.

On Friday morning, her parents always delivered groceries for the weekend to some of the elderly residents in town, many of them widows who lived alone. This morning a few calls came in after the run was made, and when Cheryl arrived for work around nine, she had to deliver the new orders in her mother's station wagon. By the time she returned, the street in front of the store had also filled with pickups. A short while later, one of the men at the meeting stuck his head in the door and told them in a low, excited voice that McElroy was in town. The meeting had broken up, he said, and the men were heading toward the tavern to face him.

She bolted the rear door, piled the potato sacks on the cellar door, and took her place by the window. Evelyn Sumy, her parents' neighbor and a clerk at the store who had been entangled in the struggle from the very beginning, stood beside her. After a few seconds Cheryl's gaze shifted from the Silverado to the men walking down the street from the Legion Hall to the tavern. As each man passed by, she spoke his name, as if she was reciting an honor roll of men who finally had the guts to stand up to Ken McElroy. She watched with fascination and apprehension as about forty men disappeared single file into the tavern, holding the screen door for one another.

As the minutes passed, she stayed focused on the Silverado. With its heavy steel running boards, chrome brush guard, red clearance lights and Cattle Country mud flaps, the Silverado was the biggest, the newest, and the fanciest of the McElroy trucks, the one that Ken almost always drove himself. The story was that he had bought it the previous December off the lot of the Chevy dealer in Mound City for $12,000 cash, carried in a paper bag.

Suddenly, the screen door to the tavern opened and McElroy appeared on the sidewalk in front of the tavern. He was wearing dark slacks and a brown tank top, and he was carrying a brown paper sack with what looked like a six-pack of beer in it. His movements were slow and deliberate, as always. Trena followed behind, carrying a small purse, and got in the passenger side of the pickup, closest to Cheryl. The men began pouring out of the tavern a few feet behind them. She noticed one farmer lean up against the front of the tavern with a beer in his hand, and it occurred to her that it was illegal to take a glass of beer out of the tavern. Others stood on the sidewalk out of her field of vision.

When she heard the first shot ring out, she was confused, wondering who was shooting at whom, and from where. Then she saw the glass splattering in the air in front of the pickup and McElroy's head fall forward on his chest. Trena turned away and threw open the passenger door and dived out onto the street. By then the men were hitting the ground, crouching between the pickups and scattering up the street to the top of the hill. Royce Clement jumped clear over the hood of a pickup.

She saw Jack Clement, Royce's father and the cowboy patriarch of the Clement family, rush over and pick up Trena, who had blood and dirt on her arms and shirt, and hustle her up the walk toward the bank, out of the line of fire. The gentleman in the cowboy made him do that, she thought later.

As the shooting continued, in bursts of two and three shots, Cheryl rushed to the telephone in the front of the store to call her baby sitter, who lived in town. More shots rang out as she explained to the baby sitter that it wasn't safe to bring the children to the store. The front door opened and a man stepped halfway in.

"It's over now," he said. "You people can sleep tonight. Just stand behind us."

The relief hit Cheryl like a blast, then flooded slowly through her body. The constant harassment, the fear for her father and her children's lives, all of it was finally over. She grabbed onto a shelf to steady herself as the tears came to her eyes. Her dad—tall, gangly Bo, the sweetest man in the world, who never understood why he had been shot—walked over to comfort her. He put one arm around her and the other around Evelyn, who also was crying and shaking.

"It's all right," he said. "It's all right now."

When she had steadied herself, Cheryl returned to her observation post and surveyed the scene. The pickups were hurriedly backing out and leaving town in all directions, and the few men on foot were also clearing out. Later, when her strength returned and she regained her composure, she would respond to her curiosity and need for confirmation and venture out for a closer view of the killing scene. For the moment, though, she simply stared at the smoke pouring out of the hood of the big Silverado, which she figured must have caught fire in the shooting. *Burn!* Cheryl thought. *Burn until there's nothing left of any of it!*

On the day of his death, Alice Wood had been involved with Ken McElroy for more than twenty years. She had lived with him for sixteen years, borne him three children, been beaten severely by him untold times, loved and hated him, and dreamed of shooting him with one of his own guns. Alice was no longer in love with Ken—those feelings had ended a few years earlier when the sex and violence had gone beyond what she could handle—but still she cared for and respected him. He was a good father to her children, and in recent years they had become pretty good friends.

Alice was a mildly attractive brunette in her mid-thirties, with blue eyes and a disarmingly direct manner. For the past year or two, she had lived in an apartment in St. Joseph with her three children.

Juarez, the oldest at twelve, slight with brown hair and clear blue eyes, had always been a favorite of his father. The feeling was mutual—Juarez worshiped his dad to the extent that sometimes Alice felt almost left out of her son's life. Ken had called Juarez the day before and told him he would be down on Monday to watch him pitch in a Little League baseball game. Tonia, named for Ken's dad and called Tony, was a sweet, sensitive eight-year-old girl, with medium-length brown hair and a round face and broad forehead like her father's. Ken, Jr., nicknamed "Mouse," was a quiet and easygoing six-year-old, seemingly unaware of the storm that surrounded the McElroy name wherever it came up.

St. Joseph had always been one of Ken's stomping grounds, and he often came by the apartment to see Alice and spend time with the children. Tonia especially looked forward to her long visits at his Skidmore farm in the summer, when she could see him every day and play with the other kids. She was in the middle of one of those visits on the morning of July 10, 1981.

Alice and her boyfriend, Jim, had planned to take the boys up to the Skidmore farm for the weekend. They would leave that Friday afternoon after Jim got off work and bring Tonia home with them Sunday night. As they often did, Alice and the two boys had driven to the appliance store around noon to take Jim his lunch. When they arrived, the boss's wife was talking on the phone. She looked up and saw Alice and an odd look came over her face. Handing Alice the phone, the woman said, "It's Trena. Something's really wrong, I can't understand her." *Strange,* Alice thought, *I just talked to her this morning about groceries and supplies for the weekend and everything was all right then.* Alice held the receiver to her ear and said hello.

"They shot him," said Trena, sobbing.

"What are you talking about?" asked Alice.

"Ken, they shot him."

Alice could barely make out the words. "Who shot him?" she asked.

"They did."

"Is he hurt bad?"

"No, no," Trena wailed. "He's dead."

Alice said, "We'll be up as soon as we can," and hung up. Jim's boss gave him the rest of the day off, and they loaded the boys into the car and headed north out of St. Joseph for Skidmore.

For most of the forty miles the four of them sat in silence, anxious to get to the farm, but holding on to the last few minutes before they would have to face Ken's death.

By the time they reached the farm, Trena was gone. On the advice of McElroy's Kansas City lawyer, one of Ken's sisters had driven her to the highway patrol headquarters in St. Joseph for her own protection (an irony not lost on the citizens of Skidmore when they later learned of it). Several of Ken's brothers and sisters had gathered at the farm and they tearfully told Alice what had happened: The people had conspired to kill Ken, and even the sheriff and mayor had all been in on it. There had been four guns firing, and Ken had been shot over eight times in the head. Trena had been in the truck beside him and had seen the whole thing. Somebody at the bank had called Tim, Ken's younger brother, to come and get her. Trena had been a mess, a whirling, bloody, blond apparition, and she blurted out the story in spasms of words and sobs, her eyes still wild with fear for herself. The people in the bank had tried to lure her into a back room and kill her, Trena had said, and they might still be coming out to the farm to get her.

Several of McElroy's sisters, who lived in surrounding towns and farms, came to the farm immediately when they learned of the killing. They found Tonia in such bad shape, crying and sobbing uncontrollably, that they took her and Oleta, Ken and Trena's four-year-old daughter, to Maitland, away from the scene, and tried to calm them down. Tonia wasn't in much better shape when Alice found her—her body was convulsed in wrenching sobs, and she was absolutely inconsolable.

Ken, Jr., sat in a corner of the farmhouse living room by himself and cried softly. Juarez, a tough guy like Ken who never showed his feelings, took his bike a few hundred yards down the road to Tim's house and rode in circles in the driveway for hours.

Someone called and warned them that it might be dangerous to stay around the farm—that some of the townspeople might be coming out to the house—so they left, vowing to come back that night to claim the family possessions. After dark, with the younger kids parceled out to Ken's sisters, Tim, Alice, Jim, Juarez, and the older girls returned with two trucks and a horse trailer. They worked through the night moving the personal items and furniture to Faucett, where Trena could retrieve them later. They made three trips that night, hauling items out of the darkened house, loading them silently onto the vehicles, and creeping down the drive to the gravel road.

By Saturday morning Tonia had calmed down somewhat. She and the boys were watching TV around noon when news of the killing came on. A picture of their father with a thick, fleshy face and cold eyes staring out under heavy black eyebrows appeared on the screen, while the announcer recounted his reputation as the most hated and feared man in Nodaway County.

The newscast also showed a photograph of the killing scene that would later become a part of almost every story that was written or produced about the incident—a close-up of the driver's side of the Silverado. The window in the driver's door was shattered, and the shards of glass around the edges framed the side of the tavern and the D & G sign. Through the window, two people could be seen examining the building for bullet holes. The right edge of the picture showed the bullet holes in the rear window behind the driver's seat. The upholstery was splotched with a wide, dark spill of blood. The television cameras had arrived at the scene just as the truck was being towed away, and the station replayed the footage of the Silverado hanging by a hook from the back of the truck, shot full of holes and looking, as it would later be described, as if it had been the target in a shooting gallery.

By the time Alice realized what was happening and got over to turn off the TV, Tonia was hysterical and Ken, Jr., had burst into tears. That afternoon, when she couldn't calm Tonia, Alice took her to a doctor, who prescribed tranquilizers for her. By evening, Tonia finally fell asleep and was put to bed.

On the morning of July 10, 1981, Highway Patrolman Dan Boyer was heading north on Highway 71, only a mile or so out of St. Joseph, when the call came over the radio to return to Troop H headquarters immediately. When Boyer pulled in a few minutes later, the dispatcher explained that someone had called in a report that Ken McElroy had been shot and killed on the main street of Skidmore. Boyer froze for a second, and then shook his head. *Probably just another one of the weird calls the patrol got all the time,* he thought as he walked back to the patrol car. *Who would have the guts—or be crazy enough—to go up against McElroy with a gun?* Skeptical but curious, Boyer headed back out north on Highway 71, driving without lights or siren and barely exceeding the speed limit.

Boyer was 32 years old, a stocky man of medium height with short brown hair and brown eyes. He lived with his wife and two kids in a small town in Worth County, bordering Nodaway to the east. Boyer liked the people and the country life, but most of all he loved being a patrolman.

Many people in northwest Missouri considered the Missouri State Highway Patrol the best law enforcement agency in the area. All the patrolmen had survived six months of rigorous training, and many of them, including Boyer, had college degrees. Patrolmen drove the fastest cars with the fanciest equipment, and they carried the most firepower. They projected a crisp, professional look with their tailored blue wool uniforms, black ties, and patent leather Sam Browne belts. Patrolmen were trained to be gentlemen cops—tough but even-handed, polite but firm, treating citizens with respect but always retaining control of every situation. As a matter of policy, they were never assigned to areas where they had grown up or lived before joining the patrol.

Boyer had joined the patrol in 1975 and was eventually assigned to Troop H in St. Joseph. His unit, based in Maryville, the Nodaway County seat, consisted of seven troopers. From the patrol office in the Nodaway County Courthouse, they fanned out over the highways and county roads of their zone. In six years with the patrol, Boyer had come to know most of the zone's small towns fairly well, and Skidmore had always seemed much like any other small farm town in northwest Missouri.

As he drove to Skidmore that July morning, Boyer described McElroy to Bryan, a young academy graduate who was riding along as the final stage of his training. Boyer didn't know what had happened, he said in his low, almost gentle voice, but he was sure that McElroy wasn't the one dead. The patrolmen had just driven through Savannah, about thirty miles south of Maryville, when the second call came over the radio.

McElroy's wife had just called, the dispatcher said, crying hysterically and sobbing that her husband had been shot and killed. Over and over, she said that they wouldn't stop firing, that the killers just kept shooting him and shooting him, and that they wanted to kill her, too.

Telling the dispatcher to call the ambulance in Maryville and the Nodaway County sheriff's office, Boyer flipped on the siren and the light. He told Bryan to hang on, and within seconds the black 1980 Plymouth Grand Fury was barreling up Highway 71 at more than 100 mph.

About twenty miles north of Savannah, at Pumpkin Center, a combination gas station and grocery, Boyer slowed and took a hard, screeching left onto Route A. Bryan grabbed the dashboard as he slid into the door. The road running west out of Pumpkin Center descended a steep hill and then broke into a wide, sweeping curve before straightening out briefly to cross a narrow bridge. Halfway through the curve, which was banked as poorly as most of the curves on the county blacktops, Boyer glanced over and saw that Bryan had turned white.

As they whipped across the bridge, Boyer thought back on the night a year or so earlier when he had stopped McElroy at Pumpkin Center. Boyer had been parked in the gas station when the green Dodge pickup sped by at 75 mph. Not until he was walking toward the pickup with his flashlight in his hand did Boyer realize he had stopped Ken McElroy. A wrenching fear had hit Boyer's gut: He was only a move away from having a shotgun stuck in his face and his head blown away.

Every law officer in northwest Missouri, even those who had never met him, knew Ken McElroy—and knew he hated cops. Only a few days before, Boyer had read a notice at the patrol office, in which an informant had warned that McElroy was traveling in a caravan of three pickups and that each truck carried guns. The two female drivers were backing up McElroy wherever he went, the informant had said, and they had orders to shoot and kill any cop who came upon them.

In the dark at Pumpkin Center, Boyer had quickly recovered from the shock and the clench of fear. He slowed his step, dropped into a slight crouch, and pulled his service revolver from its holster. Holding the revolver at his side, he continued his approach but swung out in an arc away from the cab so that he could see inside the truck before he was upon it. Backlit by the spotlight on the patrol car, McElroy sat looking straight ahead, both of his hands in plain view on top of the steering wheel. Shaking slightly, Boyer went through his routine about the radar gun, the speed of the truck, and the option of paying or contesting the fine. To Boyer's surprise, and somewhat to his consternation, McElroy just sat there. He was polite and soft-spoken and offered no argument. He kept his hands on the steering wheel at all times, except to reach for his driver's license, which he did very slowly, and to accept the ticket from Boyer. He looked at Boyer only once, and Boyer noticed the hard, flat eyes and the thin mouth. The incident seemed to be over almost before it began.

The patrolman said little on the fast ride to Skidmore. Bryan tried to relax, but he continued to grab the dash in the tight curves. Boyer's imagination spun out different versions of what might have happened, but none of them made sense: *Who in Skidmore would shoot Ken McElroy in broad daylight in the middle of town? If he really had been shot, there must be other casualties, given the firepower he always maintained around him. Hardest of all to believe*

*was that McElroy was really dead. Something that horrible couldn't
die that easily.*

The blacktops and dirt roads curved and twisted up and down
the steep hills and through the creases of the rumpled countryside.
Hitting the hills at anything over 40 was like riding a roller coaster
without rails. Boyer knew all the roads in the area and prided
himself on being an expert high-speed driver, which meant knowing exactly how fast he could take the hills and curves without
sliding into a ditch or smashing into a fence. He raced eight miles
west over Route A, flew past ZZ (which ran north and came within
a few miles of the McElroy farm), then sped through Graham and
Maitland with siren wailing and lights flashing, finally turning
north on 113 to Skidmore.

Boyer's watch read close to 11:30 by the time the Plymouth
reached the edge of town. They had covered the forty miles in
thirty minutes. Entering from the south, the Plymouth cruised
through six residential blocks before coming to the grocery store
and bank and turning east onto Elm Street. Boyer saw the ambulance parked behind the Silverado, which was angled in front of the
D & G Tavern. Two sheriff's cars were parked in the middle of the
street, and another patrol car was arriving from the east. As Boyer
pulled to a stop, he saw two attendants loading a stretcher into the
rear of the ambulance. A white sheet covered a large form.

One look at the rear of the truck cleared up Boyer's confusion
about what had happened: Somebody had taken McElroy from
behind. There was no gunfight, and nobody stood up to him face to
face. The bullets came from across the street, undoubtedly from a
rifle, while McElroy sat in his pickup facing the tavern. He never
saw his killer, and he never had a chance. A crazy act, it had to
have been committed out of a terrible well of fear.

Behind the driver's seat, the rear window had been blown out.
The driver's door hung open, its window shattered. There obviously had been a hell of a lot of shooting, probably from more than
one rifle, and much of it had been wild.

Boyer walked up to the truck and looked in. Teeth and pieces of
bone lay scattered on the dashboard in front of the steering wheel.
Blood splotched the seat and formed a deep puddle on the floor; it
had run over the edge of the door jamb and collected in a purplish,
jelly-like pool on the ground. The air was dead still. As Boyer

turned away, he felt a searing blast from the 100-degree midday sun.

Boyer stepped back and surveyed the scene. Other than the law and a few people watching the loading of the body, the town was deserted. Occasionally, a male face would peer out the window of the cafe, or someone would leave the tavern, walk nonchalantly past the truck, glance in, and disappear down the street. Now and then, a passing pickup would slow almost to a halt as the driver leaned over and stared inside the familiar two-tone brown Silverado.

Boyer reckoned that people were trying to convince themselves that Ken McElroy was really dead and was going to stay dead, that he wouldn't come cruising the streets of town that afternoon with his guns and his trucks and his women. It was too late, but for an instant Boyer wished he had looked under the white sheet before the ambulance left.

Boyer wasn't surprised that something had happened, but he was surprised that *this* had happened. He had expected that McElroy would perish some night on a back road, at the hands of a cop given half a reason to blow him away. Maybe then his death could have been dealt with quietly, in a way that would have solved the problem without creating an uproar. But Boyer hadn't realized the town was so twisted over McElroy that it would come to this.

Boyer had left his car running to provide a cool refuge from the heat, but when he returned to it, he stood outside with a foot on the bumper. Other cops came over and told him what they knew. Earlier that morning, Nodaway County Sheriff Danny Estes had been at a meeting at the town's Legion Hall, at which the sole topic had been what the town was going to do about McElroy. Estes hadn't even made it back to Maryville before McElroy was shot, and now people would think that Estes had told the men at the meeting to do it.

Estes was shaken up and excited, pacing around, arms flapping, shouting at nobody in particular, "What the hell happened? Why the hell did you do this?"

Boyer's radio crackled. The dispatcher told him to meet another car at the McElroy farm. Trena had called and asked the patrol to drive her to St. Joseph for her own safety. When Boyer reached the farm, a pickup with a woman at the wheel was pulling out of the drive onto the gravel road. He went to the house and knocked on the door several times. When he got no response, he wondered if Trena or somebody else was setting him up. Finally, Tim McElroy, Ken's younger brother, came to the door. He explained that Trena had been crouched down on the passenger's side of the truck that had just left. She had mistaken the approaching patrol car for a sheriff's car and, believing the local police to be involved in her husband's murder, had fled with one of Ken's sisters. Tim was sure they were on their way to patrol headquarters in St. Joseph.

Boyer returned to Skidmore to assist in the investigation. As the officers interviewed witnesses, a pattern developed:

"Where were you when he was shot?"

"Standing in front of the tavern."

"Did you see anything?"

"No, I didn't see a thing. I heard something, a couple of shots, and then I hit the ground. There were more shots and, by the time I got up, it was all over."

They were lying. It would have been impossible for one or two gunmen to stand across the street from the Silverado and fire ten to fifteen shots, put the guns away, and drive out of town without being recognized. Yet the answer was always the same: Nobody looked up until the shooting stopped, and nobody saw a thing.

Boyer soon realized that he had become the enemy. Normally, these people were open and friendly with the patrol, willing to help, ready to discuss the facts of any incident they might know about. Now, they were closed up so tight some of them wouldn't even speak to him.

Several locals were openly hostile. Boyer and Sergeant Barnett worked on tracing the trajectory of the bullets by lining up the holes in the tin hut next to the D & G Tavern with the holes in the front and rear windows of the truck. They were drawing a chalk line across the street when a man walked up and demanded, "Where in the hell were you guys when we needed you?"

Whether he was being charged with incompetence or cowardice, Boyer felt he had to respond. He followed the man into the cafe and joined him and several other men at a center table. The others looked away in silence, but the accuser's anger had grown.

"If you guys had caught the son of a bitch and thrown him in jail, he wouldn't be dead now!"

"I understand how you feel," replied Boyer, "but it isn't fair to blame the law for the murder. We've always come when we were called, and we have no choice now but to conduct a full and fair investigation."

The man was still cursing McElroy and insisting that the cops were too scared of him to do their jobs, when two cops burst into the cafe, apparently worried about Boyer being alone with the townspeople.

In a way, Boyer sympathized with the townspeople who felt that justice had been done in their town for the first time since McElroy started terrorizing the place. The very system that had failed to protect its citizens was now persecuting them for doing what it had failed to do.

Boyer knew lots of reasons why it had reached this point: Many of them involved the failure of the criminal justice system. But the town was partly to blame, too. People wanted to be protected, to have their little community made safe from their tormentor, but no one wanted to step forward and file charges.

Boyer and his sergeant continued to look for evidence. They followed the trajectories across the street and found two different piles of shell casings. One pile, from a .30-.30, lay in the street, a few feet west of the post office door. The second, from a .22-caliber rifle, was ten yards up the hill. The bullets from the high-powered rifle had been tumbling by the time they blew out the window in the driver's door, which accounted for the large, ragged holes in the tin building next to the tavern. The low-velocity .22 was an odd choice of murder weapon, particularly when the target was down and across the street and on the other side of a truck window.

Noting the locations, the patrolmen picked up the casings and put them in plastic bags. Boyer retreated to the cool interior of the Plymouth to write his report. Somebody came over and said that the body had been taken to the funeral parlor in Maryville. Boyer put away his notes, told Bryan to work with the sergeant, and headed east out of town toward Maryville, curious to see the remains of Ken McElroy.

2

Skidmore, a small town in the heart of northwest Missouri farm country, has always been a farming village, off by itself, every aspect of its existence rooted in the process of coaxing substance from the earth. The town's population has hovered around 450 for the past fifty years. During the town's heyday, around the turn of the century, when the railroad ran through the middle of town and carried cattle and grain to Omaha and Kansas City, the population blossomed to about 600; but it faded with the end of World War I, the coming of the Depression, and the availability of automobiles.

The town sits on a low ridge a quarter mile east of the Nodaway River, which runs south and pours into the Missouri River a few miles above St. Joseph. The hilly countryside is crisscrossed with hedge trees, or osage orange, planted by the settlers in the 1840s to mark their fields and pen their animals. Groves of sturdy oak, walnut, hickory, maple, and cottonwood grow along the edges of the fields, in the folds of the hills, and beside the stream beds. In early October the hedge and timber, adorned in autumn's reds and golds, flash like brilliant stripes through the fields of ripening grain.

White frame farmhouses, sheltered from the elements by encircling pine, maple, and walnut trees, occupy occasional hilltops. Off to the side and behind the houses are wood and metal buildings, some empty and others filled with animals or machinery. Metal hog feeders squat in the middle of barren lots. Dirt roads wind through rich fields of corn, wheat, milo, and soybeans, and large rolls of last summer's hay lean against wire fences. Small ponds, broken windmills, and tall wire grain bins with pointed metal hats speckle the hillsides.

To the north about twenty-five miles lies Iowa and to the west about thirty miles is the Missouri River and Nebraska. Northeast about thirteen miles lies Maryville, the home of Dale Carnegie and Northwest Missouri State University, and a town of about 10,000 people. St. Joseph (where Jesse James was killed), the closest city, sprawls alongside the Missouri River about forty miles south, and below that another thirty miles is Kansas City. Judging by its geographical location, northwest Missouri might appear to be a continuation of the great Midwest of Iowa, Kansas, and Nebraska, but history has shown that a good many of its roots run south.

A place out of time, Skidmore seems to have slipped outside the streams of commerce and contemporary culture. There are no launderettes, no ice cream parlors or video shops, no blacks or Chicanos, no runners or bikers. The local people pretty much dress the same way and talk about the same things their parents and grandparents did.

The town has two paved streets but no stoplights. Vehicles slide through the stop signs after only a casual glance by the driver, and hardly anyone signals a turn. The town doesn't have a marshal, the last one having been let go after only a month because he took his job too seriously, busting speeders and trying to enforce angle parking on Elm Street.

Cable television has come to town, and a few farmers have satellite dishes in their yards. Drugs hit the area like the rest of the country in the sixties and the seventies, although perhaps not as hard. A few farmers own fancy cars, but the most common vehicle is still the pickup. The high school kids go to Maryville to dance and party and listen to live music. The only airwaves that successfully cross the rolling hills to Skidmore carry country music. On moonlit nights pickups with two or three young men in the back holding high-powered rifles race across the fields in search of coyotes.

Life is steady and predictable in Skidmore. The residents have known each other all their lives; the farmers who drink coffee each morning at Mom's Cafe went to grade school together and took part in each other's weddings. They know each other's family histories and jokes as well as they know their own. From years of attending church bake sales, they know who makes the best blueberry pie and who makes the best German chocolate cake. The residents are for the most part decent, law-abiding people who share a few basic values, one of which is that the less interference people have in the way they run their farms or their lives, the better off they are. People should also take care of their own problems; to seek outside help is an admission of weakness and only invites interference.

Farmers, particularly the older ones, view work as the very measure of a person's character. How hard a man works tells you most of what you need to know about him; if he's ready to go when the sun comes up and stays until the job is done, or until it's too dark or wet to finish it, almost anything else can be forgiven.

A stoic strain runs through the character. The only legitimate complaints concern the weather, crop prices, and the government. Personal problems, physical ills, are usually borne privately.

For all the cherished sense of privacy, true secrets in Skidmore are hard to come by. A farmer passing through town can tell who is shopping for groceries, who is drinking coffee, who is in the tavern, who is buying fertilizer, and who is applying for a loan, just by glancing at the location of the vehicles parked up and down Elm Street. If a married woman or man goes out dancing at the saloons in Maryville on Friday night, it will be old news by church on Sunday.

Although the people are friendly to each other and to outsiders, there is a distinct difference between friendliness and openness. And different boundaries exist for different people. One respected community leader, who was responsible for reviving the long dormant Punkin' Show, the town's annual celebration, concluded after living in Skidmore for fourteen years that because he was born and raised elsewhere, he would never truly be accepted.

Skidmore is not class-oriented, probably because there are so few classes. With the exception of a banker, a few cashiers, a clerk or two, and a few shopkeepers, it is a blue collar town: farmers, mechanics, hired hands, 'dozer operators, repairmen, people who work with their hands. The biggest distinctions exist within farming. The rich farmer—the man with lots of land, most of it paid for —is at the top of the heap. Next comes the yeoman farmer, the one with a couple hundred acres and six kids, who makes it from year to year, until one year maybe he doesn't. After that comes the renter or sharecropper, who works someone else's land in exchange for a share of the crops.

At the bottom is the furtive subculture of the lowlifes, a midwestern version of the southern rednecks, made up of people who exist on the outermost fringes of the community. The lowlifes live in rundown houses or trailers, drink a lot, fight, never pay taxes, have probably spent time in jail once or twice—usually for assault, or stealing, or discharging a weapon—and are terribly suspicious of strangers. The men, usually unkempt with scraggly beards and dirty hair, are most at home in the timber, working their dogs or hunting coon.

Despite the commonality of values and the similarity of life experiences of most of the residents. Skidmore does not have a strong sense of community. Partly because of the values themselves—independence, self-sufficiency, dislike of outside authority—and partly because of the economic decline of the community and the continuing loss of the young people, the community doesn't steer a strong course; it seems, instead, to maintain barely enough momentum to avoid losing steerageway altogether.

Coming into Skidmore from the east, Route 113 rounds a wide curve and disappears under a canopy of tall maples, ashes, and elms. The trees bend slightly to the north at the top from the persistent blowing of the south winds. All the streets in town are named for trees, and Route 113 becomes Elm, the wide, paved main street of town. Flanked by narrow gravel shoulders, Elm runs through four blocks of quiet neighborhood before sloping into the depression where the railroad once ran. Most of the houses are one- or two-story white clapboards, plain but well maintained, set back from the street fifteen or twenty feet, with gravel drives and occasional garages. Narrow sidewalks, cracked here and there, bisect well-cared-for lawns. Metal mailboxes on posts stand where the curbs would be, if there were curbs. The houses sit far apart, and in midsummer most of the spacious backyards contain large vegetable gardens brimming with sweet corn, lettuce, potatoes, tomatoes, carrots, squash, cucumbers, beans, and peppers. Summer evenings in the neighborhood are quiet; a few people sitting out on their steps or porch swings, others working in their gardens or leaning against their pickups and chatting with their neighbors.

As the road descends into the depression, it passes the large red-brick Methodist Church. With a pair of tall spirals and several large oval stained-glass windows, it is the town's most striking building. Across the street and down a few yards, just before the bottom of the hill, is the seat of town government—a converted gas station with large black letters spelling out SKIDMORE across the top. The board of aldermen meets once a month in the former station's office, which also houses the town clerk. Attached to the city hall is the Skidmore Community Fire Department, which contains three trucks of varying vintage.

Thirty yards down the road, where the depression flattens out, sits the old Skidmore Depot, a red wooden building which was recently fixed up to serve as the town museum. Hot dog and marshmallow roasts are held here on Halloween night in a futile attempt to distract teenagers from shooting out street lights and setting bales of hay on fire in the middle of bridges.

Rising on the other side of the depression, Elm becomes the one-block business section and reveals with uncompromising clarity the extent of the town's economic decay. The few businesses that remain are barely hanging on. In place of the big hotel is an empty wooden garage with splintered wooden slats where the front door used to be. In a squat, cinder-block building attached to the garage is Mom's Cafe, where farmers, seed dealers, and the few remaining merchants gather during the day.

Further on up the hill is the D & G Tavern, named for owners Del and Greg Clement. A long building of corrugated metal, with a nearly flat roof and an air conditioner in the only window, the tavern has a bare cement floor, two pool tables, and booths along the east wall. Much larger than it looks from the outside—it sometimes hosts dances on Saturday nights—the tavern is the sole source of night life in Skidmore.

Across the street from the tavern is the post office, and a few feet to the east of that sits the Masonic Building, a two-story brick building with a large arch over the front door. The building, which has been a drugstore, a barber shop, and an opera house in years past, now serves as the town library, but it is really only an empty building with books piled in it. In the little park on the corner, just west of the post office, a flagpole has been planted in cement next to a plaque honoring local men who died in various wars. Brief services are conducted in the park every Memorial Day for the town's veterans, and frog jumping contests are held here in August during the annual Punkin' Show. A wire fence runs along the edge for posting community notices.

The intersection at the top of the hill, where Elm Street turns back into Route 113 and heads south out of town, is Four Corners, the crossroads of town. On the northwest corner, across from the little park, sits Sumy Oil, a gas station and repair shop and one of the enduring businesses in town. The Sumys are a third-generation Skidmore family, and Marvin Sumy, like his father, sells most of his gas and does most of his repair work on credit. Each spring, his gasoline truck makes the rounds to the farms, and the farmers settle up with him on the way back from the grain elevator in October. On the southwest corner sits a combination gas station and convenience store. Next door is the American Legion Building, Sam Albright Post No. 411. (Sam, from another old Skidmore family, went down with his ship in World War II.) The brick building is large (for Skidmore), with an exterior like a 1930s five-and-dime store. A battered wooden bench sits outside the door, a convenient roost for old-timers on summer days.

Route 113 emerges from Skidmore to meet the corn and bean fields growing up to the backyards of the houses on the southern edge of town. From there, the road begins a long, gradual descent, passing the water-treatment plant on the right and swinging west to cross the Nodaway River. A half mile before reaching the river, the road cuts through the river bottoms, an alluvial plain carved out by the constant meandering and flooding of the river.

Route DD, a minor artery, heads north out of town and swings west to cross the Nodaway River. On the way, the road passes the Christian Church, a homely brown stucco building with a shingled roof that slopes off in an assortment of arbitrary angles. A fundamentalist church, it is distinguished by an unshakable belief that baptism by total immersion is the only gateway to eternal life in Christ.

Just before dropping down to the river, DD passes a large house with towers and bay windows, built either by the town's founder, Martenay Skidmore, or his son William—no one is quite sure which. On a small plateau just above the river is the Masonic cemetery, where the Skidmores and many other local families are buried.

A chalkboard in front of the post office displays the weekly and cumulative rainfalls for the current summer compared to last summer, giving everyone a common basis for speculating on how high the bean plants will grow and how big the ears of corn will be by harvest.

As it always has, the weather—the sun, the wind, and the rain, particularly the rain—affects all the rhythms of life in the community. If the moisture falls in the right amount and at the right time, if the sun shines the other days, and if the river doesn't flood, there might be a good harvest. If the farmers prosper, the waitress and the bank clerk and the fertilizer salesman prosper, and there might be money to buy a new car or to put a new roof on the house. If the rain falls too late in the summer to provide the critical early nourishment, the yield per acre drops, and the farmers work only to pay their loans and stay alive. If the farmers are gloomy, everyone is gloomy.

Many of the farmers include the great-grandsons and great-granddaughters of the settlers who moved to northwest Missouri in the 1840s. Large numbers of them came from the southeastern states of Kentucky, Tennessee, Virginia, and Maryland to clear the land, work the soil, grow crops, and raise animals. Their descendants are now the town elders, approaching the end of their time on the land.

Q (for Quentin) Goslee has lived all his life on the land his great-grandfather bought two miles east of Skidmore. If a storm wakens him in the night, as it did when he was a boy, he might step out on the east porch to feel and smell the air. Or he might lie in bed and listen to the currents of the winds as they bend and twist the tree limbs, lash the rain against the house, and rattle the windows. He knows which hills are likely to run first and where the gullies will form. And he knows that if the wind picks up another notch, he will find broken limbs on the tall walnut trees behind the house. He knows without thinking where he is in the planting, growing, or harvesting cycle and what each hundredth of an inch of rain will mean to each of his crops at a particular moment. The loamy soil is a part of him like his skin or his hair, and he knows how it reacts to the sun on the back of his neck or the sting of a February wind in his eyes. Q might well have sprouted from the dark soil himself, perhaps as a walnut tree in the heavy timber to the north or a stalk of corn somewhere on the fifty acres sloping gently west to the hedge trees. When he was young, Q told his wife Margaret—who already knew it—that he couldn't even stand to *think* about living anywhere but on that piece of land.

Route V is one of two roads linking Maryville and Skidmore. A narrow blacktop with no shoulders, it twists and turns over the hilltops and through the troughs. In the spring and fall, after a heavy rain, tractors and combines track mud from the fields and dirt roads onto the highway, creating slicks that send unwary vehicles sliding into ditches and fence posts. One hundred yards before V intersects with 113 to enter Skidmore from the east, a well-maintained gravel road cuts south from the blacktop. Called the Valley Road, it runs straight for about a mile, through pasture lands and fields of beans and wheat and past white frame farmhouses, then curves east. Two miles further, the road passes the place where Ken McElroy grew up and learned to hunt coon.

3

Ken Rex McElroy was rarely called Kenneth or Rex or Ken Rex; to his friends he was Ken, pronounced something like "kin," or Kenny. To everyone else he was McElroy. Ken McElroy was not quite a month over forty-seven-years old when he died on the main street of Skidmore. At 5 feet 10 inches and 230 pounds, he was grossly overweight, but except for a huge gut, he was mainly solid flesh. His shoulders were broad, he had a massive, barrel chest, and his arms were thick as tree trunks. His hair was naturally a dark brown, but he had dyed it pure black for years. (Alice Wood had seen pictures of him when he was younger with brown hair and a pencil-thin mustache.) He always kept it oiled and slicked back, 1950s style.

McElroy was dark complected, attributable no doubt to the fact that his father's mother was a full-blooded Cherokee Indian. His eyes were dark blue, sometimes blue-black. (Many people in Skidmore recall him as having pitch black eyes and being well over six feet.) He had a broad forehead and heavy black eyebrows, and his eyes were set far apart. When he looked straight ahead, only the bottom three-quarters of the irises were visible, leaving white quarter-moons beneath. When he was young, girls saw his eyes as "sexy, but kind of cold"; when he was older, they became "icy black eyes that could see into your soul." Full, wide sideburns reached just below his ears, almost even with the corners of his mouth. Thin lips, like a slash below the prominent nose, turned down at the corners, the left side turning up slightly when he smiled. In his younger days, he was a handsome, almost dashing man, but in middle age his huge belly threw him out of proportion, making his legs seem almost a little too short for his body. And his face had become fleshy, a bit loose in the jowls.

McElroy had several tattoos. On his lower right forearm was a tattoo of a cross, and within the cross were the letters MOM (or WOW). The fingers of his right hand bore the name KEN. On his upper left arm was scratched the word LOVE and beneath that was a dagger inscribed with the name JOAN. On the back of his left hand was written the word OLETA, the name of both his first wife and his second child by his third wife.

McElroy took pride in his appearance. When he left the farm, particularly if he was going to town, he usually cleaned up, combed his hair, and put on good clothes—dark knit slacks and a western shirt or a nice T-shirt and cowboy boots. He was never seen in public looking dirty or wearing seedy clothes. He wore many of his shirts loose to conceal a .38-caliber pistol in a leather holster, custom designed to lie flat on his rib cage beneath his left armpit. Even in the winter he seldom donned a coat, and he never wore a hat.

When he wasn't angry, McElroy was usually soft-spoken. He could sit unnoticed at a bar in Maryville, talking so low the waitress would have to lean over to hear him. When he played pool, he usually won, and he always graciously bought the next game. But he seldom laughed. When he did, in the words of a family member, it "was from the outside, not the inside"—there was never a belly laugh, just a *ha, ha, ha,* and then it was over.

McElroy moved slowly and deliberately, with a heavy person's easy grace. When he stepped out of his truck, his head would turn slightly in several directions as his eyes flicked about, automatically scanning his surroundings. Outside his home ground, Ken moved about with even more caution, always very aware of everything around him. Until the very end, he sat in the taverns of Maitland, Graham, and Skidmore facing the door, with his back to the wall.

McElroy was happiest at a coon dog meet or trading hounds at a friend's house or just telling dog stories and drinking Jack Daniel's at the Shady Lady bar in Maryville. His skill as a dog handler and shrewdness as a judge of dog flesh was legendary among coon hunters and dog owners. He bought and sold dogs over the phone without ever laying eyes on them, sometimes at $200 or $300 apiece. He could control one of his hounds with a slight wave of his hand or a nod of his head.

Until the court ordered him not to carry firearms in the fall of 1980, Ken McElroy never went anywhere without a gun, whether it was a pistol in the shoulder holster, a shotgun in the window rack of his pickup, or both. But nobody remembers ever seeing him in a fist fight.

Across the Missouri River from St. Joseph, the land flattens out as though a huge steam roller had once run over it. This is the beginning of the great Midwest, cattle country, where the plains stretch far over the horizon and are broken only by occasional rises and clumps of cottonwood trees. Barbed-wire fences and telephone poles cross dry creek beds and stitch the endless windswept prairie. About seventy-five miles southwest of the river is Topeka, Kansas, and twenty or thirty miles south of Topeka is the tiny cattle town of Dover. Like Skidmore, Dover was once a thriving community, but now only a post office, a few stores, and 125 people remain. Here, on February 28, 1897, Mabel Marie Lister was born, third of five children of Oliver and Isabelle Lister. The Listers were tenant farmers, hired by the year, the season, or the month. They moved from ranch to ranch, living in little shacks without electricity or water, earning barely $30 a month. The Listers were good people who just never managed to accumulate much money.

On June 6, 1910, when she was just fourteen years old, Mabel Lister married twenty-year-old Tony Wyatt McElroy from nearby Shelton. Tony ("Tone" to his family) was known for his hot temper and terrible cursing. As a young man, he made moonshine, drank too much, and got in fights, usually over women. He was boisterous when sober, but he became downright quarrelsome when he drank. Tony farmed a little, but he mainly made a living with his wagon and horses. He hired out to haul hay for people and, when times were good, worked for the county cutting ditches and scraping roadbeds. He owned good horses and wagons and fine harnesses of oiled leather with shiny rings.

Mabel gave birth to a boy, on February 26, 1911, only two days before she turned fifteen. Hershel was the first of sixteen children Mabel would bear, losing a set of twins along the way. Seven boys and seven girls were spaced almost evenly over a twenty-eight-year span of child bearing. Ken Rex McElroy was born on June 16,

1934, followed by the last child, Tim, born on June 1, 1936. Mabel worked hard feeding and raising her steadily increasing brood, always without running water or electricity. She baked bread every day, hung endless lines of wash in the backyard, and took her turn in the fields. The family was poor then, as it would be poor up to the last few years, but the children were always clean and presentable.

Times were tough in eastern Kansas in the predepression twenties, and somewhere around 1926 or 1927, Tony and Mabel packed up the family and set out for southern Missouri, ending up in the Ozarks. In the town of Lamar, they rented a four-hundred-acre farm and planted corn, and by early July the crops were doing well. But two rainless weeks of burning sun and hot winds destroyed the entire crop, and the McElroys went under.

The complete loss broke Tony. Eventually, he went back to road construction, working temporary jobs in small towns in southern Missouri and eastern Kansas, all the while having more kids and all the while staying dirt poor. The family wandered up to Quitman, a small town six miles north of Skidmore, and Tony and Mabel, like her parents, became tenant farmers, living in two- or three-room houses and working long days in the fields.

Soon after the McElroys came up from the Ozarks a farmer hired Tony at a dollar a day because he had four healthy-looking sons and they could help clear land, cut hay, and plow fields. Tony was a good worker and was always willing to help, but he talked a lot and his loud mouth sometimes got him in trouble. Mabel had put on a little weight by then, but she was still attractive.

Ken McElroy spent the first thirteen years of his life as the child of a tenant farmer, living in someone else's house, working somebody else's land, subsisting at near-poverty level in a large family continuously struggling for economic survival. The bitterness of these years never left him.

Ken was never Tony's favorite child. (Years later, Tony would list for a Skidmore banker which of his kids were okay and which ones to stay away from, and he always put Ken in the latter group.) Timmy, born two years after Ken, made things even worse. Timmy had a sweet disposition from the beginning, and he fit right into his role as baby of the family. Although Ken and Tim were close for a while because of their proximity in age, Tony's preference for Tim, who would grow up to be the ideal son, was always evident and eventually created a distance between them.

In the mid-1940s, the McElroys bought the old farmhouse and 175 acres on Valley Road. The house was always jammed with people. Three of the married children moved in, and at one point, eighteen people were living in the two-bedroom house. Ken and Timmy slept in one bed next to two boys in another bed. The house was usually a mess, mud tracked everywhere, clothes strewn about, dishes stacked in the sink. Mabel worked twelve-hour days keeping house, cooking, canning, and butchering animals, but the only one who really helped her was Timmy. Ken and most of the other children came and went and didn't pay much attention to her. The yard was filled with broken-down automobiles, junked equipment, and hunting dogs in cages and on leashes.

Tony yelled at his children to discipline them. When Ken was young, Tony yelled at him a lot for not doing things and for doing the wrong things. But Tony spared Timmy, who had a knack for doing the right things—like feeding the pigs or sweeping the floor, and staying on the good side of his parents. Ken never did any chores, and as he grew into his teens, Tony backed off him altogether and let him do whatever he wanted. By the eighth grade, Ken essentially did as he pleased.

Except for his sister Dorothy, who seemed to care for him, Ken's brothers and sisters—even the older ones—tended to leave him alone. To the extent that Ken modeled himself on anyone, it was on an older brother who was a serious troublemaker and who supposedly went to jail for stealing corn.

During the winter Ken would skate on a creek, from his farm to school, checking his traps for opossum, coon, and beaver on the way. More than once, he showed up smelling strongly of skunk. His fifth-grade teacher, a strict disciplinarian, would take him to the basement and attempt to get rid of the pungent odor by washing his hands and face using cleaning fluids on his clothes. Sometimes the smell was so bad she had to send him home.

Ken seldom went to school that year, and when he did show up he had never done his homework and displayed little interest in what was going on. The teacher considered him an attractive boy, but his good looks were ruined by the perpetual sneer on his face. He didn't say much, but to her his sullen manner said it all.

Ken kept to himself, never mixing with the other kids, and seldom participated in any school activities. After school, when other boys played football or went to the cafe to shoot pool, Ken went off alone to trap and run his dogs. He was strong, though, and could have been a superb athlete. In choose-up football games during recess, no one could ever bring him down, and he could toss a basketball across a court as if it were a baseball.

His teacher found him mean and hard to control. He seemed to think he could do anything he wanted to, that he need not obey her or anyone else, and she couldn't do a thing about it. She held him back in the fifth grade twice because of his truancy and poor grades. By the time he made it to sixth grade, he was the biggest kid in the class, looming three or four inches over the others. The kids in school learned early to stay away from Ken. One former classmate explained it this way:

"When I came to the Graham school in fourth grade from the Elkhorn Country School, one of the first things the other kids told me was about Ken McElroy, the type of kid he was. I was told to stay away from him, not to have anything to do with him, that he pushed other kids around."

Another classmate recalled:

"I don't care who you were, you didn't mess with him. If he came up to where you were sittin' and said, 'Hey, I wanna sit there,' then you moved. He wasn't the biggest kid in class—there was one really big kid, he must have been six feet and two hundred pounds, and even he never crossed Ken's path."

Strangely, no one—students, teachers or friends—remembers an incident of Ken actually beating somebody up. Perhaps he didn't have to.

On Ken's first day on a school bus, he and an older brother got into a scuffle with two other boys. The McElroy boys pulled knives and threatened to cut the other two, who immediately backed off. After that, Ken always had plenty of room—if he sat in the back of the bus, the other kids sat in the front.

Ken was also known to steal. One winter day, the owner of the gas station and grocery store in Graham caught him and another boy stealing some items. The man called Tony and told him about it. Later in the day, Tony burst into the store with a long, curved hunting knife in his hand, slammed the owner up against the wall, and held the knife up to his throat.

"If you ever touch my boy again," Tony snarled, "I'll cut your heart out."

The school yearbooks have one or two pictures of Ken. One year the school put on a play called *The Snow Queen*. In the cast picture three rows of boys stood behind the girls, who were kneeling. In the far left corner, at the back, is a tall, thin boy with wavy hair, at least a head taller than everyone else. Ken was the stagehand for the production.

Tim, who was quiet and studious and liked by his teachers, caught up with Ken in school by the sixth grade. Ken was finally passed on to junior high, although he could neither read nor write.

Most farm boys got up at 5:30 in the morning, did their chores, and went to school. After school and sports, they went home and did chores again before dinner. Not Ken. After school he would roam the countryside on his strawberry roan horse, hunting and running his dogs, going wherever and doing whatever he pleased. If you wanted to ride across someone's land, the custom was to ask permission, unless you knew the owner and had done it before. Ken never bothered; he rode through the timber and across the fields as if it were all his land, as if nobody had the right to restrict where he went and what he did. If a fence blocked his passage, he cut it with wire snips and rode on through. A farmer called him on it once—challenged him for hunting on his land without permission—and Ken, not more than fourteen at the time, pulled up short and told him nobody was going to tell him what he could do. The landowner backed off.

By the seventh grade Ken had a best friend, a boy named John L. The two boys first met when they attended first grade together in a small country school. John would stand lookout while Ken took a girl from their class into the bushes, removed her clothes, and did something to her—John was never quite sure what—during recess. In the second grade John moved away and didn't see Ken again until he moved back a few years later.

In junior high, Ken and John both wore their hair slicked back and their shirt sleeves rolled up, and the two of them sat together in school, until the teacher split them up for disrupting the class.

The two boys were rebels with big chips on their shoulders. They played hooky a lot, and spent most of their time riding horses. Ken knew every inch of the land around there and they would ride for hours after school, checking traps and hunting. Once, as they were riding full speed alongside the timber, they came to a hidden embankment with a thirty-foot drop. Ken saw the danger first, nudged John, and turned his horse at the last second to keep him from plunging over the embankment.

When the two friends weren't hunting, they were riding around to girls' houses. Most parents didn't like Ken and John, and forbade their daughters to have anything to do with them. Several girls were attracted to them, though, and managed to meet the boys secretly after school and on the weekends. One girl used to sneak out of her parents' farmhouse and meet Ken in the timber after dark.

When John spent the night at Ken's house, people were stacked up like wood in the bedrooms and John slept in the same bed with him and Tim. There always seemed to be a lot of arguing and fighting going on. John felt sorry for Mabel because she worked hard all the time and barely seemed to stay even with things. She never had a new dress or anything for herself. The others seemed to just go on about their business. Ken stayed at John's house a few times and was always cleaned up, well-behaved, and polite to his parents.

Toward the end of eighth grade, Short Linville, the school bus driver, stopped by the McElroy farm three or four days in a row and found no one waiting. Each time, somebody came to the door and waved him on. Finally, one of Ken's sisters came out and explained to him that he needn't stop at the house because neither Ken nor Tim would be going to school anymore. (Short didn't bring the bus around to the McElroy farm until years later when he stopped for Ken's children.)

John started the ninth grade but didn't last long. He got into an argument with the principal, hit him in the mouth, and quit before he was kicked out.

Stealing wasn't a new activity for Ken and John—they had always swiped stuff—but when Ken got a 1936 Ford, theft acquired more purpose because they needed gas and parts. They took out the backseat and lined the space with plywood. At night the two boys would drive to a farm and scoop grain from a bin until the car was full to the windows. The next morning they would drive to an elevator and unload the grain for cash, usually with no questions asked. Sometimes they would spot tractors or trucks sitting in the fields during the day and come back at night and siphon gas from the tanks. When the transmission on the Ford went out, Ken and John looked around until they found another 1936 Ford sitting in a farmyard. Waiting until the farmer was gone for the weekend, they slipped in and removed the transmission in little more than an hour. They took it back to the farm and had it installed in Ken's car by dinnertime.

Ken never cared for work. He and John found jobs in a nursery in a small town in Iowa when they were about fifteen, but they were fired the first week when Ken was caught fooling around with a young girl who also worked there. The way John saw it, Ken never got over the fact that he was poor, and he resented people who had money and new cars and good clothes. He could never bring himself to do their shit work.

If you didn't go to school, and you wouldn't work, there was really only one other way to get by.

PART
TWO

4

In 1952, when he was eighteen, Ken McElroy married Oleta, a sixteen-year-old girl from St. Joe. Soon afterward, they moved to Denver, where one of Ken's sisters lived. Her husband, a construction foreman, gave Ken a job. Ken and Oleta stayed in Denver for six months, then moved to the mountains, where Oleta had a still-born child.

One day, as Ken was working on the construction crew, a cribbing form fell about thirty feet and hit him on the head, splitting his safety helmet and cutting his scalp. The accident jammed the nerves and muscles in his neck, causing him periodic episodes of severe pain and occasional blackout spells the rest of his life. (McElroy told people that this injury resulted in a steel plate being implanted in his head, and many people attributed much of his subsequent bizarre and violent behavior to the plate.)

The Colorado job was Ken's last attempt to function in the straight world. In 1955 or 1956, he and Oleta moved back to Missouri, where he initially centered his activity in the St. Joe area, although he soon began roaming the entire six-county area of northwest Missouri. The stealing he and his buddies had done in junior high school, for which they were never punished, convinced him there were easier ways to make a living than running a jackhammer, digging ditches, or hoeing beans.

He started off small time, stealing one hog or calf at a time. He rigged a toggle switch to shut off the running lights in his Ford and shored up the plywood lining in the back. During the day he roamed the gravel roads looking for calves or hogs that were fat and ready for market, noting the locations of the closest gates. He would return late at night, usually around 1 or 2 A.M., and park as close to the animals as possible. Dressed in dark clothes, he would isolate a fat hog and, if the gate was close by, guide it through by the tail. Otherwise, he would lift the beast, which could weigh 250 pounds, one arm under its neck and the other in back of its rear legs, and carry it against his chest while he stepped over the barbed wire fence. With the hog in his trunk, he would drive away, rear end low, often to another farmer's house, where he would get fifty or sixty dollars for the animal. Occasionally, if the job went smoothly, he would take the hog up to his father's farm, and then return for a second and maybe a third animal.

But even this was a meager living. His friend John had joined the Navy at age seventeen and was now out. He tracked Ken down and found him living in a squalid flat in St. Joe with a woman who wouldn't even get out of bed for the visit; Ken was obviously embarrassed by his situation. He had a long way to go if he was ever to hold his head up around the rich farmers of Nodaway County.

Nevertheless, up north, around Skidmore, Graham, Maitland, and Quitman, the legend was growing. Children in junior high and grade school grew up hearing stories about Ken McElroy. People whispered that he had raped a fourteen-year-old Quitman girl who became pregnant and died delivering twins at home because she couldn't afford to go to the hospital. A year later, according to the rumors, he returned and raped her older sister, who later ended up marrying one of his best coon-hunting buddies. People talked about what happened whenever Ken was around—the heavy drinking, sex, and violence. Just hearing his name was enough to bring a taste of fear to a child's mouth.

Adults shook their heads over the stories and asked each other why he never got punished for the stealing and raping. Most people just stayed away from him and places he hung out. For the better-off families that wasn't that hard to do—McElroy didn't pick on people who had money for lawyers or had influence in the community. He picked on the poorer country folks.

When Ken was about twenty, he befriended an eleven- or twelve-year-old boy, Larry D., who came from a poor family of dedicated coon hunters in the Quitman area. Ken didn't have much then either, only his beat-up car, but he was friendly and generous to Larry. Ken bought him pop, gave him rides, and if Larry ever needed anything, Ken gave it to him and never brought it up again. Larry admired Ken's style; once he took a gun rack and strapped it to his leg, then sawed off an old shotgun and walked around with it stuck in the rack.

Larry came to understand that Ken was also a very dangerous man. If Ken didn't like someone, or heard he was saying bad things about him or a member of his family, that person would walk out of the tavern one day and find Ken waiting for him around the corner with a shotgun or a long-bladed corn knife. When Ken drank, his grievances would eat on him. He would tell Larry what he was going to do to get even with someone who had crossed him, and then, as the wide-eyed boy watched, Ken would carry out his threats. Before long, Ken was asking Larry to come along on his nocturnal stealing jaunts.

During this period, a seventeen-year-old girl named Barbara T. was hanging out with her girlfriend at the bar in Burlington Junction, a small town north of Quitman. The girls noticed a good-looking, muscular man with dark hair and pretty, dark blue eyes begin to come around. He drove an old white Ford and was usually alone. He either sat by himself at the end of the bar, or played pool or shuffleboard. The girls got to know "Kenny," and soon they were partying with him regularly. They would be drinking and talking, and all of a sudden he would say "Let's go," and off they would go, never knowing where, usually to bars in other towns or somebody's place in St. Joe. Ken seemed happy in those days, unless he hit the liquor too hard. He had plenty of girls wherever he went, and they were always young—younger than his seventeen-year-old friends. He would laugh and tell them they didn't have to worry about him.

"You're too old for me," he would say. "I like my women young and tender. I like that young meat."

By "young meat," he meant thirteen or fourteen. One thirteen-year-old girl, Donna G., used to sneak out of her farmhouse in the middle of the night to see him. She lived with her grandparents, who owned a tavern in a nearby small town. One night, when Ken and the two girls had been running around and drinking heavily, they stopped in at the tavern. Ken teased the grandfather—asking how things were at the farm and how Donna was doing—until finally the old man lost his temper.

"You stay away from her, goddamn it, or I'll get the law on you!"

Ken stopped talking and joking. He sat perfectly still and stared at the old man. The two girls also quieted down. After four or five long minutes, the three of them left, not saying a word. In the truck, Ken announced that they were going to the farmhouse to burn it down.

On the ride, they passed around a bottle of Jack Daniel's. Once inside the farmhouse, Ken said he was hungry and wanted a sandwich before they set to work. He found the bread, and the two girls got baloney and lettuce and mayonnaise from the refrigerator. By this time, the mood had lightened, and the three were joking and laughing, Ken describing with delight how the blazing farmhouse would light up the darkened countryside. Then they heard a noise overhead—the squeaking of bed springs and footsteps in the hallway.

"That must be Donna's uncle," Ken said, startled. "He's not a bad ol' guy, doesn't deserve being burned up, anyway. We'll have to come back." Disappointed, they finished making the sandwiches and walked out the door, eating and swigging from the whiskey bottle. A year or so later, Donna bore Ken a son.

5

Not long after McElroy returned from Colorado, he began running around with Sharon, a fifteen-year-old girl from a poor family in the St. Joe area. Sharon was sweet and unworldly and seemed drawn to Ken because of his style and strength. One night, she and Ken were quarreling in his pickup, when Ken pulled out a shotgun and told her if she didn't shut up, he was going to blow her head off. Whether by accident or design, the gun discharged and tore open the underside of Sharon's chin, leaving permanent scars. The police were called and charges were filed. Ken explained to Oleta that he would have to divorce her and marry Sharon in order to avoid prosecution for assault with a deadly weapon. Oleta agreed to the divorce, and in 1958 Sharon became the second Mrs. Ken McElroy.

In July 1959, Sharon bore Ken a son, Jerome. The family moved to the farm outside of Skidmore, living in the two-bedroom house with Tony, Mabel, and Tim. Ken was gone a lot, and the family became concerned about the baby's well-being. Once Tony almost backed his truck over Jerome, who sat unattended in the driveway. Ken's sister Helen came to visit when Jerome was just over a year old and concluded that Ken and Sharon were leaving too much of the child care to Tony and Mabel. So Helen took Jerome back with her to California. Soon afterward, Ken and Sharon left the farm and moved to a tiny house outside Burlington Junction.

Sharon seemed to both love and fear Ken. More than once she tried to get away from him, but it never lasted very long. She had neither the resources nor the strength to hold out. In 1961, she bore him a daughter, Tammy Sue.

One afternoon that year, Sharon appeared with her baby in the sheriff's office in Maryville and told a story about how Ken had locked them in the house and left them for over two days. She had finally escaped and caught a ride to town. Now, she was scared about what he would do when he found out. She described the beatings she had suffered when he became angry. A social worker came to the sheriff's office to help her, but Sharon was so frightened she could barely keep track of where she was and what she was saying. Her eyes darted constantly around the room, and she couldn't sit still. The social worker arranged for both Sharon and her baby to stay with a foster family who lived on a farm outside Graham.

Linda B. and her husband loved children, but were unable to have any of their own, so they had begun taking in foster children that year. Sharon and her baby were two of their first guests.

To Linda, Sharon seemed a sweet, shy nineteen-year-old who obviously hadn't been around much. She was anxious to learn homemaking skills and followed Linda around and watched her sew, cook, and clean house. Sharon was a conscientious mother and took good care of her baby. She had one false tooth in front that popped out every once in a while and made her look kind of silly.

Linda learned from the social worker that McElroy had brought a fourteen-year-old girl named Sally D. out to their house to live with him and Sharon. McElroy had sex with both of them and frequently beat them up. Sharon couldn't handle it and wanted out.

Sharon and Tammy stayed on the farm for about six weeks. The prosecutor had filed a complaint charging Ken with abusing Sharon, and the social worker brought her to the courthouse to sign the complaint. The sheriff's office and state patrol had been alerted and were standing by to execute the arrest warrant. Somehow, McElroy found out where Sharon was and appeared in the social worker's doorway, demanding to talk to his wife. The social worker told him he had to get permission from the judge, which was granted on the condition that the meeting take place in the prosecutor's office. Ken sweet-talked Sharon and told her that if she came home, he would bring Jerome back from California. At the end of the conversation, Sharon told the prosecutor she wouldn't sign the papers. That night, McElroy came to Linda's farm and picked up Sharon, Tammy, and their belongings. Linda heard later that when Ken got Sharon home that night, he beat her terribly.

Sally was a skinny, gawky kid with pretty strawberry blond hair, brown eyes, and light freckles. Her mother had died when Sally was very young, and she lived in Quitman with her dad, who was a butcher, and her two brothers. In 1960 she was thirteen years old and very much a child—she would believe anything someone told her and do whatever an adult said. Ken McElroy hunted coons and traded dogs with one of her brothers, and soon he was hanging around and paying lots of attention to this trusting girl—picking her up after school, giving her rides home, and buying her candy.

Kirby Goslee, Q's third oldest son, who was in junior high with Sally, thought she was cute and arranged to meet her at a school dance. But when he passed by her house the afternoon before the dance and saw Ken McElroy's car in her driveway, he decided to forget the whole thing.

One night Sally was dumped out of the Ford onto a lawn in town, screaming and bleeding, her clothes torn and ripped. The people who found her took her to the hospital. In their words, she looked "like an animal hit on her." Afterward, Ken got hold of her and threatened to kill her father if she didn't do what he said. A few days later she moved in with him and Sharon.

By this time Larry had begun stealing with Ken, and he often went out to the house where Ken and the two women lived. One night, he and Ken had been out late prowling the countryside. When they came in around 1 A.M., Ken undressed and climbed into one of the three beds in the bedroom. Sharon was still up, and she started complaining to Larry that Ken was always taking Sally with him when he went places, and that Ken liked Sally more than he did her.

"You better be quiet," Larry told her. "Ken might not be asleep yet."

"Hey, Larry," said Ken, hauling himself out of bed. "Have you ever seen the Saturday night fights?" McElroy then proceeded to knock Sharon around the room until she could no longer stand up.

With his two women, Ken ran the show. He did whatever he pleased, came and went at will, and had other girlfriends, but Sharon and Sally were to stay home and keep their mouths shut. If they kept quiet and did as he said, they would be all right.

Sally told a friend that sometimes McElroy would beat Sharon and her up and then have violent sex with them, using objects. Sometimes, he would simply go from one to the other. Sally grew tired of taking turns with Sharon, and after a while, she began to feel that she wasn't worth much anymore. Being with Ken made her feel like trash, a wasted piece of flesh.

Sally's friend could never understand why Sally and Sharon put up with Ken or why so many women were attracted to him. But they were—young and old, ugly and pretty, women fell all over themselves when he was around.

Sally began having Ken's children—she had Ken, Jr., in 1961, Lisa in 1963, and Jeffery in 1964. At the same time, Sharon continued having Ken's children. After Tammy Sue, she had Teresa Lyn in 1963, Tina Renee in 1964, and Debbie Ann in 1965. At one time, both Sharon and Sally were in the Fairfax hospital having Ken's babies.

During this period, the thieving became more sophisticated. McElroy developed a network of girlfriends who lived on farms in the area. These women would take the stolen animals and sell them at various markets and auctions using their own names. Ken would stop by a few days later to settle up; he would have sex with the women and give them a little something for their effort.

Larry was a heavy drinker, and he and Ken drank constantly when they were just prowling. But Ken wouldn't let him drink when they were rustling livestock, which was serious business. Once, Ken came for Larry in a truck with stock guards on the sides, and they headed off for some animals that Ken had spotted during the day. Ken pulled over by the side of the road and put on a pair of old boots he had picked up somewhere and would discard later that night. He felt for the corn knife under the seat, and then took the 12-gauge off the rack. He pumped a shell into the chamber and told Larry to begin rounding up the cattle. "If anybody comes," said Ken, "you take off and get out of the way 'cause I'm gonna kill the sonofabitch." Larry maneuvered two five-hundred-pound steers up the ramp into the truck. He and Ken headed for St. Joe to drop the cattle off at a friend's place.

* * *

After Sally had had three children, McElroy was finally done with her. Her father had died, leaving Ken without one of his holds on her, and besides, he had started spending a lot of time with a new girlfriend in St. Joe. Sally had no friends or close family left, so she moved with her three kids into a tiny apartment in Maryville. She had trouble keeping a job, but she took good care of the children. Except for one night.

A girlfriend talked Sally into going to a party in St. Joe after promising her that she had a responsible baby-sitter for Sally's kids. The baby-sitter, a high-school girl, invited her friends over, and they partied and drank and threw bottles from the rooftop, creating such a disturbance that the neighbors called the police. The police came and, finding no responsible adult, took the children into custody. When Sally learned what had happened, she went to see her children and cried when the authorities took the little baby back from her. The county filed dependency and neglect charges and the kids were placed in foster care. Without money, without friends or family, Sally didn't fight. She simply disappeared.

Linda and her husband, the foster parents, fell in love with all three of Sally's children when they came to live with them on the farm. Ken, Jr., was about three and had blue eyes and light blond hair. Lisa was a darling two-year-old with golden hair that framed her face in a cascade of falling ringlets. Jeffery, who was just a baby, didn't stay long. Upon discovering he had a serious hernia, they decided that, because their farm was far from any medical care, they weren't the right family for him, so he was taken away. Ken, Jr., and Lisa were bright and friendly, and apparently well adjusted. They seldom cried. They didn't seem to know who their dad was, and Linda didn't tell them. She also didn't tell people in the community, who had taken a liking to the kids.

Sally had visiting rights, but in the almost two years her children were on the farm, she never came to see them. McElroy never came around or showed any interest in them either.

Eventually, the county initiated proceedings to terminate parental rights and put Ken, Jr., and Lisa up for adoption. (One courthouse observer felt that the fact that they were Ken McElroy's kids hastened the court's decision to terminate parental rights.) When Sally showed up at court for the final hearing, in which she did not contest their adoption, Ken, Jr., and Lisa scarcely seemed to remember her. After the proceedings were over, Sally played with them in the hall outside the courtroom for a few minutes, sweet and gentle, almost like a child herself. Then the kids got excited about going, the way kids will, and Ken, Jr., said to Linda, "Come on, Mom, let's get in the car and go!" Kneeling, Sally drew her children to her and hugged and kissed them. Gently brushing the hair from their foreheads, she looked each one in the eye and whispered good-bye. Then she stood and walked alone down the long hall. As the retreating figure grew smaller in the dim light, and the kids tore down the stairs in a racket, Linda was overcome by sadness.

Preparing Ken, Jr., and Lisa for the adoptive parents who were coming to get them was difficult for Linda. The children seemed all right, but on the way to their new parents' car, Ken, Jr., reminded Linda of his younger brother, saying, "You know, you gave Jeffery away, and he never came back." Right before Ken, Jr., got in the car, he turned to give her a final hug and said, "Mom, someday you'll hear a knockin' on your door, and it'll be me."

Linda had one snapshot of the three kids, with their blond hair and blue eyes, and she put it in a special place in her album of foster kids. Later, she heard that Sally had been in a mental hospital and then became a prostitute in St. Joe, although she never learned if it was true.

By the mid-sixties, Ken McElroy was creating a common cause among lawmen in St. Joe and adjacent counties. They knew he was stealing hogs, cattle, and coon dogs; they were convinced he ran a ring of thieves that stole grain from elevators and expensive chemicals from farmers' supply stores in Missouri, Kansas, and Nebraska; and they knew he carried a loaded shotgun with him at all times. They even knew how he went about his crimes.

Proving what they knew was something else altogether. McElroy had a number of places around where he stashed livestock, and the animals were usually sold in women's names. Marvin Dycus, an investigator with the Buchanan County Sheriff's Department, headquartered in St. Joe, spent a lot of time trying to nail McElroy. Dycus had an uncomplicated view of him: "He was a mean son of a bitch and a snake—you never, ever turned your back on him." He investigated McElroy many times for livestock theft, but could

never make it stick. McElroy always managed to move the livestock faster than he could catch up with him. Dycus uncovered a
farm at Willow Brook, a small town near St. Joe, where he was
convinced McElroy was holding stolen animals. But whenever the
cops showed up there, McElroy was always ready for them. He
would not talk, and he would not let them look around without a
warrant. "If you think you've got a case against me, prove it," he
would say defiantly to Dycus.

Two things made McElroy's business easier. Some sale barns
cooperated by not keeping good records and by not making readily
available to law enforcement the records they did keep. Also, Missouri law did not require branding of livestock, and farmers had
difficulty making their identifications stick in court. If a farmer
said he recognized his five hogs in a pen of fifty, he'd better be able
to point out identifying characteristics, such as a scar, a split ear,
or unusual coloration. In the larger hog operations, holding as
many as 500 or 1,000 hogs, identification was virtually impossible.
The fact was, as McElroy well knew, to make the charges stick, the
cops would virtually have to catch him loading someone else's hogs
into his truck.

Some assault charges were filed against McElroy in Buchanan
County in those days, but they never stuck either. One was filed by
a woman, and later dismissed on her request. And a farmer filed
charges after catching McElroy stealing two of his horses, but
withdrew them after McElroy smashed him across the face with a
rifle.

6

In 1961, when Ken was twenty-six, he met Alice Wood. Fifteen years old, with brown hair and pretty blue eyes, Alice worked as a clerk in Herman's drugstore in St. Joe. The boyfriend of a fellow clerk stopped in frequently, and one day he came in with a tall, dark, well-built, good-looking guy, and introduced him to Alice. Alice found him charming and dashing, with a flair for doing things his own way and spending money as if it didn't matter. She was impressed.

Alice's experience with men before this had not been good. She had not known her father, but her mother told her he was an alcoholic who had walked out on the family when Alice was a baby. Later, her mother wouldn't let him around the kids and had only bad things to say about him. (After Alice was grown, he would come to see her, but only when he wanted something.)

When Alice was four or five years old, her mother married a man named Otha Embrey, whom Alice disliked from the very beginning. If she was made to go to the store with him, she would refuse to let him buy her a candy bar. According to Alice, he would often come home drunk and abusive, but her mother didn't seem to see it as a problem. Finally, when Alice was thirteen years old, she ran away from home and moved into an apartment with a friend. When she met Ken McElroy, she was young, naïve, and on her own, without any real family support. Soon, she became fascinated with Ken McElroy, with the sheer force of the man.

In 1964, Ken left Sharon and the four girls at the farm in Skidmore, and moved in with Alice in St. Joe. In those days Alice loved him—in fact, she idolized him. She was the little girl without a father who needed taking care of, and he was the older man, knowledgeable in the ways of the world, tough, and strong. But it didn't work out that way. Ken was almost never around, and when he left, he never said where he was going or when he would be back. He could be gone for two days, or two weeks, and when he did return, he never gave any explanations. Although he was free to come and go, Alice wasn't. She was to be there for him whenever he came home, to keep his house, satisfy his needs, and make no demands. If she asked questions or tried to do things on her own, she risked a beating. When he was drinking, he often flew into violent rages over the smallest thing—a look she gave him, or another man saying hello to her on the street. Sometimes, he would crack her across the face with a backhand; other times he would grab her by the hair and yank her across the room.

He erupted when she complained about his being gone all the time or seeing other women. Afterward, the beating was always her fault; if she hadn't complained, she wouldn't have gotten beaten. He was never to blame. In all the years he beat her, Ken never once apologized. Many times, she was so black-and-blue and swollen that she was ashamed to go outside. In the later years, more than once in the middle of a beating she fantasized about grabbing one of his guns and shooting him.

One time, when he had been gone for days, he walked in the bedroom and found her packing boxes of clothes. He went crazy over her walking out on him, and before she could explain that she was just putting the clothes away, he had grabbed her by the hair and swung her into the wall. He ended up with a fistful of her hair and she was left with lumps and a bald spot.

Other times, the rage seemed to come from nowhere. He would be fine, and then he would start drinking whiskey and brooding about something that somebody had said to him two months ago, or some imagined slight in a pool game. The memory would eat away inside him until he couldn't handle it anymore, and he would explode. If Alice got involved, if she tried to reason with him, even if she just tried to calm him down, she was immediately favoring the other side and became the enemy—another person to be punished. She learned to keep her mouth shut and stay out of his way.

The other women in Ken's life were hard for Alice to accept at

first. When she met him, she had a schoolgirl's vision of fidelity
between a man and a woman in love. She knew that Ken saw other
women, but she thought maybe he would settle down once they
lived together. He didn't. The same thing that fascinated her about
Ken fascinated lots of women, and he had girlfriends everywhere.
After a while, she could tell when Ken had a new girlfriend because he calmed down, and would even be nice to her.

As the years passed, Alice learned that women were merely possessions to Ken—that he needed and used them. As far as sex
went, it was for his gratification alone: he had it with a woman, and
then went on his way. In fact, Alice felt that his real need for
women was not sexual, but to boost his ego. The way Ken saw the
world, he was always having to prove himself, always having to
show that he was more of a man than the next guy, and one of the
ways to prove it was by collecting women, the younger the better.
Another way was to screw the women of men who thought they
were better than he was, the rich farmers and ranchers. He would
laugh and remark to Alice that he was really doing those men a
favor by keeping their wives satisfied.

Ken and Alice moved to Amazonia and then Rosendale, two
small towns close by St. Joe. Alice had a stillborn child during this
period and became pregnant again in early 1968. She gave birth to
Juarez on September 19 of that year.

Meanwhile, Sharon and her four girls, who had stayed on the
farm Ken left, moved to Florida to live with Sharon's mother.

7

In the late sixties, McElroy hooked up with a man who would run with him until the very end. Like most of Ken's pals, Fred M. was a coon hunter. He met McElroy at a dog meet in Bedford, Iowa, and took an immediate liking to him.

About ten years younger than McElroy, Fred was a known rowdy, drinker, and thief. He would steal anything, but he preferred to steal guns. He threw in with Ken McElroy because McElroy was bigger and better at stealing: he knew which farmhouses had valuable furniture and guns; he knew when the residents were going to be away, and he always had plans on how to get in the house, get the goods, and dispose of them. Fred also threw in with Ken because Ken had more guts than most other guys. He would do things most of them wouldn't dream of doing, and just being around him made Fred feel stronger and tougher. Nobody ever, ever fucked with Ken McElroy. Being Ken's buddy, Fred got a little more respect than otherwise.

Ken treated him like a son. Once, when Fred said he wanted a job in a town about 100 miles away, but he had no way to get there, Ken gave him $300 to buy a car and $100 for gas. The money was never mentioned again. The two of them also played a lot of pool in the bars, and one night Ken won all Fred's money, his watch and ring, then gave it all back to him with a smile and a pat on the back at the end of the evening.

For Fred, the most exciting times were when Ken got twisted over something and decided he had to get even. He would start drinking and talking about it, and the more he drank, the madder he got. His face would get red, and he would start describing loudly and angrily just what he was going to do for revenge. He would turn to the man on the stool next to him and say, "You think I won't?" Eventually, Ken would fall silent and stare at the counter or the wall; finally he would stand up and demand of Fred, "You in or out?" Fred was almost always in, because he wanted to see what was going to happen.

Ken McElroy and his sidekicks were known characters to the law in Doniphan County, Kansas; they were suspected of regularly stealing animals, grain, and chemicals. Troy, the county seat, is thirteen miles west of St. Joe, on Highway 36, an easy jump across the Missouri River. On February 7, 1969, the farmers' co-op warehouse at Leona, a tiny town a few miles west of Troy, was broken into and burglarized. The thieves took several cases of a new herbicide which was so expensive that the trunk of a car could easily hold more than $1,000 worth. Two nights later, the warehouse was burglarized again, and the thieves took more of the chemical.

The local cops speculated that Ken McElroy was behind the break-ins, and figured that if he had come twice, he might come a third time. The co-op hired an elderly night watchman, placed him inside the warehouse with a 20-gauge shotgun, and told him to protect the goods. Five nights later, the watchman was standing guard when he heard somebody breaking in the door. He yelled at the thieves to stop, and they turned and ran. He fired the shotgun at the retreating figures, then called the sheriff's department.

When Undersheriff Jerry Dubach received the call in Troy, he jumped in his car and headed west toward Leona. The night was cold and snowy and the roads were icy; any speed over 35 or 40 mph was extremely dangerous. On the edge of town Dubach met a yellow Cadillac heading east toward Missouri at 65 mph. He flipped around and chased the Caddy, but couldn't close in on it without risking losing control. He followed the car as it crossed the bridge over the Missouri River into St. Joe and turned off at the 22nd Street exit. But by the time Dubach reached 22nd Street, his quarry was gone. He drove around a while looking for it, but the Caddy had simply disappeared.

Jim McCubbin was the special agent for the Kansas Bureau of Investigation assigned to the investigation. Like every other cop

around, he knew Ken McElroy and was anxious to nail him. Mc-
Cubbin had been unable to develop any proof of McElroy's involvement in the chemical thefts, until he learned that the night of
the third burglary, February 14, 1969, a man had had some shotgun pellets removed from his rear end in a small town not far from
St. Joe. McCubbin visited the hospital and discovered that the man
was Ken McElroy, and that the size of the pellets taken out of his
ass were the same size as the pellets from the watchman's gun. He
turned up some corroborating proof, and took McElroy in for
questioning at Troop H headquarters in St. Joe. McElroy denied
everything.

Nevertheless, on October 27, 1971, prosecutors in Doniphan
County filed an indictment charging McElroy and another man
with five counts of burglary and theft. The judge in Troy issued
warrants for their arrest, which were sent to the sheriff's department in Andrew County for execution, along with a request for
extradition. The warrants were never executed and the case was
never prosecuted.

8

In the early sixties, a man joined the Missouri State Highway Patrol who would in time earn a reputation as the only cop around who was not afraid to go up against McElroy one on one. Richard Dean Stratton—called Dean by his family and friends, Stratton by Ken McElroy, and "Lean and Mean" by his many admirers—was a tall man with a spare, wiry build, a thin face, and short brown hair. Even as a rookie trooper, Stratton had a certain presence, an air of confidence and self-assurance. As time passed, the legend surrounding him would span almost as many counties as Ken McElroy's, but Stratton never fit the image of the highway cop in dark blue, swarthy face masked in aviator glasses, swaggering with the authority of law and justice. Instead, he was an easygoing man who smiled easily and appeared very relaxed. He talked in a low, mellow voice and chuckled readily. He could have been the basketball coach at the local high school. But when Stratton was on the job, his bearing changed slightly: His spine straightened, his moves became efficient and graceful, and his voice grew steady and even. As his concentration centered, his eyes locked in on his subject. A smile lingered on his face, but his eyes became still.

Born in southwestern Nebraska in 1936, Stratton joined the patrol when he was twenty-six. His first assignment was Maryville, and he broke in under a sergeant who drummed into him the importance of getting out of his patrol car and meeting the people in the small towns. Stratton would park in front of Mom's Cafe in Skidmore and drink coffee with the farmers and seed dealers, and when his turn came, he would pick up the check. He hunted and fished with some of the local boys, tramping through the fields and timber and stream beds with them for pheasant, coon, and deer. He could talk corn prices, weather, and women right along with the rest of them.

One of the first conversations he had with his sergeant was about Ken Rex McElroy. Even in those days he was a known hog thief and cattle rustler.

"He's a rogue and a troublemaker," the sergeant told Stratton. "He's a thief and a bully who will use a shotgun—don't ever trust him and don't ever turn your back on him."

Stratton learned how to deal with McElroy the hard way. One morning around 4 o'clock, Stratton was cruising the blacktops west of Skidmore, keeping track of who was where and what was going on, when McElroy's green pickup went by, riding low in the rear. Stratton pulled him over. The patrolman was struck by McElroy's eyes up close: They were dark and cold and deep, and Stratton felt as if they were looking into the far reaches of his soul.

McElroy said he was on his way to St. Joe.

Stratton examined the hogs in the back of the truck—two red and two black, squeezed in tight—and asked McElroy, "Whose hogs are those?" McElroy gave an evasive reply, so Stratton asked him straight out, "Did you steal those hogs, Ken?"

McElroy's face darkened and his eyes seemed to get blacker, until Stratton felt as if they were piercing his mind.

"Goddamn it," McElroy said, "you're just like everyone else around here—you think I steal hogs for a living!"

As McElroy started to reach behind him, Stratton realized the deal was going bad. Turning back to the window, McElroy dropped the barrel of a 12-gauge shotgun in Stratton's face, his finger curved around the trigger. McElroy said nothing, but his dark eyes glittered in anticipation. Stratton had been caught flat-footed, out of position without a weapon drawn, and he knew it. The only thing he could do was back off and hope he didn't get his face blown away. He had no doubt that if he went for his pistol, or tried to grab the shotgun, McElroy would shoot him.

"OK," said Stratton, "this time is yours. But the next time we meet, I'll be ready for you. When I come for you, I'll get you." He walked away, and it was over.

The incident stuck in Stratton's gut. He was a rookie, young and cocky, and he had been careless in the way he approached McElroy. From that night on, he began keeping book on the man; he learned who he ran with, where he hung out, the names and descriptions of his various women, and the makes and models of all his vehicles. Through informants and other sources, he tried to keep track of him—where he was and what he was up to. He never passed up a chance to stop him; over the years he pulled him over at least twelve times for speeding, invalid registration, dragging muffler, faulty head lamp, and other infractions. Sooner or later, Stratton knew, there would come a time to even things up.

9

In late 1969 or early 1970, McElroy went on a spree of violence and stealing that would result in nineteen separate felony charges being brought against him: two in St. Joe, five in Savannah, and twelve in Maryville. He would demonstrate his ability to defeat the criminal justice system, if there were any doubt, by the application of two simple rules, one following the other: If you delay a case long enough, a witness may disappear or forget what he saw, and if there is no witness, there is no case.

Rather than getting better, as Alice had hoped, her life with Ken deteriorated after they moved to the farm outside of Skidmore in 1969. Ken was seldom home, and when he was around, the beatings were worse and more frequent. His sexual activity in the area was rampant; young girls and other men's wives took up a lot of his time. Some of the stuff she saw and heard about almost made her sick.

Mabel and Alice were close, and Mabel could see what was going on. Several times she talked to Ken, hoping to persuade him to stop abusing Alice, but the talks did no good. Ken's only reaction was to get furious with Alice for telling his mother, although Alice didn't have to say a word because the evidence was written in bruises on her face.

Finally, Alice had had enough. She grabbed Juarez, who was by then three years old, and took off for St. Joe. On April 10, 1972, Ken called Alice and told her he was coming for both of them, and

Juarez was going with him, whether she came or not. This threat—
he would take Juarez and never allow her to see him again—was
really the only one that worked anymore. But this time, Alice told
him no, she wasn't going with him, and she wasn't giving up Juarez. She took Juarez and went to her mother and stepfather's house
and got a .32-caliber pistol from the bedroom, determined to protect herself and her son. If Ken tried to carry out his threat, she
told herself, she would shoot him as he walked through the door.
Alice sat down at the kitchen table and began trying to load the
pistol. In the process, the gun accidentally discharged and a bullet
tore into her hip. She was taken to Methodist Hospital and was
admitted to intensive care. (Alice stayed in the hospital for a week,
but the bullet was never removed.)

McElroy called the house that same night, looking for Alice and
Juarez.

"She's in the hospital," Otha told him.

"Well, I'm coming for Juarez," McElroy said, "and I'll shoot
anybody that stands in my way."

"The hell you will!" Otha replied.

A short time later Otha looked out the living room window and
saw McElroy approaching the house with a rifle in his hand. Otha
went into another room and got a shotgun, but when he came
back, McElroy had disappeared. After a while, Otha put the gun
away. As he walked back into the living room, a rifle shot shattered
the window and tore into his left thigh. He saw McElroy run to the
pickup with the rifle in his hand and drive away. Otha went to
Methodist Hospital, where he was treated and released that night.

McElroy later told his lawyers that he had stood across the
street from the house and yelled at Otha to come out. He then hid
in his truck, and upon seeing Otha standing in the window with a
gun, shot him with a .22-caliber rifle.

Three months later, the Buchanan County prosecutor filed a
felony assault charge against McElroy, alleging that he had shot
Otha in the leg with a rifle with intent to do great bodily harm.
Originally, McElroy retained a St. Joe attorney to represent him.

Life for Otha and his family was hell after the assault charge was
filed. McElroy called Otha at least once every day or night, threatening to shoot him on the way to work, kill his wife at home, or
shoot his child on the school playground. McElroy drove by the
house repeatedly and followed Otha in his car. His wife and child

became scared to leave the house, and Otha began carrying a gun for protection. Several times McElroy demanded that Otha step out onto the lawn so they could have it out man to man. Finally, after a couple of months of harassment, Otha figured *what the hell*, and walked out onto his lawn with a rifle. Nobody showed up, but a little later McElroy called and said he had seen Otha standing out on the lawn.

McElroy was no stranger to Otha, and Otha knew what was going on; McElroy was becoming obsessed with him.

"McElroy was a bad dog. He'd sit and talk to you and smile and be as friendly and charming as he possibly could, but the minute you turned your back, he would shoot you if he felt like it. He used to tell me that when he got a bad coon dog, he would hook him onto the trailer and drag him behind the pickup until he was dead. With Ken, everything was always your fault. If he shot you, and you prosecuted him for it, you were the bad guy. He would beat up Alice, beat her silly, she would complain, and then she was the bad person because she was complaining. He shifted the fault onto the victim, and then the victim became responsible for his pain."

Otha, the source of his pain in this case, was terrorized, convinced that McElroy meant to shoot him again. Otha agonized as the assault case was delayed repeatedly. Several times he got a subpoena for a court date and showed up, only to be told that the case had been continued again.

Finally, on January 10, 1973, ten months after the shooting, McElroy came out of the shadows to deal directly with Otha. Otha was drinking at Garland's Tavern in St. Joe, a popular bar that attracted people from surrounding towns and was a favorite hangout of Ken McElroy's. McElroy walked in and pulled a corn knife on Otha.

"I'm going to cut your guts unless you swear not to testify," McElroy said.

Otha pulled a chair between them, and insisted he wouldn't back down. McElroy left, but returned ten minutes later in a burning rage, carrying an automatic 12-gauge shotgun. He locked the doors behind him and yelled at the owners to close the place down.

"Nobody's leaving here," he bellowed. "Nobody's even going to the goddamn bathroom!"

He walked over to Otha and stuck the barrel of the shotgun in his face.

"I'm going to kill you," McElroy said, "unless you swear not to testify." He raised the gun in the air, then dropped the barrel in Otha's face again, pulling the hammer back and resting his finger on the trigger.

"I'm going to start at your feet and shoot all the way up until there's nothing left of you," he said.

No one else in the place moved, and the room fell silent. Believing that McElroy was going to pull the trigger, Otha prepared to die. The gun went up into the air, then swung back into Otha's face.

"I'll blow your goddamn head off if you testify!" McElroy swore. McElroy repeated his threat several times, then pointed the gun at the floor and fired. A crashing boom resounded in the tavern and the frightened patrons jerked in their seats. The pellets tore a hole in the wooden floor a few inches from Otha's feet.

McElroy backed out the front door, gun pointing in the air, cursing Otha.

Sergeant Jacob (Jake) Rostock, a thirty-seven-year-old stocky ex-marine and veteran of the St. Joseph Police Department, responded to the disturbance call at the tavern that night. By the time he reached the bar, everything was over—several customers and a black bartender remained, but none of them, except Otha Embrey, had seen or heard a thing.

McElroy was arrested and released on $1,500 bond. Within a few days prosecutors filed a charge alleging that Ken McElroy did "willfully, unlawfully by menace attempt to deter a witness, to wit: Otha W. Embrey, from appearing or giving evidence in a criminal proceeding, to wit: the prosecution of the said Ken McElroy for the felony crime of felony assault, by threatening to kill the said Otha W. Embrey."

On March 2, for some unexplained reason, the state dismissed the felony charge and refiled it as a misdemeanor, Attempting to Bribe a Witness Not to Testify. At that time, misdemeanors in Missouri were heard first by a magistrate. If found guilty by the magistrate, the defendant had an absolute right to a new trial in the circuit court, by a jury if he chose.

In February, Richard (Gene) McFadin, a Kansas City trial lawyer, took over the defense of both cases. McFadin had been in Savannah on another matter when McElroy approached him about representing him. He didn't know McElroy, nor had he ever heard of him, but at first glance he didn't look like the sort who could afford his services. He listened to the story anyway and told McElroy the fee would be $3,000 for both cases, with $1,000 up front. McElroy paid cash on the spot. This was the beginning of a long, mutually beneficial relationship: McElroy constantly needed a lawyer, always paid cash, and never complained about the fees; and McFadin always (or almost always) got him off.

The second case was tried before a magistrate on April 27, 1973. Otha testified that McElroy had threatened to kill him if he testified in the assault case. The bartender, who was originally going to testify that McElroy had threatened to kill Otha, changed his mind and swore he hadn't seen what had happened. In his testimony, McElroy admitted he had a shotgun with him in the bar, but said he was showing it to someone in hopes of selling it to him. McElroy forgot the gun was loaded, and it accidentally went off. Appearing as a character witness in favor of Ken McElroy, Alice Wood told the court that Ken was a fine person and outstanding citizen. Nevertheless, the magistrate found McElroy guilty of the charge and sentenced him to six months in prison.

This was McElroy's first conviction, but it didn't stick. On May 4, McFadin filed a notice of appeal to the circuit court, which would automatically have resulted in a new trial. Mysteriously, however, the files in the clerk's offices were sealed one day later, on May 5. Under Missouri law, records must be sealed in cases where the defendant is acquitted or the charge is dismissed by the prosecuting attorney. In McElroy's case there was no acquittal (the case couldn't have been tried in the circuit court the day after the appeal), so the prosecuting attorney must have dismissed the charges. The only legitimate reason for a prosecutor to dismiss a case under such circumstances would be the loss of a critical piece of evidence —such as a key witness. Neither of the two prosecutors involved can recall either this case or the underlying assault case.

Otha never knew what happened to the bribery case, but the underlying assault charge was dismissed when he finally told the prosecutor that if after two years, he wasn't going to try the case, he should drop it, since he couldn't handle the harassment any longer. Otha never heard another word about the case.

10

Reid Miller was elected sheriff of Andrew County, which lies just to the south of Nodaway County, for the first time in 1969. A tall, lanky, easygoing type, Miller enforced the law with the help of only one deputy in those days.

When Miller took over, he had heard that Ken McElroy was a dangerous character who loved guns and hated lawmen. The first time he encountered him was in 1970, when he got a call from the highway patrol that Alice Wood had reported that Ken had gone crazy and had been shooting at her. She had fled in her car, and he had followed her and run her off the road into a ditch. She had escaped on foot to a neighbor's house to use the phone, and now she was afraid to leave.

On his way to the house, Miller saw the yellow Cadillac convertible, with the top down, barreling down the road. *That's him*, he said to himself, and flipped a U, hit the siren and lights, and ran him down. McElroy pulled over. Miller pulled the .357 Magnum from its holster and aimed at the driver's door.

"Get out of the car and get your hands up!" Miller yelled.

McElroy emerged and stood casually at the rear of the car with his hands on the trunk. Two patrol cars pulled up, and one of the patrolmen searched McElroy and the Caddy. No guns. They contacted Alice Wood and told her they had him. She was very frightened.

"I can't file any charges," she said. "He'll kill me if I do. I just want to get out of here."

They agreed that the Savannah city marshal, who had shown up by that time, would escort Alice to the Buchanan County line. Once she was across, he would radio back, and they would release McElroy.

McElroy wasn't as tall as Miller expected, but he was big; his arms looked thicker than Miller's thighs. McElroy flat out denied shooting at Alice or even having a gun. He was very nervous about having the pistol pointed at him and told Miller several times to put it away.

"If you're not careful, I'll shoot you right here," Miller said, only half-joking.

"Not if I can get a hold of a gun, you won't," McElroy responded menacingly.

"Yeah, but you ain't going to," said Miller, ending the conversation.

Miller ordered McElroy into the back of the police car, waited until he received the call from the marshal, then turned him loose. "Don't go shooting at her anymore," he said to him. McElroy walked to the Caddy, got in, and drove away, glaring at Miller the entire time.

When Miller took over as sheriff, Andrew County hadn't much of a problem with hog thefts, but soon after this incident, an epidemic broke out. The thefts started up in the northern part of the county. Every couple of days, a few farmers would call or stop in to report four or five hogs or a couple of cows stolen. Soon, the thefts were occurring almost every night, and the farmers started getting more and more upset. They began showing up at Miller's office first thing in the morning. "We lost eight hogs last night," they would say, "what are you going to do about it?" Miller began hitting the gravel roads at night looking for McElroy. He went out at around 10 P.M. and stayed out until 4 or 5 A.M., cruising first the areas of the recent thefts, and then picking other ones at random. He never managed to catch McElroy, or even lay eyes on him. McElroy used different vehicles and different methods, and his targets had no apparent pattern.

After a month or two, the pressure from the farmers became unbearable. Miller would stay up all night trying to catch McElroy in the act, and would spend all day taking complaints from the farmers who'd been hit the night before. He tried, but he couldn't cover the whole damn county.

Miller estimated that in a three-month period the farmers had lost more than $100,000 worth of hogs and cattle. There was also a rash of burglaries involving thefts of tools and antiques from farmhouses. The farmers began staying up at night, sitting by the windows in their darkened farmhouses, holding loaded rifles across their laps, waiting for McElroy. *Something's got to give,* Miller thought.

Since 1969, Ken had been running around with Marcia Surritte, a young woman from the St. Joe area. Marty, as she was called, had long black hair, a fair complexion, and large brown eyes; she was, by all accounts, the most beautiful of all McElroy's women. In 1971, Marty bore a son named Tony.

One day, Miller spotted Alice and Marty driving through Savannah in a car loaded with tools and furniture. He pulled them over and attempted to trace the items to the recent burglaries. Unable to do so, he decided to try to crack the women anyway, and he called in Sergeant Jim Rhoades, a special investigator for the highway patrol. Rhoades had a special hatred for Ken McElroy—Miller had heard him say that McElroy had been hanging around his daughter and that he would kill him if he got a chance.

Miller and Rhoades put considerable pressure on the two women to talk—they pushed them pretty hard, using a variety of techniques to loosen them up—but Miller denied threatening or coercing them. Eventually, according to Miller, Alice, whom he described as a tough, coarse woman, became very upset and angry. "Goddamn it," she said, "I'll just tell you every goddamn thing, then."

For the next two days, Miller claimed, he and Rhoades drove through the countryside with Alice and Marty, who pointed out the farms they had burglarized or stolen hogs from. The two cops developed a cooperative, supportive relationship with the women, taking them to dinner and breakfast and asking about their children. The cops had a list of all the recent thefts, and as they drove by the farms, one of the women would say, "Oh, there's one, that's where we stole some hogs," or "Over there, we broke into that house and stole some furniture."

At one farmhouse, according to Miller, Marty got out of the car and showed them exactly how they had helped Ken steal the hogs. Marty even pointed out the tracks where they had walked the animals through the gate, and explained that they quieted a squealing pig by sticking a finger up its ass. At another place, one of the women told Miller, they had served as lookouts by sitting on a hill across the road from the hog barn, where they could see approaching vehicles and signal Ken with flashlights if there was any trouble. The farmer who lost four hogs that night found the blanket the women had been sitting on. What burned him almost as much as losing the hogs was the human excrement he found not far from the blanket on the hill.

At another farm, Alice told Miller, they were hiding in the bushes when he drove by in his sheriff's car. "We were sure you saw us," she said. Until then, Miller hadn't realized he had ever been that close to Ken McElroy.

Shortly thereafter, Marty signed two statements reflecting question-and-answer sessions with Rhoades.

RHOADES: Marcia, you showed me a house in Andrew County which is one mile south of Highway 59 on Route K approximately one-half mile west. . . . Can you tell me if you were ever at this house and with whom?

MARCIA: I was there with Ken McElroy. He took several items out of the house and out of the cellar. He took several picture frames and a rocking chair out of the house.

RHOADES: How did he get into the house? Was it locked?

MARCIA: He took a crowbar and pried open the back door.

RHOADES: Was there anything unusual about the shapes of the frames?

MARCIA: They were oval . . .

RHOADES: Was one of the items an old-type churn?

MARCIA: Yes, but he got them out of the cellar. He got some jars.

RHOADES: Was there anything else he got out of the buildings at the same time?

MARCIA: He got two gunny sacks of corn out of the corn crib.

RHOADES: Was it a wooden or metal corn crib?

MARCIA: Metal bin I guess it was.

RHOADES: Would this have been about a year ago or more?

MARCIA: This was more than a year ago—about one and a half or maybe two years. I know this was last year in the fall . . .

RHOADES: Do you know what has since happened to these items?

MARCIA: Bill . . . came over and he sold them to him. He has an auction company. He owns an antique place and I think he took some of them there.

RHOADES: Did Ken tell you that Bill . . . bought some?

MARCIA: Ken told me Bill . . . came out and beat him out of all his stuff is the way he put it. He said he didn't give him enough money for it or something.

RHOADES: From your knowledge do you know if Bill . . . knew these items were stolen?

MARCIA: Yes, he did. I was there when Ken told him.

Marcia gave a second statement on hog theft:

RHOADES: Marcia, last Friday, which would have been October 15, 1971, we were driving at your direction to a location north and east of Fillmore and you pointed out a lot or field which lies in the northeast corner of the intersection as being a place where you were when some hogs were stolen there. This is in Andrew County and Herschel Clizer owns this property. Will you tell me what transpired when you were there and who you were with?

MARCIA: Well, Ken McElroy, Glen . . . and I were coon hunting and on the way home Ken said that we might as well stop and get a load for the sale. We went down to this place and they left me parked on the road and they walked up to this hog lot and they walked one at a time down to the corner of the fence and then walked back to the car and put it in the trunk of the car.

RHOADES: When you make a reference to getting a load of it, what do you mean?

MARCIA: Getting a load of hogs. They took the hog by the tail and walked it to the trunk of the car.

RHOADES: About how many hogs did they take this time?

MARCIA: They made two trips but only had two at a time. Two out of there. They drove them up and took them to his dad's place in Skidmore. Then they went back and got two more.

RHOADES: Were you with them both times?

MARCIA: Yes.

RHOADES: Were these fairly large hogs?

MARCIA: Yes, about 275 pounds, I think. They were really big. That is why they only got two at a time. Had to make two trips back. Reason they only made two trips was because it was getting daylight.

RHOADES: Do you know the color of these hogs?

MARCIA: I think they were black and white. I couldn't be positive. There was so many different colors.

RHOADES: Where were the dogs after the hogs were loaded?

MARCIA: They were still hunting.

RHOADES: Did you ever pick the dogs up from hunting that night?

MARCIA: Not that night. We went back the next day. Ken left his coat on the side of the road and the dogs would come back. We went back the next day.

RHOADES: Is this very far from the hog lot?

MARCIA: We were coon hunting around Graham.

On the basis of statements made by both women, Andrew County Prosecuting Attorney Alden Lance filed four separate felony informations against Ken McElroy on February 4, 1972. The charges included stealing four hogs on July 1, 1971; breaking and entering a dwelling house and stealing various items on August 27, 1971; breaking and entering a dwelling house and stealing various items on September 23, 1970; stealing four hogs on September 13, 1971.

The records indicated that Alice and Marcia took several hogs to the auction barn in Oregon, Missouri, and received receipts made out in their names, which they turned over to Lance. Lance and Miller decided to wait for McElroy to come to the auction barn on the day of the sale to pick up his money. When he showed up, they arrested him for hog theft and took him to jail.

Because Lance had filed four separate informations, Miller decided to issue four separate warrants and arrest McElroy three more times. That way, he would be picked up, put in jail overnight, and bonded out four separate times. The only drawback was that the law had a hard time catching Ken McElroy. Few cops were eager to execute the warrants.

In one instance, Miller came upon McElroy by accident on a

gravel road at night. After pulling him over, Miller trained the spotlights on the rear of his car and radioed the patrol. He held his .357 Magnum on McElroy and spread-eagled him at the trunk of the car until the patrol arrived. The patrolman tried putting the cuffs on him, but they lacked an inch of making it around his wrists.

"What'll we do now?" the patrolman asked.

"Tell you what," Miller replied, "I'll put him in the passenger seat of my car and you follow behind."

Miller slid behind the wheel and put the barrel of the .357 Magnum, which had no safety, under his left leg.

"Ken," he said, "if you grab me or make a move, I'll kill you."

"I won't do nothing," said McElroy.

"I hope not," Miller said, "because if I don't get you, the trooper behind us will."

"I won't do nothing."

The ride in was easy. McElroy was overly friendly, seemingly intent on convincing Miller that there would be no problem.

"I'll be out in a few hours," McElroy told Miller while being booked. McFadin was called, a bond hearing was held, and McElroy was out the next morning.

By the third arrest, catching McElroy was taking so long that Miller decided to serve the fourth warrant at the same time. For some reason, McElroy stayed in jail for two days this time before making bond. The lawmen decided to see if they could trick McElroy into admitting the thefts and burglaries. The prosecutor arranged for a patrolman to come to the jail looking and acting like a drunken cowboy. Badly in need of a shave, the patrolman wore a dirty shirt and greasy hat, stank of whiskey, and even had cow shit on his boots. He and Miller put on quite a show in the sheriff's office where McElroy could hear it. The cowboy yelled and cursed the sheriff for picking him up, claimed he wasn't drunk, and called Miller a stupid cop. Miller swore and banged into the desk as he tried to get the cowboy under control and relieve him of his personal possessions. After about ten minutes of this, Miller put the cowboy in the cell with McElroy. The poor cowboy-cop stayed up all night talking to McElroy, trying to get him to open up about what he was in there for, but McElroy didn't utter so much as a complete sentence. When Miller let the patrolman out in the morning, the man shook his head in frustration, cleaned up, and left.

During McElroy's stay the sheriff discovered some loose bricks in the wall of the common room, where the prisoners spent time during the day. The mortar between the bricks had been dug out, apparently with something like a spoon. Prosecutor Lance filed a new charge against McElroy for feloniously attempting to escape while lawfully imprisoned. McElroy denied the charges, but later admitted to Alice that he had dug the mortar out. He wasn't trying to escape, he told her, he was just trying to provoke the sheriff by proving how easily he could undo his building.

Lance and Miller's sole objective in these prosecutions was to nail Ken McElroy. Because the whole case rested on the women's testimony, Lance granted Alice and Marty immunity from prosecution in return for their cooperation. Even so, the case was precarious—Lance had little confidence that the two women would hold firm and actually testify under oath in front of a judge.

Richard McFadin had been admitted to the practice of law in Missouri in 1956. He specialized in litigation and built his reputation in criminal cases, which made up 40 percent of his caseload. Not modest, he claimed to have won approximately 90 percent of his trials, the more glorious of which he would willingly recount in detail with only the slightest encouragement. A short, heavyset man of ruddy complexion, he was easygoing and affable, with a sophisticated type of country charm. He made some people uneasy, probably because they sensed that, behind the easy laugh and relaxed manner, a shrewd and calculating mind was sizing them up and probing for a way to pick their psychological pockets. They were right, and McFadin made no bones about it. He liked to repeat, with a self-promoter's pride, a description of himself as "cunning and devious." "You can call me cunning and devious," he would say with a chuckle, "just as long as you don't call me dishonest." He loved the law and he loved the game—the strategy, the moves and countermoves—and he was good at it, particularly in front of a jury. Like all good performers, he knew his audience.

But like every good lawyer, he also knew that most cases were won by thorough preparation. He sent investigators out to interview every witness, follow up every lead, read every document, and look under every stone. Sooner or later, he usually found something, some discrepancy or contradiction, to hang his case on. And he pushed the law to its limit: His obligation to his client was to

uncover and exploit every loophole and every technicality in the
law, to use every trick in his bag, while staying within the bounds
of legality, if only by one millimeter. He was not morally concerned about or responsible for his client's behavior—he was, in his
own words, a "hired gun." His sole concern was keeping his client
a free man (and getting paid).

In the burglary and theft cases, McFadin saw clearly that there
would be no case against his client without the testimony of Alice
and Marty. McFadin took their depositions more than a year after
the charges were filed, and both women completely recanted their
earlier statements. Alice swore that Miller and Rhoades had
threatened and coerced them into making the statements, and that
none of the information was true. She and Marty had said what
they said because they were mad at Ken and wanted to get even
with him. (Their earlier statements confirmed that they had indeed
been mad at him.) Lance was not surprised, but he was angry. He
knew he had no choice but to dismiss all the charges, including the
one for jailbreaking. Right then and there at the deposition, he
threatened to file perjury charges against the women. Alice asked
McFadin to represent her, but he declined because of the obvious
conflict of interest. The cases were dismissed, confirming for McElroy the rule of "no witnesses, no case." Nothing came of the
threatened perjury charges.

The only good thing resulting from all of this, in Sheriff Miller's
mind, was that the hog theft and cattle rustling came to a complete
halt.

11

Alice returned to the McElroy farm near Skidmore. Not much had changed—Ken was gone most of the time, leaving Timmy to look after her and Juarez. Ken had a fear about being trapped on the farm, being unable to move. If a heavy snow began falling, or he heard that a bad storm was coming, he would take off and stay gone until the storm had passed and the roads were clear and dry. When he did come back, there was no telling what might be in store for her.

Tony died in 1970, and Mabel and Timmy moved to the small house down the road. Mabel took Tony's death hard, and some family members feared that she wouldn't last long, but they underestimated her strength. Alice turned to Mabel for comfort, talking to her about her problems with Ken, and Mabel listened by the hour. She cared about people in an old-fashioned way, and Alice knew Mabel could feel what Alice was feeling and understood her in her heart. Mabel consoled and encouraged Alice, and did what she could to make things better at home.

If Ken told anyone how he was feeling, if he confided to anyone his fears and anxieties about how his life was turning out, he talked to his mother. Others in the family tended to stay away from him, to leave him alone, but Mabel encouraged him to come to her and talk. She knew about some of his activities and what he was becoming—she had to go to court and put up the surety bond every time he got arrested, and she could see the marks on Alice. She talked to him about it, particularly about what he did to Alice, but she never judged him or shunned him. The most upset she ever got with Ken was when she learned that Alice and Juarez were going to leave the farm because he was going to marry the blond girl from Graham.

12

ATTORNEY: Your father's name was—your real father's name
was what?

TRENA: Clarence Otto.

ATTORNEY: Clarence what?

TRENA: Otto.

ATTORNEY: Otto was his last name?

TRENA: I think it's his middle name.

ATTORNEY: Last name?

TRENA: McCloud.

ATTORNEY: Is he alive?

TRENA: I don't know.

ATTORNEY: Do you know where he lives?

TRENA: I never have.

ATTORNEY: Was he married to your mother when you were
born?

TRENA: Uh-huh.

ATTORNEY: Never asked your mother where he was?

TRENA: Uh-huh.

ATTORNEY: Did she know?

TRENA: Huh-uh.

Trena Louise McCloud was born in the small prairie town of Whiting, Kansas, on January 24, 1957. Her mother, Treva, was the second child in a family of eight girls and four boys. In her early twenties Treva met Clarence McCloud, a county road worker, and moved in with him not long afterward. In the spring of 1956, when they had been together about a year and a half, Treva became pregnant. One October afternoon in the seventh month of Treva's pregnancy, Clarence told her he was going out for a few things and would be back shortly. He was never seen or heard from again. Treva would later tell Trena that the reason her father left her was "because he didn't want you."

Treva wasn't ready to settle down, either, and she and her younger sister Brenda set off for St. Joe to seek their fortune, leaving Trena behind in the care of her grandparents in Whiting. Eventually, the two sisters migrated north to the Skidmore and Quitman area, where Treva met Ronnie McNeely.

Ronnie was a slight, almost skinny man. A nice enough guy and a decent worker, Ronnie wasn't a strong personality. His nickname was "Muscles." Growing up, Ronnie had done what a lot of poor boys did in rural northwest Missouri: He trained and traded dogs and hunted coons. In the fall hunting season, he would go out in the timber five or six nights in a row, hunting coon for the sport and to earn, sometimes, decent money for the pelts. He became good friends with another coon hunter and dog trainer, a man who preferred running his dogs through the timber and over the creeks on a moonlit night to doing anything else, except perhaps running women.

In 1963, Treva and Ronnie married and moved into a house outside Graham, a couple of miles down the road from the McElroy place. The newlyweds' house was run-down and had neither indoor plumbing nor electricity. Several months later, when Trena was almost seven years old, Treva brought her out from Kansas to become a part of the family.

Trena was a pretty girl, with clear blue eyes, light blond hair that fell to her shoulders, and a soft alabaster complexion. A little on the chubby side, she was an easy child, gentle, quiet, and very shy, responding to overtures with a slight smile. To some, she seemed a little too passive.

Ronnie got a job working on the bridge crew, and Treva began having more children. In a few years, Trena had three brothers and one sister. As the older sister, she worked hard taking care of her siblings and doing housework. One friend of Trena's, who stayed over at her house a few times, remembered Treva sitting around drinking coffee and smoking while ordering Trena to cook breakfast, do the laundry, or fetch water. The children came to call the person who took care of them "Sissy." Although Sissy continued to use the last name McCloud, she soon came to call Ronnie "Dad."

Trena grew up a rural kid in a rural family, meaning in the case of non-landowners, lots of kids, very little money, and not a whole lot of education. The man usually worked for someone else as a hired hand, driving combines and grain trucks in season, and maybe pumping gas or tending bar in the winter. The woman stayed at home and cared for the kids and possibly waited tables at the cafe in town a few evenings a week. Money was scarce even in decent times, and the kids who were tall enough to reach the tractor pedals worked during planting and harvest seasons. Education wasn't that important; the goal was to find a decent job, get married, and have a family. Recreation consisted of hunting coons and trapping muskrat and, for some of the men, drinking. In terms of community affairs, these families usually had little interest or influence.

Although Trena went to school regularly, she seemed in some ways never to quite fit in. Classmates from better-off-families saw her as "rough" because of her poor grammar and the fact that her clothes were not the newest or the best. She was friendly enough to anyone who approached her, but otherwise she usually hung back, keeping quietly to herself. In class, she was not considered bright by her teachers or her classmates. She seldom had her homework done, and she seemed to have difficulty following the teachers' instructions. She often looked over her classmates' shoulders while doing her work. But she excelled in sports, particularly track and basketball.

Most small towns have one teacher who stands out among all the rest—one, who over the years, is a favorite of the kids in class after class. Stories of affection and admiration are passed down until she (it is always a woman) becomes a local folk hero, and the kids entering her class feel as if they'd known her all their life. What sticks with her students long after they're gone and grown up is the feeling that, as children, this adult treated them as human beings.

In the Nodaway-Holt school district, which included Graham, Maitland, and Skidmore, this teacher was Kathleen Whitney. She served as the guidance counselor, as well as teacher of algebra, art, business, psychology, and shorthand, from 1965 until she retired in 1985. As guidance counselor, she was the one students talked to about their problems and the one who talked to the parents about their kids' problems. Even the toughest characters in the area—the drinkers, abusers, and active malcontents—remember with a laugh how, on a Monday morning, when they were bragging about their weekend's exploits, she would sit them down and tell them the truth about men and manhood: "Boys," she would say with a serious face, "there's more to being a man than driving cars fast, drinking beer hard, and laying lots of women." She would chide them that, if half of their numbers were true, there couldn't be a virgin left in Nodaway *or* Holt County. She tried talking to parents about their sons' drinking and fighting, but the fathers' response was usually "Well, hell, that's what I did in high school!"

Mrs. Whitney saw Trena as young for her age. She couldn't recall her mother or stepfather coming to school for parents' night; in fact, she never met Treva or Ronnie.

To Mrs. Whitney, Trena was soft and warm, and had a nice quality of friendliness about her, like a friendly puppy, always glad to see you. She and her friend Vicki were alike, except Vicki was a little bit more bubbly.

Vicki, a pretty brown-haired girl from the Graham area, was Trena's only close friend. The girls had become friends in fifth grade, when they first attended school together and by sixth grade, they had become inseparable. They sat next to each other in class, passing notes back and forth, and hung around together, during recess and after school. They talked on the phone at least once a day about schoolwork and boys. The girls often spent the night at each other's house, and they promised they would always be best friends.

Trena gave Vicki a pendant for her birthday in the eighth grade, and a bracelet with her name engraved on it for Christmas. The pendant was a piece of oval red glass encased in a gold frame with a gold cross etched in the middle. Years later, Vicki still had the pendant and the bracelet securely tucked away in a small box in her bedroom.

Through most of the eighth grade, everything seemed fine to Vicki. Trena had a boyfriend, David, who took her to the homecoming dance, and she played basketball and competed in track, performing well against students from other schools. She seemed as happy as the average kid. Sometime that spring, Trena started to change.

"She started skipping school and getting in trouble. After a while, her attitude changed and she just didn't care about anything.

"Ken McElroy began coming to the school and sitting outside in his big, fancy car and waiting for her. When school was out, Trena would go with him. The school didn't like it, and there was trouble over it, but he kept on doing it.

"It got so she didn't have time for me anymore. We were still friends, but we didn't run around together anymore.

"After a while we weren't really best friends anymore."

Brenda, Treva's sister, had married Russ Johnson, a Nodaway County deputy sheriff and a member of the numerous Johnson clan. (Several opposing forces met in this family: One of Russ's sisters, Sue, was Ronnie McNeely's mother, whom Trena called "Grandma"; another sister was Lois Bowenkamp's mother—thus, when Ken married Trena, Lois would become his first cousin once removed by marriage.) Russ had suspected for some time that something was going on between Ken and Trena. In 1969 or 1970, when Trena was twelve or thirteen, Russ had been called to Graham regarding a shooting incident. He stopped by the junior high school to check out a dance and noticed Ken hanging around, talking to Trena. He learned later that Ken had intimidated Trena's date into picking her up at home and bringing her to him, then coming for her later and taking her home. Russ told Brenda about it, and she told Treva, but Treva adamantly denied anything was going on between her daughter and Ken McElroy.

Schoolchildren in Trena's area had to take one bus to Skidmore and transfer to another bus which took them to the school in Graham. Many mornings McElroy was waiting in Skidmore to pick Trena up. He would bring her back in the afternoon in time to catch the bus home. Her clothes were usually disheveled, and she often cried all the way home. The other kids on the bus would tell her she should stop going with McElroy, but she kept it up. At first, Ken took her to St. Joe and bought her things, like clothes and little gifts and candy. Then he began taking her to the Tic Toc Motel in St. Joe, where he molested her.

Although Cheryl (Bowenkamp) Brown was a year younger than Trena, they were in one class together—Introduction to Business. Trena sat next to her, and Cheryl felt sorry for her, so when she asked for the answers to the homework, Cheryl gave them to her. Cheryl and Trena rode the school bus from Skidmore to Graham together, and Trena would talk other kids on the bus into signing her mother's name on a note for the teacher.

In the fall of her freshman year, when Trena was fourteen, she became pregnant and dropped out of school. Kathleen Whitney, the school counselor, was furious. She had heard the stories of McElroy taking Trena off the bus and could never understand why nobody—the school or the law—had done anything about it. Whitney believed Trena wanted to be rid of Ken but didn't have the strength to free herself.

Although Vicki felt a little bitter over being abandoned by her best friend, she tried to understand what had happened.

"I know other girls thought he was good looking, but I didn't. I think the reason Trena went with him was because he was an older guy with a fancy car and a lot of money. And you know, he paid a lot of attention to her. He was a friend of the family and went hunting with her dad, and she probably trusted him at first.

"In the beginning she was more or less his captive, and then sooner or later, when everybody abandoned her, she just gave up and went along with him."

Ronnie, the skinny, likable coon hunter, was not the guy to stand up to Ken McElroy—not that he didn't try. He told Ken more than once to leave Trena alone and he even pulled her out of school a couple of times, but what was he going to do when Ken didn't stop? The law sure as hell wouldn't help him in a war with Ken McElroy.

After Trena dropped out of school in 1972 (while Ken was in trouble in Savannah for stealing and in St. Joe for shooting Otha Embrey), her life essentially narrowed down to Ken McElroy. Although both Trena and Alice later denied that the two of them lived at the farm together (the townspeople swore they both lived there for years), Trena spent most, if not all, of her time there until she had her baby. Trena would later tell how Ken used to make love to them both in the same night, going from one room to the other. It bothered Trena, but what could she do? Trena learned that the way to get along with Ken was to do as she was told without asking questions. In the beginning, it was simple obedience, as a dog minds his master or a child her father. But in later years, Trena grew to believe in him. Whatever Ken said was the way it was.

13

On June 11, 1973, two weeks after her baby boy was born, Trena made a desperate bid for freedom. The baby was still in the hospital, and Trena told Alice she wanted to get away from Ken. Would Alice help her? Would she take her to Russ and Brenda's house in Skidmore? Alice, who should have known better, said she would. They told Ken they were going to the hospital to see the baby and left, taking Alice's two babies, Juarez and Tonia. They drove straight to Russ and Brenda's house, and Trena asked Brenda if she and Alice and the babies could stay there until Russ could take them somewhere. She wanted to get away from Ken, she explained, and if she was ever going to escape, it had to be now. Brenda hesitated. She knew what she was getting into, but the two women were obviously quite desperate. Finally, she said they could stay if they promised not to leave the house; she didn't want them going out and bringing McElroy back with them. The two women agreed, but it was only a few minutes before Trena called her parents and Ronnie came over to take her and Alice to the hospital to see Trena's doctor.

Somehow, McElroy figured out that his two women had run off, taking his favorite child, Juarez, with them. He hit the streets of Maryville in his Buick, and soon spotted Alice and Trena in Ronnie's truck. Driving alongside, he ordered them to pull over. McElroy aimed the shotgun at Ronnie and made him get in the Buick, then ordered the two women to drive back to Brenda's house in Ronnie's truck. (Ronnie thought for sure he was going to die. He would later tell his mother: "Ma, I wouldn't have given a nickel for my life that night.")

McElroy burned. To think that his women and Ronnie, puny little Ronnie, were defying him, telling him to get fucked. They were leaving him! *Him!*

When McElroy and Ronnie arrived at Johnson's house, Trena and Alice had already gone inside. McElroy jumped out of the Buick and stood on the sidewalk, the stock of the shotgun resting on his hip.

"Come on out here you fuckin' bitches," he yelled, "or I'm coming inside and blow your fuckin' brains out!"

Brenda took her two kids and Alice's babies and stuffed them in a closet in the back bedroom.

McElroy was getting worse, out of control.

"Bring my little boy out here, you fuckin' bitch," McElroy screamed at Alice, "or I'm comin' inside and blow you all away!"

Alice relented and took Juarez outside. McElroy stuck him in his car. When Alice went back inside, she began clawing and scratching at Brenda, yelling, "You said you would help us!"

"Yeah," Brenda said, "but you left like I told you not to, and now look what's happening!"

Brenda's daughter escaped from the closet and looked out the front window.

"Careful!" Trena said, pulling her away, "you'll get killed!"

Now that McElroy had his son, he started yelling for Trena. She ventured out onto the porch, then came back inside a few minutes later.

"He said he just wants to talk to me," she said.

"Don't leave, or you'll never make it back," Brenda warned. "He'll get you in the car and you'll never get out."

"He said he'll come inside and kill us all if I don't," said Trena.

Brenda gripped her loaded shotgun. "Well," she said, "he'll have to come through the door first."

McElroy kept yelling about what he was going to do to Trena and Alice when he finally got ahold of them, and eventually both women gave in and went outside. Soon they all left, Trena riding in the car with Ken, and Alice riding with Tonia, Juarez, and Ronnie in the pickup.

Once at the farm, the rage inside McElroy boiled over. Worried that Russ Johnson might call in the law, he leveled the shotgun at

the two women and threatened to shoot them if anyone came to
the farm. The shotgun roared forth inches from Alice's legs to
make his point.

Trena would later describe what happened under oath in a court
of law.

> PROSECUTING ATTORNEY JOHN FRAZE: O.K., just describe
> what happened there [at the farm].
> TRENA: Oh, after we got there, he made us get out except my
> dad and he sat in the car and I was behind the corner and
> he was in front of us and he shot the gun and he saw the car
> coming up the hill so he made us line up on the side and he
> says, "You guys might as well look forward to it if some-
> body comes you are gonna get killed." And then he just sat
> and talked for a while and then he took us behind the shed
> and he was going to shoot us because he thought another
> car came and after that he said we better take Ronnie home
> and he asked me if I wanted to go home and I said, I didn't
> say nothing for a while and then I said, "I don't know."
> And then he says well you are not going to go home until
> this is cleared up. And he told Alice to get in the car and he
> was going to be right behind her and if she made a wrong
> move that he would get her. So we went and let dad off and
> went on a gravel road.
> FRAZE: O.K., after you let your dad off where did, you went
> where?
> TRENA: About a half a mile on a gravel road.
> FRAZE: What happened when you got there?
> TRENA: He made me get out of the pickup and Alice stayed in
> the car and he put the gun up on top of the pickup and he
> wanted to know whose idea it was to go to my uncle's house
> and I said I didn't know and Alice said she didn't know.
> And then he got mad at me 'cause I kept on saying that I
> was feeling sorry for my mother and he kept on slappin' me
> and then after a while when he got done we went back to
> his house.

Ken beat Alice badly that night for her role in the attempted
escape. In the midst of his fury, he whirled on her, shotgun in
hand, and yelled that he was going to blow her head off. Instead, in

a lightning movement, he drew the barrel back and brought it around full force on her face, smashing her nose and breaking both cheekbones and her brow. Alice stumbled away from the barn and managed to drive to the hospital in Fairfax. She arrived with her face puffed up and split open where the metal had hit the skin. In a few days, when the swelling dropped, her whole face turned an ugly, gruesome black-and-blue. The pain was excruciating, and it would leave her with headaches for the rest of her life.

McElroy's rage was not yet spent. He had to establish complete dominance. The next morning he told Alice, who had returned the following morning, to go to his mother's house down the road and make a phone call. Trena would later describe what happened under oath.

PROSECUTOR JOHN FRAZE: O.K., would you tell the Court what happened from the time that Alice left to make this phone call until she got back? Just tell it in your own words, however you want to tell it.

TRENA: Well, I was in the kitchen with the baby and he was in the front room with the gun, and he told me to come in and I said, "What for?" and he said, "You know what for." And the baby was crying and I said, "I don't want to put the baby down," and he said, "Put it down on the couch," so I put him down on the couch and he said, "Take your clothes off," so I took my clothes off, and he set down on the divan and I sat down on the divan and he put the gun up on top of the couch, the top, and he told me to suck his dick, and he told me to get on my hands and knees, and the baby started crying and I wanted to give the baby his bottle so I reached over and gave the baby his bottle and he came back and we had intercourse. Then Alice came and he acted like he was asleep on the couch and this was when he wanted to know what she had said, then after that he asked me to go get some water and bring some ice and some water to put in the jug.

FRAZE: O.K., Did you agree to have intercourse with him, was that voluntary?

TRENA: No.

FRAZE: Did you agree to do the other, was that voluntary?

TRENA: No.

FRAZE: Why did you do it?

TRENA: Because he had the gun, and I didn't want to—

FRAZE: Were you afraid?

TRENA: Yes.

FRAZE: Was it painful?

TRENA: Yes.

FRAZE: You had a baby sixteen days before? I think that is all.

MR. MCFADIN ON CROSS-EXAMINATION: Was there anybody at the scene that witnessed this act of forcible rape?

TRENA: No.

MCFADIN: And the reason why, you are telling the Court, is that you were afraid at the time that you allowed Mr. McElroy to have intercourse with you?

TRENA: Yeah.

MCFADIN: Well, you allowed him many other times to have intercourse with you, have you not?

TRENA: Yes, but he didn't have no gun either.

MCFADIN: Well, would that have made it, let me ask you this, I am not trying to be argumentative, but, as I say, you have had intercourse with him many times, but he didn't have a gun then, now you still would have had intercourse with him on that particular time if he hadn't had a gun, wouldn't you have?

TRENA: No.

MCFADIN: And why not?

TRENA: Because he hit me all the time.

Trena's parents also had to be taught a lesson. On the afternoon of the same day, McElroy told Trena to get in the pickup, they were taking a trip.

FRAZE: Well, after you got to your parents' house what happened there?

TRENA: Uh, well, we stopped at the station first after we went to my mother's house to tell her, he had a can, I remember a can. He got some gasoline in it and took it in the house and I never saw him pour any of it, but I saw him pour it in when he was walking out the door just on the steps and he lit the house and it started smokin'.

THE COURT: Who is he?

TRENA: Ken McElroy . . .

FRAZE: When you arrived at your parents' house that day was there any smoke coming from the house?

TRENA: No.

FRAZE: Was there any flames?

TRENA: No.

FRAZE: Did Mr. McElroy go inside the house?

TRENA: Yes.

FRAZE: And you mentioned a gasoline can, did he take that with him when he went in?

TRENA: Yes.

FRAZE: Did you at any time, while you were there, see him pour any gasoline or any other substance out of the can onto the house or in the house or anywhere about the house?

TRENA: Yes.

MCFADIN: Now, I am going to object to that because she testified a few minutes ago that she did not see him actually pour anything. I think the question is repetitious.

THE COURT: I wish you would tell exactly what happened at that time, seeing this fellow McElroy, and now who else was with you?

TRENA: Alice Wood.

THE COURT: All right. Now, where did you, what station did you stop at, where was that?

TRENA: Lawson's.

THE COURT: In where?

TRENA: Graham.

THE COURT: And what happened there?

TRENA: He had a can, and the guy came out and put some gasoline in the can. Then he threw it in the back, 'cause it was a truck.

THE COURT: OK, now just what happened after that?

TRENA: We went to my folks' house and uh, we parked on the gravel road there and he got out and took the gun with him and took the gasoline and went in the house and poured out—

THE COURT: Just exactly what did you see? Did you see him go in the house with the can?

TRENA: I saw him go in the house with the can and the gun

and then I saw him come out and when he opened the door
he was still pouring and then when he come out the door he
had the gun and my dog barked and he shot the dog.

THE COURT: He shot the dog?

TRENA: Yeah.

THE COURT: Well, there is a lot more to this than—

FRAZE: All right, after that did you leave immediately or did
you sit there for a while, or what did you do?

TRENA: Well, we left and then we turned around and came
back.

FRAZE: Did you ever see if the house was actually burning or
not?

TRENA: Yes.

With their house destroyed, Ronnie and Treva moved out of
Nodaway County to Ravenwood, Missouri, about twenty miles
east of Maryville, leaving Trena firmly in the clutches of Ken Mc-
Elroy. But even that was too close for McElroy. A few weeks later,
Brenda stopped to visit her sister and found the front door hanging
open. Wash hung on the line, and the furniture was inside, but
Ronnie and Treva were gone.

A day or two after the raping and burning, Trena went to a
doctor in Mound City for treatment. After hearing Trena's story,
the doctor notified the Nodaway County juvenile authorities and
welfare department. He also prescribed tranquilizers for Trena, because she was so frightened. Trena was placed in the custody of the
county and taken to the mental hospital in St. Joe, presumably to
keep her safe from Ken McElroy while the authorities sorted out
the situation. Her baby was placed in a foster home.

Trena remained at the mental hospital for about three weeks.
She spent the first night in a cell and then moved into a private
room. She did not have contact with other patients, nor did she
receive any counseling; the hospital was simply a safe house, a
place to stay until they found a permanent place for her. Finally,
the social worker told her she was going to stay with a foster
family at the air force base in Knob Noster, Missouri. No one
talked to her about her baby, how he was doing, or whether she
could take him with her. She left without seeing him.

On June 19, 1973, primarily on the basis of Trena's testimony,
Prosecutor Fraze filed three criminal charges against Ken McEl-

roy: rape, arson, and flourishing a deadly weapon. Fraze later filed an amended complaint alleging that McElroy had also assaulted Trena on June 12 by "kicking and slapping her, by pulling her hair, by exposing her to vulgar and obscene language, and by causing Trena . . . to exhibit herself nude before him. . . ."

14

For the first time in his life, Ken McElroy found himself in extreme jeopardy. He was subject to arrest at any moment for the four felonies, each of which would be tried separately, and he faced the possibility of a death sentence on the rape charge. However, he had the best lawyer money could buy, and three of the four cases, including the most serious ones, depended entirely on the testimony of one person. No witness, no case.

McElroy and Alice decided to clear out of Nodaway County and lay low until things settled down. They went to Kansas City, leaving the kids at the farm in the care of his sister Dorothy. A few days after they left, the sheriff came out to the farm and told Dorothy that, because McElroy had left his kids, the authorities were going to declare them neglected and take them away. When McElroy learned of the visit, he went into a frenzy and called McFadin. McFadin explained that the authorities couldn't take the children; the cops were probably trying to smoke him out into the open so they could get their hands on him. McElroy finally surrendered. He was arrested and released on a $2,500 bond.

The main problem for the prosecution was keeping the chief witness safe and secure, which meant out of McElroy's way. No one doubted that he would try to get to Trena. When they first took her to Knob Noster, McElroy lost track of her. Furious and desperate, he told his friends there was $2,000 in it for the man who located her. For days he scoured Maryville and the small towns around looking for her, often borrowing friends' cars so he could travel unrecognized.

Meanwhile, Trena was talking. Her juvenile officer listened in shock and sympathy as she described how McElroy had sex with her violently and often, coming after her wherever he wanted—on the dining room table, on the couch, in the kitchen. She told the officer there was oral sex and anal sex, and that McElroy once told her he was going to buy a ring of sausages and find out exactly how much she could take. Her parents were too afraid of McElroy to help her. He frightened her, too, and she just wanted to get away from him. She willingly went wherever the authorities took her.

Trena and the juvenile officer made numerous trips to different foster homes and to Maryville for court appearances, and the officer never felt that she was trying to manipulate him, to use her girlish sexuality to exploit the situation, the way some adolescent girls did. She was what she appeared to be—a young country girl with no worldly exposure, who had been overwhelmed by a charismatic, powerful man.

Trena liked it at Knob Noster. The husband was a lawyer, and both he and his wife were nice to her. The woman talked to Trena about her baby, and asked if she wanted to get him back. Yes, Trena told her, she very much wanted to have her baby with her, and the woman said she would help. The family was soon transferred, so Trena had to leave, but not before retrieving her boy.

Ginger and George Clement (no relation to Del and Greg) lived in a large house with their two daughters in Maryville. As foster parents, they had taken in many unwed mothers over the years, and never had any problems. Ginger, an attractive woman of earthy speech and manner, and George, a tall man with a milder personality, found it to be a rewarding experience. When the welfare and court people talked to Ginger about taking in Trena and her baby, they told her the whole story: The baby's father was being prosecuted on charges of raping and assaulting the girl; he was also charged with burning her parents' house down; Trena had been taken into custody after her parents had fled the county; and she was the primary witness in all these cases and must at all costs be kept safe. The officials also explained that McElroy would undoubtedly come looking for Trena and the baby. Ginger talked it over with her husband, her daughters, the neighbors across the street, and the police, who understood the situation and said they would be around to help if McElroy showed up. The social workers were desperate—they had no other place to put Trena and the baby—so Ginger decided to take them in.

Ginger had a room ready in the basement, and the social worker brought a separate bed for the baby. But now that Trena had her baby back, she wouldn't let him go. She insisted that he sleep with her, and when Ginger came to awaken her in the morning, she found the baby sleeping comfortably inside Trena's curled figure.

At first, Trena wouldn't let go of him for any reason; if she went to the bathroom, he went with her, and when she sat at the dinner table, he was there on her lap. Often, when Ginger came home from work in the afternoon, she would go to Trena's room and find her huddled in a chair in the corner, holding the baby closely in her arms. In those first few days, Trena explained to Ginger several times that the baby's real name was Jerome, but that Ken already had a son named Jerome and she wanted to change her baby's name to Jeffy. So that was what she called him—Jeffy.

The county officials were adamant that Trena was never to be allowed out of the house alone. This turned out not to be a problem, because for months Trena was too frightened to leave the house at all. She told Ginger again and again that Ken McElroy would find her. The search might take him a while, but sooner or later, he would track her down. Her worst nightmare was that he would come in the window, kill her, and take her baby.

The officials also insisted that Trena wasn't to have any dates or be alone with any boys. When McElroy went to trial on the rape charge, the prosecution had to be able to say that no other man had had access to Trena. Ginger, in fact, might be called upon to testify that while living in her house, Trena had not been with any man.

The first two or three weeks passed with no sign of Ken McElroy. Ginger kept expecting him, though, undoubtedly because Trena kept saying it was impossible to hide from him, that he would always find her and the baby. One afternoon, when Ginger came home from work, a large, white Oldsmobile sat about thirty yards down the street. Inside, behind the wheel was a heavyset man with black slicked-back hair, thick sideburns, and bushy eyebrows. She found Trena in the basement, sitting on the floor of her bedroom, holding her baby tightly to her chest, crying and screaming that Ken was going to come in the window and kill her and take Jeffy. After calling the police, who said they would come immediately, Ginger tried to comfort Trena. Trena explained through the tears and the sobbing that she had just happened to look out the window, and there he had been. He had sat there for more than four hours, never moving or doing a thing except staring at the house.

The police came and talked to McElroy, and a few minutes later he left. They explained to Ginger that McElroy knew the law, and that as long as he didn't trespass or do anything else illegal, there was nothing they could do.

The phone calls began not long after McElroy's visit. A man would demand to speak to Trena, and when Ginger refused, he would call her a bitch and tell her that if she knew what was good for her, she better turn Trena back over. He didn't say to whom, just "turn her back over." He said he was going to kill Trena.

"Tell my little bride that I'm coming to get her," he would say menacingly. He always called her his "little bride."

Sometimes he would ask, "Wanna trade girl for girl?"

"What are you talking about?" Ginger asked, by now recognizing the voice.

"I know where your girls go to school and what bus they take. I think we oughta trade girl for girl, don't you?"

Ginger knew the caller was McElroy, because one of the first times he called, Trena came over and stood close to the receiver. When she heard his voice she backed away, got real panicky and began shaking all over. She grabbed Jeffy and mouthed the word *Ken* to Ginger. Then she went and got a blackboard, wrote the word Ken in big letters, and held it up for Ginger to see. Whenever one of those phone calls came in, Ginger knew she would spend the night sleeping in Trena's room with her.

Ginger worked at a dry cleaner's only a few blocks away, and Trena called her there whenever Ken showed up during the day. Usually Trena was crying hysterically, screaming that Ken had driven by the house and was coming back to get her. Ginger would go home immediately. Once or twice, she found Trena in such bad shape that she thought she would have to take her to the hospital. Ginger would spend hours comforting her, assuring her that Ken was gone and she was safe in their house. Then, after the terror had subsided, Trena often said something strange, such as she was glad her baby was a boy, because Ken liked little boys, but not little girls.

Some days Ginger would see McElroy driving around the block in the white Oldsmobile. He would cruise by slowly, never quite stopping, staring at the front of the house. Ginger was afraid, not because he might have a gun and come after her, but because she might be in the way when he came for Trena. Ginger and her husband began locking all the windows and doors when they left Trena home alone.

Trena talked about her life, sometimes shocking Ginger and her two daughters. When Trena told them that she and Alice shared a bedroom together, and that Ken would come and pick one to take back to sleep with him, Ginger asked her if she didn't get jealous when Ken took Alice and she had to lie there knowing what was going on in the next room. Trena simply replied that she knew Ken really loved her, and she and Alice got along really well. Ginger's daughters sat and listened, wide-eyed.

Trena often talked about her mother and her stepfather and the house they had lived in when she was growing up. She told Ginger that Ken had burned the house down because her parents didn't want him to see her anymore. She also talked about going back there to see what was left of the house, so one Sunday the four of them—Ginger and George and Trena and Jeffy—loaded up the car and, following Trena's instructions, drove to the spot where the house had been. Only the foundation remained, but as they walked around, Trena told them stories of growing up there as a girl.

Trena talked about how Ken always had a lot of money, and how life with him was so different from the way it had been at home, where they never had anything. He had lots of vehicles and furniture and guns, always lots of guns. When Ginger asked how he got the money, Trena said, "He would steal cattle, grain, anything that wasn't nailed down and he could haul off."

Ginger's two girls spent a lot of time with Trena, and after a few months, she became almost a member of the family. The Clement girls were going to high school dances and ball games, and they were learning to put on makeup and fix their hair; they would sit in front of the mirror after school for hours and talk about boys and try on eye shadow and lipstick. Trena confided in them that she was thinking about going back to school and having a normal life

—getting married and having babies. She even began fixing up her hair and wearing makeup around the house.

Sometimes, one of her daughters would bring a boy or two home after school, and afterward Trena would talk about what they were like. Once the two girls had a party for some of their school friends. Trena met a boy she liked, and the two of them talked and danced along with the other kids. He began coming over every now and then in the afternoon, and he and Trena would talk and watch television together. The visits seemed so good for Trena that Ginger asked the social worker if the two of them could go somewhere together, perhaps to a ball game. The social worker said no.

15.

In November 1973, the court held a preliminary hearing on the charges of rape, flourishing a deadly weapon, and arson. Because the incidents had occurred in Nodaway County, and the charges had been filed there, the normal procedure would have been for the local magistrate to conduct the hearing. But in this case, as in all cases involving Ken Rex McElroy, Magistrate (later circuit judge) Montgomery Wilson disqualified himself.

Monty Wilson grew up in Skidmore, where his father worked as an officer at the bank. After obtaining his law degree, he served as city attorney of Maryville before becoming magistrate. Wilson developed a reputation as a weak and indecisive judge. According to one deputy sheriff, Wilson "had less force in his voice than an eleven-year-old girl—he had absolutely no guts at all." He seemed to be in a constant state of vacillation—should I or shouldn't I—on even the simplest matters in front of him. He agonized over basic objections, mumbling and holding his head in his hands. He seemed overly worried about being reversed on appeal. Many locals perceived him as being unable to crack down on criminals—he would hand down a stiff sentence and then suspend it, giving the defendant one more chance. Some lawyers thought Wilson was smart enough, while others thought he wasn't very bright. As one lawyer put it, "The last one to argue in front of him usually won."

Wilson's fear of Ken McElroy was well known. He admitted to one prominent citizen that "I don't want anything to do with that man, or I'll get killed."

Monty Wilson certainly didn't want anything to do with the three felony charges against Ken Rex McElroy. On November 9, he issued an order disqualifying himself from conducting the preliminary examination, and sending the matter to Magistrate Clark Gore in adjoining Atchison County.

The hearing was held in front of Gore on November 15, 1973, some five months after the crimes had occurred.

. In addition to the rape and arson charges, at which Trena was the primary witness (Alice Wood denied having seen McElroy burn the house), Magistrate Gore heard evidence on the charge of flourishing a deadly weapon.

Russ Johnson, Skidmore city marshal and special deputy sheriff, and Trena's uncle, testified that on June 11, 1973, at approximately 11:30 P.M., he was with Ronald McNeely and Wayne Johnson when Ken McElroy approached them with a gun.

FRAZE: O.K., did the defendant have a gun with him at that time?

JOHNSON: Yes, sir.

FRAZE: What did he do with the gun, did he point it at anyone?

JOHNSON: He pointed it at me.

FRAZE: What did he say to you?

JOHNSON: He told me that he was going to blow my damn brains out, that he was going to start at my feet and work up.

FRAZE: Was this done in the presence of these other people?

JOHNSON: Yes, sir.

On cross-examination, McFadin pointed out that Deputy Johnson did not immediately arrest Ken McElroy and take him into custody for threatening to kill him, but waited four days before signing a complaint.

McFadin called Ronnie McNeely on behalf of the defendant.

MCFADIN: Now, at the time this alleged incident took place, where were you?

MCNEELY: Well, I'm not sure, I just can't quote, but I was back some.

MCFADIN: Did you ever see him take a gun and point it at Mr. Johnson?

MCNEELY: I can't say I just exactly seen it, no.

MCFADIN: All right. Now did you ever see him take a gun out of the car?

MCNEELY: No, I can't say that I actually seen him take one out.

MCFADIN: Did you see him put a gun in the car?

MCNEELY: No, not actually.

MCFADIN: Did you ever see him threaten Mr. Johnson?

MCNEELY: Well, no, I was standing back a ways, I can't be sure what went on.

For each of the three charges, the magistrate found substantial evidence that a crime had been committed and that Ken McElroy had committed it. He therefore bound McElroy over for trial.

Prosecuting Attorney Fraze, a somewhat laconic but intelligent man in his mid-thirties, was determined to convict Ken McElroy of something. After Trena passed a lie detector test, and after the motel attendant confirmed that a man matching McElroy's description had rented the room, Fraze filed eight additional charges of child molestation against him. Not only would each charge increase the chance of a conviction, but molestation charges would be easier to prove. Fraze was a little uneasy about the likelihood of success on the rape charge with a rural jury, mainly because the victim had been staying with the defendant and, by her own admission, had had intercourse with him previously on numerous occasions. But anyone who took indecent or improper liberties with a person under the age of eighteen was guilty of child molestation, whether the child consented to the act or not.

The new charges, filed in February 1974, alleged that on eight separate occasions during 1971, 1972, and 1973, Ken McElroy ". . . did then and there willfully, unlawfully and feloniously detain and divert one Trena Louise McCloud, a minor of the age of fifteen years with intent to indulge in degrading, lewd, immoral and vicious acts and practices and take indecent and improper liberties with said minor by diverting and transporting said minor from Nodaway County, Missouri, to the City of St. Joseph, Missouri, with the intent and purpose of: having sexual intercourse with said minor; exposing his private parts to said minor in an obscene and indecent manner; and by language suggesting a lewd and indecent act, to wit: sexual intercourse and fellatio, and thus and thereby did annoy and molest said minor, contrary to the form of the statute in such cases made and provided . . ."

Had the criminal justice system dealt with these twelve felony charges at all expeditiously, Trena might have held. But it didn't. First, on the motion of the defendant, the cases were transferred to other counties—the rape, arson, assault, and weapon cases to Gentry County, and the molestation charges to Platte County. There they languished. At least three different trial dates were set for the various cases, and each time the court granted continuances. Finally, the first four charges were set for trial on October 24, 1974, some seventeen months after the alleged crimes, and the molestation charges were set for November 25, 1974, some two and three years after the alleged crimes.

In 1974, when Trena had been with the Clement family for about a year, the social worker called Ginger and said that Trena would be leaving. The woman didn't say why or where, but Trena told Ginger she was going to her grandmother's house, and Ginger suspected the trial might be getting near. Trena assured Ginger that she didn't want anything more to do with Ken McElroy, but Ginger was apprehensive. Although the girl seemed to be getting stronger and was beginning to laugh and relax like a normal teenager, Ginger had a feeling that she wasn't quite ready to leave, that she really needed to stay with them a little while longer.

Trena's grandparents had come to Maryville seeking to take Trena home with them. They convinced the welfare department and the judge to allow her to return with them to Whiting, Kansas. But Trena wasn't happy in her grandparents' home. Without her mom and dad, her brothers and sisters, or her friends, Trena felt as if she had no one to turn to. After a couple of months, feeling very alone, she called Ken and asked him to come get her. He gladly complied.

Lawyer Gene McFadin was sitting behind the desk in his well-appointed law office in Kansas City one morning that summer when he felt a presence in the room. He looked up and was startled to see the bulk of Ken McElroy standing by the wall, not more than ten feet away, looking at him. He buzzed his secretary: "Ken

McElroy is in my office, which is OK, but you know nobody is supposed to come in unannounced."

"But, Mr. McFadin," she protested, "we haven't seen Mr. McElroy this morning."

"How do the cases look?" McElroy asked, getting right to the point.

"They're tough cases," McFadin replied. "Going to be hard to win."

"What happens if I marry Trena?"

"Well," said McFadin, "then she can't testify against you and they would have no case." McFadin thought for a second. "But you got a problem, Ken—you're already married."

A few days later, Sharon McElroy came to see McFadin. "Ken will give me a divorce," she said, "and I want you to handle it." McFadin considered for a moment whether he had a conflict of interest, decided he didn't, and set to work.

McFadin obtained Sharon's divorce in Richmond, Missouri, freeing McElroy to marry. The question was where? First choice was a little town in Oklahoma, but the judge there refused to perform the ceremony because Trena was only fifteen. McFadin suggested Las Vegas, but McElroy said he couldn't fly because his head injury left him susceptible to serious nosebleeds. The marriage would have to be in Missouri.

"Ken," McFadin said to him, "Trena's underage in Missouri. She'll have to have her parents' consent to marry you."

On October 20, Treva McNeely showed up in McFadin's office and explained that she would consent to her daughter marrying Ken McElroy. McFadin had Treva write out and sign a notarized statement giving her consent to her daughter's marriage. Treva also signed a notarized statement that there was no coercion involved, and that she was voluntarily agreeing to the marriage.

McFadin had located an elderly judge in Plattesburg to perform the ceremony, and on the same day, October 20, Ken and Trena were married. McFadin witnessed the ceremony.

Prosecuting Attorney Fraze was sitting in his office on that day four days before the rape case was due to be tried, when he received a phone call from McFadin. Wrinkling a piece of paper close to the mouthpiece, McFadin said, "Hear that? It's a marriage license for Ken McElroy and Trena McCloud."

Stunned to hear that his only witness, his victim in eleven felonies, had married the accused, Fraze said simply, "I can't believe it." McFadin assured him it was true and promised to send him a copy of the certificate.

Both McFadin and Fraze assumed that eleven of the felony cases —all but the flourishing-a-deadly-weapon charge—collapsed when McElroy married his victim. As a matter of law, that assumption was not necessarily correct. Like most states, Missouri recognizes the husband-wife privilege, which provides in general that a person may not testify in a court of law against his or her spouse. But Missouri, as most states, also recognizes several exceptions to this rule: One of them provides that a spouse is not prohibited from testifying about crimes committed by the other spouse against him or her.

Thus, theoretically, Fraze could have continued to prosecute the cases. But his real problem was practical, rather than legal. What would the jury think when the victim got up and testified that she had been raped by the defendant, but had married him a year later?

Fraze could have explored other avenues to save his cases. He could, for example, have filed a motion for a hearing, brought the circumstances to the attention of the court, and asked that a guardian ad litem be appointed for Trena; then he could have attacked the validity of the marriage, arguing that it was a continuation of the crime itself, that McElroy was attempting to conceal the crimes by marrying the victim. Under this argument, the judge could have invalidated the marriage as a blatant fraud on the court, entered into solely for the purpose of defeating the criminal action.

Such an attack would have been difficult, and what probably made it impossible was a statement executed and sworn to in McFadin's office by the victim-wife, in which she said:

I do not wish to engage in any criminal or legal actions against Kenneth McElroy; that any and all accusations that I made against any improper or criminal conduct between Mr. McElroy and myself were made because of my feelings of frustration and jealousy toward Kenneth McElroy; that all such accusations were untrue. That I fully understand the consequences of my acts, but said accusations were made when I was under considerable mental anguish and I do not feel I was fully responsible for said accusations. This statement is true. I do desire that the charges against Mr. McElroy in which I am the prosecuting witness be dropped.

The above statement is true to my best knowledge and belief.

Trena L. McCloud

As Alice Wood and Marcia Surritte had done in the Savannah cases, Trena claimed, in recanting the felony charges, that her motivation in bringing the charges had been jealousy and frustration.

Fraze was baffled by Trena's turnabout, but did not in good conscience feel that he could proceed with the prosecutions. On October 24, 1974, he filed papers dismissing the eleven felony charges. The twelfth one—flourishing a weapon—went to trial some time later in Gentry County. A key prosecution witness could not be found for the trial, and McElroy was acquitted after trial by a jury. McElroy's rule—no witness, no case—had been elevated to the status of a criminal commandment. At this point a total of nineteen felony charges—occurring in Buchanan, Andrew, or Nodaway counties between 1970 and 1973—had been dismissed or resulted in an acquittal because the primary witness declined to prosecute, changed his or her story, or became unavailable for one reason or another.

Once the rape, arson, and child molestation charges had been dropped, the prosecutor and the juvenile officer washed their hands of the whole matter. In their view, they had tried to protect Trena as best they could, and if she chose to run off and marry McElroy, that was her business, and so was whatever happened to her afterward.

Ginger Clement felt bad when she heard about the marriage. Remembering Trena's descriptions of what Ken had done to her, she could only wonder what he had done to get her to marry him. Ginger would never believe that this was what Trena really wanted, and she often felt things might have turned out differently if she had only been able to keep her a little longer.

Shortly before the marriage, Ken explained the situation to Alice: He had to marry Trena to avoid going to jail, and Trena had made him promise that she would be the only woman living at the house. He knew Alice was going to be mad about it, but there was nothing he could do. But Alice wasn't mad; whatever love remained had vanished when he split her face open with a gun barrel. In fact, she was beginning to wonder why she had stayed around as long as she had. If anything, the drinking, the violence, and the obsessive streak in him had gotten worse. "You go your way and I'll go mine," she told him genially.

Alice left and moved to Maryville with the two kids, and took up hairdressing as a means of support. On September 20, 1975, eleven months after Ken and Trena were married, Alice gave birth to Ken, Jr. Some things were apparently easier said than done.

McElroy's triumphs shook the three small towns of Skidmore, Graham, and Maitland. For the first time, it had been their system going after him—their cops, their prosecutors, their judges—and for whatever reason, the system had failed.

16

Ken McElroy was a thief by profession. He stole everything he could get his hands on: pigs, cattle, dogs, grain, chemicals, antiques, tools, parts, and guns. His friends and family claimed he made a living raising hogs, growing corn, and buying and selling antiques. But most people never took that story seriously, and they probably weren't meant to. Any farmer in the area could tell you that the McElroy farm wasn't a true crop-producing farm: The land hadn't been cleared right or terraced where it should have been. He always had a few hogs on the place, but aside from their questionable origin, never enough to support a family. Ken McElroy wasn't a farmer, and he surely would have cringed at the image of himself as a farmer. Ken McElroy hated farmers.

McElroy may have been the best dog handler in the entire area. He knew dogs, he loved dogs, and in the trading, buying, and selling of them, he always came out ahead. A few dogs, the champions or potential champions, went for $2,000 or $3,000 apiece. And he could talk a guy into paying $500 for a dog he had just seen fall headfirst into a creek. But he would have had to make a lot of dog deals to live the way he did—to afford the women, the kids, the cars and trucks, the fancy guns, the good whiskey, and the enormous legal fees.

Ken was an honored figure at the dog meets. He had hunted and traded dogs with the other men for years, and his word was always good: If he told you that this pup came from that bitch, then it was a fact. And he was a gentleman. Coon hunters were a pretty rough crowd, arguing and cursing when they thought a judge had favored a friend or had miscounted the number of times a particular dog had barked when it hit a tree with a coon in the branches. But McElroy never joined in these disputes. If he received a bad call, he simply shrugged and walked away, without so much as raising his voice. If anything, McElroy was the conciliator, the one who tried to smooth things over. He drank quite a bit, and he made his women work hard training and exercising his dogs, but he was always polite and friendly. Everyone at the meets had heard the stories about Ken's thieving and violence, and some of them had been in on a few activities with him. But he never showed that side of himself at the gatherings.

Few people at the meets thought Ken McElroy was a farmer. He came dressed in slacks and a nice shirt, all cleaned up with his hair slicked back. His hands were soft and clean and his nails trimmed, like a woman's. He drove new, fancy pickups and he was always flashing a wad of money around. Once, he popped the hubcaps off the wheels and laughed as wads of money tumbled out on the ground.

Family members argued, with some justification, that Ken couldn't possibly have committed all the crimes he was accused of —unless he could be in twenty places at the same time. He could be, indirectly. By the time he moved back to the Skidmore farm, McElroy had graduated from popping a hog or two into the trunk of his car to stealing two or three trailer-loads of cattle in an evening and, more lucratively, fencing animals and other items for a network of other thieves. Some of the thieves were his buddies, who stole both with him and for him, and others were young boys from the area. McElroy seemed to know which boys would be amenable to his propositions—boys from poor families, misfits, malcontents, boys that would look up to him because he ignored the rules and lived life his own way. He bought them pop and beer and played pool with them, and let them drive his pickup, even though they were under age.

Sam S. began stealing for him at the age of fourteen and kept it up for ten years:

"There was a bunch of us that stole for him, kids that he trusted. He would buy whatever we would bring him: corn, tools, air compressors, chemicals, anything. We would go to a farmer's yard, scoop the grain into the back of our truck, drive to his place and scoop it out in his yard or one of the sheds. He would give us a dollar a bushel and the next day he would scoop it up and sell it at the elevator in Maitland for two or three dollars a bushel. Whatever you took him, you always got cash on the spot, usually one-third to one-half the price. There were never any confrontations or disputes—he was always fair with us."

A few of the boys formed more of a bond with McElroy. Tom L., who came from a poor rural family, was also fourteen when he began stealing for him.

"Ken always stopped to talk to us about things he had done, about his cars and women. Other times, he would buy us beer and give us money to play pool. He would talk a lot about how he didn't like farmers, that they were always fuckin' with him.

"Once, he pulled out a stack of money and asked a friend and me if we would like some of it. 'Shit yes,' we said, and he told us exactly what he wanted and where it was. He would drive around during the day and look at stuff and then tell us where it was and how much he could give us for it. He always paid cash.

"I never went out to the farm uninvited; he always came and found me. I never liked it out at his house. It was scary. His wife and kids never said a word. They would fade into the background the minute we arrived. He kept a bottle of speed in the house; I never saw him use it, but he would give it to me to keep me awake when we were out stealing at night.

"He knew when the farmers were going on vacation and how to get in all their places. He told me once that the key to this one house was in the fruit cellar, and there it was. How in the hell did he know that?

"Sometimes he would find me in town and he'd be in jeans and a jean jacket with a pistol under the jacket. 'I need you to do some things that my women can't,' he would say. We would take off in the middle of the night in his big Buick or Delta 88—they all had toggle switches on them to shut off the tail lights and brake lights when he was running—and he would slow down as we went by the place, and I would jump out the door. I'd go steal whatever it was and wait crouched in the ditch for him to come back around. He'd slow down and I'd run alongside the car with whatever I had and jump in.

"Some of his dogs were real bad. He had fifteen or twenty of them chained up outside, and he fed some of them speed to keep them mean. When he would give me a pill, he would always pop a couple down their throat—it really fucked them dogs up.

"I liked him, I really did. He was always really good to us kids. A helluva lot better than the farmers that hired us for nothing to slop around in their pens and do their nigger work. Once or twice I went back when I was stealing for Ken and nailed a couple of farmers I had worked for.

"I got a lot of respect hanging around him; people thought more of me after I was seen with him two or three times. The guy never did nothing wrong to kids. He was like a father to me."

McElroy loved to prowl the countryside at night, cruising the small towns and the back roads in his cars and pickups, stopping by bars and friends' houses, running his dogs and stealing cattle, until the early hours of the morning. He could be hunting or working, or both; more than one farmer came up on Ken McElroy on a dark night, parked alongside a gravel road, supposedly tracking down a dog he had lost in the timber.

Stories about Ken McElroy's exploits flourished. Many, though highly suspect, were repeated enough to become part of the legend. Some had a grain or more of truth to them, and others—often the wildest ones—were outright fact. One of those was the horse-trailer incident.

Fillmore, a town about twenty-five miles south of Skidmore, was a place unto itself, a grimy, wasted little rural slum where dilapidated buildings and run-down streets went unfixed for years, and rusted-out trucks and old farm equipment sat out on the street in front of ramshackle houses. Fillmore had a serious reputation for hard drinking and mean fighting, which the residents, men and women alike, did their best to live up to. It was a town of coon hunters, tenant farmers, and truck drivers. At midday people stood on the sidewalk on the main intersection of town drinking beer and spitting pools of tobacco juice on the dusty pavement, staring silently at strange cars that happened to wander in off the track. At one time, McElroy lived a few miles outside of town and used to hang out in the bar.

Nick P., a regular at the bar in Fillmore, had met Ken a few years back through a friend, trading dogs. Nick was a rough-looking dude; about forty-one, thick upper torso, bald with a little fuzz on the sides, beady eyes—"mangy," in the words of an acquaintance. His nature was decent enough until he got drunk, and then he was mean as hell. He had sold Ken a few hogs in the past and had always received a fair price for them. The night that Ken found him at the bar in Fillmore, Nick had just been released on parole after serving three months on an assault conviction. Ken had a goosenecked horse trailer hooked on behind his pickup and was out to rustle some cattle. He needed someone to stand lookout and help him load the animals into the trailer. Nick readily agreed to assist, and in the course of a few hours the two of them rustled four cows from nearby farms. They were heading south through Fillmore on their way to St. Joe when Ken spotted a sheriff's car sitting in the driveway of the park. The deputy sheriff pulled out after them.

"I haven't got time to talk to any cops," Ken said casually, and stepped on the gas.

When they came to a bridge, Ken said, "Here's where we lose them." He stopped the pickup in the center of the bridge and backed the trailer up at an angle until it blocked the road. He jumped out, unhooked it, and off they drove in the pickup, leaving the deputy, who was too far behind to see the license or the occupants of the truck, stuck on the other side of the trailer. Ken chuckled about it, continued driving south unconcernedly for a few miles, then hopped on the interstate. He got off at the Oregon exit and drove to a phone booth across from the courthouse. From there he called the highway patrol and the Andrew County sheriff's department and reported his horse trailer missing, saying that somebody must have stolen it from his farm. He dropped Nick off at the closest bar and headed home.

The next day, McFadin's investigator retrieved the trailer from the Andrew County sheriff's department and returned it to its rightful owner, Ken McElroy.

17

Romaine Henry was a typical Skidmore farmer. Forty-one years old, about medium height, with thinning hair and a pot belly, he was a quiet man with a steady-as-she-goes philosophy. Farming was Romaine's way of life; he worked from sunup to sunset and beyond. Born and raised in the area, he lived with his wife and three kids on a 1,000-acre farm accumulated over the years since 1952, when he had bought the first acreage.

About two and a half miles before Route V hits the edge of Skidmore, Route ZZ, a decent blacktop, cuts off and runs south to Graham. At the third curve, a gravel road turns off to the left and passes Romaine's farm about a quarter-mile further on. Down ZZ another mile and a half is the Valley Road, which leads to the McElroy farm.

In the late afternoon of July 27, 1976, Romaine had just returned from having new tires put on his truck in Skidmore, and was working in the shop, sharpening a sickle, when one of his sons came in and told him he had heard gunshots. The boy said it sounded like a shotgun, and that it seemed to have come from down the gravel road alongside their property. Romaine got in his 1974 GMC pickup and drove over to investigate. As he approached the area, he recognized Ken McElroy's green Dodge pickup parked along the right side of the road, and decided to keep going and forget about whatever was going on. As he swung out to pass, Ken McElroy stepped into the middle of the road, directly in front of Romaine, holding a shotgun in the air. Romaine braked, and as he did so, he noticed another man, younger, behind the wheel of the green Dodge. The man looked him squarely in the face, then ducked out of sight.

Romaine hoped that whatever was happening was something innocuous—maybe McElroy wanted to go on his land to get a rabbit or squirrel he had shot. McElroy jerked on the GMC's passenger door, but it was stuck. Romaine reached over and opened it for him. McElroy leaned in and stuck the shotgun about three inches away from Romaine's face.

"Were you the dirty son of a bitch over at my place in a white Pontiac?" McElroy demanded.

Confused and scared, looking down the barrel of the gun, Romaine said he didn't know anything about a white Pontiac.

"You're a lying son of a bitch!" snarled McElroy. He lowered the barrel and fired the shotgun. The blast tore a big hole in Romaine's stomach, spattered blood and pieces of flesh against the driver's door, and ripped holes in the panel. Romaine tried to move, but McElroy quickly pumped another shell into the chamber, thrust it in Romaine's face, and fired again. Romaine ducked just as the gun went off, but he felt a stinging as the pellets tore a huge gash in his forehead and cheek.

By now, Romaine was moving. He jumped from the pickup and crouched alongside the front fender, intending to take off across the fields and head for home. He heard the gun fire again, but felt nothing. He had gone about ten feet when he heard the sound of Ken working the gun and swearing. *Those guns only hold three shells,* Romaine thought, *and he must have jammed it reloading.* He turned back, jumped into his truck, slammed the gearshift into first, and stomped the accelerator.

"Get the hell out of here!" yelled McElroy. "I don't want to see you again!" Looking in the mirror to see if the Dodge was following, Romaine noticed blood streaming down his face and neck. The green pickup, with McElroy at the wheel and a shotgun hanging out the window, was coming after him.

Because he was heading away from home, Romaine had to make a series of right-hand turns along section lines to get back on ZZ and the gravel road to his farm. Shaking and spattered with blood, he drove as fast as he could. McElroy hung right on his bumper, and at each turn Romaine figured McElroy would take the angle and fire at him. After the third turn, for some reason Romaine would never understand, the green Dodge dropped back and gave up the chase. The pain in Romaine's stomach sharpened and he came close to losing consciousness before he turned into his drive.

Finally, he stood in the doorway of his house, blood streaming from his face and stomach, and told his wife, "I think we better get me to the hospital."

At the hospital in Maryville, doctors found a gaping tear from the first gunshot, running eight inches to the left from his navel. He had powder burns, and x-rays revealed seven pellets in his abdominal wall. A doctor cut away the damaged skin, placed a drain in the wound, and closed it. No pellets had penetrated the skull, so the lacerations in his forehead were cleaned and sutured. The doctor dressed the wounds and admitted Romaine to the hospital for continued treatment, which lasted a week. (The pellets were removed later. The wound became infected, and the doctors eventually had to go back in and clean it up.)

McElroy was arrested the next day, and Prosecuting Attorney Fraze charged him with feloniously assaulting Romaine Henry with the intent to kill him or do him great bodily harm.

McElroy's defense was simple from the very beginning: He wasn't there, and he didn't do it. Romaine Henry had obviously been shot, but he was mistaken about who had shot him.

Five people, other than McElroy and Romaine, initially claimed to have knowledge of McElroy's whereabouts at the time of the shooting: Three people placed him on the roads in the vicinity of Romaine's farm, and two swore he was at home.

Short Linville, the man who drove McElroy, Trena, and later McElroy's kids to school, lived in Graham in a house right across the street from a stop sign where ZZ dead-ended into Route A. A friendly man with a huge gut, Short happened to be in his yard around 5:30 that July afternoon. He looked up to see Ken McElroy's green Dodge come barreling down ZZ about 50 miles an hour. Ken was driving and a young man wearing a felt hat was hanging on to the dash. McElroy barely slowed as he hit the corner, and the Dodge went into a four-wheel sideways skid that ended about half a foot shy of the ditch. Short, who had been standing only a few feet from the ditch, jumped back in alarm. *"Goddamnit, Ken,"* he swore to himself, *"you knew that corner was there. What the hell's wrong with you?"* The instant before the truck came to a stop, Ken downshifted, hit the gas, and roared out in a screeching fishtail.

Danny Kinder, a hand on Romaine Henry's farm, lived with his wife and kids about a mile away from Romaine. Kinder was driving home at 5:30 after the day's work, heading west on Route A, when Ken McElroy passed him in a green Dodge going east faster than hell. There was no question in his mind that it was McElroy's truck and that McElroy was behind the wheel.

Two farmers who lived close by Route ZZ also saw Ken McElroy around 5:30 that afternoon, traveling east at a high rate of speed on ZZ.

But Maurice O'Connor and Alvin Smith told a different story. Both men were from Bedford, Iowa, a small town over the Iowa border and a favorite hangout of Ken McElroy and other coon hunters. They claimed that they were at Ken McElroy's farmhouse doing carpentry work the afternoon of July 27, and that McElroy had been there from shortly after 5 until 6 P.M.

Lawyer McFadin, with one of his best clients in trouble again, set about methodically constructing a defense. First, he took Romaine's deposition, spending considerable effort nailing Romaine down as to the exact time the shooting had occurred. Romaine couldn't say what time he left home, but he was very clear on the time he returned: "Well, all I know is when I got home I looked at my watch and it was twenty-five minutes till six and so from the time I left home until I got back home I wasn't gone over five or six minutes."

McFadin had him repeat time and again that he was positive he arrived home at twenty-five to six. Under McFadin's questioning, Romaine acknowledged the incident could have occurred fifteen minutes earlier, thus setting in concrete the time period for McElroy's presence from 5:20 to 5:35.

McFadin also asked Romaine a routine question: Had he ever been convicted of a felony? No, Romaine answered, he had not.

O'Connor's and Smith's affidavits rebutted the time periods perfectly, although they contained some slight inconsistencies. On September 29, O'Connor signed a handwritten affidavit stating that on the day in question he had been working as a carpenter at Ken McElroy's house and that Ken McElroy was "at his home from 5:10 P.M. and left with Alvin Smith and myself at 5:55 or possibly 6 P.M. Mr. McElroy was driving his own station wagon." After his signature O'Connor added that he remembered the time because they started picking up their tools a few minutes after 5 P.M. On November 9, O'Connor executed another statement, this one typed, in which he stated that McElroy arrived around 5:10 in his green Dodge truck and asked them to fix a flopping tailgate. He and Smith talked to McElroy, fixed the tailgate, and all three left around 6 P.M. Smith's statement, also signed on November 9, said the same thing, adding only that his record book indicated that they billed McElroy for services from 8 A.M. until 6 P.M.

Next, McFadin, looking under every stone, found that Romaine had been convicted of common assault some twenty-four years earlier. The charge stemmed from an adolescent fist fight, and Romaine had paid a $10 fine. He had completely forgotten about it.

To no one's surprise, Judge Wilson disqualified himself from the case on his own motion. Wilson told a prosecuting attorney in another county that McElroy had threatened to burn his barn down, and that not very long after the threat, the barn *had* burned down. Wilson was terrified of McElroy. In a previous case, before Wilson had disqualified himself, deputies had brought McElroy into the courtroom for a hearing and left him alone. Wilson motioned a lawyer over and said in a panic, "He's in here all by himself! Where are the deputies?" Wilson scurried from the bench, and in a minute the courtroom was crawling with bailiffs and deputies.

With the defense in relatively good shape, McFadin, relying on the tried-and-true principle that delay would always benefit the defendant, sought to have the trial continued. He succeeded in having the case transferred to Gentry County and the original trial date of February 14 continued to April 25. That date was continued again to August 2, 1977, when it finally went to trial.

McElroy used the time to go after witnesses. When the visits first began, Romaine didn't know what to expect; he spent several nights sitting in his bathroom with a rifle in his lap, waiting to shoot McElroy if he came through the door. The Henrys' bedroom faced out on the road, and many nights after the family was in bed, Romaine and his wife awakened to find a bright light flashing around on their bedroom walls. Romaine would peek out the window and see the green Dodge with a hand-operated spotlight parked on the side of the road. Sometimes Romaine or his wife would look out the door in the middle of the day and see McElroy down the road a hundred yards, standing alongside his pickup, fooling around in the back or under the hood. Suddenly, the truck would start up, the engine would·race, and McElroy would tear out in a spray of gravel. Other times, the truck would just cruise by the farmhouse very slowly, several times in a night, the lights off and the engine rumbling loudly. McElroy might come around every day for a week or stay away for ten days at a time. The Henrys' closest neighbor, who lived three-quarters of a mile away, grew accustomed to the sound of scrunching gravel as McElroy drove back and forth in front of Romaine's house.

Romaine estimated that McElroy visited him on at least one hundred separate occasions. He figured McElroy was trying to provoke him into doing something foolish, such as coming after him with a gun, or to intimidate him into not testifying. Romaine never considered backing down. He complained to the sheriff, who said he would talk to McElroy. The sheriff did drive by a couple of times, but never when McElroy was there.

One morning, a week or two before the trial, Romaine couldn't start two of his tractors. On investigating, he determined that someone had put sugar in the gas tanks. He called the sheriff, who sent the fuel filters to the lab, which confirmed the presence of sugar. But without proof that McElroy had put it there, the sheriff said he couldn't do anything.

Danny Kinder, who had told his story to the prosecution, feared for his life and the lives of his wife and children. Several times, he saw McElroy drive slowly by his house with a shotgun hanging out the pickup's window. Kinder also got word from various sources that if he testified at the trial and McElroy was convicted, he was a dead man. When he was working, he worried about his wife and kids at home. He asked for police protection but was told that it would be impossible. Nobody came around and asked how he was doing or whether he needed any help; he was on his own. Eventually, deciding that he couldn't stand up to McElroy alone, Kinder took his family and moved to Florida.

In the fall of 1976, Prosecuting Attorney Fraze was elected magistrate to replace Wilson, who had been elected circuit judge. The new prosecutor, Amy Davis, sent Short Linville a letter requesting that he come into the office and talk with her about the case.

To hell with that, Short thought, *she can come talk to me if it's that important.* Finally, the sheriff came to his house and asked what he had seen. By then, Short had all but decided he didn't want to get involved in the case. He had been on the witness stand once before, and had gotten worked over pretty badly. When he saw the sheriff's tape recorder running, Short became vague about when he saw McElroy barreling around the corner.

"Oh, it was around 5:30," Short said. "But it could have been a half hour either way."

Romaine came by one day to see him, and demanded, "Are you going to testify at my trial?"

"I haven't been asked," said Short, "and I don't even know that you've been shot."

"Here, I'll show you," Romaine said, pulling up his shirt and revealing a huge, ugly scar across his stomach.

"OK, now I know you been shot, but why were you shot? Nobody shoots somebody without a reason." Short had heard the rumors that McElroy and Romaine had been involved with the same woman.

"Well, there wasn't any reason, he just came up and shot me."

Short figured, *To hell with him. Why get in all that trouble if the man wasn't going to tell the truth?*

This was Amy Davis's first big trial. She was graduated from law school in 1975 at age thirty-four, and ran for prosecuting attorney in Nodaway County the next year. She knew McFadin and McElroy from having clerked for Fraze when he was handling the rape, molestation, and arson cases. She had poor opinions of both men.

Davis was confident and the cops were hopeful—with Romaine's eyewitness identification, the case should be a winner. Romaine, after all, had known the accused all his life, and the shooting had occurred at point-blank range. What possible defense could there be?

In preparing her case, Davis came to understand how terrified people really were of Ken McElroy. In addition to Short Linville backing off, the two other witnesses who had seen McElroy on the road close to the scene of the crime simply refused to testify. Davis sensed their raw, mortal fear that McElroy would kill them if they came forward. No threats or appeals to conscience could change their minds.

McFadin had previously told Davis he *might* have two alibi witnesses, but when she had pressed him for their names and addresses, he had said he couldn't locate them. On the day of the trial, McFadin pulled the two carpenters out of his hat. In Missouri, as in most states, the law requires both sides to disclose the names of their witnesses in advance of trial so that their depositions may be taken and, if necessary, investigated. The court may prohibit the testimony of witnesses who have not been previously disclosed, or it may grant a continuance in order for the opposing side to take their depositions and prepare a rebuttal. When Davis saw the two carpenters on the morning of trial and learned they were defense alibi witnesses, she objected vociferously to their testifying. To her surprise, the judge overruled her objection, refused a continuance, and said she could instead interview them on the spot. In talking to them, Davis became convinced their stories were concocted. While there was lots of information in the notebook about the day of the crime, little was written in the surrounding pages. Davis was furious with McFadin and the judge. Given a couple of weeks, she felt sure she could have broken the alibi.

From the very beginning, the trial seemed strange to Davis. During her opening statement she noticed that several of the jurors were looking away from her. As the trial progressed, she realized that the rest of them had also stopped looking at her, almost as if she were invisible. She felt as though everyone but her knew what was happening, as though the outcome were predetermined, and they were just going through the motions. A friend of hers in the gallery, a reporter, noticed the same peculiarities.

As the first witness, Romaine firmly identified McElroy as his assailant, and described the shooting in detail. On cross-examination, McFadin couldn't shake Romaine's testimony, but he hammered him unmercifully over his failure to admit the assault charge in his deposition. If a witness had lied previously under oath, McFadin implied, why should he be believed this time?

The prosecution's second witness was Danny Kinder. His marriage had broken up (in part, he felt, because of the stress over the shooting), and he had returned to Clarinda, Iowa, right across the border. In Davis's view, he was a reluctant witness. On cross-examination, McFadin first got him to state unqualifiedly that he saw McElroy at 5:30. Then the lawyer played an old game. "Isn't it possible," asked McFadin, "that it could have been ten minutes later? Isn't it possible?" After getting Kinder to admit that it was possible, McFadin got him to admit that it could have been fifteen minutes later. After repeating this process several times, McFadin said that Kinder had, in effect, changed his testimony and was, therefore, an unreliable witness and not worthy of belief.

Encountering McElroy in the hallway and observing him at the counsel table, Davis found his menacing attitude unnerving. He acted as if the consequences didn't mean anything to him; prison and punishment didn't apply in his case. His eyes seemed to say to her, "I'll get away with it, and then I'll come after you." She wondered if he knew where she lived.

McElroy's testimony was firm and consistent: He had been at home that afternoon until 6 P.M. and hadn't shot anybody.

Davis could not shake him on cross-examination, partly, she would admit to herself, because she felt intimidated by him. She also thought she saw hand signals coming from McFadin's associate to McElroy during the cross-examination.

By the time the evidence was in, Davis had become almost paranoid. She felt something was very wrong, but she couldn't get a fix on it.

The temperature in the jury room was a humid 100 degrees. Initially the jurors disagreed on a verdict; two men argued that McElroy was innocent, while several women felt he was guilty. After further discussion, a consensus developed that, while McElroy may have shot Romaine, he had to be found innocent based on the evidence presented. The jurors couldn't ignore the fact that two independent witnesses placed McElroy at his home at the time of the shooting. A few jurors couldn't figure out whom to believe, and the way they understood the law, the defendant won a draw. After two hours of deliberation, the jury voted unanimously for acquittal.

When the clerk announced a verdict of "not guilty," Davis felt certain that the jury had been tampered with. She was too angry and upset to talk to the jurors, but she seriously considered investigating the matter. She knew, however, that she would have trouble getting the resources for an inquiry. More important, she knew law enforcement would not be able to protect her from Ken McElroy. She let the matter drop. (She was defeated for reelection by Robert Nourie in 1978.)

When the verdict was read, Romaine noticed McFadin wink and smile at his client. McElroy looked over at Romaine with a half-grin, half-sneer on his face.

After the verdict McFadin came up to Kinder and in Kinder's words, apologized for his cross-examination and explained that he was just a hired gun. In the hallway, McFadin genially told Romaine the same thing, "I'm just a hired gun. I work for whoever pays me."

Short Linville received a lot of criticism from his friends and neighbors. If he had testified as to what he saw, they told him, McElroy would have gone to jail. But Short stuck by his guns: If Romaine wouldn't tell him what had really happened, he wouldn't testify on his behalf.

Skidmore residents reacted to the acquittal with disbelief and amazement. How could Romaine not know who shot him? Why would a jury believe Ken McElroy and a couple of guys from Iowa over Romaine and his hired hand? Was McElroy totally immune from the law? Could he roam the countryside blasting people with a shotgun and walk away a free man?

Romaine took the verdict philosophically. He had told the truth, but if the jury chose to believe someone else, that's just the way it was. He felt the matter was done and over with, and now he could get on with his life. He was mistaken. One October afternoon after the trial, during harvest, Romaine was returning from the elevator in Maitland, where he had taken a load of beans, when he met McElroy coming the other way. He watched in his mirror as McElroy made a U-turn and began following him. When Romaine turned into his field, McElroy stopped at the gate. Romaine had a good idea what was going to happen if he got out of the truck, but he stepped out anyway. He saw McElroy lift something up to his shoulder, and, a second later, heard the crack of a high-powered rifle and a bullet whiz by about two feet over his head. Romaine climbed into his combine, cranked it up, and started running it down a row of beans. If he was going to die, then he was going to die.

After about ten minutes, McElroy left without firing again. Romaine didn't even consider reporting the shooting; if a jury wouldn't convict McElroy for shooting him in the stomach and face, it sure as hell wouldn't convict him for firing a rifle into the air.

To McElroy, the acquittal was a triumph. He knew, and he

knew everyone else knew, that he had shot Romaine Henry. Everyone also knew that he had intended to kill Romaine. McElroy even laughed and joked about it, rubbing it in, "I thought I had the bastard shot deep enough that he'd die before he got home!"

18

After their marriage in 1974, Ken and Trena moved to Cameron, Missouri. In April 1975, Trena gave birth to her second child, a girl named Oleta. Not long thereafter, Ken and Trena and their two children moved back to the farm on Valley Road. The old house, with its faded wood siding and peaked roof, had two small bedrooms upstairs, and a kitchen, small dining room, and living room downstairs. The house had no electricity or running water; an outhouse stood at the end of a path leading from the back door.

Ken was determined to provide a better life for his family, and he had the cash to make it happen: He told friends that he was earning $10,000 to $15,000 a pop burning buildings for the insurance money. At first, he intended to tear the house down and start over. But Mabel, who was living with Timmy in the small house down the road, objected because she had raised her children in the old house. So Ken set about remodeling it. He tore up the linoleum floor and laid nice carpet throughout the house. He rebuilt and paneled the walls and put in a new kitchen with large cabinets. After having the house wired and plumbed, he installed a bathroom downstairs. He added a pantry and converted the dining room into a third bedroom. He reshingled the roof, put on storm windows and constructed some outbuildings. To Mabel, the house no longer seemed like hers.

McElroy's four daughters by Sharon visited the farm frequently. After one vacation, three of them (all but Teresa) informed their mother that they wanted to live with their father. Sharon resisted for a while, but eventually gave in. By 1977, the household consisted of Ken, Trena, Derome (formerly Jerome and Jeffy), Oleta, Tammy, Tina, and Debbie. The final addition would be Reno, born to Ken and Trena in 1978.

Trena lived an isolated existence on the farm. Ken was gone more than he was around. He would take off for ten or twelve days at a time, then show up unannounced. She stayed home, kept house, cared for the kids, and did as she was told. She knew he was seeing other women, but she felt there was nothing she could do about it. Trena lost contact with her family and friends; her mother and Ronnie had fled to the Ozarks, Ken wouldn't allow her to see her "grandmother" (Ronnie's mother, Sue McNeely) or her Aunt Brenda (Treva's sister), and Alice, whom Trena considered a friend, had moved to St. Joe.

When people she had known before ran into her, they noticed that she had changed; the sweet blond with the beautiful complexion and pretty blue eyes had gotten rough; her soft smile was gone, replaced by a hard, flat look; her mannerisms seemed tough, like a feminine version of Ken's. One former classmate, to whom Trena had always said hello with a shy smile in high school, passed her on the street in the late seventies, and she looked right through him.

Vicki, Trena's best friend, worked as a secretary in the sheriff's office and saw Trena every time the cops brought Ken in to be processed after an arrest. Trena would come over to her, and they would go down the hall and around the corner to talk, because Trena didn't want Ken to know she was friends with anybody in the sheriff's office. The women talked about their kids and what they were doing, and Trena would say, "He's good to me and he supports my kids." But when Trena was with Ken, she acted tough and mean, like she didn't know Vicki.

In the mid-seventies, Ginger and George Clement opened a bar in Maryville called the Shady Lady, which became famous as the toughest, rowdiest bar in the county. It was a rare Saturday night that at least one fight didn't develop between two drunken lowlifes over a called shot on the eight ball or a demeaning reference to somebody's pickup or girlfriend. The Shady Lady became one of Ken McElroy's favorite hangouts. Trena sometimes came in with him and sat around while he drank beer and shot pool. She was friendly enough, but Ginger saw little that reminded her of the frightened girl who had lived at her house. Trena had taken on a hard edge, and her voice had a flat, almost dull quality. She looked and acted rough, particularly when Ken was around. Trena would talk about her kids, how they were doing, but neither of the women mentioned Trena's stay with Ginger and her family.

Ken McElroy's triumph over the legal system apparently did not relieve the pressure he felt. He could hear people at the cafe and the tavern saying Ken McElroy had gotten away with breaking the law again, that he never worked a day in his life and was nothing but a thief. And he wasn't imagining things: People *were* talking about him more often, and every time something was missing or stolen, it *was* blamed on Ken McElroy. As the complaints grew louder, his rage increased.

Ken would always pay well for a tool box, whether it had any tools in it or not, as long as it came from a farmer. One night, Tom and a friend stole a set of Snap-on tools from a farm off Route ZZ and another big tool box from a farm south of Graham. When they went to Ken's farm, he gave them $250 cash. The two boys hung around talking until after midnight, when Ken said, "You boys want to have some fun?"

Of course they did.

Ken loaded the tool boxes into the green Dodge pickup and said, "Follow me."

He drove into Skidmore and then swung south on Highway 113 about a mile, down the long hill and across the Nodaway River bottoms. On the other side of the bridge, he made a sharp right onto a narrow dirt road that ran between a cornfield and the river. About 300 yards down the road, they pulled up at a clearing on the river's edge. The autumn night was clear, and the rippling water reflected a bright, crisp half-moon. Ken backed the Dodge up to the river and dropped the gate. He rolled the tool boxes off the truck onto the ground, not more than a foot from the bank, then grabbed a can from the truck and poured gasoline on the boxes, shaking the can over them until it was empty. He lit a match, dropped it on the boxes, and watched as they whooshed into flame. The orange light danced in his dark eyes, and a wide smile crossed his face. The boys glanced at each other and then joined in, smiling in appreciation. McElroy laughed a long, low laugh, then stepped forward. With his booted foot, he pushed the boxes one after the other into the river. The orange flames splashed on the white moon as the boxes fell hissing into the water.

"Like I told you," Tom said to his friend as they drove away, "getting back at people is the most important thing to Ken."

PART THREE

19

In 1865, Martenay Skidmore, a forty-year-old man who had knocked around the country as a farmer, boatman, and trader after leaving his native Virginia, purchased 700 acres of land, at ten dollars per acre, along the Nodaway River. Over the next few years, he added 300 acres, and in 1880, he platted and organized the town of Skidmore. He gave twenty acres to the Kansas City, St. Joseph and Council Bluffs Railroad, and envisioned Skidmore becoming a cattle and grain shipping center like Omaha.

For a while, his dreams looked possible. With plenty of moisture, the climate was perfect for dry-land farming, and the silty, glacial soil was suitable for growing heavy grains. The railroad laid track through the town, and farmers fattened hogs and cattle and drove them down the main street for shipment to Omaha and Kansas City. By 1910, the town had two banks, a hotel, two doctors, a justice of the peace, a lawyer, a newspaper, a dentist, and twenty-six businesses. A sawmill was operating, and a huge apple orchard produced 45,000 bushels of apples a year. Soon there would be liveries, an opera house, a theater, a funeral parlor, and a bandstand in the middle of the Four Corners intersection for Saturday evening concerts. Chautauquas were held in tents in the fields outside town on summer evenings. The population surged to 600, and businessmen foresaw a new St. Joe.

But if the railroads made towns like Skidmore, the automobile destroyed them. When the average farmer found he could afford a Model T, he also found he could save money by making one trip to

Maryville or St. Joe to do all his shopping, particularly after the main roads were paved in the thirties. Also, the railroad discovered there were too many towns along the line seeking to become shipping centers, so the trains began skipping stops. The Depression sank a number of banks and businesses, and they never reopened. By the thirties, young people were moving away for better opportunities. New people seldom moved to town. Skidmore, like Graham and Maitland and countless other small towns, settled into a long, gradual economic decline, managing to survive only because it was surrounded by farms and provided a few essentials, such as fuel, food, a bank, a place to drink, and a post office. The schools of Skidmore, Maitland, and Graham consolidated in 1964, and the churches of the three towns shared ministers. There has been no sense of forward momentum for a long time. Slowing the decline has been the most that could be hoped for.

In late July of 1930, a terrible event occurred in Maryville—an event that would be endlessly cited by those who argued that what happened in Skidmore some fifty years later was the work of a vigilante town.

Velma Coulter was an attractive nineteen-year-old schoolteacher at the small Garett schoolhouse about three miles southwest of Maryville. As was the custom, she boarded with a farm family and walked a half mile to and from the schoolhouse every day. She usually stayed after school and swept the floors, emptied the trash, and erased the boards before going home. She followed this routine even after reporting some suspicious happenings around the school and telling friends she was frightened. On the night of December 16, 1930, when she hadn't come home by dark, her host family was not unduly concerned because they knew she was making Christmas decorations for the schoolhouse. When the farmer finally went to the school to investigate, he found her brutally beaten and stabbed to death.

Within three days, the police had picked up Raymond Gunn, a twenty-seven-year-old black man from Maryville. The only reason to suspect him initially was his previous conviction for assaulting a white college girl, for which he had served four years in prison. After eight hours of interrogation by three detectives, Gunn confessed. The police claimed they corroborated his confession with other evidence. He was immediately whisked in secrecy to the St.

Joe jail, but crowds gathered and violence seemed likely, so he was moved to the jail in Kansas City, where he remained until his arraignment on January 12, 1931.

In the interim, the schoolhouse became a local attraction. On Sunday afternoons the road was lined with cars, and a long line of curiosity seekers formed at the door of the building. Fathers and sons walked slowly through the small structure, looking unashamedly at the remnants of the scene by the teacher's desk. One six-year-old boy cringed when the dried blood on the wood floor crackled under his feet.

The press and local authorities predicted that mob violence would occur when Gunn was brought back to Maryville for arraignment. The National Guard was put on alert, but never mobilized. Cars full of people began arriving in town on Sunday afternoon. By Monday morning, January 12, more than 700 people had gathered around the courthouse in 20-degree weather. A car pulled up, and a sheriff, a deputy, and Gunn started to get out. Gunn never made it to the door of the courthouse. He was "wrested" away from the sheriff and led across the fields, barefoot and shirtless, on the end of a seven-foot chain, to the schoolhouse. The authorities made no attempt to intervene. The action was well organized: twenty-five men with clubs formed a cordon around Gunn as they walked across the fields, and others drove to the school and removed all the furnishings of any value, including desks and slates.

By the time Gunn and his captors reached the school, an estimated 3,000 people had assembled. A few shouted, "To hell with the law!" when he arrived. Gunn was taken inside, where he allegedly confessed again to his captors. While some men pushed and pulled Gunn up a makeshift ladder to the roof of the schoolhouse, other men tore shingles off the roof and punched holes in it. Once on top, Gunn was told to spread-eagle himself on the crossbeam, and his legs were stuck through the holes, dangling inside the schoolhouse. One man looped a chain around Gunn's body and through the leg holes and drew it tight. Others doused the roof with gasoline. Several people shouted, "Want some water?"—a reference to the published reports that Velma Coulter had begged her killer for a glass of water just before she died.

An eyewitness account in the *St. Joseph Gazette* described what happened next:

The Negro was then left alone on the roof facing the swarm of people below with an impassivity that was marked. The building was now fired and within a few minutes flames and a dark cloud of smoke burst forth obscuring the figure on the roof. Then the flames began swirling about Gunn and he strained back in a futile effort to escape the uprush of heat. He twisted and revealed a huge blister ballooning on his left upper arm. Pieces of his skin blew away to the wind as the blistering heat became more intense and soon his torso was splotched with white patches of exposed flesh. His hair burned like a torch for a moment and then his head sagged. His body writhed. It took on the appearance of a mummy.

Gunn screamed once in agony. Twice he swung an arm outward despairingly. He was conscious for perhaps ten or fifteen minutes. Within half an hour from the time the flames reached him, he was dead. The flesh was burning from the top of his head and his neck, exposing the white skull to the view of the hundreds massed on the hillside east of the burning building, and on the west, the watching crowds saw his legs draw upward with the heat as in a kneeling position before the body fell with the roof.

When the fire had died, souvenir hunters supposedly combed through the ashes for bones and teeth.

The *Maryville Daily Forum* reported the next day that the "Negro Murderer" had been "Burned to Death by Mob," and in a subsequent editorial the paper condemned the burning and expressed fear that Maryville would become forever identified as the place where they "burned the nigger." The prosecuting attorney called the event a "regrettable incident" and the sheriff, who was in bed with a sore shoulder from the "wresting," said he was "very sorry it all happened and [he] hated it very much." Gunn's mother said she wanted to go "back there and search around. There might be something left [she] could bury as a body."

A few men from Skidmore attended the burning and can recall it vividly fifty years later, but none of them was ever implicated in any way.

20

Like their ancestors, many people around Skidmore were independent farmers who held the same strong beliefs in self-determination and self-reliance. A man should be able to make his own way in life; what he did with himself was his own business, as long as it didn't interfere with others. Old ways died hard, new ideas were slow to be accepted, and people wasted little energy keeping up appearances.

These characteristics, coupled with the steady economic decline, created a community without a strong center. Skidmore had no real leaders, no person or persons who held things together in times of crisis. To be sure, the respected elders—Q Goslee, Pete Ward, Sandy Lemon, Junior Linville, and Charlie Lawrence—had served the community over the years and could influence events when they chose to, but they did not chart the course of the community. Skidmore had fraternal organizations, the most important of which was the Lions, but their purpose was to raise funds for charity and to hold social gatherings. The two churches in town were well attended on Sundays, but neither church exercised the strong influence of, say, a Baptist church in a small southern town.

A sense of community did exist in Skidmore: The residents organized a volunteer fire department; the Community Betterment Association converted the old railroad depot into a museum and tore down numerous derelict buildings; and tremendous energy went into staging the annual Punkin' Show. But the sense of community was passive, surfacing only when specific tasks needed to be done. The *group* was not necessarily more important than the *individual.*

Government was a minimal proposition in Skidmore. The town had a mayor and a board of aldermen, consisting of five people elected every two years from different sections of town. Little or no campaigning occurred, and most candidates ran unopposed. The board met once a month to deal with issues such as loose dogs, vandalism, cable TV rates, water and sewage systems, road grading, and missing street signs. Many competent people wouldn't run for the board, because they understood that their fellow citizens might complain about their neighbors' activities one day and then condemn the board for interfering the next. Also, membership on the council was limited to residents of the town, and many respected citizens lived on farms.

City elections were held on April of 1980. Steve Peter ran unopposed for mayor. At twenty-seven, with a college degree in engineering, Steve was one of the younger and better-educated members of the community. Ruggedly handsome, with bushy brown hair, a thick mustache, and dark brown eyes, Steve was soft-spoken and hard working. He understood when he ran for mayor that it was primarily a caretaker's job, carrying little prestige or responsibility. He would preside at meetings of the board of aldermen, present awards at a rodeo or two, and mediate an occasional dispute.

Mayor Peter took a passive approach to his responsibilities. If a problem arose—a neighbor's dog running loose in another's flower garden, or neighbors arguing about trash in the alley—Peter figured the parties should settle the matter themselves rather than involve the town. He also knew that he could easily lose at least one friend if he stuck his nose into a dispute.

Mayor Peter's attitude reflected the community's general tolerance of minor rule-breaking. No one wanted to point a finger at a neighbor's kid for vandalism or petty theft, for flipping a high-speed U-turn in his pickup at the main intersection, or for towing sheds down the main street on Halloween. Most residents had pulled these pranks or similar ones at some point, and someday their children or their grandchildren would, too. But more than that, minding your own business and letting the other fellow mind his was how people got along.

Having grown up in the area, Steve knew all the stories about Ken McElroy. But he had never had any trouble with McElroy, and as far as he knew, McElroy did not have any particular problem with Skidmore, at least no more than with Graham or Maitland. McElroy wasn't something Steve Peter thought much about when he decided to run for mayor in the spring of 1980.

The community had always felt ambivalent about having the law in its midst. The police were nice to have around when you needed them, but most residents did not feel a need for them very often. A small town like Skidmore had few rules to enforce anyway, and the problems that generally arose—a fight at the tavern, vandalism at the gas station, or kids climbing the water tower and peeing on each other—were minor. Many residents felt that the presence of the law created problems: A sheriff's car sitting in the gas station at midnight was a tempting sight to bored highschool kids who had drunk a few beers.

When a serious problem did occur, however, the law seemed far away and slow to respond.

Skidmore was within the jurisdiction of the Nodaway County Sheriff's Department, but Maryville was a hard fourteen miles away, and the sheriff didn't have enough duputies to patrol all the county roads and small towns with any sort of regularity. A good half hour usually elapsed from the time the call came from Skidmore until a car arrived on the scene. Sheriff Danny Estes, a big, burly guy from Quitman, was generally considered to be a good cop, but concerns about his willingness to take on McElroy would develop as time went on.

The highway patrol was respected, but the patrolmen stayed mainly on the interstates and the main highways, chasing speeders and drunk drivers and handling accidents. As a matter of policy, the patrol entered local matters only when asked by the local cops or when a citizen called directly.

Because of the town's isolation, many residents felt better having someone in town with a badge and gun. So, off and on over the years, the town had hired a marshal. For a long time the marshal was Russ Johnson, who also served as a Nodaway County deputy sheriff. Russ Johnson was a great storyteller and a controversial character. Some people in the community felt he was totally incompetent and inept, while others thought he was a good man and a fine officer. Ever since the incident in 1974, in which Ken McElroy backed Johnson down with a shotgun, many people thought that he did not have the guts for the job, at least when it came to Ken McElroy. There were also complaints that Johnson was shooting stray dogs that weren't really stray to collect the $10 bounty.

Larry Rowlett, then the mayor of Skidmore, thought the town could do better than Russ Johnson. Rowlett's choice was David Dunbar, a friend and coworker on the Maitland pipeline. Dunbar had moved to Skidmore in 1979 from Lamoni, Iowa, a small town about a hundred miles away, where both he and his wife, Dana, had grown up. At twenty-four, Dunbar was a former wrestler, handsome and imposing with powerful shoulders and arms. Soon after coming to Skidmore, he earned a reputation in Skidmore as a good fighter, someone who could take care of himself and wasn't afraid to mix it up.

In April 1980, Larry Rowlett bet Dunbar a case of beer that he could win the upcoming election for marshal. As a newcomer with absolutely no law enforcement experience, Dunbar laughed and said there was no way he could get elected, even if he wanted to.

"It'll be an easy case of beer for you then," Rowlett taunted.

When Dunbar finally agreed to run, he did so as a lark. He had no idea that people were seriously dissatisfied with Russ Johnson, and he had heard only the faintest rumblings about Ken McElroy.

Rowlett called Dunbar on election night and told him to bring a case of beer and come get sworn in—he had won by four votes. After the shock wore off, Dunbar decided to approach his new responsibilities in a low-key fashion, trying to calm things down rather than escalate them. He paid little attention to demands that he crack down on speeders and teenagers running loose at night. But after an attempted burglary at the tavern, and after several people warned him that if he fucked with Ken McElroy he could get his head blown off, Dunbar asked the board of aldermen to buy a gun for him. To his surprise, the board refused. The town would buy his ammunition and a light and radio for his car, give him $35 a month for gas, pay him a salary of $200 a month, and that was all. Dunbar bought himself a Ruger Security .357 Magnum and practiced with it until he felt reasonably proficient. With no training or orientation, he pinned the badge on his shirt, put the pistol in the glove compartment of his car, and proceeded to attempt to keep the peace in town. David Dunbar became the law in Skidmore.

21

In March the hilly countryside began to awaken from winter's long slumber. Cold, gray dawns gave way to streaked pink sunrises, and the stubbled fields absorbed the yellow-white rays of the morning sun. The bitter winds began to lose their sting; the earth, still frozen solid two feet down, began to warm; and the small animals ventured from their dens into the timber and fields.

By early April light southern breezes blew gently over the drab landscape, washing away the lingering traces of winter. The air was fresh and fragrant and stimulating. Tiny alfalfa shoots punctured the earth like millions of needles, casting a light green haze over the black soil. The grass began to turn green and the hedge sprouted bright yellow buds.

In town, Mom's Cafe filled earlier than usual. Around the tables, the talk intensified as the farmers forecast the weather, comparing this April with Aprils past, and argued the merits of no-till farming and a new strain of seed corn from Illinois. Soon the streets would fill with machinery and the tractors would run day and night, crawling over the hills, churning the compacted soil. But for a few weeks in early spring, after the redbuds had popped but before the ground was ready, when the nights were still cool and the days were brisk and sunny, the farmers basked in the feelings of renewal.

As the days passed and the farmers performed endless tasks in preparation for planting, the urge to get in the fields and break winter's seal grew stronger. The farmers felt the earth for warmth and studied the sky for moisture, anticipating the precise moment of confluence.

In 1972, Bo and Lois Bowenkamp bought the large white house on the east edge of Skidmore that greets travelers coming from the north as they round the curve on 113. Five years later, they bought the B & B Grocery around the corner from the D & G Tavern. The store never made much money, what with the poor farm economy and people buying most of their groceries in Maryville or St. Joe, but savings and Bo's Social Security enabled the couple to get by without a lot of worry. They fixed up the big house with new windows, a new roof, and a paint job, making it one of the more attractive places in town.

Bo loved to spend spring and summer evenings in the large garden behind the house, tending to his corn, tomatoes, squash, and beans. Fishing was his other love, and he knew many of the ponds and rivers in Nodaway County.

For her part, when the work day was done, Lois preferred to sit on the porch drinking coffee and chatting with Evelyn Sumy, her neighbor from across the street.

At the store, Lois ran the show. She kept the books, ordered the products, prepared the tax records, and handled the money. Bo spent most of his time behind the meat counter at the rear of the store, sometimes helping out at the cash register or stocking new goods.

Bo had grown up in Elmo, a small town twenty-five miles north of Skidmore. At sixty-nine, he was a good twenty years older than Lois, who had grown up in the Skidmore area. Bo stood close to 6 feet 5 inches, and weighed around 220 pounds. His large hands and feet seemed to hang from his limbs, and his nose jutted out from underneath glasses that magnified his blue eyes two or three times their actual size. His voice rose from deep in his throat, like a gurgling brook. Wearing overalls, short-sleeved plaid shirt, and a baseball hat, Bo occasionally joined the men for coffee at Mom's, gradually folding his lanky frame into one of the chairs at the center table, leaning forward on his elbows, and mainly listening. Slow and easygoing, Bo did not talk unless he had something specific to say. At the store, he tended to business from behind the meat counter, greeting the customers kindly and courteously. A gentle giant, his way was the path of least resistance.

Lois, however, took a harsher, no-nonsense approach to life. A short and stocky woman with dark brown hair and glasses, not unattractive, she bristled easily and jabbed back at life. If anyone asked her how she was doing, she was apt to reply, "Well, I'm here." To "Beautiful day, Lois," she might respond, "I guess." Some townspeople saw her as bossy; others perceived her as a genuinely decent, caring person. One thing was sure: Lois was not one to be pushed around.

On the afternoon of April 25, 1980, Bo was behind the meat counter and Lois sat at a small table nearby, smoking cigarettes, drinking coffee, and tending to her books. Evelyn Sumy was working at the checkout counter, which was at the front of the store in the middle of four aisles running from front to back. At about two o'clock, two girls, a teenager and a blond pre-schooler, came in the front door. Evelyn wondered why the teenager was not at school. The teenager walked to the aisle where the cookies were kept while the child picked around in the candy rack.

After five or ten minutes, the teenager approached the counter with a candy bar and a sack of cookies, and asked for a pack of cigarettes. The child stood close by, holding a couple of pieces of bubblegum and a jawbreaker, probably worth no more than a dime. As Evelyn rang up the third item on the register, the teenager handed her some money and said, "Here's for the candy bar and the cigarettes." Realizing that the girl wanted to split the order, Evelyn voided the tape and started over, ringing up the cookies separately. She asked about the candy in the child's hands and the teenager replied, "She has her own money."

Evelyn returned the change to the teenager and, noticing that the child was not moving to the stand, asked about the candy again. Becoming distraught, the older girl took the candy from the younger girl's hands and put it back in the boxes. Up until this point, the child had been fine, a pleasant little girl interested only in the task of selecting candy. But as the teenager was leading her out the door, she broke away and returned to the candy rack and grabbed the items she had selected. As the teenager opened the door, Evelyn said loudly, "Ma'am, she still has the candy in her hand."

The teenager whirled, grabbed the candy from the child and threw it into a box on the rack. The child immediately began to fuss, and by the time she reached the door, she was wailing and trying to pull away from the older girl.

From her table at the back of the store, Lois had heard the little girl start to fuss and cry, so she wasn't surprised, after hearing the tinkling of the bells on the door, to see Evelyn coming down the aisle toward them, very upset. Evelyn had no sooner begun to explain to Lois what had happened than the door opened and a third, still older girl came in. Walking back up front, Evelyn recognized her as Tammy McElroy, a girl who had gone through school with her son Greg. Tammy had come in the store off and on during the summer.

"May I help you?" asked Evelyn.

"I want my money back!" Tammy said angrily.

"What money?" Evelyn asked. "Is something wrong?"

Tammy stepped closer and dropped a sack on the counter. "Whoever in here waited on my little sister accused her of trying to raid the store."

According to Evelyn, she tried to explain about the two purchases and the fact that the older girl had put the candy back, but Tammy wouldn't hear it.

"Debbie has no reason to lie to me," she challenged.

"Well, neither do I," Evelyn responded evenly.

Overhearing part of the exchange, Lois figured she had better take charge and straighten things out. She didn't recognize Tammy.

"Is there a problem?" Lois asked. "If there is, I'm sure we can work it out."

"Nobody," declared Tammy, "accuses my little sister of stealing!"

"What are you talking about?" demanded Lois in her sharp reedy voice.

"Don't get snotty with me!" Tammy shot back.

"I'm not getting snotty with you. I just said if there's been a mistake, we can straighten it out. If you'll just bring the girl back in we can talk to her."

"She's only four years old!" Tammy said.

Evelyn refunded the money to Tammy and began replacing the items on the shelves.

"Nobody in our family will ever buy anything in this store again!" Tammy said, starting for the door.

"OK, that's fine," pronounced Lois huffily. "That's your privilege."

Tammy left, and Evelyn immediately burst into tears. She had never in her life been accused of anything so hateful, particularly toward a small child. Walking to the back, Evelyn told Lois and Bo that Tammy was a McElroy and that the other two girls probably belonged to Ken McElroy, too. Neither Bo nor Lois knew Ken McElroy by sight, although Lois had known him years before, and both had heard stories about him.

Lois decided to take a look at the two younger girls so she would recognize them if they ever returned to the store. She stepped outside and saw the three girls sitting in a green pickup just north of the store. Tammy was at the wheel. Lois stepped back into the store, and within moments, all three girls tromped back in, Tammy in the lead.

"Is there something else you want?" Tammy demanded, standing a few feet inside the door, glaring at Lois.

"No," replied Lois evenly, "I just wanted to see the other two girls, so if they come in here again, I will know them."

By this time, Evelyn had calmed down a little and, hearing the commotion, returned to the front of the store. When she saw the teenager she had waited on earlier, Evelyn said, "Debbie, you know I didn't accuse your little sister of raiding the store."

"Yes, you did!" said Debbie defiantly.

The three girls flounced out the front door, and the two women retreated to the back of the store to sort things out and regain their composure. About twenty minutes later, Evelyn heard the bells jingle and looked up to see a hulking figure striding down the cookie aisle toward them. "Batten down the hatches," she told Lois, "you're about to meet Ken McElroy."

Well that's fine, thought Lois, *I don't know the man, haven't seen him for years, and I know Bo has never seen him.* She stood up and walked around the table to meet him. Bo came out from behind the meat counter to back her up. McElroy's huge shoulders spanned the aisle, and in his hand he cradled a large pocket knife, holding it about chest high with the blade open.

"You can put that knife away," said Bo. "There's no need for that in here."

"Nobody tells me what to do," McElroy said, then smiled slightly. Almost chuckling, he said, "I have a right to stand here and clean my fingernails, don't I?" He fiddled with the knife, running the blade along the tips of his fingers.

A woman Lois didn't recognize burst out from behind him and stopped a foot or two from Lois and Evelyn. According to Lois, Evelyn and Bo, she opened up with a string of profanities that left both women speechless.

"I wanna know," the woman yelled in a rising falsetto, jabbing the air in front of the two women, "which one of you fuckin' bitches accused my fuckin' kid of comin' in this fuckin' store and raidin' it!"

Lois and Evelyn stood mute, in a state of shock. The woman, her face reddening and her blue eyes flashing, continued to spew forth, teetering on the edge of hysteria.

"I'm gonna take one or both of you fuckin' bitches out here in the fuckin' street and whip your fuckin' asses off!"

Still, neither Lois nor Evelyn could react. The language was horrible, but they had heard it all before; what stunned them was the viciousness of the attack and the fact that it came from a woman. Lois knew that there was an elderly woman at the front of the store, and she had seen the milkman come in a few minutes earlier. (The milkman, upon seeing McElroy with a knife, hid in the cooler.)

My God, thought Evelyn, suddenly recognizing the woman hurling abuse at them. *This raving woman is Trena McCloud, that shy little blond girl.* She noted a slurring lisp in Trena's voice, something she had never heard before, and wondered whether it was permanent or simply a result of her excited state. Recovering enough to respond, Evelyn said, "I waited on the girl."

But Trena was out of control.

"Which one of your bitches is the fuckin' boss around here?" she screeched.

Lois came to and puffed up a little. "I'm the boss around here and she works for me."

"If you'll just shut up a minute," Evelyn said to Trena, "I can explain to you what happened, but you'll have to come up front to the register."

Trena began yelling again. Finally McElroy, who had said nothing so far, told her to be quiet and let the woman explain. Trena shut up immediately.

At the register, Evelyn reenacted the entire incident. Trena paid attention and seemed to understand. McElroy appeared almost nonchalant, asking no questions and making no comments. When Evelyn had finished, Trena said, "Why would Debbie lie to me? She had no reason."

"I don't know, Trena," Evelyn responded, "I really don't know." *Maybe,* thought Evelyn, *Debbie didn't want to bring the little girl to town in the first place, or maybe she just had to have some explanation for why the little girl was crying when the two of them left the store.*

At that point, McElroy, who had been watching Lois replace the roll of tape in the register, turned to her and said he wanted a pack of Camels. Pride and pugnaciousness rising within her, Lois looked Ken McElroy in the eye and said in an accusatory singsong, "Sir, I understand that nobody in your family wishes to do business in this store anymore."

"That's right," McElroy responded.

"So be it," said Lois, closing the conversation.

McElroy and Trena walked out, saying nothing.

After the door shut behind the McElroys, Bo doubted he would ever see them again. Evelyn, who had been terrified from the moment McElroy walked in the door, felt sure she and the Bowenkamps hadn't heard the last of it. Lois was nervous but she had no regrets over her behavior. McElroy had tried to threaten them with a knife, his wife had cursed them, and his kids had called them liars. She would hold them to their word: Neither he nor any member of his family was welcome in her store.

McElroy told various versions of what had happened that afternoon. To one friend, he said that Bo had thrown the girls out of the store, accusing them of stealing and yelling at them that they were all a bunch of thieving McElroys and not to come back. To another friend, he said that the little girl had her own allowance with her that day, but that when she put a jawbreaker in her mouth, Lois started raising hell. When Debbie tried to pay for the candy, Lois told her and the child to leave. McElroy apologized, but Lois told him to "Get out. We don't need your type of people in here, and we don't want your business." Ken also told Alice Wood that Evelyn Sumy called him one night and told him that he and Trena weren't raising their kids right.

Marshal David Dunbar had his first encounter with Ken McElroy that same pleasant spring afternoon. Dunbar was passing time in Larry Rowlett's liquor store when a couple of kids came in and said that McElroy had been sitting in his car just a few feet south of the B & B Grocery for a while. The kids were afraid he was going to rob the bank on the corner. Dunbar did nothing, but about ten minutes later McElroy parked in front of the liquor store, with Trena beside him. Dunbar and Rowlett watched them sitting there and wondered what was going on. Suddenly, McElroy opened his door, got out of the car, and came into the store.

"You're the new marshal," McElroy said, his eyes boring in on Dunbar. "What would you do if my wife got in a fight with Lois Bowenkamp?"

Dunbar, who had been on the job less than two weeks, paused for a moment to consider the possible implications of this question. McElroy continued: "I just wanted to know what you'd do if it happened."

"Well," Dunbar replied, "if both of them agreed to it, I'd referee the damn thing. If that's all it amounts to," he said, "it can't hurt too much."

Having taken the new marshal's measure, McElroy got back into his car, drove across the intersection, and parked in front of the B & B.

That evening, Bo and Lois had just finished supper when Lois looked out the window and noticed a caravan driving slowly past the house. Spaced about ten feet apart were three trucks, each carrying a rifle or shotgun in its rear window rack. Ken McElroy drove the lead truck, a green Dodge. Trena came next, driving a green Chevy, and Tammy followed in a red Chevy. Once, they turned around at the end of the block and came back. Another time, they circled the block. For a while, Bo and Lois simply stayed inside the house and went about their business. Finally, Lois, unable to repress herself any longer, stepped out on the porch just as Trena drove by. Trena looked at her and did a double take.

Well, thought Lois, *if they weren't sure where we lived before, they are now. We are marked and located.*

Lois retreated inside the house and telephoned Russ Johnson, the newly defeated town marshal but still deputy sheriff, and told him the story. Russ's response was typical and prophetic:

"Now, don't worry about it," said Russ. "He won't do nothing. Oh, he may harass you a little bit, but he won't do nothing serious."

22

Bo and Lois heard and saw nothing of Ken McElroy for four days. Then, on Tuesday, April 29, they noticed McElroy's Buick parked in front of the tavern most of the afternoon. The car was still there when Evelyn Sumy left the store at five o'clock, an hour before closing time. When Lois walked out the front door at six, she noticed McElroy sitting in his car a little way down the street, watching the front of the store. Seeing Lois, he backed out and began easing up the street toward her. Lois got in the Bowenkamp station wagon on the passenger's side and waited for Bo, who was locking up. Just as he finished, an elderly lady approached him and insisted that she needed a ham for dinner. Bo unlocked the door and went back inside with the woman. At that moment, the Buick pulled in beside the station wagon on the driver's side. Lois stared straight ahead, but in her peripheral vision she could see that McElroy was staring at her.

They sat like that, without speaking, for nearly five minutes. Bo finally appeared in the front door and bid good night to his customer, who hurried away with her wrapped ham. Bo walked between the two vehicles and started to open the driver's door of the station wagon.

McElroy leaned over and said in a low, clear voice, "Hey, is she still the boss in the store?"

"Well, yeah, she is," replied Bo.

"Is she the boss on the street?" said McElroy.

Bo didn't answer, just slid behind the steering wheel and closed the door. Lois, however, jumped out of the station wagon and marched over to the passenger side of the Buick. She leaned against the door and stuck her face in the window.

"Mr. McElroy," she said, punching each syllable, "as far as I know, there is no boss on the streets."

"Yeah," said McElroy. "Well, you accused my kids of raiding your store, didn't you?"

Lois stood her ground. "Nobody ever accused your kids of stealing in my store."

McElroy glared at her.

"You know," she said, softening a bit, "it took me quite a while to figure out who your wife was, but I'm more or less related to you. My mother was a Johnson, a sister to Russ Johnson and Sue McNeely, Trena's step-grandmother."

"I don't give a damn who you're related to," McElroy spat out. "Russ Johnson is nothing but an asshole and a coward, and I could whip his fuckin' ass with both hands tied behind me." He leaned over closer to Lois. "Russ Johnson is the biggest chicken shit in town."

McElroy stopped suddenly, and his faced relaxed.

"I'll tell you what," he said calmly, "I'll give you a hundred dollar bill if you'll try and whip my old lady's ass, right here on the street."

"What purpose would *that* serve?" Lois asked. *Nothing,* she answered herself. *I'm not a brawler, I'm a businesswoman.*

McElroy reached in the back pocket of his knit slacks and pulled out his wallet. Fishing through it, he pulled out a $100 bill, leaned over, and held the bill in Lois's face. Lois pulled back a little.

"It's yours," he said, "if you'll do it. All you gotta do is try and whip my old lady's ass. You just wait right here, while I go get her."

"I don't want your money," Lois responded, "and I'm not going to fight with Trena in the middle of the street!" She hammered the words, drawing out the last few syllables for finality.

"I'll pay the fine," McElroy said. "I'll pay the fine."

"What fine?" Lois asked.

"Don't worry about it," he repeated. "I'll pay the fine."

"If you will tell me what fine you're talking about, then maybe I can understand you," she said, her irritation growing.

"I'll pay the fine," he said again.

Lois finally had had enough of the whole situation—the money, the fighting, his obnoxious repetition about the fine. Turning on her heel, she summed up her feelings in one word. "Bullshit!"

She marched defiantly back to her car and got in, slamming the door. Bo started the engine, and the station wagon pulled away and rounded the corner down the main street. McElroy remained sitting in the Buick in front of the B & B Grocery.

As soon as she and Bo got home, Lois immediately crossed the street to tell the Sumys what had happened. As she was explaining about the $100 bill, Evelyn, who was looking over Lois's shoulder, said, "Oh my God!"

"What's the matter?" Lois asked, knowing the answer from the tone in Evelyn's voice and the look on her face.

"Look who is parked just south of your drive," said Evelyn.

The big Buick and the green Dodge pickup with the white camper top sat a few feet beyond the Bowenkamp drive. Both vehicles were empty.

"Where're they at?" asked Evelyn, glancing nervously up and down the street.

"I have no idea," responded Lois anxiously. She worried about Bo, alone in the house.

Then McElroy and Trena appeared, walking down the street, approaching the Bowenkamps' house from the north. They swaggered as they passed the house, walking slowly and glancing from side to side, as if daring Lois or Evelyn, or anyone, to say or do anything.

"We're going to have to get some help," Lois said. She went into Evelyn's house and called her parents, then crossed the street to her own house. A few minutes later, her parents pulled up, parked a few feet north of the drive, and went inside. The four of them sat at the kitchen table and looked out the window, watching as McElroy lifted the hood on the Dodge pickup and stuck his head in the engine compartment. His huge belly flattened against the fender. After a minute or two, he emerged and stood with Trena, looking at the house, looking at the truck, then looking up and down the street.

Lois called the highway patrol, and a few minutes later McElroy dropped the hood on his pickup and drove away. Although the cops knew McElroy's truck had the most sophisticated communication equipment available, the patrol and the sheriff always broadcast their plans, giving McElroy plenty of warning.

Trooper Cash and Deputy Sheriff Johnson showed up within twenty minutes, and Lois explained what had happened. This time, she was a little more emphatic and antagonistic. "Now, is there anything you can do?" she asked testily.

Cash and Johnson responded that as long as McElroy stayed on public property, there was not a darn thing they could do.

"What about the time McElroy had an open knife in my store," Lois asked.

Nothing they could do about that, either, the officers said. If they pushed it, they would get him all riled up, with little chance of a successful prosecution.

Finally, the two officers left, Russ Johnson saying he would cruise the streets for a while and submit a written report later. Lois never found out whether he cruised the streets, but she did learn that no report of the incident was ever filed.

Not more than an hour had passed when McElroy showed up again in the green Dodge with Trena at his side. He parked in exactly the same spot as before, and up went the hood. Car trouble again. About forty-five minutes later, just as night fell, they left.

This time, Lois did not bother to call the patrol. She was beginning to understand that, as far as the law was concerned, she and Bo would be left to deal with Ken McElroy by themselves. She was also developing a bitter appreciation of McElroy's cunning. *He is smart,* she thought. *He knows just what he can get away with.* Lois sensed that McElroy had no fear of the law; taunting the lawmen seemed to be part of the fun.

Evelyn began keeping detailed notes of every incident. She found it strange that McElroy had focused his anger, or whatever it was, not on her, the person who had waited on his children, but on the Bowenkamps.

For his part, McElroy made light of harassing Bo. To his friends, Ken seemed to be enjoying the whole thing tremendously. He would laugh about scaring the old man and say he needed to be taught a lesson. The one thing he didn't laugh about was Lois. "The real problem," he would declare, "was that old bitch Bowenkamp." Whatever happened was her fault. "How could a woman be the boss of a man?" he would ask. "How could a man let a woman be the boss?"

One evening a few days after McElroy parked outside the Bowenkamp house, Cheryl Brown realized that, like it or not, she had become a part of what was happening to her parents. As she was driving home from town, she glanced in her rear-view mirror and recognized McElroy's green Dodge. She could make out a large form behind the wheel. As she slowed, the Dodge slowed, staying about ten yards behind her. When she turned into her drive, the Dodge slowed almost to a stop, but when she got to the house and looked back, the truck was gone.

McElroy let almost a full month pass before visiting the Bowenkamps again, just long enough for them to begin to relax and think maybe the trouble was over. On May 29, Bo and Lois arrived home from the store a few minutes after six and ate a light supper. The evening was bright and airy, with only a soft breeze from the south, and Bo and Lois decided to work outside a while. They were pulling grass and weeds from the cracks in the sidewalk in front of the house when the green Dodge appeared from the south, heading toward them. The truck stopped a few feet away. Lois looked up and saw Ken and Trena in the cab, a hound in the back, and guns in the rear window. McElroy stared at Lois for a few seconds, then got out of the truck, put on a pair of gloves, raised the hood, and began fooling around in the engine compartment. Trena watched every move the Bowenkamps made. Loud enough for them to hear, Lois said to Bo, "Maybe if we just ignore them, they'll take the hint and go away."

They didn't.

When Bo and Lois finished their chores, they sat on the porch outside their kitchen. Still, McElroy and Trena stayed. As night began to fall, Bo and Lois went inside the house and watched through the window. McElroy walked around his truck, thumped the side, and said something to the hound, which started barking. McElroy waited for the dog to stop, then he set it barking and howling again. He did this three or four times, then got in his truck and drove away. *Well,* thought Lois, *at least it's over for tonight.*

About forty-five minutes later, the green Dodge reappeared, moving slowly along the dark street until it reached the driveway.

BOOM! BOOM!

The reports shattered the evening stillness like cannon fire. Lois looked out the window and saw a large figure standing at the front of the truck, holding a shotgun, its barrel pointed to the sky. She turned off all the lights in the house, locked the doors, and went back to the window. Bo had gone to bed before the shooting and he stayed there, figuring he couldn't do much about it anyway. Across the street, the Sumys turned on their rear porch light. After a few minutes, the gunman got into the Dodge and left. Lois recognized Trena in the passenger seat as the truck passed by.

Lois kept watch by the window, thinking McElroy might be back. Sure enough, thirty minutes later, the Dodge crept alongside the house to the same parking spot.

BOOM!

This time, McElroy fired only once, but the explosion seemed closer and louder than before, and the sound rattled around inside the house.

After a few minutes of silence, the truck pulled slowly away.

Guns were part of everyday life in Skidmore. Probably half the pickups passing through town had gun racks in the rear window, and about half of those regularly carried rifles or shotguns. Kids grew up with guns, learning to shoot with .22s and hunting pheasant, deer, and raccoons in the fields and timber. A rural rite of passage occurred when a boy received his own shotgun or deer rifle for his thirteenth birthday. But the use of guns against fellow human beings was no more acceptable here than it was anywhere else. Males bragged about guns and 'scopes and steel-jacketed ammunition, about who was the best shot and how far away last fall's deer was when it fell, but pulling guns or discharging them in public or within the city limits was uncommon.

Word of the shooting spread throughout the community with dawn's light. The gunfire was the first indication that the candy incident might result in somebody getting hurt, and it was the focus of conversation at the cafe. McElroy's brazenness set the men on edge. Shooting at a farmer on a country road was one thing, but firing a shotgun over a house in town was another. As the day passed and nothing happened—no word of an investigation or an arrest, no police cars in town—the sense of McElroy's immunity from the law seemed confirmed.

For Bo and Lois, the gunfire began the transformation of anxiety into fear. McElroy was no longer simply an annoyance, he was a menace.

But the Bowenkamps hadn't given up completely on the law.

Although Lois didn't call the cops that evening for fear of provoking McElroy, who was undoubtedly monitoring the police bands, she and Evelyn went to the sheriff's office in Maryville the next morning to report the incident. They spoke with Sheriff Roger Cronk, who said he would file a written report with the county prosecutor's office and see what happened. Sheriff Cronk told Lois she might be able to get a restraining order, but it would expire in thirty days. He promised nothing and, as far as the two women could tell, did nothing. His only advice was for Evelyn and Lois to "watch McElroy."

Legal remedies did exist. In addition to a local ordinance against discharging firearms within the city limits, the crime of assault in Missouri included discharging a weapon with the intent to put another in fear of bodily harm. Yet McElroy was neither charged nor arrested. He was not interviewed, nor were any formal statements taken from the witnesses. At a minimum, say veteran rural lawmen from the area, McElroy should have been rousted. Two or three cops should have gone to his farm the next day and told him that life would be hard for him if he hassled the Bowenkamps again. That was what the cops would have done to anyone else, and it was what they should have done to him. The cops knew it, McElroy knew it, and the community knew it.

Two days later, McElroy came again. Bo arrived home from work in the evening to find an empty McElroy pickup parked by his drive. Trena and Tammy were strutting up and down the street in front of the house, swaggering and acting tough, as if nobody could touch them. They did not speak to Bo or Lois or each other. They just kept walking back and forth in front of the house. At about seven o'clock, McElroy drove up in a second pickup and parked only a few yards from the drive. The barrel of a shotgun poked out the driver's window and exploded. BOOM! BOOM! Both pickups drove away immediately.

By ten o'clock, Bo had been in bed for two hours. Lois joined him and was just dozing off, when she heard another explosion, followed by the sound of wood cracking and splinters flying. *My God,* she thought, *he's shooting into the house!* She made her way through the darkened rooms and peeked out the kitchen window. The Sumys had turned off their lights, and the street was dark.

Lois could see McElroy standing at the front of his pickup beyond the cedar tree, facing the Bowenkamp house. A shotgun rested on his hip, the barrel angled up over the roof. He climbed in his truck, backed it up four or five feet, then got out. He stepped forward, holding the shotgun in front of him. BOOM! The sound faded and the night fell silent. BOOM! The shotgun roared again. Shaking, Lois waited for the sound of wood splintering or glass shattering, but heard nothing.

After a minute or two, McElroy cranked up his truck, revving the engine, until finally it reached a full roar. He held it there for a few seconds, then dropped it to a low, rumbling idle. He did this several times, until finally he clunked the gearshift into first and drove off.

Bo remained in bed, and Lois stayed frozen at the window for a few minutes, wondering whether he would come again, and whether next time he would fire into the house. Around midnight, sensing that the siege was over for the night, she went to bed.

In the morning Lois found the place in the tree where the pellets had chewed up the wood. She and Bo had never owned a gun, but after this incident Lois bought a 20-gauge shotgun, and after learning how to load and fire it, put it in her bedroom closet.

Lois didn't bother to call the highway patrol or the sheriff's office. For her last hope, her last line of defense, she turned to David Dunbar, who had now been marshal for six weeks. She called and asked him to come to the store. When he arrived, she took him to the back. "Did Russ Johnson tell you anything about Ken McElroy?" she asked.

"No," he replied, "the only thing Russ ever said was to kind of watch him, that he was a rough character."

"Well, David," she said, "we're having big problems with him. I know you have a family, and we've tried to keep you out of it, because I don't want him camped on your doorstep. But," she bore down on the words, "it's come to the point where one of these nights we're going to have to have some help."

"You know I don't have any police background," Dunbar said. "I've hunted a little, and practiced with my pistol, but that's it for my shooting experience."

"Well," said Lois, "we don't have any choice—we have to depend on you."

"I'll do my job," Dunbar said.

The thought of Lois going around town saying "Dunbar won't do his job" and the knowledge that the townspeople had knocked

Russ Johnson for being afraid of McElroy made Dunbar decide he had better do something.

One evening, in late June, Dunbar spotted McElroy parked in front of the Bowenkamps' house. He drove up alongside the driver's window and said, "What are you doing here?"

"Just sitting here," McElroy replied, friendly enough.

"Have you been shooting your shotgun near the house?"

"Could be, but you know," McElroy grinned, "we're getting real close to July Fourth, and maybe it could have been firecrackers."

Dunbar shook is head and drove on.

The next night, after dark, Dunbar was sitting in his driveway fooling around with his kids. Hearing a low rumble, he looked up and saw three pickups creeping by at about three miles an hour. *A goddamn caravan,* he thought. McElroy was driving the first truck, the green Dodge. A woman followed in the red Chevy, and another woman brought up the rear in another Chevy. The trio drove with their lights off and maintained a distance of about five yards between vehicles. They circled once and were gone.

It's true, David realized, *what Lois said and everyone else in town believed: If you stick your neck out, if you try to help somebody that McElroy is after, then he turns on you.* Dunbar felt a twinge of sympathy for Lois and a burst of anger toward the town. *Why had McElroy gotten away with it for so long? Why hadn't somebody stood up to him before?*

If the townspeople were concerned about the shooting, they did little to help the Bowenkamps. Aside from the Sumys, no one called and offered support, no one stopped by to see how they were doing, and no one offered to keep an eye on their house or to check in on them periodically. Occasionally, a friend would call to warn that McElroy was in town, but most people kept their distance. Business began to drop off at the B & B Grocery.

Although Lois had grown up in the area, she and Bo had not moved to Skidmore until 1972, which made them outsiders to some degree. And, while everybody in Skidmore liked Bo, many people found Lois a bit prickly, and some folks thought she was reaping what she had sown. After all, why on earth would a rational person refuse to sell Ken McElroy a pack of cigarettes?

As they had in the past, most people simply ignored McElroy's misdeeds, hoping he would settle down. At the same time, faint tremors of fear rippled through town. Only a few of the residents had actually met Ken McElroy, but everyone knew who he was, and that he was a mean, unpredictable, and dangerous man. They understood that you could offend him without knowing it, and once your name was on his list, it never came off.

As McElroy waged his campaign of harassment against the Bowenkamps and met no resistance from the lawmen who were paid to keep the peace, the townspeople began to realize that the community was standing alone, and that anyone who tried to do something about McElroy would stand alone, as well.

During this period, Ken McElroy spent a lot of time visiting friends in the small towns nearby. He sat and drank beer and played with the children, picking them up by their feet and telling them their ears were going to fall off. Over and over, he listed his grievances against Bo and talked about going back to straighten him out. "I go into town and see him regularly, just to check up on him," McElroy would say, laughing. "He needs to know I'm there all the time."

McElroy didn't laugh about Lois Bowenkamp. "She is a real mouthy lady," he would say. "She has the biggest mouth in northwest Missouri." Then he would smile and say, "The only thing wrong with Lois, beside her big mouth, is that I won't take her out. She wants to get personal with me, and I won't do it."

On the evening of June 27, shortly after getting home from the store, Bo went outside to do some yard work. He was watering flowers beside the house when McElroy pulled up in the Buick and parked in his usual spot by the drive, only a few feet away. Bo kept on watering the flowers and paid no attention to him, while Lois watched from the window. McElroy sat and stared at Bo through the car window for about thirty minutes, then started the car and slowly drove away. As he passed the house, McElroy stared long and hard at the window where Lois stood.

23

Bo's seventieth birthday, July 8, 1980, dawned hot and muggy. The dew lingered in the fields until the sun finally climbed over the trees and burned the moisture from the stalks and leaves. By midmorning the sun ruled the hazy sky, scorching the air and baking the earth. The south winds rose and swirled clouds of dust inside the tractor cabs, covering the farmers' skin with a sticky brown film.

In midafternoon, the air conditioner built into the wall at the rear of the B & B Grocery broke down. Bo called the electrician, who said he couldn't make it until early evening.

About the same time, Ken McElroy stopped in Birt Johnson's service station and ran into Eldon Everhart, whom McElroy had known since they were kids. McElroy began talking about Bo Bowenkamp.

"That old man needs a lesson taught to him," McElroy said. "I know he's an old man, but he still needs a lesson taught to him."

Red Smith had been tending bar at the D & G off and on since he had come to Skidmore a couple of years earlier. In his early fifties, Red was short and slight and had light orange hair speckled with gray. He was soft-spoken and easygoing and had few ambitions other than making it to the next day with a full belly, a roof over his head, and a few beers in the refrigerator. He did whatever work was available: driving a combine, hauling corn to the elevator, or tending bar.

On July 8, Ken McElroy spent a good part of the afternoon in the tavern drinking beer. To Red, who stayed out of his way and minded his own business, McElroy seemed almost calm, keeping to himself at the end of the bar. This was, in fact, one of the few times in the last month or so that McElroy hadn't been going on about what he was going to do to the old man.

Outside the tavern, four teenage boys were standing around and sitting on the fenders of various vehicles, passing the time with talk of cars and girls and jobs, hoping that something still might happen to interrupt the boredom of the small-town summer. Earlier they had noticed McElroy's green Chevy pickup parked in front of the tavern. Now, they watched as McElroy left the tavern, got into the truck, and moved to the other side of the street, where he had a clear view of the rear of the grocery store.

Every year the whole family gathered on the Bowenkamp lawn after dinner to celebrate Bo's birthday with cake and ice cream and gifts. But not this year—such a gathering would have been an open invitation to trouble, so Bo and Lois closed the store at the usual time and ate a light supper alone. At about 7:30, Bo drove back to the store to meet the electrician. After bringing the stepladder out onto the loading dock so the electrician could get to the air conditioner, Bo began collecting cardboard boxes. He intended to cut them into pieces to put over the slats of the dock, so the parts could be set there without falling through to the ground. But first, he rested in his chair on the dock.

Earlier in the day, Bo had also noticed McElroy's green Chevy parked in front of the tavern. Now, the pickup was parked across the street in front of the post office, and Bo could see McElroy sitting alone in the truck, watching him. McElroy must have sat there for half an hour, while Bo waited for the electrician.

Bo was getting ready to start cutting up the boxes with an old butcher knife when he saw the green Chevy pull away from the post office. The truck headed up the hill, and Bob thought, *Well, maybe it's over for the night.* But McElroy circled the block, came in from behind, and pulled up alongside the loading dock, leaving just enough room to open his door.

McElroy got out of the truck and closed the door.

"Have you called the police?" he asked, looking up at Bo, who had put down his knife and come out onto the loading dock.

"No, I haven't," said Bo. "I don't have no reason to call the police."

"Are you mad at me?" said McElroy.

"No," said Bo. "I'm not mad at you."

Bo looked at McElroy, his T-shirt, slacks, and polished boots. Suddenly, something in him flared. "This is private property, you know." He looked McElroy in the eye. "And we want you off it."

McElroy flushed. "Nobody tells me what to do," he replied in a low, taut voice.

He turned away from Bo and walked over to the drive beside the tavern where the four boys lounged in clear view of the loading dock. Handing the boys a $5 bill, McElroy told them to go inside the tavern and get something to drink. Then he turned and walked back to the loading dock.

Bo had stepped back into the store to retrieve the knife and finish cutting up the cardboard boxes. When he turned around, he found himself staring into both barrels of McElroy's shotgun.

Is he just bluffing? Bo thought. *Or is he really going to shoot?* Sensing the answer, Bo jerked to his right. At the same moment, he heard the boom of the shotgun and felt a searing pain in the left side of his neck. He crumpled to the floor.

When the teenagers came into the tavern, they found Red Smith sitting on the customers' side of the bar and, behind it, Greg Clement, one of the two owners. One of the boys said that Ken McElroy had given them five dollars to get something to drink. Another one, John, said, "I think Ken's about to thump ol' Bo." An instant later a shotgun boomed only a few yards away, and the sound reverberated inside the tin building. Greg yelled for Red to lock the doors, and Red, figuring that McElroy might come in the rear door, rushed to lock it first. He then locked the front door and sat down. Stillness reigned in the bar for a few minutes, as if people feared that the sound of their voices might draw the malevolence inside.

Finally, Steve Day, another of the boys, started for the back door. Somebody yelled, "I wouldn't go out there if I was you, boy!" Steve unlocked the door and stepped into the drive. Looking around, he noticed one of the doors on the loading dock move slightly.

Steve rushed up the stairs and stopped short at the sight of Bo lying on his back two or three feet inside the door. Blood gushed from two gaping holes in his neck, and his shirt and the floor around his head were drenched a deep red. He wasn't moving, but his mouth was open slightly. Steve knelt by his head, and the old man whispered, "Get help!"

Steve raced back to the bar and pounded on the back door, which had been locked again. "The old man's been shot!" he yelled. Finally, the door opened, and he went in and told what he had seen. Greg Clement called an ambulance, and Steve and John took off looking for the marshal.

The two boys found Dunbar at his friend Larry Rowlett's liquor store, along with Jim Jones, Rowlett's brother-in-law. Breathless, John blurted out the story. Rowlett and Jones took off for the grocery store. Dunbar got in his car, checked his pistol in the glove compartment, and drove over. Because only a few minutes had passed since the shooting, he thought McElroy might still be in the store somewhere. Envisioning a Starsky-and-Hutch-style shootout, Dunbar drew his gun, crouched slightly, and entered through the front door. He walked slowly up and down the aisles, but found nobody. He returned to his car, radioed Maryville to report the shooting and then looked for Bo.

Meanwhile Jones and Rowlett climbed the stairs and found Bo lying in a pool of blood, like a dying bird. The air was stifling. Jones whipped off his T-shirt, and Rowlett helped him apply it to Bo's neck as a compress to stop the bleeding. Bo was gurgling and mumbling, but the only words they could make out were "I'm dying. I know I'm dying." Bo kept trying to get up, saying he wanted to go, but Jones and Rowlett held him down and tried to keep him calm.

When Dunbar reached the back of the store, blood was still pumping from Bo's neck into a trickle that ran across the floor and collected in a small puddle. Bo tried to talk, but he was swallowing blood and could make only gurgling noises. He was trying to tell Dunbar who shot him, and Dunbar reassured him he knew who did it. He told Bo not to talk.

Lois and Evelyn Sumy were sitting on the Bowenkamps' porch drinking coffee and enjoying the summer evening. About 8:30 Evelyn called her husband, Ronnie, to tell him they were moving to the north porch, where the air was cooler. Ronnie had his scanner on and he had heard the calls for the ambulance and police assistance at the grocery store. He asked where Bo was. When Evelyn told him, he said, "You better get up there. I think he's been shot."

When Lois and Evelyn arrived at the store, Russ Johnson was sitting in his patrol car in the driveway talking to one of the boys.

"What happened?" Lois asked, as she approached his door.

"Bo's been hurt," Johnson replied.

"What *happened*?" she demanded.

"He's been shot."

"If the law had done its job," Lois said bitterly, "this wouldn't have happened."

At the top of the stairs, Lois could see Bo lying inside the door, covered with blood. Jim Jones was kneeling at his head, dipping his fingers in a glass of water and bathing Bo's head. Larry Rowlett was pressing the T-shirt to his neck and trying to keep him quiet. Seeing Lois, Jim turned to Bo and said, "She's here, Bo, she's here."

Although Bo was barely conscious, he was making sounds, repeating the same word over and over. Jim thought he was saying his wife's name, "Loie, Loie." But Lois understood what he was really saying: "McElroy, McElroy."

The repairman was at the store when Lois and Evelyn arrived. The cops told him to leave, but Evelyn pleaded that he be allowed to stay and repair the air conditioner, which he did.

Lois and Evelyn began calling the children to tell them that their father had been shot and to come to the hospital in Maryville.

Evelyn reached Cheryl at home. "I don't know how to tell you this," Evelyn said, "but your father's been shot. He's at the store." Cheryl began screaming for her husband and grandfather, who were in the basement. They rushed up the stairs, and she blurted out what had happened. Her husband called the baby-sitter, Cheryl changed her clothes (something that would later strike her as strange), and they left.

The patrol arrived about half an hour after the shooting. Rowlett and Jones left, and Dunbar maintained order outside the store.

Patrolman Bruce Richards had been in Maryville when the dispatcher radioed that there had been a shooting in Skidmore and ordered him to proceed there immediately. He fired out with siren wailing and lights flashing, and arrived at the scene shortly before nine. Deputy Russ Johnson, who had arrived a few minutes earlier, motioned him up the back stairs. Richards knelt beside Bo and administered first aid, checking the wound and redoing the compress. Because of the heat and Bo's age, Richards was worried about shock. He checked Bo's pulse and found it a bit rapid. Bo was awake and agitated, and Richards tried to calm him down, urging him to relax and simply lie there and wait for the ambulance. He asked Bo what happened.

"I was shot," Bo gurgled.

"What were you shot with?" Richards asked.

"A shotgun."

"Who shot you?"

"Ken McElroy."

Bo managed to give him a brief version of what had happened. While he talked, Richards glanced around and noticed the butcher knife lying in a stack of boxes about fourteen or fifteen inches behind Bo's head. He stayed with Bo for another twenty minutes, trying to keep him calm, until the ambulance came. Paramedic Steve Jackson checked Bo's blood pressure and pulse and gave him medicine to stabilize his heart. By then, thirty or forty people had gathered in the drive and the street, and the paramedics had to push their way through the crowd.

The first person Cheryl saw when she got to the store was the repairman, who looked pale and sick. Somebody brought Bo's cap over to her, and it was covered with blood. *My God,* she thought, *if there's blood on his hat, he's got to be dead.* She watched as Bo was loaded onto the stretcher, then stepped out onto the loading dock. People were standing around in small groups, talking and staring up at them. In their faces she thought she saw guilt for not helping her family before, guilt for letting the persecution go on for so long that her dad finally got shot. *Maybe this will shock them out of it,* she thought bitterly.

When the ambulance took Bo away, Lois followed in the station-wagon. Evelyn stayed behind to clean up the blood and mess.

On the ride to Maryville, Bo politely answered all of Jackson's questions, but didn't volunteer anything. He was undoubtedly in severe pain, but he didn't complain.

Bo was still conscious when the ambulance reached the emergency room around 9:30. Dr. E. R. Wempe, the attending emergency-room physician, asked him what had happened. Bo replied that he had been shot by a man with a shotgun about four feet away. Dr. Wempe checked Bo's vital signs, and everything seemed stable. After removing the dressing from Bo's neck, the doctor noted four wounds, measuring from one to two inches in length and about two or three inches apart. One wound was behind Bo's left ear and the other three were on the left side of his neck. All four wounds were oozing blood, and the entire area was swollen.

The profusion of blood prevented Dr. Wempe from determining the presence of gunpowder burns or residue. When the x-rays revealed no evidence of metal in the neck, the doctor cleaned out the wounds and tied off the bleeding points. Then he sewed the wounds, inserted rubber drains in them, and applied a bulky dressing to the neck. Bo received a unit of blood and was transferred from the emergency room to intensive care at 10:40 P.M.

Dr. Wempe had treated patients with rifle wounds in the army. While exit wounds from rifle bullets were almost always larger than the entrance wounds, the holes in Bo's neck were the same size, leading the doctor to conclude that they had been made by shotgun pellets. He also believed that two of the wounds were entry wounds and two were exit wounds, because when he stuck his finger in one wound, it came out another.

The doctor was amazed that Bo was alive. The pellets had passed within half an inch of two major vessels, the jugular vein and the carotid artery. If either one had been hit, Bo would have bled to death on the floor of the grocery store.

As soon as Bo arrived in the intensive care unit, police officers asked to talk to him. Dr. Wempe gave his permission and accompanied them to Bo's bedside. Present were Sheriff Estes, Deputy Russ Johnson, and patrolmen Bruce Richards and Alvin Riney. Dr. Wempe described Bo's wounds and pulled the gauze back to show them to the lawmen. Bo seemed traumatized and in substantial pain, but rational. He supplied his age and date of birth and answered other general questions.

Richards asked Bo to tell him again what had happened, and Bo repeated in a croaking whisper that Ken McElroy had shot him with a double-barreled, side-by-side shotgun.

Then, for the third time that night, Richards asked, "Who was it that shot you, Mr. Bowenkamp?"

For the third time, Bo told him without hesitation, "Ken McElroy."

At about one in the morning, shortly after Evelyn Sumy had finished cleaning up the blood and had locked up the B & B Grocery, Bo was transferred by ambulance to the Methodist Hospital in St. Joe, where all his medical records and his personal physician were. Bo would remain there for ten days before being released to go home. He would talk in a hoarse whisper for months, and his left shoulder would develop a permanent droop.

Estes and Richards had begun investigating the crime scene before going to the hospital. First, they talked to the four boys who had been loafing by the tavern. They had told essentially the same story—McElroy sent them into the tavern to buy some pop moments before they heard the shotgun blast. One boy remembered hearing McElroy's pickup drive away seconds later. Estes and Richards found no other witnesses to the shooting, nor could they locate any weapons or spent shotgun shells.

The Maryville chief of police came over and drew a sketch of the scene, and a photographer took pictures. The sketch and the bloodstains showed Bo to be about three feet inside the door.

In the ceiling of the store, Richards and Estes made a critical find—fourteen holes grouped in a tight pattern in the ceiling tiles. Richards climbed up on the meat counter and dug out some of the pellets. Most of them had penetrated the ceiling and had either gone into the roof structure or been deflected by the lumber into the insulation above the ceiling. Estes climbed up onto the roof, tore up the tar, and dug out a few more pellets. The men looked around the floor of the grocery for more pellets, without success. All in all, they came up with eight of the fourteen pellets. After weighing, the pellets would be found to be 00 buck. Estes stepped off the distance between the rear doors and the pellet holes and estimated it to be seventeen feet, a measurement later confirmed by taping.

The only other piece of physical evidence was the butcher knife. Estes later described it as being about a foot long with a long, thin blade and a wooden handle. Although both Estes and Richards noticed the knife near Bo's head, neither officer took it into custody.

That night, before Dunbar went home, two cops took him aside and said, "Look, Dave, if you ever get McElroy alone somewhere, all by himself, blow him away." Irritated, Dunbar said, "Hey, guys, you're the real cops. If you can't handle him, how in the hell do you expect me to?" Dunbar knew as well as they did that Richard Stratton was the only cop that McElroy feared.

24

The heat of the sun had become so intense on the afternoon of July 8 that the blacktop had begun erupting and cracking, causing dangerous fissures in several places on the highways. Early that evening, Corporal Richard Dean Stratton was flagging traffic for the repair crews on the Interstate 29 and Highway 71 overpass just north of St. Joe. To break the boredom, he was snooping on other police bands, checking the activity. He had just flipped to the Nodaway County sheriff's frequency when he heard a call about a shooting in Skidmore. The dispatcher said that an elderly man, believed to be the grocer, had been shot. The assailant had used a shotgun and was driving a green Chevy pickup.

Hearing the words *shotgun, Skidmore,* and *grocer,* Stratton knew immediately what had happened. The patrolman didn't know the green Chevy as well as he knew the Dodge with the white camper top, but he would bet his life that it had a white CB antenna on the roof and that the driver was listening to police bands.

Realizing he was too short of fuel for an extended chase, Stratton headed immediately back to Troop H headquarters in St. Joe, not bothering to call in. He was pumping gas in his car when the dispatcher frantically yelled his number over the radio: "507, where are you? Where are you?"

As the dispatcher repeated the information, Stratton formulated his plan: He had to get between Ken McElroy and the Missouri River.

Over the years, Stratton had tried to learn everything he could about Ken McElroy. When he pulled McElroy over, he talked to him, and when he went to the farm looking for him, he drank coffee and chatted with his mother, who was always very hospitable and somewhat apologetic about Ken. He talked to other cops about him, kept track of his whereabouts, questioned his friends, studied his cases, and tried to figure out how he worked, and, especially, how he got away with everything he did. Stratton couldn't account for his immunity from the law; eventually he came to believe that McElroy either got to the prosecutors, the judges, or the witnesses. This made Stratton more determined to pull him up short at every possible turn.

Stratton's reputation had grown over the years. In addition to incidents involving Ken McElroy, there were many stories about how he stuck his neck out for people in trouble, and how he personally broke up fights in the meanest, most derelict bars in the area, like the dive in Fillmore. People considered him to be a friendly cop, a good guy who became unpleasant only if he thought somebody wasn't being straight with him. If someone broke the law, he would do his best to nail him; but if he needed a break, he would give it to him. Above all, he was considered to be fair, a cop with nothing to prove.

When word spread in Nodaway County in 1979 that the patrol was transferring Stratton from Maryville to St. Joe, people protested. Residents circulated petitions at gas stations, taverns, fertilizer stores, auctions, and door to door. When the petitions failed, several people sought to convince him to resign from the patrol and run for sheriff of Nodaway County. One morning Stratton and his wife woke up to find a sign saying STRATTON FOR SHERIFF stuck in their front lawn. Most people believed he would have been elected easily.

Stratton had not forgotten the feeling of McElroy's shotgun in his face, and he had never stopped believing that one day things would settle out. So when the call came about the shooting, Stratton was ready. He swung out of the driveway of patrol headquarters and headed north. *I'm coming for you now, you son of a bitch,* he said to himself.

The call went out to law enforcement officials in a four-county area, but Stratton knew that if they didn't use their heads, McElroy would get away. It had happened before; McElroy would head south to St. Joe and jump the Missouri River into Kansas at Elwood or Atchison or Leavenworth, and stay out of the state until the situation cooled down. If he was charged and a warrant was issued, his lawyer would call the patrol and say he would bring in his client in a couple of days. By then, McElroy would have disposed of the evidence and arranged his alibis.

McElroy knew every blacktop and gravel road between Skidmore and St. Joe, and the cops could not possibly cover them all. But Stratton knew them as well as McElroy, and he meant to nail his quarry before he got to the crossings. McElroy wouldn't come down Interstate 29 because the police would easily spot him there. And he wouldn't come down Highway 71 because that would bring him through Savannah, where he was too well known. The gravel and dirt roads were too twisty and slow for a man in a hurry. McElroy would run the blacktops for both speed and secrecy.

Stratton pulled onto the interstate and drove a few miles north to the Amazonia exit. From there, he headed north on CC, then west on Highway 59 until it ran into H. He stopped at the intersection and pondered his options. If he stayed on H and headed north, he would end up in Fillmore, only about fifteen miles away and a favorite stomping ground of McElroy's. Or he could head west on B until it intersected 113 and watch for McElroy around Oregon. But according to the radio chatter, Trooper Monahan was already in the Oregon area. Besides, Stratton felt in his gut that McElroy would come through Fillmore. He chose H.

Stratton resisted the temptation to radio for a blockade of the bridges over the Missouri. He had seen the CB equipment in McElroy's trucks and had no doubt that McElroy knew the call numbers of the patrol cars. McElroy would be listening and planning a counter-strategy. Stratton would stay off the airwaves and keep his plan to himself.

Stratton monitored the radio traffic as he approached Fillmore. The patrol was dispatching steadily on the incident, and he could tell that sheriffs' cars from Nodaway, Andrews, and Buchanan counties, as well as local police departments, were in on the chase.

Stratton slowed down as he entered Fillmore and came to a halt at the center of town, where H crossed A. At almost the same instant, a green Chevy pickup pulled up opposite him, heading south. Stratton looked up at the driver and recognized the hulking form of Ken McElroy. In the passenger seat was a blond woman,

Trena. Stratton could make out their features clearly, and McElroy's jaw seemed to drop two inches when he looked across the intersection and recognized Stratton. *I told you there'd be a payback for the hog deal,* Stratton thought. *What goes around, comes around.*

McElroy turned and said something to Trena. Then he looked back at Stratton. Stratton himself was somewhat taken aback; he had figured running down McElroy would be a lot harder than this. He grabbed his mike to call in the sighting, just as McElroy began driving slowly across the intersection. Sure that McElroy was listening to every word, Stratton described the truck to the dispatcher, noting the white CB antenna, the chrome mirrors, and the white brush guard. He let McElroy come on through the intersection, then made a U-turn and dropped in behind him, staying about twenty-five yards back. His radio crackled, and the dispatcher reported that the truck was registered to a Tammy McElroy, and matched the description of the one seen in Skidmore at the time of the shooting. The adrenaline hit Stratton's system in a blast: *I've got the bastard cold!*

The truck picked up speed to about 40 miles per hour, and Stratton maintained a distance of about 100 feet, using neither top light nor siren. The dispatcher told him to hold his position until assistance arrived. Reluctantly, he agreed; McElroy was always dangerous, but to take him on single-handedly when he had just shot a man and was probably still armed would be foolhardy.

The two vehicles passed the schoolhouse and the double-S curve a few miles south of Fillmore, Stratton still hanging back, not crowding McElroy. As the other deputies and patrolmen heard Stratton's dispatch, the chatter of locations and instructions increased. Stratton could tell they were closing in from all directions, and he could sense their excitement. He would dog McElroy until three or four other cars were in position, probably around Route 59, and then he would close in quickly.

McElroy must have understood the transmissions and sensed the trap. His left-turn signal blinked and he turned east onto a gravel road.

He's trying to take me into the bush, thought Stratton. *No way I can let that happen.*

The gravel roads wound around and forked off in all directions in that area. If Stratton let McElroy pull him into the maze, the other cars would never be able to find them. He was headed for isolated country, no place for a gunfight, particularly not with two against one. He radioed his position and told the dispatcher that he was going to take McElroy alone, then and there. Figuring that McElroy might run for it, Stratton checked his seat belt and equipment, then flipped on his red light. The Chevy pickup eased onto the shoulder and stopped.

Stratton pulled up about twelve feet behind the Chevy, angling his front end slightly toward the center of the road so he could use his door as a shield. He flicked on his bright lights and trained the spotlight on the rear window of the truck. Stratton grabbed his riot gun, a Remington Wingmaster 12-gauge pump, loaded with shells containing nine 00 buck pellets. With its barrel sawed off to nineteen inches, the riot gun was a short-range weapon designed to stop a human being by ripping him apart or an automobile by shredding its block. Stratton wanted all the firepower he could get, and he wanted it from the very beginning. If McElroy came out shooting, there would be no time-out while Stratton got his gun. As he pushed the door open with his elbow, he pumped a shell into the chamber. He flipped the safety off with his thumb and wrapped his finger around the trigger, which didn't take much of a squeeze. He stood behind the door with the shotgun at a forty-five-degree angle, ready to lower the barrel and fire in an instant.

Stratton had been trained to exercise restraint with firearms, to avoid firing until absolutely sure that the other person had a weapon and was going to use it. But Stratton had no intention of holding back this time. That split second could be the difference between living and dying. If McElroy appeared in the door with a shotgun, if Stratton saw a shotgun in motion, he would shoot to kill.

Stratton had a buzz in his system, but he wasn't shaking. Concentrating on survival, he was methodically planning each move he would make. First he had to get McElroy out of the truck, then Trena. Afterward, he would get both of them to the back of the truck, cuffed and under his control.

"Ken McElroy," Stratton said, not yelling, but commanding, "open the door and step outside." Thinking that McElroy might roll out of the truck onto the ground and begin firing, Stratton lowered his shotgun a couple of degrees in the direction of the driver's door.

The door opened slowly, a brown cowboy boot gingerly pushing the bottom edge out. Gradually the door widened, and Stratton could see blue jeans and then a leg from the knee down. McElroy's left hand appeared in the light, about shoulder level, palm out and fingers spread wide. Stratton knew the open hand was for his benefit. Then the right hand appeared, palm out and fingers spread. Stratton's eyes flicked to the rear window and Trena's blond head. He considered her to be every bit as dangerous as Ken McElroy, but as far as he could tell, she hadn't moved since he put the spotlight on them. She appeared to be looking straight ahead. McElroy pivoted in his seat, and his right boot stuck out. He slid from the seat and stood erect, arms outstretched, palms out and fingers open. *He's never been dumb,* Stratton thought. *He's buying all the insurance he can.*

"Ken McElroy," he said, "you're under arrest for investigation of assault with a deadly weapon."

Stratton looked McElroy over. His rust-trimmed beige knit shirt stretched tight over his huge belly. His jeans were tight, too, and his belt disappeared under a massive layer of flesh. Knowing that McElroy often carried a .38 on his person, Stratton looked for the bulge of a hidden handgun in the tight clothing.

"What do you mean?" Ken asked.

"You're wanted for a shooting in Skidmore," said Stratton.

"Who got shot?" McElroy asked innocently.

"Turn around."

Stratton came out from behind the door but kept the shotgun angled only a degree or two over McElroy's head. Both men seemed to understand that one quick move, a lunge by McElroy or Trena's door flying open, and Stratton would blow McElroy's head off. Although Stratton held the weapon, they were still two to one against him.

McElroy turned around slowly, feet spread, hands out. No bulges showed in the small of his back or in the belt line of his rear pockets. McElroy might have a weapon in his boot, but he would have to make a move for it, and Stratton felt sure he could beat him.

"Walk to the back of the pickup and put both hands on the tailgate with your feet spread," Stratton ordered. McElroy obeyed, moving slowly and deliberately, uttering no arguments or curses. Stratton turned to the other source of danger.

"Trena, get out of the truck," he said loudly. He stepped toward the center of the road, out of her line of vision in the rear-view mirror. He didn't want her to know exactly where he was. Stratton had known Trena for a long time, having first met her when she was fifteen. At twenty-five, she looked sorrier than hell.

"Slide over under the wheel and come out the left side of the truck," he said. He didn't want the truck between her and him. But the right door popped open.

Here we go, thought Stratton, lowering the barrel a fraction. *Here's where it all comes undone.*

The door opened the rest of the way, and Trena stepped out. She stood on the far side of the truck bed, which covered her from her chest down. She was wearing a light blue T-shirt. She looked first at Stratton, then McElroy. Stratton could not see her hands.

"Hold it right there," he said. "Put your hands above the bed." He glanced over at McElroy, who hadn't moved an inch.

"Do what he says," McElroy said, probably realizing that he was in the line of fire between Stratton and Trena. She put her hands up, and Stratton directed her to the back of the truck. He moved McElroy to the left taillight and put Trena at the right one. Stratton thought of handcuffing them one by one, but decided it would be too risky. He had the situation under control. *I could sit here until midnight,* he thought, pointing the barrel of the shotgun over their heads. The voices on the radio told him that the other cars were getting close and would arrive in a couple of minutes.

"Who was it got shot?" Trena asked, not turning her head.

"The grocer in Skidmore," Stratton replied.

"I ain't shot nobody," McElroy protested.

"He was home with me," Trena said. "All night. He didn't go anywhere."

Stratton was still in the center of the road, out of their sight. He kicked some gravel, then crept back behind the door. If they moved, they would go for him in the center of the road, and that would give him the advantage he needed. He checked the safety to make sure it was off, then just stood and waited.

He could hear the motors humming and see the red lights flashing in his peripheral vision as two cars arrived from opposite directions—a patrol car heading south and an Andrew County sheriff's car coming north.

"It's all right; it's secure," Stratton said to the two officers as they jumped from their cars, guns drawn. They covered McElroy while Stratton reached inside his car, grabbed the mike, and reported in that he was O.K. Two other patrol cars arrived, followed a few seconds later by three or four more police cars.

Stratton walked up to McElroy and cuffed him, hands behind his back, while another officer cuffed Trena. McElroy's forearms were as big as an ordinary man's legs, and his wrists were only slightly narrower. The cuffs only clicked one or two notches, and Stratton worried that they might not hold.

"The cuffs are too tight," complained McElroy.

"You'll live," replied Stratton.

Stratton pulled McElroy's jeans up and felt around inside his boot for a weapon, then put him into the right front seat of the patrol car. Patrolman Riney sat in the backseat, and Stratton pulled out his plastic card and read McElroy his Miranda rights. In the background, the radio broadcast the details of the arrest. McElroy sat quietly, staring out the window.

Before driving away with his prisoner, Stratton walked over to the truck and searched it. It was clean—no guns, no ammo, no casings, no boxes, nothing. McElroy must have run home, cleaned out the Chevy, and grabbed Trena before heading for the river. *Another fifteen minutes,* Stratton thought, *and he would have made it.*

Because the arrest was made in Andrew County, Stratton drove his prisoner to the sheriff's office in Savannah. Trena rode in another patrol car, and a deputy drove the green Chevy. While McElroy was being booked and fingerprinted, Stratton and a deputy talked with the Nodaway County sheriff, who had primary jurisdiction in the shooting. The sheriff told Stratton that because McElroy had been alone when he shot Bo, they had no grounds to hold Trena, and she should be released.

Sergeant Rhoades and Stratton felt sure that McElroy wouldn't talk, but they asked him a couple of questions, just in case.

"I don't know anything about it. It wasn't me. I didn't shoot anybody," he responded each time. "I want to talk to my lawyer." After a few minutes, Stratton and Rhoades looked at each other, shrugged their shoulders, and gave up.

About ten minutes after Trena was released from custody, the telephone rang in Stratton's home. His wife, Margaret, answered, and a man's voice said, "Something bad's going to happen to your husband. He's not going to live until the trial." Click.

Margaret called 911 and within three minutes, a St. Joe policeman was at her door. The officer called Troop H and learned that Stratton had busted Ken McElroy. The officer then called his supervisor, who told him to stay with Mrs. Stratton until ordered to do otherwise. A patrolman called Stratton at the sheriff's office in Savannah, where he was still processing McElroy, and told him of the phone call.

Stratton called home immediately.

"What's going on?" Margaret said anxiously.

"I got Ken McElroy tonight," he responded.

Stratton thought he understood the call: As soon as Trena was released, she probably called one of McElroy's friends in St. Joe and told him what had happened.

Later, as Stratton and Rhoades were talking, McElroy approached them, looked Rhoades in the eye, and said, "You got an oak bookcase in your study that has a top shelf filled with books bound in leather. Three of the books are red, three are brown, and two are black."

Saying nothing, Rhoades and Stratton turned and walked outside. "He's never been inside my house and, as far as I know, he's never even been at my door," Rhoades said. "He's right on the bookcase and the colors, but wrong on the number of books."

The men went back inside and asked McElroy how he knew about the books.

"I saw them through the scope on a high-powered rifle," McElroy replied nonchalantly, a slight grin crossing his face.

McElroy was locked up for the night, and Stratton wrote his report. He described his captive: Ken McElroy, 5 feet 10 inches, 240 pounds, eyes blue, occupation "farmer," tattoo "Oleta" on his left arm.

Stratton headed for home. By the time he arrived, Margaret was scared and angry.

The following morning, July 9, 1980, Sheriff Estes and troopers Riney and Richards transported McElroy from Savannah to Maryville, about twenty-eight miles. Afterward, Trooper Riney drove to Skidmore and retraced McElroy's route from the B & B Grocery to his farm on the Valley Road and then to Fillmore, verifying that

McElroy could have made the drive in the time that had elapsed between the shooting and the arrest.

Robert Nourie, the prosecuting attorney for Nodaway County, filed a felony complaint against Ken McElroy, charging him with the class A felony of assault in the first degree. The complaint alleged that on July 8, 1980, Ken McElroy had "attempted to kill or to cause physical injury to Ernest J. Bowenkamp by shooting at him with a shotgun causing wounds to the neck and shoulder and defendant committed this offense by means of a deadly weapon."

At a hearing that morning, Nourie strongly urged the magistrate to set a surety bond in the amount of $50,000. The magistrate instead approved a bond for $30,000. Under Missouri law, a surety bond required only a written promise by two qualified citizens to produce the defendant at the preliminary hearing and all future court hearings. If the defendant failed to appear, the sureties would have to pay the state the amount of the bond. In this case, as usual, the sureties were Tim and Mabel, the record owners of the 175-acre farm on Valley Road. Thus, McElroy was released from custody and sent back into the community on the written promise of his mother and brother that he would appear for the preliminary hearing.

McElroy and his sureties also signed a document entitled "Additional Bond Conditions," stating that he would "keep the peace and be of good behavior until the case was finally disposed of." The document said nothing to prevent McElroy from carrying firearms or returning to Skidmore. The magistrate set McElroy's preliminary hearing for August 18, more than five weeks away.

25

July was often the hottest month of the year. Temperatures slid effortlessly up to 95 or 100 degrees by noon and hung there until well into the evening. The south wind rose in late morning and blew hard by midday, alternating between steady blasts and gusty swirls. On humid days, the hot, moist air was suffocating. Sometimes, when nature relented, the rain fell in the late afternoon, washing the heat and dust from the air and leaving the evening light and cool.

For the farmers, this was a good time of year, a time for "laying by." The planting had ended, the weeds had been sprayed, and the corn and beans had turned the countryside a bright, shiny green. Plenty of work remained to be done, as always. Winter wheat planted the previous October was ripe and ready for harvesting in early July, and if the wheat was combined early enough, the farmers could plant beans in the same fields. A second cutting of hay might be ready to cut. But the long days on the tractor, from seven in the morning until nine or ten at night, had passed. Now, the farmers quit early and played softball or took their kids to fairs or bought fireworks. The small towns held their annual festivals, civic organizations sponsored fund-raising barbecues, and families had picnics on Sunday afternoons. Teenagers roamed the blacktops, driving from Skidmore to Maitland and Graham and back three or four times a night in a never-ending search for excitement.

In the fields, the corn was pollinating. The stalks had tasseled, and the wind and insects carried the pollen to the shiny yellow corn silk. The process was delicate; if the wind blew too hard, the pollen would fly away, leaving blank spots on the cobs; if no rain fell, the cobs would be stubby and the kernels small. The farmers could only worry and wait.

Mom's Cafe opened at 6 A.M. every day. The pickups began collecting at first light, parking at whatever angle to the broken curbs pleased the drivers. Inside, the men walked to the counter, helped themselves to coffee, and signaled the waitress for a breakfast of bacon and eggs. The center tables filled first, then the smaller ones along the walls. The worn spots on the linoleum floor underneath the chairs told of work boots resting on and rubbing the same places year after year. The bulletin board on the west wall announced auctions and sales, calf-roping contests, and specials on seeds. The screen door opened and closed with a long creak for each new arrival. A few flies buzzed around, hats stayed on heads, and people smoked wherever they sat.

At this time of year, the talk usually centered on the lack of rain, the early morning forecast from station KMA in Iowa, the price of cattle, the Kansas City Royals' latest victory, or the plans for the Punkin' Show, which was less than a month away. But on July 9, 1980, the talk was of the previous night's violence.

Most everyone knew that McElroy had shot Bo with a shotgun and that Bo had survived. The conversation continued all morning, with each newcomer asking questions and adding twists, creating a version of events that was continually taking new form.

The mood was curious. Anything like a fire or a fight always created a stir in the community, and provided a welcome break in the monotony of small-town existence. There was a little of that feeling on July 9, but people were mainly subdued, uncertain what to make of the shooting. They rehashed the details again and again, pinpointing where Bo was standing, naming the boys that McElroy had sent inside, and describing the nature of Bo's wounds. Everyone had a favorite part.

"Ol' Stratton nailed his ass around Fillmore, right off H going south."

"Took him by himself, I guess. Ran him down and dropped a shotgun on him before he could twitch. Got Trena, too."

"I hear he slapped those cuffs on so tight that McElroy whined all the way to jail."

"Stratton is a tough son of a bitch. He probably would have loved to blow ol' Ken away."

"McElroy's goddamn lucky to be alive. Stratton could have dropped him on the spot."

"McElroy knew better than to fuck with Stratton."

The community was stunned at McElroy's brazenness. Before, the townspeople had always been able to ignore McElroy, or to somehow rationalize his behavior. (Even when he shot Romaine Henry, many people speculated that Romaine had given him a reason.) But now that had changed. McElroy, the illiterate son of a poor farmer, had turned from a barn-burning braggart and hog thief into a murderous renegade.

The craftiness of the attempted murder also unnerved the community. McElroy had gone about his crime quite methodically—sitting in his truck and watching Bo on the dock, noting the empty streets, getting rid of the boys. If Bo hadn't jerked to the right, he would have died, and McElroy would surely have gone free. If a jury wouldn't convict him in the Romaine Henry case with an eyewitness, it certainly wouldn't convict him without one.

But if McElroy's actions were methodical, his crime was crazy. Bo was not some lowlife who had provoked McElroy by slurring a member of his family in the tavern. Bo was a nice old man who had never met Ken McElroy until the confrontation in the grocery store and, even then, he had had nothing to do with the little girl and the candy. The arbitrariness of the attack was frightening. If it could happen to Bo, it could happen to you, or your brother, or your daughter.

But, although the shooting appalled the townspeople, they did nothing more than they had when McElroy had been simply harassing Bo and Lois. Perhaps they thought this was the end of the feud between McElroy and the Bowenkamps; maybe now he would go back to stealing hogs and cattle and running crazy in Savannah and St. Joe. Besides, what could you do? If you proposed something, if you did anything, you would be hanging out on a limb the way the Bowenkamps were. The safest course of action was to watch and wait and look out for yourself.

Ken McElroy now stood unmasked. The hatred and jealousy he felt toward the rich farmers, the ones who inherited their land and then looked down on him and his family, the rage that consumed him when he heard they were talking about him, calling him a thief, had boiled over. In a way, he must have felt relieved. Everything was in the open now. It was him against the community, and he was strong and it was weak. The days of brooding and agonizing and thinking about what he should do, the days of stealing the farmers' tools and throwing them in the river, the days of firing shotguns in the air, those days were over. No one would ever call him or his kids thieves again.

McElroy wasn't worried about the criminal case. McFadin hadn't failed him yet. The only witness was still in the hospital, and maybe he would die. Whatever happened, McElroy knew one thing for sure—he wasn't going back to jail. He'd rather die than spend another night locked in a cage.

The D & G Tavern usually experienced a midafternoon slump. A few lowlifes, sucking beer and spitting tobacco juice in cups, might hang around after lunchtime, but the pickups didn't start arriving at the tin building until four or four thirty. By six on the evening of July 9, about twenty people were inside, some playing pool, others playing Ping-Pong, and some sitting at the bar drinking beer and shooting the breeze.

An hour or so later, the door swung open and in walked Ken McElroy, with Trena a step behind him. The place stopped in midstroke: People froze as if they were all wired to the same circuit and somebody had just thrown the breaker. Without missing a beat, McElroy walked up to the bar, ordered a beer, and settled on the same stool he had sat on the previous night, before he shot Bo.

McElroy turned and spoke to the man next to him and drank his Budweiser. The electricity came back on, and people began moving around. The crack of the billiard balls and the click of the Ping-Pong balls sounded again. But everything—people, movements, voices—angled away from the malignancy sitting at the bar, as if anyone who came too close or looked at it would be infected. A few conversations started up, mainly to alleviate the awkwardness of the silence. After serving McElroy's beer, Red Smith walked to the other end of the bar and perched on the cooler.

Marshal David Dunbar wondered whether McElroy had broken out of jail. In reporting the previous night's shooting, he had mentioned Ken McElroy as the probable assailant. McElroy had undoubtedly been listening on his CB. Perhaps McElroy had come for him.

Jim Jones, who had applied the T-shirt to Bo's neck, felt strange vibrations the minute McElroy walked in. *This is pretty weird,* Jones thought, *a guy sitting at a bar drinking beer not thirty yards from where he shot a person the night before.*

In a loud voice, McElroy asked, "What was all the commotion about last night? Was there a burglary in the grocery store?" When no one answered, he chuckled and turned to Trena.

A few people left, trying to walk out nonchalantly, as if they had been intending to leave anyway. More trickled out, until only two or three remained.

Word had not reached town that McElroy had been released on bail that morning, so when he appeared at the D & G, he might as well have been an evil apparition returned to its haunt. The townspeople couldn't believe that after the cops (or one cop, anyway) had finally done their job and put McElroy in jail, the court had turned around and released him back into the community. Bill Everhart, a former town marshal, spoke for many when he said simply, "If a man shoots an unarmed man at point-blank range, he ought to be kept in jail until trial." To Lois Bowenkamp, the question was simple: "What the hell was he doing back on the street?"

Missouri law provided that, with the exception of people charged with capital crimes, every person was entitled to be released on bail, regardless of the nature of the crime or the threat posed to the community. The court could not consider the fact that the defendant might commit further crimes or intimidate witnesses before the trial. The reasoning behind the law was that the defendant had a constitutional right to be presumed innocent and, therefore, should not be punished before conviction.

Several states and the federal government had adopted the concept of "preventive detention," which allowed courts to consider factors such as the seriousness of the offense, the strength of the prosecution's case, and the defendant's criminal record, in deciding whether to set bail. But in Missouri, as in most states, the court had to set bail without regard for the welfare of the community.

McElroy knew this, of course, just as he knew what effect his appearance in the tavern would have on the town. He had come back to shove those farmers' faces in their own weakness, and he had enjoyed doing it. Their hero Stratton could bust him, but the courts would turn him loose, and the people in Skidmore couldn't do a thing about it.

The people who were already targets, who could find no shadows to fade into, took what precautions they could. Across the street from the Bowenkamps, Evelyn Sumy loaded her shotgun. West of town, Cheryl Brown got out the 4-10 shotgun, loaded it, and began carrying it on the seat beside her in the car.

At the cafe, conversations turned inevitably to McElroy's appearance at the tavern. People shook their heads and swore over the easy freedom of a would-be murderer. Inevitably, the more people talked about McElroy, the bigger and more fearsome he seemed, and the more intimidated and helpless they felt.

McElroy had a few sympathizers who sat in the cafe and the tavern and listened to the talk and told him later what people said about him. These reports fed the fires of his paranoid rage and kept things going full circle.

Word of the shooting spread far and wide, mainly because Ken McElroy's finger had been on the trigger. To his friends, McElroy explained that the shooting was pure and simple self-defense: The old man came at him with a knife, and he had to shoot him or he would have been stabbed to death. In recounting his capture, his face darkened, and he rubbed his forearms and told how Stratton had handcuffed him so tight his wrists hurt like hell for weeks.

To his family, his brothers and sisters, Ken gave a more elaborate story. He had driven up the alley and found a pickup blocking his way. When he stopped, Bo yelled at him to get out of the alley. Ken shut the motor off so he could hear what Bo was saying, and Bo yelled again, "Get out and stay out!" By then Ken's pickup had developed a vapor lock and wouldn't start. He got out of his truck to explain it to Bo, but Bo started coming at him with a knife. Ken reached in the truck, grabbed his shotgun and fired, intending only to scare him. Had he intended to kill the old man, McElroy would explain, he would have blown his head into a million pieces.

The Bowenkamp family feared McElroy would do exactly that. He might not have had any reason to shoot Bo before, but he certainly had one now. Without Bo, there was no case. From the hospital, Bo went into hiding at his daughter's house in Elmo for two weeks. Bo badly wanted to go home, and he cried at the end of the first week when his family told him he couldn't go home yet because he wouldn't be safe there.

When Bo eventually left Elmo, he stayed with Cheryl and her family for a few days. Cheryl was glad to have him, but she worried that McElroy would track him to her house. She asked the sheriff for protection and was told, as usual, that the cops couldn't do anything.

Finally, almost a month after the shooting, Bo went home. For his protection, the family established one iron-clad rule: Bo was never to be left alone. If he crossed the street, someone crossed the street with him. If he drove to work, someone drove with him. The Bowenkamps' primary defense, other than the loaded shotgun, was to make sure that Bo was never isolated again. After a while, Bo had had enough of the women looking after him and announced that he was going out by himself and wanted to be left alone. They let him go.

The Bowenkamps and the Sumys took other precautions, as well. They hooked up an intercom system between their two houses and kept track of each other. Cheryl's sister would call from Maryville and say she was driving to Skidmore; if she didn't show up in twenty minutes, Cheryl would start phoning around looking for her. When Lois left the store, she would call Cheryl or Evelyn to let them know, and would check in when she got home. The key was not to get singled out and picked off.

The nighttime, when McElroy did most of his prowling, was the worst. Someone would call and tell the Bowenkamps that McElroy's truck had pulled up in front of the tavern, or that he had been circling a block in town, and they would lock the doors, turn off the lights, and wait and watch. Evelyn and Lois had decided shortly after Bo was shot that someone needed to be awake at all times. So Evelyn would lie down and rest from six to nine in the evening while Lois stayed up, then Evelyn would sit up until midnight or one while Lois rested, then they would repeat the cycle two more times. The intercom buzzed through the night as they moved through the cycle. Lois cleaned house and did chores, running a vacuum cleaner and dusting table tops at 3 A.M. to stay awake.

Some people in town continued to believe that the Bowenkamps had brought their troubles on themselves. Cheryl's father-in-law told her that what was happening to them was their own fault.

Others in town felt sorry for Bo and sympathized with the family's plight, but were afraid to get involved. Knowing that any neighbors who tried to help them would find McElroy on their own doorsteps before the day was out, Lois understood her family's isolation and partly accepted it. But she was also bitter. When you were in trouble, friends and neighbors were supposed to help. That's what small towns were all about.

One person who did offer assistance was Tim Warren, minister of the Christian Church. A short, rotund man, with a small head and a high voice, Warren had been the minister for only a short time when Bo was shot. Returning from vacation in Colorado a few days after the shooting, Warren paid a visit to Lois and told her to please call on him if he could do anything to help.

He also visited Bo in the hospital, where security was tight. After getting permission and showing identification, Warren entered Bo's room and sat by his bed. In his raspy, crackly voice, Bo described what had happened and showed him the holes in his neck. Once or twice, when Bo's voice broke altogether, he stopped talking and turned his head away, and tears welled up in his large blue eyes. He feared for his life and his wife's life, he told Warren. They talked for about an hour, then Warren left.

He hadn't been home more than forty-five minutes when the phone rang, and a male voice told him not to go see Bowenkamp again. "If you don't mind your own business, we'll have to hurt you."

"It's my job," Warren responded, "and I'm going to continue to do it no matter what you say."

"You're going to be sorry," the caller said, then hung up.

Two days later, a church member told Warren that Lois was very upset, so he stopped by to visit her. She was a frightened woman, and he did what he could to comfort her.

A few minutes after he returned home, the phone rang, and the familiar male voice said, "I told you to mind your own business, and now we're going to take your little boy and kill him and throw him out in pieces in your front yard."

"If you want to try it," Warren shot back, "go ahead!"

Warren knew the voice belonged to Ken McElroy. The threat bothered the minister, but the fact that somebody apparently was watching his movements bothered him even more.

Twenty minutes later, the phone rang again. The familiar voice said, "We're going to get you, you fat son of a bitch!"

Warren saw himself as a peace-loving man—"most of the time." He believed in God, Guts, and Guns and in his right to keep and love all three. He was not a violent man, he would say, but he had a right to protect himself and his family. He had been around guns since he was ten, and he understood and respected them. At the time of the incident, he had a .32 automatic, a .38 snub-nose, a .38 police pistol, a .22 rifle, and two or three shotguns. After the first call, he loaded the shotguns with deer slugs and 00 buck. After the second phone call, he began sleeping with the .38 snub-nose under his pillow and carrying the .22 rifle and the other .38 in the car with him. Some days, he would also carry a shotgun on the front seat.

Warren kept up his visits after Bo came home. The minister would stop at the Bowenkamps' house, and he and Bo would talk about what had happened and what it all might mean in God's plan for Bo. For the first month or two, the phone calls came every other day or so, even on days he hadn't seen Bo. The voice called the minister "fat boy," "stupid," "cocksucker," and other vulgar names. Sometimes the threats were short descriptions of what would happen; other times, the caller rambled on in lurid detail, as if he were enjoying it.

"If you keep on minding other people's business instead of your own, we're gonna rape your wife in front of you, and then we're gonna cut your little boy's sex organs off and make him eat them while you watch," the voice would say. "We're gonna tie you up and cut him into little pieces, and then all of us are gonna fuck your wife in front of you, and then we're gonna kill her."

"If you're so brave," Warren finally yelled, "come ahead and do it!"

The caller hung up.

Not long afterward, the trucks began coming by, as if by his challenge Warren had called them down on himself. Sometimes only McElroy came, sometimes Trena followed in another truck, and sometimes a third truck, with a woman driving, would make it a caravan. Sometimes they came in daylight, and sometimes at night. Some nights they circled only once, and other nights three or four times.

* * *

The distinctive sound of the Chevy pickup could be heard half a block away, approaching slow and steady. The deep-throated rumble of the big V-8 engine with its double exhausts would seep into the victim's consciousness, gradually growing loud enough to jolt him from his sleep. The sensation was like awakening in a darkened room to find someone sitting across the room staring at you. As the truck approached, it would go slower and slower until it was creeping, crawling almost to a standstill in front of the house. The rumble would dissolve into separate beats that floated singly through the air, rising and falling almost imperceptibly. For an instant, the truck would fill the window frame, a green apparition on huge tires with red running lights, white CB antenna, and shiny running boards. Then it would start to move, the beats would connect with each other, and the pitch would rise. The pickup might return a few minutes later, after an hour or two, or not at all. Into the night, the victim would listen, waiting for the faint rumbling to return.

McElroy kept the pressure up—pushing a little bit here, twisting that person over there—almost every day. He worked on anybody who might be a witness at the trial, and he paid particular attention to the four boys he had sent into the tavern before gunning Bo down.

Before the shooting, McElroy didn't seem to mind Red Smith much one way or another. When McElroy sat in the bar, drinking and cursing Bo, Red simply stayed out of his way. After the shooting, everything changed. McElroy would come in and sit and brood and drink and stare at Red, following his every move behind the bar. Red felt like McElroy's eyes were boring through him, and he tried to look away and ignore it, but he couldn't shake the sensation. A day or so after the shooting, McElroy started asking about the boys, who their parents were, where they lived, how old they were and where they went to school—always speaking in a low, soft voice. Red figured that McElroy knew the answers and was just asking to see if Red would lie to him.

Red also assumed that McElroy wanted the boys to know he was interested in them, because if he could get one witness to break, the others would probably scramble for cover as well. McElroy wanted

Bo hanging out there all alone, seeing nothing but huge distances between himself and everybody else in town.

Late in July, a few weeks after the shooting, McElroy came in with Trena and sat at the bar. Red left for a few minutes and returned to find McElroy staring at him. McElroy nodded at Trena and she left the bar. She came back in carrying a paper sack, which she gave to McElroy. He motioned Red over.

"What do you need?" asked Red. "Another beer?"

McElroy reached into the sack and pulled out a .38 special.

"What the hell you doing with that thing in here?" Red blurted.

"I'm going to give you a memento of me," McElroy said softly.

"What the hell for?" Red protested, moving away from the counter, hands in the air, palms out. "I don't want no gun or anything."

McElroy twirled the chamber, ejected a shell, and pushed it across the counter to Red. "I just want to give you a shell out of it."

"What the hell do you mean?" Red asked. "I don't want nothing."

"One of us ain't going to be around," McElroy said.

"What the hell do you mean?" Red repeated.

"Just what I said, one of us ain't going to be around. I saw when you came back in," said McElroy. "You had a bulge in your front pocket. You carrying a rod?"

"Hell no," Red protested. "I don't even *own* a pistol!"

"By God, you are!" McElroy said, his voice rising. "I see the bulge in your pocket."

"Hell," Red said, feeling some relief, "that's my billfold, that's where I keep my billfold."

Red started to reach for the billfold, and the barrel of the .38 swung around, stopping in the middle of his chest.

McElroy turned to Trena, "You go out to the truck, and if you hear any shooting, shoot the first guy out the door, if it ain't me."

As Red would later say, he thought he'd "done had the green wienie right then and there." He hesitated, with the tip of the wallet sticking out, then pulled it out very slowly. This seemed to satisfy McElroy, who put the gun back in the sack and turned away to play a game of pool with one of his friends.

Red nonchalantly picked up the bullet and put it in his pocket.

Ken McElroy with a mixed-breed coon hound. *(Courtesy Trena McElroy)*

Ken McElroy posing a coon hound. Next to him is his daughter Oleta. *(Courtesy Trena McElroy)*

Ken McElroy with daughter in the kitchen of his farmhouse. *(Courtesy Trena McElroy)*

Corporal Richard Stratton of the Missouri State Patrol, perceived by the townspeople as the only lawman feared by Ken McElroy. (*Courtesy Richard Stratton*)

Cheryl Brown, daughter of Bo and Lois Bowenkamp, whose strength helped her family survive fifteen months of terror. Cheryl watched from her parents' store as Ken McElroy was murdered the morning of July 10, 1981. (*Courtesy Cheryl Brown*)

Bo and Lois
Bowenkamp
in their home.
*(Courtesy
Cheryl Brown)*

Richard (Gene)
McFadin, the Kansas
City trial lawyer who
succesfully defended
Ken McElroy against
twenty of twenty-
one felony charges.
*(Courtesy Richard
McFadin)*

Alice Woods and three kids by Ken McElroy: Juarez, 13, Ken Jr., 7, and Tonia, 8. *(© Dale Wittner)*

Ernest "Bo" Bowenkamp, the elderly grocer shot in the neck by Ken McElroy in July 1980.
(© Dale Wittner)

Juarez and Ken "Mouse" McElroy, Jr. Juarez holds a shotgun that was a gift to him from his father. *(© Dale Wittner)*

Trena McElroy and Alice Wood, before the end of their long friendship.
(© Dale Wittner)

The McElroy farmhouse, which mysteriously burned to the ground fifteen months after the killing. *(© Dale Wittner)*

David Baird, the Nodaway County prosecutor, was the only prosecutor to obtain a conviction against Ken McElroy. *(Courtesy David Baird)*

The post office where the shooters stood. (*Harry MacLean*)

Ben Espey, Nodaway County Sheriff at the time of the murder of Bobbi Jo Stinnet. See 2006 Epilogue. (*Courtesy Ben Espey*)

For the next few months, things seemed to be all right between them.

Before the candy incident in the grocery store, McElroy seldom came to Skidmore more than once or twice a week, usually to get gas or play pool and drink beer in the tavern. Now, after the shooting, he became a constant presence. He drove into town at least once a day, sometimes by himself, sometimes followed by other trucks. Some days, he would just drink in the tavern, his truck parked out front, guns hanging in the rear window. Other days, he would park in front of the Legion Hall and stare across the street at the B & B. Often, he would just cruise up the main street, by the tavern, by the store, swing by Dunbar's house, then back by the tavern, and eventually head out of town, driving slowly, steadily, never rushing, letting the low rumbling of the Chevy truck announce his presence.

If McElroy stayed in the tavern for hours, the women in the back-up trucks sat in position for hours. When he left, they followed him out of town single file. McElroy explained to others in the bar that the women stayed out there so he could relax and enjoy his beer and play pool.

His mere presence in town became intimidating. The fear spread to people who had never met him and to those who barely recognized him. Cheryl Brown's sister-in-law, a young farm wife, was getting gas at Sumy's station one afternoon in August when McElroy's green Chevy pulled in and stopped a few feet from her. When she saw who it was, she turned away and went about her business, doing her best to look at the ground, across the street, or inside her own truck—anywhere but at him. She felt terrified that he would catch her eye or say something to her, and she would somehow become entangled in his web.

Larry Rowlett's wife, Karen, taught school and occasionally worked in their liquor store during the evenings and on weekends. McElroy liked Jack Daniel's and, whenever he came in, he would ask for a pint or fifth of Jack. Each time, she would explain that they couldn't afford to stock it because they would have to buy a case of it and Jack Daniel's was so expensive that very few of their other customers ever bought it. She understood how things got started with Ken McElroy, and turning him down time and time again made her nervous, although he usually just bought a pint of Seagram's V.O. and left without a fuss.

When McElroy wasn't harassing Tim Warren or the Bowenkamps, he headed south to St. Joe. He didn't want Corporal Richard Dean Stratton to forget about him.

Stratton knew that setting up a patrolman would be easy. Anyone with a scanner could learn the police codes and a patrolman's car number, which was the same as his badge number, and tell where and when he was on duty, what routes he took home, and when he would arrive. So Stratton was not surprised that the phone calls to his house always came while he was out on the highway working. The St. Joe cops, well acquainted with McElroy, kept a close watch on the house at night, but during the day they came only when called.

The voice on the phone was always the same. Sometimes, the man would simply tell Margaret that her husband wouldn't live to testify, or that he wouldn't last until morning. Other times, he told her where her two daughters lived, described their houses, listed the number and ages of their children, mentioned which children went to school, and recited the addresses of their baby-sitters.

"If your husband testifies at the trial," the low voice would say, "several members of your family are going to die."

Sometimes the caller would say, "Your house is going to burn," and then hang up.

At first, the calls frightened Margaret. Then they made her mad. "Why are you bothering me?" she would demand. "I'm not the cop. If you hadn't shot Bowenkamp, Richard wouldn't have had to arrest you, and you wouldn't be in all this trouble!"

The phone calls bothered Stratton, but he wasn't afraid, at least not initially, either for himself or his family. He figured that McElroy was too smart to do any actual harm, that he was bluffing, just trying to get at a cop through his wife and two girls. He figured he could best handle McElroy by not reacting to the calls, by ignoring them.

One afternoon, when Stratton was in the shower, Margaret received a phone call from the patrol. Trooper Kincaid explained that someone from Skidmore had called and reported that McElroy had a machine gun in his pickup and was telling people that he was coming to St. Joe to kill Stratton. Stratton remained fairly composed, but he had a hard time calming Margaret down and getting rid of the trooper who came over after the call. McElroy never showed up.

Stratton's daughter Pam worked in Maryville as a checker at Pamida, a discount store named after the owner's three sons, Paul, Mike, and Dave. Not long after the shooting, McElroy began standing in her line with a basket jammed full of items. After she had rung up about half of them, he would turn and walk away, empty-handed. She had to cancel each item, one by one, on her register. After McElroy's fourth or fifth visit, her irritation turned to anger.

Stratton's other daughter, Vicki, worked as a nurse at St. Francis Hospital in Maryville. On two or three occasions, she noticed Ken McElroy standing around in the halls on the floor where she worked. She checked and could never find anyone he might have been visiting or any business he might have had there. He never said anything to her or even acknowledged her; he would be there one minute and gone the next. Once, he followed her to the grocery store and the shopping mall and home again. Stratton assured Pam and Vicki that although McElroy would hassle them and try to intimidate them, he was unlikely to actually harm them.

News that McElroy was harassing Stratton began filtering back to Skidmore. People had mixed reactions. Stratton was obviously absorbing some of the heat, and there was always the possibility that he would take McElroy out, once and for all. But picking a fight with Stratton was a crazy thing to do, so either McElroy was completely out of control, or he had never really feared Stratton in the first place. Either interpretation was disconcerting.

Not long after the shooting, Marshal David Dunbar was sitting in the tavern in the late afternoon drinking beer, when Ken McElroy came in and sat down on a stool next to him. The two guys playing pool put up their sticks and left, and one or two others at the far end of the bar departed after a respectable five minutes. Red Smith served McElroy a beer and moved away.

After three or four beers, McElroy turned to Dunbar and began talking about Stratton. McElroy's eyes hardened as he looked at Dunbar and described how he was going to drive by Stratton's house at night and nail him while he was sitting out in his yard. Or else he would wait for him in the bushes by his drive and blow him away with a shotgun as he got out of his patrol car. While McElroy talked, he massaged his wrists. The hate spilled out of him as he talked, his icy eyes glittering, his mind searching for the best way of avenging himself.

He hates Stratton because he's afraid of him, Dunbar realized. *He knows he doesn't have the guts to do anything about him.*

26

Rain could be hard to come by in August. Days of 100-degree heat and cloudless skies rolled by without interruption. By mid-morning, the fenders of the pickups in front of the cafe were blistering hot and the cabs were throat-searing ovens. Only the dumbest creatures ventured out of the shade. In the fields, the crops had reached the last phase of their growth. The beans were blossoming, and the kernels were filling in on the corn cobs. At the cafe, the farmers studied the northwest horizon for signs of rain and debated the various forecasts. Without moisture, the grains would be tiny and shriveled.

In early August, before the ground had hardened too much, the farmers began plowing under the stubble from the wheat harvest to prepare the soil for sowing in early October. Their minds turned to the big harvest six or eight weeks away, and they wondered if, in the end, all their work would leave them with anything other than more debts. They listed chores and purchases to be made—new tires and a new license for the grain truck, a new clutch for the combine, more fuel.

Preparations for the Punkin' Show began the previous fall with a smorgasbord to raise operating cash. Another smorgasbord on Mother's Day had raised more money, and in June and July the committees met and planned and organized and built and bought and promoted, all leading to the four-day celebration in August, when Skidmore became an open town with parades, dances, frog-jumping contests, beauty contests, tractor-pulling competitions, huge barbecues, and a midway with rides behind the schoolhouse.

On Saturday night, August 10, 1980, the third night of the Punkin' Show, people milled around outside the tavern, drinking beer and sitting on the hoods of the pickups. Inside, many of the seats at the bar were taken and most of the tables were full. Ken McElroy sat at the northeast corner of the bar with his daughter Tammy. He was apparently not the center of attention in the midst of all the partying.

Kriss Goslee, the youngest of the Goslee boys at twenty-eight, came into the tavern looking for the Clement brothers. Somebody had told him that three of the Clement boys had dragged one of his older brothers outside and roughed him up: two supposedly held him while the other hit him.

Kriss had a loud boisterous manner, and a reputation as a vicious fighter who wouldn't let up until he had broken his opponent's face. Tonight he was slightly drunk and exuding a reckless, macho bravado. He was looking forward to getting a shot at two or three Clements at one time.

The only empty stool was next to Ken McElroy, so Kriss joined him. He got to talking with McElroy about things. McElroy bought him a beer, and Kriss soon forgot about the Clement brothers. He relaxed too much. As he stood up to go to the restroom, he put his hand on McElroy's shoulder and, in a display of alcoholic camaraderie, said loudly: "Ken, if you're such a great coon hunter, such a good shot, how come you missed those two old boys?" In other words, how come Romaine Henry and Bo Bowenkamp were still alive?

McElroy didn't respond.

When Kriss came back from the restroom, the bar talk continued, but he noticed some whispering between McElroy and Tammy. She went to the phone, then came back and leaned over and whispered something to her father. A few minutes later, McElroy stood up, took a huge wad of money from his front pocket, and asked Kriss, "How would you like to have some of this?"

"What have you got in mind?" asked Kriss.

"Why don't you come outside?" McElroy said genially. "I want to show you something."

The two men walked outside and turned left up the hill, then left again into the drive behind the bank and the grocery store. As

McElroy walked toward his truck, which was parked next to the loading dock, Kriss noticed Trena and two other people standing by the corner of the bank, where the drive crossed the sidewalk. He realized uneasily that they were watching him and he sensed that McElroy was pulling him into the darkness.

By the time Kriss reached the truck, he was shaking, and his insides were queasy. Only a month ago, McElroy had shot Bo from this very spot. McElroy reached over into the bed of the pickup behind the driver's seat and grabbed a rifle. As he raised the gun, Kriss grabbed the barrel and got a good, firm hold before Ken could swing the weapon all the way around.

"Let go of the rifle and move back a few steps," McElroy commanded in a hard, flat voice.

Every muscle and fiber in Kriss's body, every ounce of physical and mental energy, concentrated on gripping the barrel. The knowledge that he was dead if McElroy freed the gun gave him tremendous strength.

"No," he replied, shakily. "What's wrong, Ken? What the hell is going on?"

Kriss felt McElroy's grip tightening on the gun, then he felt a slight tremble in the barrel. Kriss began moving his right leg back slowly, intending to knee McElroy in the balls, grab the rifle, and run. Another slight shiver ran through the gun-barrel. McElroy took his eyes off Kriss, leaned slightly to look over his shoulder, and jerked his head upward. Kriss, still with a death grip on the rifle, turned and saw Trena move from the corner of the bank to the driver's side of a pickup a few feet away. She opened the door and pulled out a shotgun, turned toward them, and bumped into three or four Punkin' Show celebrants on the sidewalk.

"Get back in between those trucks!" Ken hissed at her.

Wide-eyed, Trena stopped immediately and moved back in between the two trucks.

In the streetlight, Kriss saw the revelers' faces—gray, foreign, unrecognizable. Whoever they were, he would realize later, they saved his life.

"If I hit the ground," Ken said forcefully but more calmly, "shoot him."

Noticing that the witnesses had moved on, Kriss began babbling. "I've always liked you, man. Tell me what happened, what I've done. I'm sorry, man, whatever I did, I'm sorry. Tell me what the hell is wrong, I'm sorry, man." Kriss was shaking, and he wished for tears to come into his eyes, but none did.

McElroy looked at him silently for a moment with cold penetrating eyes and said, "You think you're such hot shit because your mother works in the courthouse."

The absurdity of the statement and the reference to his mother jolted Kriss out of his obsequiousness. "What's my mother got to do with it? She's not involved at all!"

McElroy said nothing.

Kriss slipped back into his rap. "Hey, man, I'm sorry. Tell me what I did, and I won't do it again."

McElroy stared at him for a few seconds, and then slowly moved the gun to the bed of the pickup. Kriss moved with him, and when McElroy let go of the rifle, Kriss let go of it, too.

McElroy fixed his dark, glittering eyes on Kriss and said, "Now just get off the streets!"

"I'm sorry, man," said Kriss. "I wish I knew what I did."

"Get to going!"

Kriss backed up in the direction of the sidewalk. McElroy kept his eyes on him, and Trena tracked him with her shotgun, aiming it at his chest until he was inside the tavern door.

Kriss walked straight to the ladies' room, sat down on a stool, and dropped his face in his hands. He took several deep breaths, trying to stop himself from slipping into shock. He sat there for fifteen minutes, thinking of his pregnant wife at their house in the country and wondering if this meant McElroy would be coming after him the same way he had been going after the Bowenkamps and all the others. *Christ, McElroy had been going after Stratton! Fuck, what the hell had happened!*

Finally, Kriss realized he couldn't stay in the women's john forever, so he stood up and left. As he passed the bar, bartender Kathi Clement said, "Kriss, are you all right? You look white as a ghost!"

"I'm just fine," he said. "Don't worry about it."

On his way to the door, he brushed off another question from a friend, not wanting to say anything that might get back to McElroy.

To reach his van, Kriss had to pass McElroy. The minute Trena saw Kriss, she moved to the truck, pulled out the shotgun, and pointed it at him.

"Hold it, hold it," Kriss said. "I'm getting in my van and going home. I'm sorry for whatever I did."

"Get movin'!" McElroy yelled at him.

Kriss Goslee would carry a .38 pistol concealed in a cigar box in his truck for the next several months, until he moved away. But for now, for him, the incident was over.

For Marshal David Dunbar, it had just begun. Saturday was the big night of the Punkin' Show and a large crowd was in town. Everything seemed mellow, even with Ken McElroy around. Dunbar had no particular love for Kriss Goslee, but he had paid attention when McElroy pulled out the wad of money and Kriss followed him outside. Noting that Kriss looked a little strange when he came back inside, not his usual cocky self, Dunbar decided he had better check the situation out. He had just stepped off the curb when he heard McElroy's voice.

"Hey Dave, come over here a minute. I want to talk to you."

David walked over to the drive, where McElroy stood by his truck.

"What do you think of Russ Johnson?" McElroy asked.

"I get along with him all right."

Dunbar was wearing his badge for the first time, and McElroy glared at it, unable to take his eyes off the metal shield.

He must be drunk, Dunbar thought, *because his eyes are glassier than hell.*

"Are you going to testify against me at the trial?" McElroy asked.

"I have to," Dunbar said. "It's my job."

"I'll kill anybody who'd put me in jail for the rest of my life," McElroy said in a low, mean voice. With that, he leaned over, grabbed the rifle from the bed of the truck, and swung the barrel around.

Dunbar pushed the weapon away with his right hand and calmly said, "What's going on here, Ken? There's not been any trouble between us. Let's not have any tonight."

McElroy flicked his right ear with his hand.

In Dunbar's peripheral vision, a form moved forward. Trena came up behind him holding a pump shotgun and stopped about three feet away. Dunbar could feel the cold steel against the back of his neck. At the same time, McElroy swung the rifle around again, and once more Dunbar pushed it away.

"Put that thing away and just calm down."

McElroy began talking about Russ Johnson again, cursing Russ for pulling a gun on him.

"Did he pull it on you?" Dunbar asked. "Or did you pull it on him?" Dunbar had heard two different versions of the incident.

The gun swung back, and McElroy said, "Goddamn it, if I'd pulled it on him, he'd be dead right now! Let's get in your fuckin' car and go down there and call him out and I'll shoot him right on his front step!"

Dunbar heard a step behind him, and his heart jammed up in his throat. *David,* he thought, *what the hell are you going to do now?*

McElroy was standing next to the open door on the driver's side of the pickup, and Dunbar figured he could smack him with a left, knock him into the seat, and grab the gun and run. Of course, that would leave Trena still holding a shotgun to the back of his head. Dunbar's mind whirred wildly, and his body tensed for action. Then, for some reason, McElroy seemed to calm down. Dunbar noticed some activity on the sidewalk, people walking by.

"Let's go get a beer," McElroy said.

Sensing a setup of some sort, Dunbar declined.

The rifle swung up again, and Dunbar pushed it away again. The only way out was to simply walk away.

"Now you just calm down," he said. "I'm going on my way."

Clenching his teeth, he turned and walked past Trena. She had backed up a few feet and was standing with Tammy beside the green Dodge pickup. Dunbar could see the pump shotgun lying on the seat.

"You women take it easy," he said as he walked by.

Trena and Tammy just looked at him.

He got in his car, checked the .357 Magnum under his seat, and radioed the Nodaway County sheriff's office. Dunbar told the dispatcher that McElroy was drunk, that he was pulling guns on people, including himself, and he was going to kill someone. More than two thousand people were in town for the Punkin' Show, and something very unfortunate was likely to happen if the cops didn't get McElroy off the streets, at least for the night.

"Don't provoke him," the answer came back over the radio. "If we arrest him, he'll just be back on the streets in two hours. Just observe him and make sure he doesn't kill anybody."

"You mean you're just going to let him run around loose tonight?" Dunbar asked incredulously, his anger beginning to rise.

"There's nothing much we can do, marshal. Just keep an eye on him."

Dunbar dropped the mike on its hook. *To hell with it,* he thought. *If I'm not going to get support from the county sheriff, I'm getting the hell out of it.* Dunbar had no intention of taking on McElroy alone, not for $240 a month, maybe not for anything a month.

A few minutes later, while he was sitting in the car recovering, Dunbar saw the two McElroy trucks drive by, heading east out of town. He knew that Ken McElroy had heard the entire conversation on his scanner. The law might as well have issued him a license to roam and ravage at will.

Monday morning, Dunbar walked over to city hall in the converted gas station, turned in his badge, and formally resigned as marshal of Skidmore.

News of the incident in the drive began to spread around the community on Sunday, but not until Monday morning, when word of the resignation spread, did the reaction set in: Incredulity, outrage, and fear greeted the revelations that a person out on bond for shooting an unarmed man could come to town a few days later, point a shotgun at the marshal, and threaten to kill him if he testified, and nothing happened, except that the marshal resigned.

Most people didn't blame Dunbar. He wasn't a trained lawman. He had been hired to keep the peace, to deal with vandalism and loose dogs and cars speeding down the main street. Nonetheless, with his badge and his gun, he had been the law. Now, nothing stood between the community and Ken McElroy, and the wait-and-see attitude of most people began to give way to feelings of helplessness and isolation.

As the date for the preliminary hearing drew near, the residents wondered how the formal judicial system would deal with Ken McElroy this time. Would the witnesses show up? If they showed up, would they change their stories? Would new witnesses appear from nowhere? Would McElroy get to the jury?

The real question was whether Bo would hold up. He was a nice old man, but was he tough enough? Could he handle McElroy harassing him outside the court and McFadin, the Kansas City lawyer who could turn witnesses upside down, working him over in the courtroom?

McElroy also understood that Bo was the key. McFadin could probably delay the trial for at least a year—a long time for a sick, old man. Maybe he would die, or his memory would fail. Maybe he would simply move away to another town in another state. Without Bo, McElroy would have no problem.

So McElroy did not idly pass the days before the hearing. He fired no more shots, but he did plenty of cruising and glaring and staring. Lois would look out the front window of the store and see two McElroy trucks parked across the street facing the store. They would sit there for hours, Ken in one truck and Trena in the other, staring at the front of the B & B. At closing time, Lois and Bo would walk out and get in their car under McElroy's fixed gaze. Shortly after arriving home, they would hear the rumbling engines as the two trucks, sometimes joined by a third one, rounded the corner from the south and crept by their house.

A customer at Sumy's station was startled one afternoon, when he looked up and saw four McElroy trucks cruising up the main street. McElroy backed his truck into a space directly across from the grocery store, another truck parked in front of the bank, the third parked about thirty yards south in front of the hardware store, and the fourth parked twenty or thirty yards south of McElroy on the same side of the street. Carrying a shotgun, McElroy got out and walked to the front of his truck. When he pointed the gun at the front door of the grocery store, the customer figured that McElroy was going to blow the place to pieces. McElroy stood there for about five minutes, got back in his truck, and pulled out, heading south. The other three trucks fell in behind him.

The pressure began to wear on Bo and Lois. Business at the store continued to drop off; as long as McElroy's truck was parked near the store, nobody would come in.

Although her parents tried to be understanding, Cheryl Brown was less forgiving. The terror she had felt since the day McElroy shot her dad continued to affect every moment of her life. If her husband went to sit with Bo and Lois, Cheryl was nervous about being alone with the kids. Sometimes, when she was planning to visit her dad, her mother would call to say that McElroy was parked out front, and she shouldn't bring the kids to town. More than once, she looked in her rear-view mirror and saw the green

Chevy following at a distance. Every sound in the night would jerk her bolt upright in bed, and she would grab a shotgun and prowl the house. And watching the physical and emotional strain on her dad wrenched her daily.

Whenever anyone blamed the Bowenkamps for inciting McElroy, Cheryl would snap, "OK, we'll move back to Nebraska, but we're not taking him with us." That seemed to put matters in a different light for them.

McElroy didn't let up on Dunbar either, even after he resigned. The phone would ring at Dunbar's home, and McElroy would say, "Dave, why don't you come over to the house? I've got some friend here from Kansas City I'd like you to meet." Dunbar didn't know whether it was a joke or a setup. Sometimes, he would be sitting in his front yard at night, and the trucks would come by. First, he would hear them, then he would see them creeping along with their lights out, guns silhouetted in their rear windows, McElroy in the lead, the women following behind. On those nights, nobody spoke a word.

27

The preliminary hearing began on the afternoon of August 18, 1980, at the Nodaway County Courthouse in Maryville. McFadin was there to represent McElroy, and Robert Nourie was the prosecutor. Presiding was Judge John Fraze, the man who five years earlier had been ready and anxious to prosecute Ken McElroy for rape, child molestation, assault, and arson. Now, the alleged victim of three of those crimes sat in the first row, wife of the accused and mother of three of his children. On the other side of the aisle sat Lois, Bo, Evelyn Sumy, Cheryl, and Cheryl's sister. They were nervous and scared, but they were there. A state trooper had spent most of the previous night parked in the Bowenkamps' driveway.

The purpose of the preliminary hearing was to determine whether a crime had been committed and whether there were reasonable grounds to believe that Ken McElroy committed it. Bo's presence in the courtroom, unless he were to repudiate his former statements, made the outcome of the hearing predictable, because an eyewitness identification normally provided reasonable grounds for believing that the defendant had committed the crime.

The preliminary hearing would also give McElroy his first real look at the prosecution's case. McFadin would have his first opportunity to try to wear Bo down, to shake him up, and to develop inconsistencies to use against him at the trial. Because of McElroy's Fifth Amendment right not to incriminate himself, he would not be required to testify or make any statements to the prosecution. The prosecutor would hear McElroy's story for the first time —if he heard it at all—at the trial.

The only two witnesses were Bo and Sheriff Estes. Nourie called Bo to the stand and explained to the court that because of the injury to Bo's neck, his voice might sometimes be difficult to hear. Several times during the course of the hearing, Nourie and Mc-Fadin had to ask Bo to speak up or repeat his answer. Once, the effort brought him close to tears.

In response to Nourie's questions, Bo told about sitting in the chair on the loading dock, waiting for the repairman, and noticing McElroy in the Chevy pickup across the street. Shortly after 8 P.M., Bo said, McElroy drove up to the dock in his truck, then got rid of the boys standing around and came back to the dock. Bo walked into the store to get a knife to cut up the boxes and turned around to see the shotgun: "The only thing I know is I was looking down two barrels, and I was debating with myself, is he going to scare me or is he going to shoot. As I studied it over, and I run in my mind he might shoot, I fell sideways, and he got me right here."

Under Nourie's questioning, Bo repeated that he had been standing about three feet inside the door and fell to his right to avoid the blast. McElroy had been standing about eight feet away. Bo also identified the shotgun blast as the cause of the scars on the left side of his neck.

On cross-examination, McFadin tackled the two vulnerable parts of the prosecution's case—the knife and Bo's location. Bo described the knife as a long-bladed butcher knife used only for cutting cardboard. McFadin came back time and again to Bo's location.

"Isn't it possible you took two or three steps backward after you were shot?"

Bo held firm. "No, I was two or three feet inside the door."

Bo admitted telling McElroy that the drive was private property and to get off it. He also acknowledged that he didn't actually see what McElroy gave the boys or hear what he said to them.

Estes' testimony was brief. He recounted his investigation of the scene and stated that he had recovered seven or eight pellets from the ceiling. The pellets had penetrated the ceiling tile in a two-foot-wide pattern about seventeen feet inside the doorway.

McFadin moved to dismiss the charge against his client, but

Judge Fraze denied the motion and found that there was reasonable cause to believe that McElroy had committed the crime of felony assault in the first degree. The judge ordered McElroy bound over for trial, continued the bond, and set the next court date for September 5.

Nourie, citing the strong possibility of intimidation, asked the judge to order McElroy not to have any contact with either of the Bowenkamps. Judge Fraze granted the request after being assured by McFadin, "as an officer of the court," that there would be no intimidation by his client.

When Trena and McElroy walked down the aisle, the Bowenkamps remained seated, and six troopers stood like a shield between the two families.

That day provided one of the few heartening moments for Bo and Lois. With the next court date less than three weeks away, perhaps the system would finally work.

The next order of business, from McFadin's point of view, was to get the case transferred out of Nodaway County. Accordingly, three days before McElroy was due in court to enter a plea, McFadin filed a motion for a change of venue.

Venue, the Latin word for "place," meant the location in which the trial would be held. In criminal law, venue normally lay in the county or district where the crime occurred. One obvious reason for this was that the community where the crime took place had the most direct interest in seeing the matter brought to trial and justice done.

At the same time, the Sixth Amendment granted the defendant a right to a trial by an impartial jury—a jury that would decide the case strictly from the facts presented at trial and not from bias or prejudice. The courts in many jurisdictions had held that where pre-trial publicity was so egregious and inflammatory as to prevent any twelve jurors from being able to put aside their opinions and decide the case only on the facts, the defendant's right to a fair trial would be violated. But these courts had cautioned that neither pre-trial publicity nor widespread knowledge of the defendant's criminal past was sufficient, in and of itself, to render a trial unfair. If the defendant could show that a "circus-like atmosphere" had developed to such an extent that *no* juror could be unbiased or fair, the case would have to be moved to another jurisdiction.

The law in most jurisdictions thus attempts to strike a balance between the interests of the offended community in administering justice and the interests of the defendant in receiving a fair trial. In Missouri, however, the law regarding venue created a tremendous imbalance in favor of the defendant. By statute, in counties of fewer than 75,000 people, if a defendant filed a petition supported by affidavits of "five or more credible, disinterested citizens residing in different neighborhoods of the county" saying that a fair trial would be impossible, the judge had to grant the change of venue. Even if no affidavits were attached, a judge who believed the allegation to be true could grant the request without any actual proof.*

McFadin filed his motion for a change of venue on September 2, 1980, and argued it in front of Judge Wilson on September 5, the day that had been set for a plea hearing. The motion was simple and straightforward. Ken McElroy swore under oath that he could not receive a fair trial in Nodaway, Atchison, Holt, Andrew, DeKalb, Grundy, or Clinton counties, because the inhabitants of those counties were biased and prejudiced against him. The motion did not mention pre-trial publicity, of which there was very little, nor did McElroy state why the citizens of a seven-county, 250-square-mile area were biased or prejudiced against him. No affidavits by "disinterested citizens" were attached to support the request.

Based on McElroy's allegation, Judge Wilson, probably with relief, granted the request and transferred the case to Bethany, the

---

* In 1982, the Missouri Supreme Court went even further, adopting a rule that in communities of 75,000 or fewer inhabitants, a change of venue would be granted automatically to any defendant who asked for it. "The defendant need not allege or prove any reason for change. The application need not be verified and shall be signed by the defendant or his attorney." Thus, the court delegated to the criminal defendant the absolute right to move the location of the trial. By simply filing a slip of paper, the defendant could deprive the community of the opportunity to judge and punish its own offenders. The state supreme court also adopted a rule allowing the defendant to obtain a new judge merely by asking for one. The defendant did not have to state any reason why the judge should be disqualified. To avoid a judge who, for example, had a reputation for meting out tough sentences, the defendant needed only to file a written application. Thus, the defendant controlled not only where the case was heard, but who heard it. The community had no say in either of these decisions.

Harrison County seat, some eighty miles east of the community where the crime had occurred.

The third tilt in favor of McElroy lay in the discovery procedures allowed by law in Missouri. By statute and state supreme court rule, the defense could issue subpoenas and take the oral deposition of "any person" in accordance with the rules of civil procedure. The defendant, however, was protected by the Fifth Amendment from being compelled to testify against himself, and thus the prosecution was not entitled to take his deposition. The state, upon permission of the court, could take depositions of persons other than the defendant and his spouse, but only for the purpose of preserving the testimony of witnesses who might be unavailable at trial. If depositions were allowed, the court had to enter orders guaranteeing that the rights of the defendant would not be violated in the process. Finally, the state was required to pay the travel expenses of the defendant and his attorney incurred as a result of the state's depositions. One result of these one-sided discovery procedures was that the defense was in a far superior position to uncover the prosecution's case (and devise ways to rebut and impeach it) than the prosecution was to learn the defendant's case.

This unlimited right to take depositions also provided the defendant with a ready-made excuse to delay the trial by claiming that discovery hadn't been completed. If he couldn't locate a witness, for example, the defendant would be entitled to a continuance in order to locate him and take his deposition.

McFadin wasted no time in starting the discovery process. On the day Judge Wilson transferred the case to Harrison County, McFadin sent Nourie a Request For Discovery, asking for any reports or statements by experts; any books, papers, photographs, or other evidence the prosecution intended to introduce; and the names and addresses of all persons the prosecution intended to call as witnesses at the trial. Five days later, Nourie responded, listing twenty possible witnesses, including Bo and Lois Bowenkamp, the four teenage boys, troopers Richard Stratton and Alvin Riney, David Dunbar, Eldon Everhart, Evelyn Sumy, and Dr. E. R. Wempe. Within days, McFadin had issued subpoenas to all the people on Nourie's list, requiring them to make themselves available for sworn depositions. In response to the prosecution's request for disclosure, McFadin replied with a list that repeated verbatim the witness list Nourie had given him. Absent from the list, of course, was the name of McFadin's client, although McElroy would be called to testify at the trial.

The majority of the depositions were conducted in a small room off the prosecutor's office in the Nodaway County Courthouse. In addition to the witnesses and the attorneys, a court reporter and Ken McElroy were present at each deposition. As the four teenage boys answered McFadin's questions under oath, McElroy stared across the table at them.

To ensure that decisions involving life and liberty were made through the dispassionate application of principles of law to the facts of each case, the judicial process was insulated from the rest of society. An intricate set of rules and procedures had been designed to immunize the process from contamination by outside influences. The courtroom became an arena in which each side struggled to prevail, using every allowable procedure and technique in a strategy of controlled combat. The assumption was that if the fight were fair, truth and justice would prevail in the end. The judge's job was to ensure that the fight was fair, that all the rules were observed and the procedures followed. Like the lawyers, the judge bore no moral responsibility for the outcome of the trial as long as everyone played by the rules. The jury, after watching the struggle staged for its benefit, would make the judgment of guilt or innocence, turning thumbs up or thumbs down on the defendant.

The focus was on process, the critical assumption being that the correct substantive result would occur more often than not if the right process were followed. The purpose of this artificial environment—fair treatment for the defendant—was certainly laudable, but often the results were not. Some judges became remote authoritarians who felt no accountability to the community at large, and juries were often asked to make complex decisions on incomplete, sanitized facts. What often fell outside the constricted vision of the judge and the jury was the very cornerstone of the system—the community.

The case of the *State of Missouri vs. Ken Rex McElroy* was assigned to Judge John Morgan Donelson, Circuit Judge of Harrison County. Donelson was known for being very formal and concerned with proper procedures in his courtroom. He showed little warmth and rarely smiled. Lawyers considered him a good judge because he was intelligent and ran his courtroom with a firm hand, but he also had a monumental ego that reacted strongly whenever he perceived a challenge to his authority. He was the judge, and you weren't, so to speak.

Donelson showed promise of being the perfect judge for Ken McElroy's trial, a judge who would run the show by the book and suffer no shenanigans from the lawyers. His isolation from the community he was supposedly helping to protect would only become apparent as the case worked its way through his courtroom. His first judicial act in the case was to schedule the trial for December 5, 1980. If the date held, McElroy would be called to account for his behavior some five months after the shooting—certainly not swift justice in the eyes of the people of Skidmore, but not unconscionably slow, either. The community geared themselves psychologically for a resolution on that date.

McElroy's two appearances in court seemed to inflame his obsession with his enemies and to incite even more flagrant and provocative behavior.

Corporal Stratton came home from work one day in early September to hear a strange story from his wife. The other unit in their duplex was for rent, and she had noticed a couple apparently interested in the unit sitting in the driveway in a brown Buick, staring at the building for hours.

Stratton asked what the couple looked like. The man was older, Margaret said, heavy-set, dark with black hair, and the woman was younger, a washed-out blonde.

Stratton didn't say what he thought—he just told her to get the license number the next time the Buick showed up.

The following week, the car appeared in the driveway again. This time, Margaret stepped out on the deck overlooking the driveway and wrote down the license number.

"Would you know the man if you saw pictures of him?" Stratton asked her.

She would.

The next day, he ran the license number through the computer and picked up five or six photos, including one of McElroy. That evening, he dropped the photos on the dining room table and asked

Margaret if she recognized any of them. She picked out McElroy immediately.

The brown Buick appeared in the drive again the following week, and Margaret walked out onto the deck for a closer look. Through the windshield, she could see a can of Budweiser in McElroy's left hand and a shotgun lying across his lap. McElroy looked up, white quarter-moons glistening beneath his dark irises, and held her gaze.

As the calls and appearances continued, Margaret grew increasingly upset. Stratton became concerned as Margaret's anxiety increased. He thought about filing a formal complaint with the prosecuting attorney alleging intimidation of a witness, but wondered whether he could prove the charge. McElroy always came when Stratton was away and left before he got home. It would be their word against his.

On the first Sunday in September, Tim Warren was outside playing ball with his son, when the phone rang. Warren ran inside to answer it.

"I'm tired of warning you and telling you," said the familiar male voice. "I'm going to come over and castrate you, and then I'm going to cut your little boy up in pieces and feed him to you while you're laying there bleeding from the castration, we're going to send you pieces of your wife's body in an envelope, and you're going to know that we're killing her bit by bit. It's too late now, you fat son of a bitch, you pushed me too far."

"You're so brave on the phone," Warren practically yelled. "And I'm tired of your threats. If you're so brave, I'm going to set my little boy and my wife on the porch right now, and you come on and try and get them. You want to use knives, we'll use knives, you want to use guns, we'll use guns. But I tell you what, you're not going to walk away alive if you show up!"

No one came and the calls stopped, for a while.

Word of the Stratton and Warren incidents made it to the cafe and the tavern, and from there to the families and the farms, causing new fears to ripple through the community.

28

On September 13, Ken and Trena McElroy loaded six of his best hounds into the cages in the back of the green Chevy and headed out to a meet in Bruckner, Missouri. After stopping for lunch in St. Joe at the Dinky Diner, Trena was backing the Chevy out of the parking lot onto 6th Street, when an old Dodge swerved to avoid hitting them. A young woman was behind the wheel, and in the passenger seat her ex-husband held their six-month-old son. Their two-year-old daughter sat in back. The woman honked her horn, yelled "asshole!" out the window, and gave Trena the finger. As the Dodge sped away, the Chevy took up the chase and tried to cut it off several times. After four or five blocks, Trena stopped the truck, and McElroy came around to the driver's side and climbed in behind the wheel. The pickup flew down the street and pulled ahead of the Dodge and swerved into it, bashing its left front fender.

McElroy came out of the truck and headed for the man in the Dodge. Trena headed for the woman and began swearing at her. When the man emerged from the car, McElroy went back to the truck, brought out the shotgun, and strode back to the car. By this time, the police were on the way.

Sergeant Jake Rostock, the officer who had answered the call when McElroy fired a shotgun into the floor of the tavern to terrorize Otha Embrey, was only a few blocks away when he got the call about a man with a shotgun threatening people in the street. When Rostock pulled up, he recognized the driver of the truck as Ken

McElroy and the passenger as McElroy's wife. Rostock could see the weapon, a model 916 Eastfield 12-gauge, sawed off to nineteen inches, lying on the dash, the barrel pointing out the driver's window. Knowing that McElroy was fully capable of picking up the gun and blowing him away, Rostock pulled out his .357 Magnum, aimed it right in the middle of McElroy's forehead, and approached the pickup in a crouch, his heart thumping in his ears.

"Kenny, you're under arrest, and if you touch that gun I'll blow your fuckin' head off!"

Rostock reached in the window and grabbed the shotgun, keeping his pistol leveled on McElroy's forehead, then backed off a few feet and waited for help to arrive. After McElroy had been cuffed and put in a patrol car, Rostock checked the shotgun. The safety was off, one round of 00 buck was in the chamber, and three rounds of 00 buck and one round of deer slugs were in the magazine. Under the seat of the Chevy, he found a large corn knife and a bottle of Jack Daniel's.

Next, Rostock talked to the man in the Dodge. He was small—about 5 feet 5 inches and 135 pounds. He shook as he told Rostock what had happened. "The guy told me he was going to blow my fuckin' head off!"

The woman was hysterical, telling Rostock that the lady in the truck had been yelling and screaming that she was going to "whip her ass."

"He pointed a gun at us," the woman told him. "He said he was going to kill us. My children were in the car, and that's not right! Who is going to pay for fixing my car?" She went on and on, crying.

Rostock thought they looked like poor folks, welfare types, and he doubted they would stick to their guns. He wouldn't be surprised if their stories changed before the day was out.

After being arrested, McElroy seemed to worry most about his four expensive coon hounds. He demanded that they not be put in the pound, where they might catch a disease, and he insisted that they stay in the truck parked in the shade and be watered every couple of hours.

Rostock drove McElroy to the station, and Trena drove the truck. While waiting for McElroy to be processed, Rostock noticed Trena becoming acquainted with the victims and heard her apologizing to them for McElroy's behavior.

A felony complaint was filed that afternoon charging McElroy with violating state law by "exhibiting a deadly weapon, to wit a shotgun, in a rude, angry and threatening manner." If convicted, McElroy would face five years in prison. McElroy could also have been charged with carrying a loaded weapon in public, a violation of a St. Joe ordinance, but he was not. The magistrate released him on a $10,000 bond that afternoon and set the preliminary hearing for the following Monday. At the time, the officials were not aware that McElroy was already under a $30,000 bond in Nodaway County.

Notice of the arrest appeared in the Sunday *St. Joseph Gazette.* By Monday morning, the incident was cafe talk in Skidmore. Although the details were skimpy, the farmers knew that McElroy had been busted for pulling a shotgun on someone in St. Joe and had been out on bond before the sun had set. They debated the implications: Would this cool him down or only make him worse? Could he go to jail for violating his bond in the Bowenkamp case?

Assistant County Attorney Dean Shepard was assigned to prosecute the St. Joe case. By midmorning on Monday, he knew he was in trouble. He had heard that McElroy had told the couple in the Dodge that any person who would testify against a friend ought to have his house burned down. And McFadin had sent his investigator around to talk to the victims on Sunday afternoon.

On the day of the incident, the woman gave the following statement:

He [McElroy] jumped out of the truck and came over to the passenger side of my car where my husband and baby were. He started cussing and pointing his finger at us. A white female came out of the passenger side of the pickup and came over to the passenger side of my car. The girl and the man were cussing at us. My ex-husband Pat got out of the car and the man and Pat were yelling. The man started walking toward Pat and Pat was backing away from him. The woman came over to my side of the car. She told me if I had anything to say to get out of the car. I kept asking her why did you hit my car. Then the man went back toward the pickup. I didn't watch him to see what side of the truck he went to, but when I saw him he was walking toward my car from the truck. He was carrying a rifle-type gun in his hand. He was holding it in both hands above his hip and he had it pointed directly at Pat, my ex-husband. The man stopped in front of Pat about four or five feet from him. He still had the gun pointed at Pat's stomach.

In his statement, the man said that when McElroy came at him with the gun, he backed off, saying he didn't want any hassle. While McElroy hadn't pointed the gun directly at him, he had waved it around in the air.

At the hearing on Monday, both of the victims testified that they had not been scared by McElroy; he had not intimidated them, nor had he approached the vehicle in an angry manner. The woman testified that she had not seen McElroy point the gun at her ex-husband, and the man said McElroy had been holding the shotgun with the barrel pointing down. Nevertheless, because of Rostock's testimony, the judge bound McElroy over for trial and a date was set for December 12, 1980.

The felony complaint in St. Joe was transmitted to Nodaway Prosecuting Attorney Nourie on September 19, and Nourie filed a motion in Judge Donelson's court to revoke McElroy's bond. The hearing was set for October 2, almost two weeks away.

Meanwhile, the pot was boiling in Skidmore. McElroy came to town every day and usually stopped at the tavern, leaving at least one backup outside, engine running. He would sit at the bar, drinking and talking about what he was going to do to Bo: The next time, McElroy said, he was going to do it right; he was going to kill Bo, and there would be no witnesses. The tavern would empty in a few minutes, leaving McElroy alone with bartender Red Smith. McElroy would sit and stare at Red, drilling holes into his mind, and Red would wonder what McElroy was going to do next.

In desperation, Lois wrote to everyone she could think of, seeking help. Her state representative, Truman Wilson, forwarded her letter to the Missouri Department of Public Safety. The department's executive director, F. M. Wilson, wrote back that McElroy had a record of arrests dating back to the 1950s, but that he had never been convicted. Wilson offered no assistance. Senator Eagleton sent Lois a letter stating that the problem was a matter for state law enforcement, and that he did not intend to interfere in the affairs of the state attorney general. The attorney general responded that his office had no jurisdiction, that McElroy's actions were a matter for local law enforcement. Governor Teasdale didn't bother to respond at all.

One night during this period, a thief broke into a feed and chemical store in Tarkio, a small town about forty miles northwest of Skidmore, and took chemicals worth about $20,000. In the report over the police radio, the highway patrol identified McElroy as the chief suspect. In an angry letter to the patrol, McFadin complained about his client's name having been broadcast on the air in connection with a burglary, and he demanded an apology. The patrol sent an ambiguous letter to McFadin stating that it wasn't aware of the incident but would call his letter to the attention of all patrolmen. McElroy took the patrol's response as an apology and was proud of the letter; he carried a copy with him everywhere and showed it around. In the tavern, he would wave the document in the air and brag and laugh about the great highway patrol apologizing to him. "See this?" he would say. "The patrol says I ain't done nothing, that I been a good boy!"

To the townspeople, he was becoming invincible, untouchable, like some creature in a nightmare or an ancient myth. Their fear made him even stronger.

McFadin was busy taking depositions and preparing for the Bowenkamp case. He focused on the four teenagers because their testimony supported the element of premeditation in the shooting and undermined McElroy's claim of self-defense. The first boy, frightened that McElroy would come after him, changed his story. Under oath at his deposition, he said he had been fetching a bicycle tire from behind the pool hall and had not been there when McElroy approached the other boys.

The second boy said that although it was customary for McElroy to give them money for pop, he had always done so inside the tavern. This time, the boy said, McElroy—after talking to Bo—gave them $5 and told them to go inside. In responding to Nourie's questions, the boy said that he had talked to McElroy since the shooting but that the conversation had been about nothing in particular.

The third boy had previously given the police a written statement saying that he was present when McElroy gave them the money to go inside. But at his deposition, the boy claimed that he had left the group before McElroy came over to talk to them. He hadn't heard or seen a thing, the boy now said. He admitted that he had had two conversations with McElroy since the shooting, and that McElroy had asked him in detail what he had and hadn't seen, but the conversations had occurred during chance meetings.

No deposition was taken from the fourth boy. (McFadin would later claim that he had been unable to locate him.)

On October 2, 1980, in Bethany, Judge Donelson held the hearing on Nourie's motion to revoke McElroy's bond because of the St. Joe charge. No real issue was in dispute: The conditions of the existing bond explicitly stated that the bond would be forfeited if a subsequent felony charge were filed against McElroy, and there was no question that such a charge had been filed. Moreover, his bond required him to "keep the peace" and "be of good behavior," which obviously precluded his running around St. Joe with a loaded shotgun. Forfeiture of the bond should have been ordered on the spot. Inexplicably, Donelson refused to rule on the motion and instead set the matter for another hearing twelve days later. The authoritarian judge, who supposedly ran a tight ship and maintained control of his docket, was spending more than a month disposing of a routine motion on a clear-cut violation of a bond condition—a matter that should have been resolved within a few days.

On October 14 Donelson issued an order finding the inevitable—that Ken McElroy had violated his bond by having a felony charge filed against him. Donelson ordered the $30,000 bond forfeited and a new bond set in the amount of $40,000, but McElroy did not have to spend a day in jail or pay any money. The only inconvenience was that his mother and brother had to sign a new promise to pay an additional $10,000 if he failed to appear for trial.

Donelson added two conditions to the bond: McElroy could not carry firearms on his person or in any vehicle; and he could not travel outside of Nodaway, Atchison, Holt, Leavenworth, and Harrison counties, except that he could go to Buchanan County for medical treatment in St. Joe. The first condition, prohibiting firearms, should have been imposed in the first bond, and the second condition would have been laughable had it not been so serious. By restraining McElroy to Nodaway and adjacent counties, the court was ordering the fox not to stray from the hen house. Ken McElroy must have chuckled all the way from Bethany to Skidmore.

The interests of the town of Skidmore had again slipped through the cracks in the judicial process as the prosecutor from Maryville, the judge from Bethany, and the defense lawyer from Kansas City, all doing their narrowly defined jobs, overlooked what their courtroom moves and countermoves meant to the small community of 437 people.

Donelson also committed an error, undoubtedly unintentionally, that would give McFadin the opening he needed to delay the trial: The travel restrictions prohibited McElroy from going to McFadin's office, which was in Clay County, to confer with him in preparing the case.

McElroy kept up the pressure on Skidmore. He patrolled regularly, creeping down the street in front of Dunbar's house, Warren's house, and Bowenkamp's house. Gary Walker, a local farmer and seed dealer, drove through town early one evening and saw four McElroy pickups parked side by side in front of the tavern. Each truck had a gun rack holding two or three rifles. Women sat behind the wheels of the trucks. To Gary, it looked like the McElroys had come for a war. He called the sheriff's office, but, as usual, the cops did nothing.

29

Charlie had grown up on a farm a couple of miles south of the McElroy place. In his youth, Charlie had hunted coons and traded dogs with Ken, although he couldn't say the two of them had been friends. In those days, Charlie had gotten into more than his share of trouble drinking, fighting, and carousing as a bona fide member of the lowlifes. Then he fell into the ways of the Baptist church and was born again. To him, this meant accepting God as a God of love and Jesus Christ as the only perfect being. Charlie also believed that God had a plan of salvation for every human being, and that if a man accepted Christ, he was obligated to spread the word and try to save others from sin.

Charlie lived with his wife and kids on a farm outside Clearmont, Missouri, and worked weekends in a gas station. Although he had been hearing about McElroy's troubles for a long time, Charlie didn't give a whole lot of thought to the subject until he heard that McElroy had shot the grocer and was firing guns over people's houses. Charlie realized that McElroy was living in sin and could use some help. Charlie had counseled prisoners at the county jail and the state prison, relying on his own background to help him understand their situations and help him point the way. He knew what McElroy was feeling: You see two people standing on a street corner talking, and you know they're talking about you; you hear a person walking behind you, and you wonder if you're going to get clipped. McElroy needed a friend, thought

Charlie, and he could be that friend. He would convince McElroy to change his life.

On a dreary fall morning, Charlie finally summoned up his spiritual courage to try to save the soul of Ken McElroy. Charlie was afraid to go, afraid of getting shot, and afraid of getting cussed, but McElroy was in a state of sin. The local pastor had planned to go with Charlie, but at the last minute the pastor remembered he had something else to do that day. *Just as well,* thought Charlie. *Now I can talk to Ken man to man.*

Charlie had not been on the Valley Road in a long time, maybe twenty years, and he wasn't dead sure which was the McElroy place. When he got to about where he thought the McElroy house was, Charlie saw a large man standing motionless at the end of the driveway.

"Do you know which house is Ken McElroy's?" Charlie asked, leaning out the window. He figured the man, who was watching him intently but without expression, was probably Ken.

"That's it right there," the man said, pointing to the farmhouse at the other end of the drive.

"Do you know where Ken McElroy is?"

"I'm him," the man said, looking neither friendly nor unfriendly.

"Well," said Charlie, reaching down inside himself for the strength to get out of the car, "you probably don't remember me. I used to hunt coons with you when we were kids. Had a black-and-tan bitch, good hunter. Name's Charlie."

Nodding as if he vaguely remembered, Ken relaxed his stance a little. Charlie got out of the car and shook Ken's hand.

"Well, Ken," Charlie said, trying to sound confident, "I'd like to talk to you about life and death and what's going to become of your soul."

Charlie told Ken about his life, explaining how he had been a fighter and a drinker but had finally straightened up. A couple of Ken's kids wandered up and asked if they could go hunting.

"OK," McElroy said, "but stay on our property."

Charlie found that strange, because most local people had permission to hunt and fish as a matter of course on their neighbors' property. But he also knew that hunting in the day was a good way to spot farm machinery and animals for stealing in the night, so the neighboring farmers might not welcome any McElroys on their property.

A light drizzle materialized as Charlie and Ken talked. Gradually, the sprinkle picked up, turning into a shower and then rain. The two men stood in the downpour, talking about salvation, and Charlie kept waiting for McElroy to invite him into the house. Finally, Charlie said, "Ken, I'd like to talk to you some more. Let's sit in my car."

"Sure," said McElroy, with a smile on his face, and they climbed into the car.

Charlie picked up his Bible, opened it, and read a passage about God's plan for salvation and then a passage about how God would allow evil to go only so far before He cut it off and smashed it. "Yes," Charlie said, "lives could be cut off before their intended time of death, if the sinner didn't change."

The rain began to fall harder. Every now and then, the steady patter of drops on the roof would be interrupted by a sheet of driving rain that would pound the roof like a clattering of marbles for a minute or so and then let up, leaving a stillness inside the car.

Charlie reached up and turned on the overhead light. Listening attentively, Ken looked over at the Bible while Charlie read from it.

Finally Charlie closed the Bible and turned to Ken. "Tell me something, Ken. Do you think there are some things in your life that are not quite how they should be?"

McElroy shrugged and said, "I guess so."

"Well, Ken, God has a better way for you, if you'll just open your heart to Him."

McElroy shook his head and smiled. "I guess I'll change one day, but I'm not ready yet. I'm not a hypocrite like all those farmers who sit in church when they don't mean it."

Ken explained that he was poor as a kid and didn't have good clothes to wear to school. School had been tough for him—the older kids picked on him, teasing him and pushing him around, and in the fourth grade, when they found out he couldn't read, they made fun of him.

And you've been pushing back ever since, Charlie thought.

Ken seemed to be opening up, and Charlie felt good. God had prepared the way for His messenger.

"I just felt I had to warn you, Ken, about how God punishes

unrepentant evil." Ken nodded, then turned away, and stared silently through the rivulets of water on the window.

Charlie tried to soothe him by explaining that everyone failed, that Jesus was the only perfect one. A sinner was saved through grace, not words.

As they sat in the car, the windows steamed up, and the air became stuffy. They talked for half an hour, and although Ken agreed with much of what Charlie said, Charlie realized that he couldn't change Ken in one day. God would work the changes in His own way, in His own time.

Finally, Ken opened the door to leave. Charlie offered his hand to him, and Ken took it. "I'm glad I got a chance to visit with you," Charlie said.

Ken nodded, gave a little smile, and heaved his bulk from the car. Charlie watched as the large form moved off in the rain, walking down the drive toward his house. *In God's own time,* Charlie thought, *in God's own time.*

30

During this period, the townspeople began to lose sympathy for Trena. Many people had known her from their own school days, or their children's school days, and had always thought of her as a shy blond girl, not terribly smart, but nothing out of the ordinary. They had watched helplessly as she fell into McElroy's clutches and her parents abandoned her. When she married McElroy and the rape charges were dropped, some thought, *Well, she's made her choice now.* From that point on, for many people, she became a McElroy.

After Bo was shot, Trena definitely became one of the enemy. By trying to help McElroy escape that night, she became a partner in the crime. She was no longer a child but an adult, no longer a captive but a willing participant, no longer a victim but a tormentor.

The police had neglected to take Bo's knife into custody on the night of the shooting. When McFadin discovered this during depositions, he thought he smelled a rat—an attempt to destroy evidence that was beneficial to McElroy's defense. However, Bo testified in his first deposition that he still had the knife and was using it at the store. Pursuant to McFadin's subpoena, Bo brought the knife to his second deposition.

If Bo stayed alive and held his ground, the knife would be the only possible defense. In Bo's second deposition, McFadin tried again to shake Bo's story, coming at it from several angles, and got nowhere. Finally, McFadin attacked head-on.

MCFADIN: Did you in fact pick up this knife and attack Mr. McElroy with it?
BOWENKAMP: No sir.
MCFADIN: That's what you're saying under oath?
BOWENKAMP: That's right.

When this deposition was over, McFadin had had three shots at Bo. If the strategy was to wear him down or intimidate him, it wasn't working. If anything, Bo was getting stronger. He knew where he had been and what had happened, and nothing would change his mind. McElroy, the expert on techniques of fear and intimidation, had overlooked one important point: If you push someone hard enough, if you corner him, his fear will turn into hate, and hate, a powerful emotion, can be a source of strength.

The Sixth Amendment to the Constitution provides that in a criminal prosecution "the accused shall enjoy the right to a speedy and public trial . . ." Like most of the other amendments in the Bill of Rights, this one was designed to protect the individual from a corrupt, incompetent or overzealous state. The Sixth Amendment prevents the state from charging someone with a crime when the state is not prepared to proceed with the case and prove the charges. The remedy for the violation of a defendant's right to a speedy trial is dismissal of the charges.

The *victim,* however, has no right to a speedy trial. No law or constitutional amendment says that the injured party has the right to have his assailant brought to trial within a certain time. Only the defendant has a right to a speedy disposition of the case, and if he wants to waive that right by seeking continuances or causing other delays, that is his privilege.

Because the state has the burden of proving its case beyond a reasonable doubt—and because the defense need not offer any evidence—fading memories or missing witnesses usually work to the advantage of the defendant. For the victim and the community in which the crime occurred, justice delayed is justice denied.

The law in Missouri required that a defendant be brought to trial within 180 days of being charged, unless delays beyond that period were occasioned by the defendant. Because the entire case against McElroy would stand or fall with the testimony of a seventy-year-old man with a heart condition, McFadin's job was to occasion those delays.

On November 24, 1980, four days after taking Bo's second deposition, McFadin and his associate, Charles Spooner, filed a motion asking that the trial be continued from December 3 to some future date. The motion alleged three grounds for the continuance: first, teenager Steve Day, the first person to see Bo after he was shot, had not responded to subpoenas; second, the defendant sought to take the depositions of the two ambulance drivers and the electrician and had been unable to locate them; and third, the bond conditions had prevented McElroy from traveling to Kansas City to confer with his attorney.

The first two grounds were weak. The lawyers stated that Steve had been served with a subpoena to appear on October 2 for his deposition, but had failed to appear. Although McFadin knew Steve was in Des Moines, Iowa, they had been unable, despite their "best efforts," to arrange to take his deposition in the intervening six weeks. Also, despite their "best efforts," they had been unable in four months to determine the names of the two ambulance drivers. And, although McFadin and Spooner had learned the name of the electrician on November 7, they had not yet taken his deposition. (McFadin apparently forgot that Bo had given him the name and address of the electrician at the preliminary hearing on August 18.)

The travel restrictions in McElroy's bond condition provided the strongest ground for the continuance. McFadin had discovered the inadvertent error within a few days of Donelson's October 14 order. McFadin conferred with the judge and Nourie, and they agreed that the order should be modified. The defense and prosecution signed a stipulation to that effect, and on October 18 Trena mailed it to the clerk of the court in Harrison County, where it languished for nearly a month. After several phone calls, McFadin finally received the stipulation on November 19, only to find that the judge had neglected to sign it, so it had to be returned. Finally, seven weeks after the order was brought to the judge's attention, a corrected, signed order was issued. During that time, according to their motion for a continuance, McFadin and Spooner had been extremely busy, and they had not been able to travel to Skidmore every time they wanted to confer with their client.

The judge's initial error, compounded by his lengthy delay in signing the modification, gave McFadin sufficient grounds for a continuance. The restriction had prejudiced the right of the defendant to effective counsel, a fact that would undoubtedly be raised on appeal and, perhaps, exposed in a published opinion. Much better for the judge to avoid public chastisement from a higher court by simply granting the continuance.

Donelson had no trouble scheduling this motion for an immediate hearing, nor did he have to take it under advisement. The motion for continuance was filed on November 24, and heard and granted the next day.

A few days later, Bo and the other witnesses received notices that the trial had been continued to February 5, 1981. Resignation and anger reverberated through the community: McElroy and his Kansas City lawyer had done it again, and this judge was no better than Nodaway County's own Monty Wilson. The system was as screwed up as ever.

McElroy didn't let up. One day Cheryl Brown drove into town and spotted the green Chevy in front of the tavern. Hanging in the truck's rear window was a Thompson .45-caliber machine gun. Cheryl began shaking. She wobbled into the grocery and told Lois, who called Sheriff Estes. He told her the gun was legal as long as McElroy had a tax stamp for it. In fact, possession of a machine gun was a felony under Missouri law and carried a penalty of two to thirty years. Other people also saw the machine gun, and Trena later admitted under oath that McElroy owned one.

Corporal Stratton had begun taking several precautions. He pulled his patrol car into the garage to make his whereabouts less obvious. He used the radio on the patrol car less and less frequently; instead, he phoned in from home before leaving for work and stopped to use private phones along the highway. He found himself making fewer checks on vehicles, and overall he knew the stress was decreasing his effectiveness as a patrolman. And Margaret's nerves were frayed. McElroy had called her one night and described the Early American couch and chair in the living room. He talked about the color of the wood and the pattern of the material, and he described where the couch and chair sat in relation to the hutch and the fireplace. Stratton thought about sending his wife to her sister's home in Texas and getting an unlisted phone number but decided not to, realizing it would only acknowledge McElroy's power.

The St. Joe police continued to watch the house, sending unmarked cars around several times a day. Once, Margaret phoned in the license number of a car that had been lurking nearby, and it turned out to be an unmarked car the patrol had forgotten to tell her about.

The tan Buick continued to appear in the driveway, always when Stratton wasn't home, sometimes every other day, sometimes every other week. Ken and Trena usually sat there for ten minutes to half an hour, staring at the house occasionally, never saying or doing a thing. A shotgun lay across McElroy's lap, and a beer can perched in his hand. To Margaret, his face seemed fat, and his hair looked wavy and greasy, as if it were plastered with Brylcreem. The expression on his face seemed empty, rather than mean. She tried to maintain her dignity and composure—after all, she was a cop's wife. She also knew that as long as McElroy thought he was getting to you, he'd keep it up.

As for Trena, Margaret felt just as much enmity toward her as toward McElroy. Her neighbors told Margaret that they had seen Trena look in the Strattons' garage window on several occasions. Margaret remembered Trena from a gathering held when she was in state custody. At the time, Trena was young and pretty with long blond hair. Now, sitting in the car, she was older, plumper, with a dead look on her face.

Meanwhile, in St. Joe, Prosecuting Attorney Mike Inscoe was reviewing the case against Ken McElroy for the "rude and angry display of a deadly weapon." Inscoe was a good politician and an aggressive prosecutor. He had heard of Ken McElroy and knew his reputation, including his ability to beat cases. Inscoe questioned Assistant Prosecuting Attorney Shepard about the case: Did it make any sense to proceed when neither one of the victims would testify against McElroy? Shepard felt confident that he could get the case to a jury and put McElroy in jeopardy. After that, who could tell what a jury would do? Additionally, Inscoe felt strongly that his office should demonstrate that wrongs committed in St.

Joe would be prosecuted, even if there were problems with the evidence. They decided to proceed.

McFadin made no motions to delay this trial, requested no additional time for taking depositions. Since the two victims favored his client, the quicker the matter could be brought to trial, the better.

As the trial date drew near, Judge Donelson still had not managed to clean up his error-ridden travel restrictions. As the order stood now, McElroy would be prohibited from attending his own trial in St. Joe. On December 3, Donelson sent a letter to McFadin giving McElroy permission to attend his trial on December 12.

Shorter and stockier than Shepard had expected, McElroy did not come off as a bully or even as a tough guy in the courtroom. He seemed more like an average Joe. In the hallway, however, away from the judge and jury, McElroy adopted a blustery and pushy manner in standing close to the two victims and looking down at them.

The state's first witness was Sergeant Rostock. When he testified about what the two victims had said to him at the scene, McFadin objected that the testimony was hearsay—the witness was repeating statements made out of court.

Shepard argued that testimony fell within the "excited utterance" exception to the hearsay rule. (The rationale for the "excited utterance" exception was that a statement made in an obviously excited emotional state was likely to be reliable, because the person who made the statement had little opportunity to lie.) The judge overruled McFadin's objection, and the statement came in.

"I talked to the girl," testified Rostock, "and she said, 'That son of a bitch pointed a shotgun at me and my ex-husband and threatened to shoot us, and we had kids in the car, and that's not right.' "

During cross-examination, Rostock felt as if he were on trial. McFadin's questions implied that Rostock was a dumb, brutal cop and that he had tried to steal a fancy pocket knife of McElroy's. Rostock had seen the technique before—put the cop on trial to shift the focus away from the defendant—and it pissed him off, because he felt he had done everything by the book.

Out in the hallway, Rostock had remarked to another cop that the only way McElroy would be acquitted was if the two victims perjured themselves. Spooner made a motion to dismiss the charge on the grounds that Rostock had been intimidating the witnesses. The judge denied the motion, but it further infuriated Rostock.

The judge refused McFadin's motion to dismiss the charge at the end of the prosecution's case. McFadin then called the victims to the stand, and they denied that McElroy had pointed a gun at them or threatened them. They also denied seeing the truck stop to change drivers. They didn't understand why McElroy was being prosecuted; the incident had been a simple misunderstanding, and they were all friends now. Shepard attempted to impeach the woman with her earlier statements, and she explained that she had been angry and excited at the time, but now she was under oath and telling the truth. McElroy had never pointed the shotgun at her ex-husband.

Dressed in a white shirt and slacks, McElroy behaved like a gentleman during the trial. He knew when to sit down and stand up and to allow his attorneys to speak for him. Testifying in his own defense, he denied pointing the shotgun at anyone. He explained with a straight face that he and Trena had been on their way to coon-dog trials and had stopped in a bar on Sixth Street to cash a check. He had taken the shotgun from the window rack and put it on the floor so it wouldn't be stolen, and he had forgotten to put it back in the gun rack upon his return to the truck. When he opened the door to confront the people in the Dodge, the gun fell out, and he simply picked it up.

On cross-examination, Shepard handed McElroy the shotgun and asked him to identify it. When Shepard picked up two of the 00 buck shells, McFadin leaned over to Spooner and said, humorously, "If he hands him those shells, let's hit the floor." Shepard handed him the shells and asked him to identify them. (The judge would later tell McFadin that at this point, "I looked over my shoulder for the door, because I figured I had about two seconds to get through it.")

"And what do you use that weapon with those shells for," asked Shepard. McElroy became visibly nervous for the first time in the trial. He rolled the shells back and forth in his hands and squeezed them while thinking about his reply.

"I hunt coons with it," he finally responded.

Shepard asked several questions about why somebody would hunt coons with a sawed-off shotgun and shells designed to stop human beings in riot situations. McElroy gave vague answers and kept rolling the shells around in his hand, squeezing them.

On re-direct, McFadin took the shells away from McElroy, and on re-cross, Shepard gave them back. McElroy resumed rolling them and squeezing them in his hands during Shepard's brief questioning.

The trial was over in a day. When the jury came in with a verdict of not guilty, Shepard was disappointed, but not really surprised. An instant after the judge's closing gavel, McElroy stood up and demanded his shotgun and shells back from the prosecution. When he retrieved the gun, he told McFadin he wanted him to have it as a gift. McFadin protested, but McElroy insisted, explaining that the gun had become bad luck to him. McFadin later took the gun into the country and fired it. The 00 buck spread out in a pattern that would have obliterated a human being within twenty yards.

After the trial, Rostock talked to one of the jurors about the verdict. The juror said he didn't believe McElroy and figured the two victims were lying, but he also figured, what the hell, if the victims didn't care enough to tell the truth and put him in jail, then neither did he. No witness, no case.

The *St. Joseph Gazette* carried news of the acquittal, and most of the regulars at Mom's Cafe knew about it by breakfast the next morning. People in Skidmore never quite got straight what had happened—they thought that the witnesses hadn't shown up and the case had been dismissed—but the effect was the same. McElroy had beaten the system again, this time in a big city. The legal system was in such a shambles that it couldn't punish a man who pulled loaded guns on people in public, not even in St. Joe.

As the community watched the criminal justice system fail time after time, it began to lose faith in the basic rule of law that people who committed crimes would be caught and punished. With this gradual loss of faith, the fabric of the community began to unravel. Perhaps a man's first duty was to his family, and his neighbors would have to take care of themselves. Perhaps he should just stay inside his house, lock the doors, and try not to do anything that would bring the animal to his doorstep.

People around Skidmore began to arm themselves. Men, in particular, began carrying guns in their pickups or loading their deer rifles and putting them in their front closets.

Ken McElroy continued to run free. Several times he and Trena circled the sheriff's office in Maryville during the day, cruising by slowly and peering through the windows. After a few circuits, the blinds would close, and McElroy would cruise off.

McElroy seemed convinced that he would beat the charge for shooting Bowenkamp. He laughed about it in the D & G Tavern in Skidmore and in the Shady Lady in Maryville. He offered to bet thousands of dollars that he would never spend a night in jail.

"I've already paid my goddamn lawyer $30,000," McElroy would say. "He better get me off."

Meanwhile, McElroy had to return to work. McFadin filed a motion in Judge Donelson's court seeking to have the travel restrictions lifted, citing the acquittal in the St. Joe case. McFadin swore under oath that his client made a living buying and selling livestock and antiques, and that he could not be fully employed, while restricted in his traveling. (Interestingly, McFadin did not ask the judge to remove the prohibition on his client carrying a weapon in his vehicle. Perhaps McFadin wanted to avoid drawing the judge's attention to the fact that in the St. Joe trial, his client had admitted having a loaded shotgun in his vehicle, a crime with which he was not charged.) Nourie did not contest the motion, and Judge Donelson removed the restrictions in early January of 1981.

One bitter-cold evening shortly before Christmas, as McElroy and his friend Fred sat drinking at the Hickory Bar in St. Joe, McElroy began talking about how he needed a new pickup. The more he drank and the more he talked about it, the more he needed a brand-new truck that night. The two men left the bar and headed north to Crouse Motors in Mound City, arriving a few minutes before closing time. McElroy went into the showroom and sent Fred across the street to look over the pickups parked on the dealer's lot. The salesman thought it odd that Ken never looked at any of the pickups himself; he just pointed at them through the window, one by one, and asked, "How much?"

When he came to the 1981 Silverado, he didn't go any further. The Silverado sat by itself, its polished chrome and fancy two-tone brown paint job gleaming under the bright outdoor lights. The three-quarter-ton pickup had four-wheel drive, a 350 four-barrel engine, and all the extras—sliding rear window, air conditioning, tilt, cruise control, and dual gas tanks. The fanciest, hottest truck on the lot, the Silverado was loaded and ready to roll.

"That one is $10,775," said the salesman.

"Reckon you could throw in a grill guard, since I'm paying cash?" asked McElroy.

"No," said the salesman. "That would be another $175."

McElroy pulled a four-inch-thick wad of money from his shirt pocket, dropped it on the desk, and laughed, saying, "You better count it, I'm a little illiterate." When the salesman finished counting, he had $9,000 sitting in a pile on his desk.

McElroy and Fred came back the next day, December 23, with the rest of the cash. McElroy was in a good mood. When the transaction was completed, he said, "A man sure could use a Christmas present or two for making a good deal in a place like this." The salesman went to the manager's office and came back with a box of candy and a bottle of Jack Daniel's.

McElroy thanked him, then climbed into his powerful, shiny new truck and drove off.

31

In January, the Nodaway County earth lay cold and dormant. A light snow had settled on the frozen ponds and the hillsides were blanketed in a white dust. Abandoned by the geese, deer, and other creatures in the closing days of autumn, the fields stood empty of man and animal, except perhaps for a cow wandering here or there. The shattered cornstalks of the previous year's harvest formed a dirty yellow stubble against the white snow. The skies remained the same leaden gray, day after day, casting a dull light without shadow, freezing the landscape in a black-and-white still frame. The only movement came from the icy wind blowing across the fields, swirling shreds of leaves and stalks in its wake.

Behind the large farmhouses, the tall walnut trees stood black and naked, their skinny limbs fanning out in veined symmetry against the gray sky. The squirrels' nests, built the previous fall, sat low in the crotches of the limbs, like well-anchored clots, in anticipation of a long, hard winter. The big machines of planting and harvest, the tractors and combines and grain trucks, hunkered in the barns and sheds, hibernating through the frozen months. The farmyards were quiet except for the clatter of hogs hitting their metal feeders and the occasional rumbling of a pickup, the only vehicle that still fired up and roamed the hard earth.

Nestled among the trees, the farmhouses offered the solace of heat and light. The days were short and the months long, and the farmers had settled easily into winter's peaceful lethargy.

* * *

A few miles east on Route V, a man and a woman tramped through frozen pastures until they came to a fence in front of a small hill. The man set three beer cans on the fence post, then took a .22-caliber pistol and a box of shells from his pocket. Patiently, he showed his wife how to load the shells, work the safety, hold the gun for a steady aim, and squeeze the trigger. He would be leaving for the stock show in Denver in a few weeks, and she had insisted that he teach her how to shoot the pistol before he left. She had never met Ken McElroy, but she knew he scared her husband. He told her how, when he helped out behind the bar at the tavern, he avoided looking at McElroy. She could handle a rifle and a shotgun, but she wanted to be able to shoot a man coming down the hall to her bedroom. She practiced shooting until her arms were so tired she could no longer hold the pistol level.

The Strattons continued to face the harassment stoically, trying to ignore McElroy. Stratton's captain had complained to the attorney general's office but was told nothing could be done. The McElroys continued to appear in the driveway and the St. Joe police continued to spot-check the area, but the tan Buick always left before the police arrived. Then, one Sunday morning, McElroy finally pushed the Strattons too far.

Stratton had left early to work the highways with a spotter plane. Before Margaret got ready for church, she had moved the Monte Carlo from the garage to the driveway to warm it up a bit in the winter sun. Now, dressed in a suit, she went out, locking the back door and dropping the house key into her purse. She crossed the deck and was starting down the stairs when she saw the tan Buick in the driveway, right behind the Monte Carlo. Her first impulse was to rush back into the house, but she knew finding her key quickly would be difficult. As she hesitated, wondering whether to turn back or go on, she noticed about six inches of a double-barreled shotgun poking out of the driver's window, angled in her direction. Inside the car, she could see the red light moving up and down the scanner, and McElroy's thick right hand clutching a red-and-white beer can. Trena sat beside him, unmoving.

Finally, Margaret decided to call McElroy's bluff. Her legs shaking, her hand gripping the rail, she slowly descended the stairs. As she walked by the Buick, passing within a few feet of the gun barrel, McElroy stared at her. For an instant she looked back into his flat eyes, without flinching. She got in the car and sat still for a second. *Well, I've got my best clothes on,* she thought. *If he shoots me, I'll be in good shape for the hospital and the funeral parlor.* She turned the key and started the car, but she was so nervous that her leg jumped, and the engine died. She started the car again, thinking that if he didn't back up, she would push the button to open the garage door and pull forward. When she shifted into reverse, McElroy started the Buick and began backing slowly out of the driveway.

Margaret drove to the Greenhills Shopping Center to pick up some items before going to church. McElroy followed, staying about five or six feet behind her. Inside the store, standing at the checkout counter, she looked out the window and saw the Buick parked next to her Monte Carlo. *I can't even go to church in peace anymore,* she thought angrily.

After telling the clerk what was happening, she asked for the number of the patrol. The two women fumbled unsuccessfully in the phone book until the manager came over. By then, Margaret was running late and realized that she might miss church. Besides, McElroy had already pointed the gun at her and hadn't pulled the trigger. She thanked the clerk, picked up her sack, and left. As she walked by the Buick, McElroy crushed an empty beer can and dropped it in her path, staring at her with that empty, expressionless look. Trena looked straight ahead as Margaret got in her car.

As she drove out of the parking lot, Margaret decided she had had enough. She pulled onto the beltway and drove to Troop H headquarters.

"Where's five-oh-seven?" she demanded of the sergeant at the desk when she walked in.

"He's out working the airplane," the officer responded.

"Well," said Margaret, "Ken McElroy was sitting in my driveway with a shotgun this morning when I left for church, and now he's following me, and I've had it. I can't take it anymore!"

"Do you have a CB in your car?" the sergeant asked.

"Yes," said Margaret.

"Turn it to channel nine and go on ahead to church," said the sergeant. "I'll contact the plane and the patrol car."

The Buick was nowhere around when she drove out, but about two miles away she saw it sitting at a stop sign, waiting for her, as if McElroy had a map of her route. When she drove past, the Buick pulled out and swung in behind her. Just then she heard the plane overhead.

"Can you see the plane?" the Troop H dispatcher asked on the radio.

"Yes," she replied.

"We've got you under surveillance," he said. "Just keep on going to church."

The plane hovered overhead, while she drove to church. After a block or two, the Buick dropped from her rear-view mirror. McElroy had undoubtedly picked up the transmission from the dispatcher.

Stratton decided that the harassment had gone on long enough. Only a few days earlier, McElroy had blocked the entrance to the parking lot at St. Francis Hospital and made Vicki late for work.

Stratton's captain, Fred Roam, cared about his men and tried to help with any problems they might be having. "How is Margaret taking it?" he would ask Stratton. "Is there anything we can do?"

Once, Captain Roam had asked Stratton why somebody hadn't already shot the son of a bitch.

"You trained us too well for that," Stratton responded, the frustration showing in his voice.

Now, Stratton explained to the captain, the time had finally come to do something about Ken McElroy. Stratton had no intention of embarrassing the patrol, and he would be happy to resign before carrying out his plan. He would also listen to any alternatives the captain had.

Roam didn't want Stratton to resign, but neither did he want to hear about the plan. "Be careful," he said. "Don't do anything rash."

Later, Stratton ticked off a mental list of McElroy's buddies and selected a character McElroy had run with for many years and would probably listen to. Both men had supposedly been involved in killing a man some years earlier in St. Joe by stretching him over a set of railroad tracks minutes before a train came. Stratton found his quarry in the lobby of a seedy hotel frequented by winos and prostitutes and other lowlifes in the industrial part of St. Joe.

"What do you want?" the man asked nervously as Stratton approached him.

"Come outside," Stratton said. "I want to talk to you."

When they reached the sidewalk, Stratton told him they were going for a ride and ordered him to get in the patrol car. Stratton headed north on Waterworks Road, an isolated stretch of gravel road that ran along the river bottoms below the bluffs. As he drove, Stratton told the lowlife what McElroy had been doing. He then explained that the harassment was over, that he wasn't going to put up with it anymore.

"That shit's going to stop," said Stratton. "I could set McElroy up and blow him away and be all legal about it, and it's very near to happening. Darkness will cover me as well as it'll cover him."

"Why are you telling me?" the man asked. "Why would I care what he's doing?"

Stratton looked at him and said nothing. They rode in silence for five minutes, then Stratton turned the patrol car around and headed back to the hotel.

Neither Stratton nor McElroy ever found out whether Stratton was indeed capable of setting a man up and shooting him down in cold blood. The phone calls, the appearances in the driveway, the visits to the Pamida store, all stopped. As Stratton had always believed, McElroy couldn't handle strength.

As McElroy's February 5, 1981, trial date approached, his case did not look good. Bo was still alive and well and seemingly as determined as ever. McElroy needed a break, and he needed time for the break to happen. In short, he needed a continuance.

On January 22, 1981, two weeks before trial, a powerful state senator named Richard Webster filed papers with the court stating that he had been retained by McElroy on January 5 to represent him in the case. Webster also sought a continuance, alleging that the Missouri General Assembly would be in session on February 4, and that his attendance would be required there.

Webster was invoking a law referred to as the legislative continuance statute, certainly one of the most self-serving laws ever adopted by any legislative body in this country. The law provided that in any criminal or civil case pending in the state courts, a continuance would be granted if the lawyer for either party was a member of the general assembly, if the assembly was then in session, and if the attendance of the lawyer was necessary to a fair and proper trial or other proceeding in the suit. The lawyer-legislator had only to file an affidavit setting forth the above facts, and the court had to continue the trial until ten days after the general assembly adjourns. The Missouri Supreme Court had held that a judge cannot question the legitimacy or truthfulness of a legislator's assertions. Thus, any party who wanted a case continued could hire a lawyer-legislator during the session, and the continuance would be automatically granted.

McFadin had played the game beautifully, of course. First, he got the case continued from December 5, 1980, into the legislative session, which began on January 6, 1981. Then, he retained a lawyer-legislator to obtain a continuance past the legislative session. McFadin did not hesitate to use this statute to obtain continuances for clients in criminal cases. In fact, he used it as often as once or twice a year, and he made no apologies for it. In his view, he was simply using an appropriate procedural tool to advance his client's case. Technically, McFadin believed that the legislator-lawyer need never actually appear in court or participate in the proceedings, but he always insisted, as a matter of ethics, that the legislator actually participate in the case.

The hearing on the motion for a continuance was held on January 27, 1981. Judge Donelson understood what was happening, and he wasn't happy about it. He stated plainly that if Webster didn't participate in the trial, he would be held in contempt of court. With no other choice, Donelson continued the case to June 25, 1981. Thus, in a county where the average criminal cases went to trial in thirty to sixty days, McElroy's first-degree assault case had been delayed for almost a year.

February could be the coldest month of the year. The ground was frozen solid, and the temperature often hovered around zero. The chill, damp winds swept unhindered across the fields and through the valleys. Although spring was only a month away, the countryside lay in the depth of winter, the trough of the lull before the new cycle began.

Farmers with livestock mucked about in ice-slickened barnyards, hauling feed, giving shots, cleaning pens, and going through the twice-daily round of chores. In the evening, they went over their books, making calculations about acreage and loans and costs for the past year and thinking about how to present their requests to the bankers and the FHA for another year's financing.

After the second continuance, fear about what McElroy might

do next grew and began, in one way or another, to affect the lives of nearly everyone. People started closing up shop early to avoid trouble, whether he was in town or not, and people became more careful of what they said and how they said it. Something could get twisted and get back to him.

In the past, one of the bank tellers had gone home around three o'clock each afternoon, leaving her fourteen-year-old daughter, who worked after school in the B & B Grocery store, to walk the few blocks home alone when the store closed. Now, the woman walked back up the hill to the grocery, went inside, took her daughter by the hand, and walked her home. Often, the big Silverado would be parked directly in front of the store, and McElroy would sit silently and stare at them as they passed.

Another woman, a God-fearing Methodist born and raised in Skidmore, had heard stories about McElroy all her life. Although she knew Ken by sight, she had never met him. When the woman went to the grocery store to buy bread and she saw his truck parked in front of it, she thought about whether she really needed the bread or not. She worked evenings as a janitor in the bank, and was scared to go to work when she saw his pickup around. It was a horrible nightmare. Like everyone else, she just wanted to stay out of his way.

For years, the senior citizens had met every third Wednesday night at the Legion Hall to eat supper, play games, and socialize. But in 1981, the dinners were canceled, because the older people didn't want to leave their homes after dark.

One elderly couple had moved to town in the mid-1970s after a lifetime of farming. The wife became upset soon after the Romaine Henry shooting and, when the rumors and threats started flying around after Bo was shot, she became so fearful that she locked all the doors whenever her husband was away, even during the day. Her fear of Ken McElroy, whom she had never met, became all she could talk about to her friends.

Cheryl Brown had begun working regularly in the store to keep an eye on her dad. Certain that something further was going to happen, she worried about him constantly. She would wake up two or three times each night, check her kids, and phone her parents to see who was with her dad. She felt helpless sitting and waiting for McElroy to make his next move, but she also felt guilty. She wanted her dad to come to her house, but she was afraid that

McElroy would find out he was there. Birthdays usually appeared in the Skidmore *News,* a monthly paper, and she didn't want her children's names published next to the Bowenkamp name because she was afraid that McElroy might see them. She also felt guilty about carrying the shotgun in the car with her kids. Once, when she forgot the gun, one of her daughters asked, "Mommy, how come you aren't taking the gun with us today?" And the mere sight of McElroy had come to terrify her. One time she missed the Silverado when she drove into town, and walked nonchalantly into the tavern. McElroy was sitting at the bar and turned to stare at her. She began shaking, and her legs nearly gave way beneath her.

Former mayor Larry Rowlett, who had talked his friend Dunbar into running for marshal, encountered McElroy in the tavern one night. McElroy walked up to Rowlett and asked if he knew where to get any copperhead snakes.

"I'll pay $50 apiece for some copperheads," said McElroy, "if you know where any are."

"Sorry," Rowlett said. "I don't know how to get any. What do you want them for?"

"If I can get two or three snakes," McElroy said, "I'm going to put them in the old man's car and let them crawl around inside and bite him."

Another night, McElroy walked in and emptied a sack of money onto the counter. Rowlett guessed there must have been between $2,000 and $3,000 lying there in a heap.

"How would you like some of this money?" McElroy asked him.

"Hell, yes," Rowlett responded. "Everybody can use money."

"I'll give it to you," said McElroy, "if you'll do something for me."

McElroy nodded toward Trena, and she left the tavern. She returned in a few seconds carrying a long, sharp corn knife.

"You just take this corn knife up there to the store and run it through the old man," said McElroy, "and you can have all this money."

"No way," Rowlett replied, "I don't want to go to jail."

"You can make it look like an accident," McElroy insisted. "Just carry it in, stumble around, and accidentally run it through him."

McElroy kept insisting that the killing could be made to look like an accident, and Rowlett kept refusing, although saying no made him nervous as hell every time.

"He's the only goddamn witness against me," McElroy would say, "and I ain't going to jail. It's going to be done right this time."

32

Spring appeared in late March. The music of the songbirds after a warm morning rain signaled the end of winter and the emergence of the new season. As the moisture in the top foot of the frozen ground began to thaw, the earth turned to mush. The fields became impassable, and many cars traveling the dirt roads in the hilly areas ended up in the ditches, leaving behind deep ruts like the paths of huge earthworms.

March was shakeout time for the farmers. Those who fared well last year had money for planting, but others were still hustling for financing, trying to convince the lenders to carry them for another year. This was also the time of year for foreclosure sales, and many farmers attended them religiously to get a sense of the value of land, equipment, livestock, and grain. Standing in small groups, the farmers discussed their neighbors' fates, crying on each other's shoulders and wondering out loud who would take over the farm now, and what the displaced neighbors would do for a living. All the while, they were eyeing the machinery, thinking about whether they might get a good deal on the big green and yellow John Deere combine sitting in the shed, or whether they could use that twelve-row planter in the middle of the yard.

The Great Planting Debate began in March and was in full swing by early April. The discussions went on continuously in the cafe, at the gas station, in the tavern, in the grocery store, on the sidewalk outside of the post office, over the dinner table, inside the farmers' heads. An early spring intensified the debate, because the farmers could start planting earlier, and the earlier they planted, the more time the corn would have for growing, and the bigger the yield would be.

A week of 70-degree weather usually warmed the soil to the necessary 58 degrees, but that alone didn't mean the time was right for planting. If you planted too early, the ground might not be ready, or the kernels might mature during the hot, rainless month of August, or you might lose your crop to a killing frost in May. If you planted too late, you might miss the early spring moisture. Then the seed would sprout, but the roots wouldn't go deep enough to find the water, and the ears would be stunted.

The older farmers tended to be conservative, and some followed hard and fast rules passed down by their fathers and grandfathers. The younger farmers pushed to get the seed in the ground early, worried that the warm days would give way to steady rain that could keep them out of the fields for days. If the ground was too wet, the earth would clump and clod when turned, providing a poor bed for the seeds. The tractor would compact the dirt, the roots would be unable to spread wide and deep enough, and the resulting stalks might be too short and weak to hold the ears of corn. The views of successful farmers like Q Goslee and Pete Ward, who consistently got good yields, were listened to with respect. The older farmers backed their arguments with stories of years past, and the younger farmers argued that nothing stayed the same and that recent advances in seed quality or equipment had to be taken into account.

One story was always repeated. Two bulls, one old and one young, came to the top of the hill at the beginning of mating season. They spied a herd of cows in the valley, and the young bull said, "Let's run down there and screw one of those cows." "Why don't we *walk* down there," said the older one, "and screw them all."

Before the great day arrived, the farmers had to loosen and turn the earth, preparing the soil for the planter. Some farmers plowed in the fall, after the harvest but before the ground froze. They chopped up the stalks and perhaps spread a layer of fertilizer at the same time. This allowed them to make one less pass over the earth in the spring, resulting in less compaction of the soil; but the plowing in the fall could work against the delicate soil by exposing it to wind and water erosion after a thaw.

So, a few days before planting, most farmers hooked up the discs or chisel plows behind their tractors. The newer models had two rows of twelve discs, one behind the other. These steel saucers sliced into the ground at angles, picked the dirt up, and turned it over. The discs on either end were attached to arms that folded up for road travel.

In the mornings the highways were clogged with tractors pulling the discs to different fields. Wings folded, lights blinking, the machines looked like huge insects seeking a place to light. Cars lined up behind them and darted past in the stretches. Once in the fields, they moved steadily across the earth, crawling up and down the hills, leaving trails of dust floating in the afternoon light. The tractors chugged on into the night, weaving back and forth across the fields and streaking the darkness.

The town came alive and bustled with energy. Machines and people were everywhere and in constant motion. The cafe was noisy by 6:30. Voices mixed and competed with backfiring trucks and chugging tractors. The farmers ate quickly, then hurried off. The seed dealers sat with their order books open, touting the excellent match of soil and weather conditions with their brands of seed. Now that the machines were running, opinions about planting were voiced with more conviction. The soil was about right, the consensus seemed to be, and if the sky held, planting could begin in a day or two.

As winter yielded to spring in 1981, Tim Warren stayed in touch with the Bowenkamps. One day in March, he was parked in front of Maurer's hardware store, a half block south of the grocery store, when McElroy pulled up beside him in the Silverado and leaned over toward him.

"You fat son of a bitch," McElroy said. "You're going to be sorry!"

"Why?" Warren asked.

"Because you ain't been minding your own goddamn business," said McElroy.

"I am."

"You are not, you lying cocksucker!" McElroy leaned forward as if to retrieve something from under the seat, and Warren was sure it was a gun.

Warren had forgotten his .38 that day, so he figured his only chance was to bluff.

"You better not do that," he said, "because I've got a gun, too, and I'll use it."

McElroy stopped short and looked back at Warren.

"You're going to pay for this," McElroy said in a low, mean voice. "This whole fuckin' town's going to be sorry!" He backed the Silverado into the street and drove off.

Warren was not so foolish as to leave home without his pistol again. In late April, he noticed a caravan of four McElroy trucks rumbling down the main street, just a few yards apart. McElroy took the lead in the Silverado, and women followed in the other vehicles, which had rifles in the rear windows. Seeing them turn north at the top of the hill, in the direction of the church and his house, Warren took off. He went the back way and parked behind the church, which was north of his house. The Silverado was parked in front of his house, another truck was in the driveway, the third was in front of the church, and the fourth was across the street.

McElroy got out of the truck, holding a Thompson .45-caliber submachine gun in one hand and a 21-bullet clip in the other.

Beside the house, Warren checked his pistol to make absolutely sure it was loaded. He cocked it and climbed up on his porch. Holding the pistol at waist level, he pointed it at McElroy. The machine gun still in one hand and the clip in the other, McElroy stood and glared at Warren for a minute or two. Finally, McElroy turned back to his truck and put the machine gun in the rack. The four trucks sat there for a while and then pulled away, single file, like ducks in a row. To see whether they left town, Warren got into his car and followed at a distance, until they pulled into Birt Johnson's gas station.

Physically, Ken McElroy was sliding downhill. At forty-seven, the weight he had put on was there to stay. His face was flabby, and his gut hung out over his belt like a fifteen-pound ham. In the door pocket of the Silverado he carried a bottle of pills for high blood pressure, which was worsening, and cough drops for his throat, which was sore from smoking two or three packs of Pall Malls a day. The doctor had told him to wear tennis shoes rather than cowboy boots, because his feet were swollen. He chewed Rolaids constantly for the pain in his stomach. Sometimes he coughed and coughed until he spat out chunks of blood and mucus. His old neck injury periodically flared up in the middle of the night, and at times the pain was so severe that he could barely get out of bed to call the doctor. Despite his ailments, his drinking never subsided. In fact, he probably drank more than ever. Each day, he replaced the bottle of Jack Daniel's under the seat of the Silverado, and whenever he stopped in a tavern, he had at least five or six bottles of beer.

Ken McElroy also grew more sullen and moody. Slipping into an obsession with the town and what people were saying about him and his family, he quizzed his friends and sympathizers in the community. His informants not only repeated the usual stories but they began telling him that some people were talking about doing something about him. McElroy was worried that somebody would come by one day while he was gone and gun down his kids in the yard, or shoot the propane gas tank alongside the house and blow the place up.

McElroy had about twenty dogs at his place at the time. Most of them were hunting dogs, but he had two German shepherds and two Dobermans. The dogs were usually tied up, but when a friend stopped by one day, he found two dogs running loose, growling, and snarling. They were so vicious that he crawled up on the roof of his car and yelled for McElroy, who eventually came outside and chained them up. He chuckled as he explained how they got that way.

"You'd be surprised what'll happen to a dog when you keep him chained up and give him speed and don't feed him for three or four days in a row."

One day in the spring of 1980, Ken McElroy spotted Beech Vogel, a local farmer, at the car wash in Maitland. After bringing his truck to a stop directly in front of Vogel, McElroy got out of the driver's side with a .38 in his hand. Trena got out with a .357 rifle, and his daughter got out with a shotgun. McElroy leveled the pistol at Vogel and demanded to know what he had been doing hanging around his place. Realizing that McElroy had him confused with someone else, Vogel managed to calm him down. McElroy stuck the .38 in the holster that lay against his rib cage beneath his shirt. He tilted his head and made some hand signals, the way a hunter would with his dogs. The daughter got back in the car with the two guns, but Trena stayed outside. McElroy, who seemed paranoid as hell, explained that a guy had been hanging around the house, acting weird and scaring his women. McElroy had cornered him one day, and the guy confessed that some man from around Mound City had offered him $2,000 to kill McElroy.

In mid-April, as if in response to the falling of a conductor's baton, the farmers drove their tractors into the fields and began planting. On the main street, stock trucks lined up at the city water pump to fill the large tanks of water that would be taken to the fields for mixing with herbicides. Huge machines, called Big A's because they sat on three wheels about ten feet off the ground and could spray twenty-four rows at a time, moved slowly down the main street like intergalactic vehicles. Spirits were high in the stores and at the gas stations. By the end of the month, however, some farmers had become anxious over the lack of rain. If the seed lay in the hot soil without water, it might dry up. Finally, rain began to fall, and it kept on falling. By the fourth day, those who drank hit the tavern early, and those who didn't became restless and irritable, doing endless chores at their farms, taking naps, watching the soaps, and going to the cafe three or four times a day. If the seeds received too much moisture and no sun, they would become susceptible to rodents and cutworms.

As Ken McElroy's trial date drew near, the farmers worried about more than just the weather. Every day, sooner or later, McElroy came to town. The minute the Silverado hit the main street the word spread. In the cafe, heads turned as the truck cruised by. When he walked into the tavern, the farmers drained their beers, shot the eight ball in the pocket, and put up their cues. Within ten minutes, the place emptied, except for McElroy and Red Smith. Red, who didn't have any choice, was tense; his two coon dogs had disappeared, and he heard that McElroy had bragged about stealing them and then shooting them.

One afternoon, someone walked in and told Red that the Silverado was parked in front of the grocery store, and the two-tone green Chevy was across the street in front of the Legion Hall. Red said to hell with it, closed the tavern, and went home. The next day, McElroy came in early and asked him irritably why the tavern had closed so early the day before.

"Wasn't no business," Red said.

Ken McElroy's presence hung over the town like the threat of a May frost. In the early hours of a spring morning, the temperature sometimes dropped below 32 degrees, freezing the moisture in the air and in the veins of the plants, whose tiny stalks were about three inches high. By early afternoon, the tips of the rich green leaves would have darkened, and by the end of the day, the leaves would be black to the stalk. To a passerby, the fields looked as if some evil, punishing plague had passed over. Such a frost was so rare that the farmers couldn't plan for it, and so devastating that some couldn't recover from it. The killing frost was a freak, a moment when the forces of nature fell out of their delicate balance, reminding the farmers, as if they needed reminding, of their dependence on the harmony of the elements and the precariousness of existence. The farmers who had survived the disease wondered whether they were now immune.

By mid-May, as the farmers began planting beans, the thin stripes of green running across the earth were becoming fuller and brighter each day. The lustrous green balanced with the deep brown soil, and the light spots, where the water had washed away the topsoil, stood out on the hillsides.

By May, the struggle between McElroy and his victims pervaded the entire community. The tavern began closing around 6:00, whether McElroy was in town or not. Business in the grocery store dropped to almost nothing. Kids were called home by 4:00, and the streets were silent and empty by suppertime. People stayed in their homes with the doors locked. Business got so bad at the liquor store that some evenings Rowlett didn't have a single customer. Finally, he just gave up and closed the store for good.

A coon hunter from south Missouri came to town one day looking to trade a dog or two with Ken McElroy. When the man asked around for McElroy, people mumbled nervously, as if they were afraid even to have a conversation about him. They wouldn't say where McElroy lived or whether they had seen him in town that day.

Some of the cops understood what was happening, but they felt helpless to do anything about it. Among themselves, they often said that if they ever caught McElroy alone on a back road, they would blow him away. Patrolman Dan Boyer, who had been trained to kill and was nonetheless nervous around McElroy, tried to imagine what the people in the community must be feeling.

"I would get a call about McElroy sitting somewhere in his truck, and I would drive into town, and it would be like a graveyard, quiet and empty. It made my hair stand on end, to tell you the truth. Now and then, a face would poke out the window and stare at the patrol car. It seemed to make it worse, because my presence meant he was somewhere around. They didn't really see us as a source of protection anymore."

The Bowenkamps waited for the trial and simply tried to survive. Except for Tim Warren and the Sumys, most people left them alone. Everyone felt sorry for Bo, but nobody gave him any support or help. Nobody walked up and said, "I'm on your side, Bo. Let's see what we can do to take care of this bastard." They talked about helping him out, but nobody ever did.

Ever since his talk with McElroy's friend in St. Joe, Stratton felt that he and McElroy had a clear understanding that Stratton—if he got the chance, if he found McElroy with a weapon and had the slightest provocation—would nail him. One afternoon, Stratton went looking for McElroy and found him on a blacktop south of Graham, cruising in his new Silverado. Deciding to check out the truck, Stratton turned on his top light. McElroy pulled over immediately. Trena was with him, and no guns were visible. Stratton checked McElroy's driver's license and called in the registration, which was in Tammy's name. Neither McElroy nor Trena said a word, but McElroy glared as Stratton gave back the documents and said they could go.

Tom, one of the boys who stole for Ken, had been spending some time with him in the spring of 1981. At the farm, the mean dogs were off their chains, growling and snarling as they circled Tom, even after Ken called them off. Ken had been going on two- and three-day binges, drinking whiskey from the bottle constantly. When that happened, he talked a lot and acted scary, as if he could go off on anybody any minute. By the third or fourth day of a binge, Ken was really weird, talking about how he didn't like somebody and was going to kill him.

One day, Ken stopped in town and picked up Tom in the new Silverado, saying, "Get in and drive." Ken drank heavily from a fifth of Jack Daniel's as he gave Tom directions to a certain farmer's house. When they neared the house, Ken reached behind the seat and pulled out a shotgun. He laid it on his lap and fondled it, saying, "This goddamn farmer has been talkin' about me." As they rode, Ken drank more and got crazier and scarier. Looking out the window at the farmhouses, he stroked the metal barrel and said he was going to have to kill somebody because "they were always fuckin' with me." He went on and on about the Bowenkamps, how they had fucked with his kid, and how he was going to have to take care of the old man and do it right this time. His voice grew louder, and he took longer swigs from the bottle and smoked one cigarette after another. Toward the end of the ride, he reached inside his shirt, pulled the .38 out of its leather holster, and laid the pistol on his lap alongside the shotgun.

"I'm gonna get that goddamn Bowenkamp," he said, again and again.

Tom knew what Ken was doing to the town, and that night, the last time they rode together, Tom understood in his gut that Ken meant to push the struggle to the point of destruction.

Rain fell for three straight days, soaking the earth and turning everything into mud. Finally, the morning sun reappeared on the hilltops and threw a soft white light across the fields. The air smelled fresh, and the countryside emerged in full bloom. The timber awoke to the music of meadowlarks and robins and mourning doves. Orange butterflies in black trim fluttered about, skimming the verdant raspberry bushes. Masked cardinals monitored the morning activity from their stately perches.

In the fields, the earth remained a damp black, and the spikes of corn ran over the contours of the land like a pattern stitched in light, shimmering green.

33

In April 1981, Robert Nourie resigned as prosecuting attorney for Nodaway County to return to the Marine Corps in the judge advocate general's office. Some people in Skidmore said that he must have left because he couldn't take the heat that came with prosecuting Ken McElroy, but they had no evidence to substantiate this charge. Nourie's departure could have been a break for the defense. The prosecuting attorney's job was not highly sought after by lawyers in Nodaway County. The annual pay was $21,500, and the job was so time-consuming that the opportunities for an outside practice were limited. Probably none of the senior experienced attorneys in Maryville would be willing to abandon their practices to accept the position, and if one of them were to accept the case as a special prosecutor, his busy schedule might well require a postponement to allow him time to prepare for trial. A younger, inexperienced lawyer might not be anxious to go all the way to a jury trial, so a deal for a misdemeanor might be possible.

Neither the townspeople nor the defense anticipated the skills and abilities of the twenty-eight-year-old legal-aid lawyer, three years out of law school, who accepted the appointment as the new prosecuting attorney.

David Baird seemed more like a man born and raised in a refined Boston suburb than a man from agricultural northwest Missouri. Studious looking, with dark-rimmed glasses, he had an educated demeanor and an easy professional poise. He was well spoken, thoughtful, and sure of himself—without a trace of a typical barrister's arrogance. Baird had attended grade school and high school in Maryville, and had been graduated from Notre Dame in 1975. He obtained a degree from the University of Missouri at Columbia School of Law in 1978, then worked for legal aid in St. Joe. In June 1978, he returned to Maryville as a legal-aid lawyer.

In April, when Nourie spoke to Baird about accepting an appointment as prosecuting attorney, the two of them reviewed the existing caseload. When they came to the McElroy case, set for trial only two months away, Nourie suggested that because Baird was new, he might want to ask the state attorney general's office to try the case. Baird didn't consider the possibility for a moment. If anything, he anticipated the challenge and welcomed the opportunity to try a major felony case right out of the gate.

Baird had run into McElroy and McFadin before when, as a legal intern, he had assisted Amy Davis in the prosecution of the Romaine Henry shooting, doing legal research and preparing witnesses. He had been absolutely amazed when the jury acquitted McElroy. The two cases were very similar in that the prosecution's case rested entirely on the testimony of one key witness. If that jury had not believed Romaine, maybe this jury wouldn't believe Bo, either. Baird compensated for his lack of experience in criminal cases by meticulous preparation. He reinterviewed all the witnesses, studied the transcripts, visited the crime scene several times, and ordered charts and diagrams of the scene drawn up for presentation to the jury.

Objectively, the prosecution had a strong case. If Bo maintained his story, and nothing untoward happened, they should have had a decent chance for a conviction. Then the call came from McFadin; he had a witness, a woman who had actually seen the incident, and he intended to call her at trial. He would send Baird a copy of the handwritten statement she had made in his office on May 8, 1981.

In her statement, Selina O'Connor said that she lived in Blockton, Iowa, about forty miles from Skidmore. She and her husband, a coon hunter, had seen McElroy off and on at coon-dog meets, and her husband had done some work for him in the past. On July 9, 1980, she had driven to McElroy's home to see about a parvo shot for her dog. Upon learning from his wife that he had gone into Skidmore, Selina drove into town. As she passed the tavern, she noticed Ken McElroy's pickup in the alley. She turned around at the intersection, parked in the street, and walked toward the alley.

"When I went around the corner," she wrote, "I saw a white, tall and thin older man holding a knife in his hand. The knife appeared to be a very large knife at least a foot-and-a-half long. The other man was shouting at Ken McElroy, who was standing beside his pickup. I turned around and left the area."

O'Connor's statement startled and concerned Baird. He knew that McElroy's cases often involved allegations of jury tampering and last-minute witnesses, and he was concerned that the defense had "created a witness." The testimony of a credible third party supporting McElroy's version of events could easily create a reasonable doubt in the jurors' minds.

Her statement contained some obvious holes: Why had she left when she saw Bo coming after McElroy with a knife? And why had she waited this long before coming forward? On May 22, Selina O'Connor produced a sworn statement, typed in McFadin's office, in which she stated that the older man had been angry and "coming toward him [McElroy] holding a very long knife in his upraised hand." She had become frightened and left the scene hurriedly. She had not come forward earlier because she didn't want to get involved. When she ran into McElroy later, she told him what she had seen and he asked her to testify.

The name O'Connor didn't ring a bell for Baird. If it had, and he had looked into it, he would have discovered that Selina O'Connor's husband, James, was the son of Maurice O'Connor, one of the two alibi witnesses for McElroy in the Romaine Henry case.

Baird took O'Connor's deposition and explored in detail why she had waited from July 8, 1980, to May 8, 1981, to come forward. He managed to turn her explanation into mish-mash. At first, she said that she had seen McElroy a couple of weeks later and they had not discussed the incident at all. Then she modified the statement and said she had told him she had been there, but he told her it was no big deal. She said she had run into him again "a long time later," and he had asked her then if she would be a witness. She had thought about it and decided "it would be the only right thing to do."

Baird asked her when her last conversation with McElroy had occurred, and she said, "Oh no, this was like winter, fall, you know winter and spring thing."

Under McFadin's questioning, her version of what she had seen became more dramatic and more beneficial to McElroy's claim of self-defense. Now she said that the old man had been holding the knife in front of him at about the top of his head and pointing it in McElroy's direction and talking in an angry voice. She had left hurriedly, she said, because, "I was scared. I had my kids with me and stuff."

Would the jury buy it?

By the second week in May, the corn stood about three inches tall in the hill country, and nearly half a foot in the rich bottom land near the Nodaway River. A slightly overcast morning sky spread an even, bright light over the fields, and the thin rows of plants glittered a rich green. The soil was dry, and the recently planted beans needed a light, soaking rain to germinate. The sky cleared, and by late afternoon the trails of dust left by tractors crossing the dry earth were back-lit a hazy yellow-orange by the falling western sun. Large green rolls of newly cut hay lay in even rows, curving over the hills into the blue sky. The radio called for a 30 percent chance of rain that evening, but the northwest horizon was clear and bright and empty.

During the last week of May, Gallatin, Missouri, about twenty-five miles south of Bethany and fifty miles east of St. Joe, hosted an annual dog meet, which drew coon hunters from Missouri, Nebraska, Iowa, Kansas, and Arkansas. The Gallatin meet was always one of McElroy's favorites. He had been hunting and trading dogs with many of the men who came there for fifteen or twenty years. He always brought four or five hounds, one or two of them usually champions. The meet was a social gathering as well as a contest with plenty of storytelling, dog trading, and betting, and Ken McElroy was always in the middle of it—a happy man with his dogs and his women and his coon-hunting buddies.

The meet was held in a park just outside of town. The parking lot at the top of the hill was jammed with pickups—some new and some battered—with wood cages in the back containing a variety of hounds: red bones, walkers, black and tans, blue tick, English red tick. Some of the hounds were tied to trees, and a few managed to sleep in the midst of the incessant barking. The hill sloped down to a few sheltered picnic tables and beyond to a lake about the length of a football field. In the shelters, the owners had their dogs up on the tables for show, stretching the dogs' back legs out and raising their muzzles for the judges.

One owner, a typical timber dweller with a long, scraggly beard, stood by his dog, waiting for the judge. The man's body was thick, with short stubby arms, and his head seemed to sit directly on his torso. A couple of his teeth were missing, the remaining ones were yellow, and his nose was short and bent to the side. His eyes were beady and didn't track each other. A grease-stained baseball cap sat on matted, tangled hair, and strings dangled from the shoulders of his denim shirt where the sleeves had been ripped away. A white circle on his lower right jean pocket outlined his tin of chewing tobacco. He communicated in grunts to a friend as the judge came by, pad in hand, to evaluate the structure and form of his dog. The judge examined the dog's muzzle, checked its posture, popped its nipples, then grabbed the animal's balls and held them in his hands for a few seconds, before scratching on his pad and moving on to the next table.

Down the hill, closer to the water, a cage containing a coon was hanging from a rope slung over the lower branches of a tree. A name was called, a dog was released, and the cage was lowered by means of a pulley to within eight or nine feet of the ground. The dog was supposed to strike the tree—run to it, stand up against it, and bark at the coon. The number of barks would be counted and the dog was supposed to hold the tree until released by its owner. The first dog, a red bone, walked over, sniffed the bottom of the tree, and didn't bother to look up. The coon looked down at him curiously. The owner cursed, and pulled his dog away.

About twenty yards to the right of the lake, at the top of a small rise, was a picnic table and a shade tree. McElroy's Chevy Silverado was parked under the tree, and he stood alone beside the truck. Trena and another woman were at the back of the truck, watering the dogs.

In the afternoon, the water races were held. At the far end of the lake, four hounds waited in cages at the edge of the water. Overhead, the coon sat in a cage, waiting to be pulled across the lake on a steel cable. As the coon moved slowly out over the water, the cages opened and the dogs tore into the water, barking and splashing. The first dog to reach the far side would win one category, and the first dog to strike the tree where the coon sat in its cage would win the second. Frequently, the same dog won both categories. The air was filled with cursing and yelling and the yapping of excited dogs.

McElroy's women ran around the lake, leashes in hand, to capture their dogs at the end of the race. The weather was hot and handling the dogs was hard work. The large figure remained in the shade of the truck and watched the performance with interest.

To McElroy's friends, his behavior seemed strange. His water champion had been doing well in the races, and he should have been in the thick of things, cajoling and joking and betting and trading. But he kept to himself, watching as his women worked the dogs. After hearing stories about Ken for so many years, the men at the meet had come to believe them. They knew he had shot the old grocer in Skidmore, although conceiving of such a thing was difficult because he was such a gentleman around them. Now, they saw him on the grassy rise, aloof, and they left him alone.

The hunt was held in the evening. The men and dogs went out in groups with judges, roaming the timbered countryside in search of coons. A dog had to be able to run the track, smell it, and follow the scent to the tree. The first dog who "opened," or barked, on the track, and the first dog to hit the tree would win points. If a dog hit the wrong tree, or if it did not hold the tree until its owner arrived, points would be subtracted. A coon hunter could recognize his dog's bark, and most could tell whether the dog was jumping a fence, running flat out, or had the coon in the tree. Some could even tell from the sound of their dog how high up in the tree the coon was.

McElroy didn't participate in the hunt that night in Gallatin. A hunter had to follow his dogs across fields and through timber, crossing fences and streams and battling through thorn bushes. Perhaps McElroy had gotten too fat and couldn't move fast enough, or maybe the old coon hunter's drive had faded. In any event, he loaded up and headed out shortly after the water races.

Ken McElroy wasn't just sitting around waiting for his trial to happen. He appeared one day in early June at the home of his friend Ray Ellis, outside Gilman City. Usually, the two men stood outside and talked about dogs and maybe traded one or two. If Ken went into the house for a beer, Trena stayed outside and tended to the dogs or just sat in the truck. But this time, Ken brought Trena inside with him; she sat quietly in a chair and didn't say a thing. Ken didn't mention dogs. Instead, he told Ray about his upcoming trial and explained why he had shot the grocer.

"He was coming at me with a knife," McElroy said vehemently. "I had to shoot him or he'd have killed me. I had no choice."

Ken had a piece of paper with a list of names on it. These were the possible jurors in the case, he explained, and he was going around to dog meets finding out who knew people on the list. Someone had told him that Ray knew one of the potential jurors, Daryl Ratliff.

Ray said that Daryl was an old friend who lived in Gilman City and ran a garage there.

"Could you do me a favor?" McElroy asked.

"If I can," Ray responded.

"Could you talk to him about hanging that jury for me? I'll give him a thousand dollars and fix it so nobody ever will have to know. He'll find it in his mailbox one day, and that'll be it."

"Sure, I'll talk to him about it," said Ray.

McElroy showed Ray the list. "Is there anybody on the list that I should get rid of?"

Ray pointed to one name and said, "Get rid of him. If he gets the chance, he'll hang you for sure."

During this period, two extremely agitated teenage boys showed up on Corporal Richard Dean Stratton's doorstep one evening and claimed that McElroy had offered them money if they could get hold of some rattlesnakes. At first they had agreed to do it, but when he told them they would have to put the snakes in mailboxes belonging to the jurors at his trial, the boys had backed out of the deal. They wanted Stratton to know how it had happened, in case he heard about it.

By mid-June, all the seed was in the ground, and everything that was going to grow had popped up, including the weeds. The corn was now twelve to eighteen inches high, and the bean plants were full and green. This was the early growing season, a time of nourishment. In the fence rows, the plum, mulberry, gooseberry, and elderberry bushes were bright with fruit. Marijuana plants, known derogatorily as Missouri ditchweed because of their impotence, grew in clumps five and six feet high along the road. Red-winged blackbirds, killdeer, and mourning doves nested in the timber by the river. A gray-brown great horned owl flapped off his perch in a cottonwood tree in a great commotion. Cliff swallows darted along the riverbanks in the quiet dusk. A red-tailed hawk swooped onto the field and clutched a long black snake in its talons. As the bird rose, the snake caught on the barbed-wire fence and hung there, wriggling on the sharp barbs. The hawk swung around from behind and, raring back, sank its talons deep into the snake, snatched it into the air, and wheeled off with a triumphant shriek.

PART
FOUR

PART

FOUR

34

Prosecutor David Baird made two strategic decisions. First, he decided against introducing the candy incident or any of the subsequent incidents of harassment in the trial. Although the evidence might have been admissible under Missouri law, and would have shown a motive for McElroy's attack and demonstrated what a malevolent character he was, such testimony would also show a history of ill will between the two men and lend credence to the theory that Bo was attacking McElroy with a knife. Baird was worried about the long butcher knife—he knew it would be presented to the jury—and he didn't want any support for McElroy's claims that Bo had come after him with it. Baird wanted the jury to see Bo as the elderly victim of an unprovoked attack.

Second, Baird amended the complaint to delete the language that McElroy had "attempted to kill" Bo. The complaint now read only that McElroy had "knowingly caused serious physical injury to Ernest Bowenkamp" by means of a deadly weapon. The charge remained first-degree assault, and the penalties remained the same, but this amendment allowed the jury to convict McElroy without finding that, at the moment he pulled the trigger, he intended to kill Bo.

Both of these moves were conservative decisions aimed primarily at obtaining a conviction. Baird was trying to close any of the doors that might allow McElroy to walk out of the courtroom a free man. The important thing was to get a conviction, and to get one that would stick.

Two nights before the trial, Baird and his assistant brought Bo into the courthouse for a dress rehearsal. Bo sat up on the witness stand, and David led him through direct examination, then Baird's assistant cross-examined him hard for more than an hour. Bo didn't budge. Baird was impressed.

June 25, the day of the trial, was a Thursday. Cheryl stayed in Skidmore to run the store. She had decided not to go to Bethany. Watching McFadin work her dad over at the preliminary hearing had been painful, and she had no desire to see it again. Lois and Bo made the hour-and-a-half drive to Bethany with Evelyn Sumy. Their support consisted of Tim Warren and Cheryl's husband, who drove over together. Alice Wood and Trena came in the green Chevy, and Ken McElroy drove by himself in the big Silverado.

The welcoming sign on the edge of Bethany, a farming town of about 2,500, read "Tomorrow's Town Today." The courthouse, a large cement structure, sat in the middle of the town square like a bunker. The floors and walls were marble, and on the first level hung a black and gold plaque honoring the men of Harrison County who had died in America's battles. In the courtroom, the benches, counsel tables, jury box, and railings were made of polished blond oak. The walls and columns and ceiling were pink, the floors gray-and-black linoleum. Hanging from the ceiling were gaudy glass-and-brass chandeliers. The building was not air-conditioned, and although the windows were wide open, the hot June air was motionless.

The offices of the county sheriff and the highway patrol were down the hall from the courtroom on the second floor, and the officers had alerted the other courthouse personnel to the notoriety of the defendant in this case. They all watched as the players in the game gathered in the courtroom. The observers chuckled at the notion of two Kansas City lawyers and a state senator representing a Skidmore farmer on an assault charge. Sitting at the counsel table, wearing expensive suits and carrying leather briefcases, the three defense attorneys looked like gangsters.

The Bowenkamps and Sumys soon learned another quirk of the American legal system—the victim was not entitled to observe the trial of the alleged offender. If a defendant chose, he could ask the court to "sequester," or exclude, all witnesses from the courtroom, on the theory that witnesses to the same event should testify without benefit of having heard each other's testimony first. McElroy was not excluded, of course. As the defendant, he was entitled to listen and observe the entire case against him, and then decide whether he wished to testify. Thus barred from the courtroom, Lois, Bo, and Evelyn spent most of the day sitting in a sideroom, wondering what was happening in the trial.

The possibility of a plea bargain was never raised. The attorneys for both sides felt their cases were solid, and McElroy undoubtedly thought that he had a good shot at hanging the jury. The trial went smoothly from the very beginning. No one on the jury panel, most of whom were farmers or had farm backgrounds, had heard of McElroy, and the attorneys did not challenge any potential jurors for bias. Baird struck the younger members, thinking that they might be a little less shocked by gunplay in a public place.

The only real issue was whether McElroy had assaulted Bo or had shot him in self-defense. No one disputed that McElroy had been two feet from the edge of the dock when he fired. Because the defense could place a knife in Bo's hand at the time he was shot, the critical fact was Bo's location. If he had been anywhere close to McElroy, the defense stood a chance of creating a reasonable doubt that McElroy had been in fear of his life.

Bo claimed that he had been in the store, and McElroy claimed that Bo had been at the edge of the dock, hovering over him with the knife. Through the testimony of the investigating officers, the use of diagrams, and the introduction of other physical evidence, Baird methodically laid the foundation for the case that Bo had been in the store. The diagrams indicated that the dock was six and a half feet wide. A pool of blood on the floor was thirty-nine inches in from the doorway. The damage to the ceiling tile was another thirteen feet in from the door. By drawing a line from the holes in the ceiling to McElroy's position, Baird demonstrated that Bo could have been shot in the neck only if he had been standing inside, about three feet from the doorway. If Bo had been outside on the dock, the pellets would have hit the outside of the door frame, not the ceiling seventeen feet inside the building.

After establishing Bo's location, Baird tried to prove McElroy's intent. The prosecutor called the one boy who had not changed his story, and he testified that McElroy walked over and gave them money for pop. On cross-examination, the boy admitted that McElroy had given them money for pop before. The man at the gas station testified that McElroy had threatened to teach the old man a lesson only a few hours before shooting him.

Bo took the stand and told his story straightforwardly and without hesitation. Not wanting to risk appearing insensitive to the elderly injured victim, McFadin went easy on Bo, asking him such questions as "Isn't it possible that you fell backward after you were shot?" or "Isn't it possible that you are confused about where you were standing?" Bo flatly denied the possibilities. Baird and his assistant had been rougher on Bo in their rehearsal.

Corporal Stratton had been around most of the morning, either in the hallways or in the patrol office. Still considering Trena to be dangerous, he made sure that he knew where she was at all times. Word had come to him that she had a gun in her purse, but he never saw any evidence of it, and without more he couldn't shake her down.

Called to the stand to testify about the arrest, Stratton looked over at Ken McElroy, who was glaring at him with cold, penetrating eyes. Stratton stared back at him, and their eyes locked. As the lawyers conferred and fumbled with their papers, the two men, one on the stand in a uniform and the other at the defense table in slacks and a shirt, stayed focused in on each other. Neither man moved. Stratton was determined not to break away; if necessary, he would not answer questions until the impasse was broken. Finally, just as Baird was ready to begin the questioning, after what seemed to Stratton like the longest five minutes in his life, McElroy looked down. During the fifteen or twenty minutes that Stratton testified, McElroy did not look back at him.

Baird led Stratton through the details of the arrest, the fact that Trena was present, and where McElroy lived. Senator Webster cross-examined him, but it was brief and friendly. "Were there any guns in the pickup?" "Did McElroy give you any trouble that night?" Webster asked Stratton whether he had had trouble with McElroy before, and Stratton described the time he had caught McElroy with a truckload of hogs, and McElroy had stuck a gun in his face. Stratton did not mention the time his wife had stared down the barrels of McElroy's shotgun on her way to church.

At the end of the prosecution's case, McFadin made a motion to dismiss the charges, but Judge Donelson denied the motion. McFadin then called McElroy to the stand. Calling a defendant to the stand was always risky, but in this case McFadin had no choice.

His whole case rested on self-defense, and McElroy had to take the stand and explain why he was scared enough to shoot the old man in the face.

With his hands in his lap, McElroy calmly explained that he had parked his truck and walked over and given the boys money so they would go in the tavern and set up a pool table for him. When he returned to his truck, he testified, it wouldn't start. He figured the vehicle had a vapor lock. While he was standing there waiting for the engine to cool down, Bo began yelling at him to get off his property. McElroy was about ready to get in the truck and try the engine again when he felt something behind him. Turning, he looked over his shoulder and saw Bo on the dock coming at him with a knife, as if to stab him. Fearing for his life, McElroy reached into the truck and grabbed a shotgun from the dash. He turned the gun around in the truck and fired from the hip. Intending only to scare the old man, he aimed over his head. Bowenkamp disappeared from sight, but McElroy didn't realize he'd hit him; he thought he had just scared Bo back into the store. McElroy drove home, picked up his wife, and was on his way to St. Joe, when Stratton arrested him.

Baird knew that McElroy wouldn't recant any of his testimony on cross-examination, so he didn't attack head-on. He handed McElroy the diagrams and had him describe for the jury where everything was placed—the location of the dock, where his truck was parked, where the boys were standing, and so on. In his first couple of questions, Baird referred to words already on the diagram, such as *store* or *tavern,* and McElroy seemed confused and unable to locate them. Baird realized that McElroy might not be able to read or write. In order to avoid the jury's developing any sympathy for him, Baird began asking the questions without referring to the printed words. McElroy placed Bo right on the edge of the dock. Baird showed McElroy the curved knife and asked him what Bo was doing with it. McElroy said that Bo was holding it up in the air and stabbing down with it.

The only other witness for the defense was Selina O'Connor, who testified that she had seen Bo coming at McElroy with a knife. Terrified, she had climbed into her truck and driven away. Baird spent a great deal of time cross-examining her, aware that if the jury believed her, McElroy would very probably be acquitted. Baird tried to get the jury to see her as a "created witness." Why had she driven forty miles to get a parvo shot? If she had never been to McElroy's farm before, how was she able to find it as easily as she claimed? Most important, why would she, seeing her friend in mortal danger, simply get into her truck and leave? She hadn't even bothered to call the cops. And, the critical question, why had she waited nine months to come forward with her story? She had admitted hearing about his arrest on the radio, so she knew he was in trouble. She was scared, she testified, and hadn't wanted to get involved. She just kept hoping that the problem would work itself out.

The presentation of evidence was completed by 5 P.M., and the judge sent the jury home. That evening, the lawyers and Judge Donelson met in conference and hammered out the jury instructions, over which there was no serious disagreement. One instruction permitted the jury to find McElroy guilty of the lesser included offense of second-degree assault.

While preparing for the trial, and during the trial itself, Baird had had the feeling that, one way or another, he was going to lose. Knowing that no prosecutor had yet obtained a conviction against McElroy, he waited for the devastating cross-examination of his witnesses, or the surprise testimony that would knock a hole in his case. The blow never came, and when he went home Thursday evening, he thought for the first time that he might actually win the case.

Friday was a big grocery day, and Cheryl stayed in town to run the store. Her husband accompanied her parents to the trial. Now that the evidence had been completed, Bo and Lois were allowed into the courtroom to hear the closing arguments.

Baird's closing argument was factual and unemotional. He compared the physical evidence—the blood stains and the holes in the tile—with McElroy's diagram of where people were located. The undisputed physical evidence, argued Baird, completely contradicted McElroy's version of events, while it matched Bo's version. "You decide whom to believe," Baird told the jury. Holding the knife in the air, he demonstrated for the jury that a man on a dock trying to stab a man on the ground would be more likely to stab himself in the leg. Baird hit Selina O'Connor's testimony hard: Who would leave a friend in mortal danger and then keep quiet about what she saw for nine months? She simply was not to be believed.

The defense tried a variety of approaches. Senator Webster, whose retention had delayed the trial for four and a half months, addressed the jury in good ol' boy fashion and talked about how good it was to be back in this part of Missouri. Charles Spooner, McFadin's associate, took the analytical approach, going over the evidence piece by piece, arguing that the prosecution hadn't proven this element or that element. Finally, McFadin stood and made an emotional appeal to the jury: His poor client didn't deserve to go to prison for the simple act of defending himself.

Baird, having the final say, brought the jury back to the physical evidence, which proved that Bo was at least ten feet away from McElroy at the time he was shot.

When the jury went out to deliberate, Tim Warren was close enough to hear and observe McElroy and his women. McElroy gathered the three women in the halls, patted Trena's purse, and said, "If it goes bad for me, you know what to do. Do it just like I told you, and everything will be okay."

McElroy must have sensed that things were going badly for him. Tim Warren saw McFadin walk over to McElroy in the hallway and begin conferring with him. Suddenly McElroy exploded: "I don't give a damn, I'm not going to spend one night in jail. I don't care what it costs, or what it takes, I'm not going to jail!"

Warren heard McFadin calmly explain that there were only certain things they could do, and McElroy had to go along with it. McElroy shouted in his face, "I told you, I ain't going to fuckin' jail!" McFadin stood his ground and went over the various things they could do if McElroy were convicted. (McFadin later denied the entire incident, saying that McElroy was never angry with him, and was always pleased with his representation.)

McElroy was right to be worried; things weren't going his way in the jury room. His friend Ray Ellis had not kept his promise. Although Daryl Ratliff was on the jury, Ray hadn't approached him about McElroy's offer of a thousand dollars to hang the jury. Ratliff was arguing strongly to the other jurors that Bo was telling the truth, and McElroy was lying.

The jurors talked and argued some, and reviewed the facts and the law as the judge had told them to do, developing various theories of what had really happened. The jurors accepted the prosecution's theory that Bo was inside the store when he was shot, and thus there was little doubt that they were going to convict McElroy. The only questions were what crime to convict him of and what penalty to set. When the jurors took a preliminary vote, several people favored second-degree assault and a two-year sentence, while others sought a four-year sentence. After more discussion, they took a second vote, and reached a consensus on second-degree assault and two years. According to one juror, the reason they didn't give McElroy five years was because he wasn't charged with trying to kill his victim.

The jury foreman, a farmer, gave the verdict to the clerk, who stood and pronounced the defendant guilty. McElroy showed no reaction. The judge excused the jury and announced that the defendant would have thirty days to file a motion for a new trial.

McFadin wasn't entirely displeased with the verdict. His client had been facing life imprisonment and had received only two years. Even then, with luck and good behavior, he could wind up serving less than eight months.

Several peculiarities in the Missouri criminal law regarding the functions of the juries work to the benefit of defendants like McElroy. One rule of the Missouri Supreme Court required the jury to "assess and declare the punishment" within the range set for the crime of which the defendant had been convicted. The maximum sentence for second-degree assault was five years; for first-degree assault, life imprisonment. A second rule allowed the court to reduce the punishment if the judge found "that the punishment [was] excessive." The judge could not raise a sentence that was too light, however. The only option was to reduce a sentence, presumably where the jury had been carried away by emotion.

The bias in favor of the defendant results from the fact that the jury had to declare the sentence with absolutely no information about the defendant's criminal history or personal background. In many states, before a sentence was imposed, the judge or the jury reviewed the defendant's criminal record, background, and other information that might have bearing on the appropriateness of the sentence.

In Missouri, however, the jury's decision was deliberately uninformed. Without hearing anything other than the specifics of the crime in question, the jury could only presume that this was the first and only crime committed by the defendant. Even if the defendant had been convicted of rape and murder the previous month, the jury would be unaware of it. In reviewing the jury's recommendation, the court might learn of the prior conviction, but then the judge could only reduce the sentence, not raise it.

In this case, as it turned out, the jury assumed that McElroy and Bo had had a dispute over the use of the driveway, and that in the course of the argument McElroy had lost his temper and shot Bo. Seeing the shooting as a singular, isolated incident, like a confrontation between two drivers, the jury felt that two years was appropriate.

But what if the jury had heard testimony in a pre-sentencing hearing about the candy incident in the grocery store and the incidents in which McElroy had threatened and intimidated the Bowenkamps, Tim Warren, David Dunbar, Margaret Stratton, and others? Would the jury still have prescribed the minimum sentence? Much of the derogatory information about McElroy might not have been allowed before the jury, but certainly the jurors would have heard enough to disabuse them of the notion that the defendant was a simple hog farmer from Skidmore who had happened to be in the wrong place at the wrong time.

Shortly after being released by the court, two deputies told them who McElroy was and gave them a thorough run-down on his past. The jurors felt deceived and misused, and a few of them were downright mad. Many regretted not having given McElroy at least five years. The anger the jurors felt over having been forced to make a decision in the dark was nothing compared to what they felt when they learned that McElroy had walked out of the courtroom a free man.

Missouri law allowed the defendant twenty-five days in which to file a motion for a new trial, setting forth the reasons why the judge should overturn the jury's verdict. This provided an opportunity for the judge to correct any mistakes he or she might have made and to develop a record for an appeal to a higher court. In Missouri, the jury verdict was not final until the court entered a judgment, and the judge could not enter a judgment until after disposing of the motion. Although the motion had to be filed within twenty-five days, months might pass while the lawyers filed briefs and made their arguments, and while the judge made findings and filed a written decision. If the motion was denied, only then could a defendant be considered guilty. Until that time, he walked the streets a free man, as if the jury had not spoken. Even after entry of judgment and imposition of sentence, a defendant in Missouri had the absolute right, except in capital cases, to remain free on bond while appealing his conviction.

On the Friday afternoon after the trial, Gary Walker headed into town to find out what had happened in court. Having seen the result of the Romaine Henry trial, he half expected Ken McElroy to walk away from this one. When Gary spotted the Silverado parked in front of the tavern and the back-up Chevy across the street, he figured that's what had happened. Finding Red Smith and Ken McElroy alone in the tavern, Gary asked McElroy what had happened.

"The jury convicted me," he said, "and they gave me two years. But I'll tell you what, I'll never go to jail. I'll appeal it and get off." McElroy seemed almost to be bragging about the conviction. "I been fighting prosecutors since I was thirteen years old and I'm almost fifty. I've been arrested for over fifty-three felonies and this is the first one I ever lost.

"I'll tell you what," McElroy continued. "My fuckin' lawyer better get me off. I've already paid him $30,000 and now he wants another $20,000 for an appeal."

Word of McElroy's return spread through town. Some people had heard about the verdict; others had seen the two trucks in town. After disbelief came shock: What the hell had happened? The man had been found guilty by the jury; what was he doing back out on the streets?

After the guilty verdict, Baird could have made a motion to increase McElroy's bond on the grounds that the likelihood of his fleeing had increased because of the verdict. Such a motion might have been a futile gesture—unless the new amount were really high, McElroy probably would have been able to meet it—but he might have had to spend a few days in jail, and the motion would at least have indicated that the jury verdict wasn't a worthless piece of paper. Baird might have had more luck—and provided a greater service to the community—if he had sought to have McElroy prohibited from entering the town of Skidmore as a condition of his bond. Such restrictions were clearly permissible under Missouri law, and Judge Donelson had previously restricted McElroy's ability to travel after the St. Joe incident. If grounds were needed to support such a request, Baird could have sought a hearing to present evidence on McElroy's harassment of Skidmore residents. Baird, however, made no such request, and Donelson simply ordered that the bond be continued as it was.

35

Many people in Skidmore felt that it would have been better to acquit McElroy rather than convict him, tell him he was going to jail, and then send him back into the town. The community felt exposed and unprotected.

One housewife remembered it this way: "The last few weeks were pretty scary. Nobody would come to the business area because they didn't want to run into McElroy or confront him. Somebody would see his pickup downtown and the word would spread. My biggest fear was for my kids. Kids are pretty much allowed to run free, playing all over town, with a few rules about coming home for meals and chores. But, after he was turned loose, I kept my kids at home, and I know most other mothers did too. If he went on a rampage, I wanted them in the house."

Cheryl Brown: "Day after day, he sat on the street in front of Mom and Dad's house. The town emptied out every time he came to town. Everyone was so uncomfortable and scared. The guys down at the pool hall didn't like to be around when he was in town, I suppose because they were nervous and scared too. You just couldn't be sure what was going on in his mind. To wake up every morning afraid, be scared and nervous all day long, and terrified when the dark came and you couldn't see him, and every time there was a noise in the night, to prowl the windows and to wonder if everything was okay in town. That's how it was for me."

* * *

The townspeople weren't the only ones in shock that Friday afternoon. Ken McElroy had spent his life creating an image of invulnerability, and now the image had been cracked. McElroy could see the effect of the community's little victory: While he was not allowed to carry a gun, more and more of the farmers were carrying weapons in their trucks, and he knew they were talking in the tavern and on the street corners about taking care of him.

In the late afternoon clouds began to move in from the northwest, and by evening the sky roiled with deep blue-black thunderheads. In the middle of the night, the rain fell and the farmers rose to the surface of their slumber and absorbed the sounds and smells of a long, hard rain that would soak the earth and rise through the roots of the plants to the veins in the tips of their leaves. The rain continued through the night and in the morning, the fields were muddy and impassable, the dirt roads treacherous mud slicks. In town, pickups were splattered brown, and the main street of town was littered with chunks of mud.

By 6:30 A.M., the tables at the cafe were filled with farmers, and the floor was muddy from work boots and galoshes. The cafe was noisy with the ritual bragging about whose rain gauge showed the most moisture, and as usual the first liar was in the worst shape—if he said one and a half inches fell on his land, the next guy claimed two inches fell on his.

The rain slowed in the afternoon and stopped altogether around dinnertime, but still the dark clouds hung in the sky. The morning of the following day the sun rose hot on the eastern horizon, and by noon the countryside was a shimmering mosaic of vibrant greens and golds. Vast dark green seas of corn rose and fell with the rolling land. Fields of winter wheat, their golden stalks heavy with grain, danced and swayed in the wind. Long parallelograms of light green soybean plants, on the verge of blossoming, merged with the pale blue sky. A doe, dark and lustrous this time of year, pranced up the viridescent hillside, pausing every few steps to look carefully about. Her black eyes glistened in the sunlight.

The corn was five feet tall in the hill country and seven feet on the bottoms; the stalks were sturdy and the leaves were wide and long. The wheat would be ready to harvest within a few days. As soon as the fields were dry, the red, green, and yellow combines would come rumbling out of their sheds and roam over the golden fields, devouring the ripened grain with their whirring blades.

36

The world seemed to be slowly closing in on Ken and Trena McElroy. They became convinced that the townspeople were planning to get rid of Ken. The son of a neighboring farmer had come to the farm and told Trena that some men were going to pay him if he'd shoot Ken. Trena saw a shotgun and a pistol on the passenger seat of the man's truck. She told Ken about the visit, and later that night, when the man came back in his truck with the lights off, Ken confronted him and told him to stay off the property. He never came round again.

A few days after the trial, Ken and Trena were sitting in the D & G Tavern when a farmer they knew sat down beside them and said that the townspeople were circulating a petition to ban Ken from Skidmore, and that everybody in town was signing it. Del Clement and Red Smith were standing behind the bar, and Red Smith made a face at the farmer. Another time, Del told Ken not to come in the tavern anymore, because whenever he came in, the tavern lost money.

Ken told Trena that Sheriff Danny Estes had pulled him over one day and told him that "he was going to catch him one of these days on a gravel road and shoot him and say that he had resisted arrest." One night not long afterward, when Ken and Trena were driving home, a car parked off the road shined a spotlight on them as they passed. Rounding a curve, they looked back and recognized the sheriff's car.

Another time, Ken and Trena pulled up to a stop sign by Birt

Johnson's gas station and noticed a group of people standing on the corner. One of them looked at Ken and Trena and hollered, "We don't want you in this town!"

McElroy's loss of face and the prospect of going to jail caused wild swings in his behavior. Sometimes, he bragged and laughed it off. Two or three days after his conviction, he walked into the tavern and poured a sackful of bills on the counter. "There's more than $20,000 there," he said. "I'll bet anyone here that I won't spend one day in jail." No one took him up on it.

Other times, he seemed to sense his power slipping away. In the Shady Lady one night, as he talked with two women about the people who had testified against him at his trial, his mood grew increasingly foul. "I'm going to get 'em," he said menacingly.

Just then, the boy who had testified about getting the pop money from McElroy walked into the bar. Ken nodded in the boy's direction and said, "And that's one of them right there."

The boy walked over to Ken. "You're not mad at me, are you, Ken?" the boy asked nervously.

"No, I don't have a thing against you," Ken replied sarcastically.

Ken and Trena asked Alice Wood if she would be custodian of their children if both of them died. Alice agreed, and papers were drawn up, executed, and put in lawyer McFadin's safe. At the time, Alice noticed that Ken seemed to have put on even more weight, not just in his stomach, but also in his face. He complained about the pain in his neck from the old injury and seemed drained. His eyes, the deep blue eyes that had always danced, were now flat. To Alice, he seemed tired of everything, looking for a way out, but doubtful of finding any.

To Trena, the fight seemed to simply have gone out of Ken, as if he didn't care anymore. When they were driving down the middle of a gravel road and met a car coming the other direction, Ken would wait to swerve out of the way until the last second.

Lying in bed one night, Ken turned to Trena and asked, "What are you going to do when I'm gone?"

Trena was silent.

"These people won't let you stay here," he said.

"I don't want to talk about it" was all she could say.

"Well, when it happens," he said, "I want you to take the girls and get the hell out of Skidmore."

He talked to the girls about what was going to happen to him, and they became upset and told him they didn't want to hear him talking like that. He told them where he wanted to be buried and what clothes he wanted to be buried in.

One day Trena asked him, "Why do you go to town when you know there's going to be trouble?"

"I have to do something to get back at them," he replied.

To a long-time partner in crime, the man who had been with him when he shot Romaine Henry, Ken admitted that the world was closing in on him. To another friend, he talked about men being hired to kill him.

"You know, Jack," said Ken, "I don't give a shit no more. I don't care if I fuckin' live or die, I just don't care."

37

On June 30, 1981, four days after his conviction, Ken McElroy drove into town in the Silverado, and Trena followed in the green Chevy. As had been the practice since Donelson prohibited him from carrying weapons, Trena carried a gun with her in the Chevy. Today, an army M-1 rifle hung in the rear window. In the tavern, Red Smith stood behind the bar, and Pete Ward, his two sons, Wesley and Wilson, Gary Dowling, a local farmer, and Larry Rowlett sat on barstools. Trena followed McElroy into the bar, which was strange, and none of the men left immediately, which was also strange. McElroy sat a few stools away from Rowlett, and ordered a beer from Red. After a few minutes, McElroy got up and walked over to where Pete Ward was seated beside his sons.

"You're an old war man, aren't you?" said McElroy.

"Yes, I am," replied Pete.

"Well, I've got a gun out here I want you to look at," McElroy said.

Ken turned to Trena, nodded to the door, and she left.

On the sidewalk, one of the boys whom McElroy had sent inside prior to shooting Bo saw Trena emerge from the tavern, walk over to the green Chevy pickup, reach in, and take out a rifle. As she turned and started back toward the tavern, the boy realized that McElroy was inside, and that she must be taking the gun in to him. The boy wavered for a moment: Going inside a tavern where Ken McElroy had a gun was scary, but, damn it, there was sure to be some action. In a snap, the boy turned and reached for the doorknob. The door was stuck, so he pushed and fumbled with the knob. By the time he had it open, Trena was upon him with a rifle in her arms. He had no choice but to step back and hold the door for her. She neither looked at him nor said anything as she walked by him into the tavern. *This could look real funny,* he thought, following her inside.

McElroy was at the north end of the bar, so Red Smith was hanging around at the south end. Red had not paid much attention when Trena left, but now he looked up and thought he saw a blade flashing in the air. As he looked closer, he realized it was a bayonet attached to the barrel of an army rifle.

Trena handed the gun to McElroy, and he began showing it off, asking everyone what they thought of it, waving it around, and talking about what a neat gun it was. Then he reached inside his pocket and brought out a five-round clip. He slapped the clip in the rifle, jacked a shell into the chamber, and began talking about what he was going to do to Bo, all the while popping the clip in and out and jabbing the air with the bayonet. Once or twice, the rifle came to rest with the bayonet pointed in Rowlett's face, and McElroy described how he was going to cut the old man in half. Scared shitless, Rowlett figured he'd seen enough. He sucked down his beer and left. The Wards and Gary Dowling stayed, and McElroy demonstrated for them how he was going to shoot Bo in the face, then roll him over and rip him open from his ass up his spine to his neck.

Looking McElroy in the eye, Pete Ward said, "Like hell you will!" then stood up and marched out of the tavern, his sons behind him.

The grizzled former army officer had decided that the terrorizing had gone on long enough, and that the folks on the east side of town needed some help. The time had come to do something about Ken McElroy, and Pete was going to do it. He walked west up the hill toward Four Corners, past the bank, and another block west to his house. A minute or so later, he reappeared on his porch with a high-powered rifle and proceeded to walk back down to Four Corners. He stopped at the corner in front of Birt Johnson's gas station. If McElroy was coming for Bo, he would have to come up the hill toward Pete. He stood on the corner holding the rifle, shell in the chamber, the safety off.

"If that son of a bitch comes up this way with that rifle," said Pete, "I'm going to blow him away."

Perhaps McElroy sensed danger as he walked out of the tavern door, or perhaps he saw Pete Ward out of the corner of his eye. In any event, he got into the Silverado and drove in the other direction out of town, with Trena following in the Chevy.

Pete Ward's action was like a drover cracking a whip over a dozing animal's head or a hypnotist snapping his fingers in the face of an entranced subject. Although only one or two people saw what Pete did, the word spread like fire on a dry prairie. In the cafe, the story was told and retold and people shook their heads in admiration. Pete Ward was one guy you didn't mess with. With his white, short-cropped hair, a white mustache, and a gravelly voice, Pete was the subject of a lot of stories, many about his heroics in World War II, always told with respect. Pete wasn't afraid of the devil himself.

More important, Pete was also a local boy and a highly respected farmer. If Pete said someone had crossed a line, then he had indeed crossed it.

For the community, Pete's action meant the long season of running and avoiding was over. It signaled the possibility that the community was not totally helpless in the face of this man, that there *were* things people could do to take care of themselves, that they *could* stand up to him. Fear would still pervade the town, but Pete Ward's simple act rekindled a spark of self-respect in the community, and began to transform the fear from a fragmenting force into a coalescing force.

Although Pete had pulled a weapon and had been prepared to defend Bo's life with it, this was not the way he would have chosen to deal with Ken McElroy. In Pete's eyes, he had fought to keep the country free, and he believed that a man should respect the law and play by the rules. So that same day, he turned to the law for help. Knowing that McElroy had violated his bond by carrying a firearm, and assuming that threatening to kill a witness was a crime, Pete called the sheriff, told him the story and asked him what he was going to do about it. Estes said he would talk to Baird. Baird told Estes to get affidavits from the witnesses spelling out what they had seen and heard. When he brought the affidavits in, Baird would file a petition with the court in Bethany to revoke McElroy's bond. Baird told Estes to explain to the witnesses that even if he were successful in court, McElroy would not necessarily go to jail.

This was when people usually backed off, when they had to come forward and point the finger for all the world, including Ken McElroy, to see. This was when they thought about Romaine Henry and Bo Bowenkamp, and what happened to them and their families. But Pete Ward didn't waver. He signed the affidavit himself, persuaded his sons and Gary Dowling to sign it, and took the document to the sheriff.

On July 2, 1981, only two days after the incident in the tavern, Baird filed a motion seeking to revoke McElroy's bond or, in the alternative, to add certain bond conditions. If the court wouldn't put him in jail, then Baird asked that the court prohibit McElroy from traveling through, crossing into, or being in the corporate city limits of Skidmore. Baird also requested that McElroy be prohibited from frequenting bars and taverns and from having any contact with any witness in the criminal case.

When Stratton heard of the M-1 incident, he assumed that McElroy had cracked up, that his obsession with the town and his fear of going to jail had pushed him over the edge. Flashing a gun in the middle of the day in front of several witnesses seemed contrary to his usual calculated approach.

Sam T., a Skidmore resident who knew McElroy from the bars and the timber, but wasn't really a friend, had spent some time in prison in Jefferson City a few years back. When he heard that McElroy had been convicted he wondered how the big guy was going to handle the time.

A day or so after the M-1 incident, Sam was standing in his yard when McElroy pulled into his drive. McElroy appeared anxious and asked if he could drive the Silverado inside Sam's garage. Sam asked why, and McElroy said only that it wouldn't be a good idea for anybody to see him there. McElroy had a case of beer in his truck, and the two of them stood around in the garage drinking. McElroy remarked that Sam's sweet corn and potato patches looked nice, that he noticed them when he drove by. Then he fell silent for a bit. Finally, he asked Sam about his time in prison. What was it like inside? What were the prisoners like? The guards? What did they do all day? Where did Sam think he would be placed? Sam answered as best he could and tried to assure McElroy that he could do his sentence standing on his head. But McElroy didn't seem to feel any better. At one point, he turned to Sam and said matter-of-factly that if he went to prison, he was dead, and that if he stayed outside, he was dead, so it didn't really matter anyway.

McElroy pulled his .38 out of the glove box and showed it to Sam. "I'll tell you what," he said emphatically, "I'm going to take a few of them with me."

McElroy stayed for about forty-five minutes and four or five beers. As he was preparing to leave, he asked Sam if he needed any money.

"I can always use money," Sam responded.

"Here," said McElroy, "here's five hundred dollars."

"Ken," said Sam, "I could never pay you back."

"It doesn't make any difference," said McElroy. "I won't live out the week, anyway."

Sam chuckled nervously, and Ken grinned at him. "I'll see ya," he said, then he backed out and drove off.

Possessing a gun in public place was against the law in Missouri, and, as Ken well knew, displaying a gun "in a rude and angry manner" in the presence of one or more persons was a felony. Tampering with or threatening a witness was also illegal, and if the threat was for the purpose of inducing the witness to testify falsely, the act was a felony. Sheriff Estes could have, when he first learned of the M-1 incident, arrested McElroy for violating these laws as well as the conditions of his bond. David Baird could have directed the sheriff to arrest McElroy and detain him until he could obtain a hearing on his motion to revoke the bond. Under Missouri Supreme Court rules, Judge Donelson had the specific authority to order that McElroy be arrested and held until a hearing on the bond petition could take place.

None of these things happened. Baird explained his action by saying that in a tampering charge the threat usually has to be made to the witness and, further, that if McElroy had been picked up, he probably would have been released on bond immediately, anyway. Estes and Donelson would not discuss their behavior.

In the cafe, the conversation turned briefly to the lack of rain, the rising price of fertilizer, and the falling price of winter wheat: Should they take the wheat to the elevator or store it in hopes that the price would rise? But the main topic was the petition that had been filed to revoke McElroy's bond and put him in jail. All the men knew that Pete, his sons, and Gary Dowling had signed the affidavits, and that, in effect, the four of them were walking around with targets on their backs—or would be as soon as McElroy learned their names. Unlike the Bowenkamps, however, the four signers did not experience the distancing of their neighbors. In fact, most people felt that the men had done the right thing and that they shouldn't have to fight the battle alone. What Pete had done, he had done not for himself, but for the Bowenkamps and for the community.

38

Heading west out of town on Road DD, McElroy drove past Cheryl Brown's farm and another two or three miles to Burr Oak Road. Heading north on Burr Oak, McElroy cruised by the farms of some of Skidmore's most respected citizens: on the west side was Pete Ward's farm, and another mile or two down was the Clements' ranch. To McElroy, Burr Oak was a rogues' gallery, a road lined with wealthy farmers and their sons who had always looked down on him and who were now trying to put him in jail out of spite and envy.

Pete Ward had retired from farming a few years earlier and moved to town. He lived with his wife, Helen, in a comfortable, two-story yellow clapboard house on the corner, one block west of Johnson's service station. Although Pete spent a lot of time in the cafe, he was out at the farm almost every day, doing one thing or another. Helen, who was nervous to begin with, became extremely upset and frightened when Pete made his stand against Ken McElroy.

On July 5, McElroy showed up at the Wards' house in town. After parking the Silverado in front, and leaving Trena inside, he went up to the porch.

"Pete," said McElroy, "did you sign the affidavit against me?"

"Yes," Pete replied.

"Why?"

"Because you threatened to shoot Bo."

McElroy insisted that Pete tell him who else had signed the

affidavit, but Pete refused. Trena overheard Helen ask Ken how many children he had, which was a source of great speculation in the community. Finally, McElroy left and drove slowly east down the block.

Bill Everhart, who lived across the street from the Wards, watched the exchange from his porch. When the Silverado reached the end of the block, by the gas station, it turned the corner and stopped. McElroy emerged from the truck with a pistol in his hand, and Trena slid over behind the wheel. As the pickup slowly pulled away, McElroy started up the alley in the direction of the Wards' house. Everhart figured that Trena was going to drive around the block and pick up McElroy at the other end of the alley after he did whatever he was going to do.

Everhart yelled across the street to Pete, "He's got a gun! He's running up the alley!"

Pete turned, but couldn't quite make out his words.

McElroy, who was in a slight crouch and had just started up the alley, turned his head and looked at Everhart. McElroy continued up the alley and got in the truck without further incident.

Bill Everhart was the garrulous sort, and the story of McElroy stalking Pete with a gun in the middle of town was on everyone's lips within hours.

The next afternoon, Helen was alone in the backyard when McElroy walked up the alley. As he passed by, not looking at her, he said just loud enough for her to hear, "I might have to burn this fuckin' house down someday."

McElroy may have assumed that one of the Clement brothers had signed the affidavit, or perhaps he simply lumped the Clements together with the rich farmers on Burr Oak Road. In any event, he turned his attention to Greg Clement's wife, Kathi. She told Cheryl Brown that as she drove into Maryville one afternoon, she noticed McElroy following her in the Silverado. He turned off in town, but she was frightened enough to begin carrying a pistol in her purse.

Now that McElroy had added the Wards and the Clements to his list of targets and had begun prowling Burr Oak Road, the Bowenkamps and Sumys found a snowballing number of allies. By bothering the Wards and the Clements, McElroy had bothered their many friends.

Cheryl Brown remembered the feeling:

"As I remember, during the time from the filing of the motion to the day it was supposed to be heard, underneath the current of fear there was a strange calm. Anyway, there was for me and my family. I guess deep down there was a sense that something was going to happen one way or another. Either they would revoke his bond and put him in prison, or the tension would finally break someone and they would get rid of him, or at least attempt to. I can't say that anyone actually thought that way, but there was a feeling of some kind of inevitability."

McElroy continued to twist the situation. One afternoon, a few days after the petition was filed, he was in the tavern alone with Red Smith. McElroy was drinking hard, and he was angry.

"Who signed that petition?" he asked Red.

"I don't know, Ken."

"Whoever signed that son of a bitch is going to pay for it," growled McElroy. "I'm going to shoot their cattle and their horses and their hogs."

During the first week of July, one of the Ward boys was on a tractor when a Silverado parked alongside the fence about fifty yards away. Ken McElroy was sitting in the driver's seat, and the long barrel of a high-powered rifle poked out of the window. McElroy sat there for fifteen or twenty minutes, then drove off. Two days passed, then the same thing happened again. Later, McElroy was seen parked alongside a field on the Clements' ranch, his rifle pointed in the direction of some of their horses. After these incidents, many farmers began carrying weapons on their tractors as well as in their pickups.

David Baird had been pleased when the jury found McElroy guilty. He had hoped for a more severe sentence, but he was confident the conviction would stand on appeal. Assuming that any man convicted of assault and out on a $40,000 bond would stay out of trouble, he had not been worried about any further trouble between McElroy and the people of Skidmore.

When Baird received the affidavits concerning the M-1 incident, he immediately prepared the petition and sent it to the court. He also advised the clerk of the court that the petition was being filed and asked for a hearing date as soon as possible. The judge scheduled a hearing for July 10, and Baird sent notices of the hearing to McFadin and McElroy, along with copies of the petition.

On July 5, the three Wards and Gary Dowling received notice of the July 10 hearing, along with copies of the petition and affidavits, and were informed that they should be available to testify on that day. The signers had five days to wait.

The Masonic cemetery, below the old Skidmore house on DD, overlooked the bridge on the route into town from Burr Oak Road. Across the road from the cemetery, on a high bluff overlooking the cemetery and the river, the Hubbell family lived in a sizable house in the midst of the pine, maple, and walnut trees. One afternoon, Whitey Hubbell, a popular man of forty-nine or fifty, with wavy blondish hair, was riding his horse down his winding rock driveway, when he noticed a pickup parked in a clump of pines in the cemetery. The truck's cab pointed west toward the river and the bridge. When he got a little closer, Whitey recognized McElroy's Silverado. He felt uneasy: What legitimate reason could McElroy have to be parked in the pines? When Whitey reached the bottom of the drive and turned his horse east toward town, the Silverado moved slowly out of the pines and wound its way out of the cemetery. As Whitey rode on, the Silverado pulled in a few feet behind him and stayed there, creeping all the way up the hill. At the top, the Silverado swerved out and around him. Whitey took it as a warning not to mention what he had seen. After that incident, Whitey carried a shotgun with him in his pickup. He also began checking the cemetery and surveying the grounds around his house for any sign of a pickup before pulling into his drive.

The line of fire from the clump of pines in the cemetery to the bridge was clear and unobstructed, a downward sloping shot of 150 yards. To hit the driver of a pickup just as it left the bridge would be difficult—but not impossible for a good marksman using a high-powered rifle with a telescopic sight.

People began discussing the best way to take care of McElroy, although most of what they said was just bar talk. Chatting with Dave Dunbar and Larry Rowlett in the tavern one day, Kirby Goslee noted that when McElroy left town, he frequently drove east on V, then turned south on Valley Road to his house. At the intersection of Valley and V stood a clump of trees and brush large enough to hide a pickup and a man with a rifle. Crouched in the brush, with the butt of the rifle pressed against his shoulder and the stock against his cheek, a man could snap off a clean shot when

McElroy slowed to make the right turn. The shot would be easy, no more than ten or fifteen yards. Within seconds of firing, as soon as the Silverado started veering for the ditch, the shooter could head for his pickup and be on his way.

A few of the local boys circulated a petition demanding that the board of aldermen bar McElroy from coming into Skidmore. After only a few signatures had been collected, someone on the board told the men that such a law would be illegal, so they dropped the effort. The significance of a petition lay in its existence: Before Pete Ward stood up and said, "The hell you will!" few people would have dared to sign such a document.

On Thursday, July 9, McElroy roamed the countryside in the Silverado, eventually finding his way to the home of his friend Larry. Larry had a serious problem and needed Ken's help. A few weeks earlier, Larry had gone out with another man to steal some hogs from a farmer who lived north of Skidmore. Larry had planned to take the hogs to Ken's place and let Ken take them to the auction barn in St. Joe or Rockport. The other man, whom Larry had met in jail, turned out to be a stoolie for the Nodaway County sheriff's department.

The whole operation had been a setup. Eight policemen in three cars sat outside Larry's house in Quitman and watched as he hooked a trailer to his pickup and drove with his girlfriend and the stoolie to Burlington Junction, where they drank for a while in one of the bars. Somehow, the cops managed to lose Larry on the way from the bar to the farm, and the three thieves were alone when they backed the trailer up to the hog chute and loaded ten hogs into the trailer. The truck had moved about a foot when its right rear tire went flat from the weight. Larry wanted to let the hogs out and leave, but the stoolie insisted that they keep going. After about ten feet, the rubber tore off the wheel, and the rim carved a groove in the dirt road for the entire three miles back to Quitman. Larry dropped the hogs off at a holding pen, and the stoolie went looking for the cops. Following his directions, the cops went to the farm, where they found the gate hanging open and hogs running loose. The cops then followed the groove to the holding pen and on to Larry's house, where they arrested Larry and his girlfriend. The trial was coming up, and Larry's prospects didn't look too good.

As Ken and Larry rode around that afternoon, going from Quitman to Skidmore, then on to the bars in Maitland and Graham, and finally to Fillmore, they drank heavily. Before the day was done, they had finished two fifths of Jack Daniel's. Ken was wearing blue slacks and a nice shirt, and seemed to be in a good mood, joking and laughing. He didn't mention the petition to revoke his bond, and he didn't rail against the farmers. When Larry brought up the problem of his own upcoming trial, McElroy turned to him and said reassuringly, "I'll never do a day's time, and you won't either. I'll get you out of it." Larry hoped that meant Ken would hire his Kansas City lawyer to represent him, which would be a lot better than having the public defender.

When Pete Ward had learned on Monday that the hearing was set for Friday morning, he knew that the community had to prove to McElroy and to themselves that he could no longer isolate people and terrorize them. Pete didn't intend to drive to Bethany alone on Friday morning, as the Bowenkamps had. He had in mind a caravan of trucks filled with farmers driving over together in a long steel line. The farmers would fill the benches in the courtroom and make it clear to the judge and McElroy and the cops, and anybody else around, that the old days were gone.

Farmers were not natural followers. They liked to think things through for themselves, and anyone who tried to tell them what to do was immediately suspect, especially another farmer. And getting farmers to agree on anything was an almost impossible task. But when Pete Ward said he wanted some company on the trip to Bethany on Friday, the others listened.

Pete appealed directly to the farmers. He showed up at a friend's house on Tuesday night and explained that the four signers of the affidavits were trying to recruit a group of farmers to go with them to Bethany. The farmer said he would go. Pete's sons talked to other farmers, and they also agreed to the plan.

Gary Dowling called Steve Peter and said, "A bunch of us guys, four of us, we're going over to testify that McElroy had a gun, and we'd like to have some people with us, the support of the community, when we go in the courtroom over there."

"Sure," Mayor Peter replied, "I'll go."

The recruiting spread beyond the original four. The mayor called Dave Dunbar, and he agreed to go. Soon, the word was all over town, eventually reaching Graham and Maitland. A feeling of enthusiasm developed, with people seeking out their friends and offering them rides. The farmers were going to stand up to McElroy this time.

The plan was loose: They would meet at the cafe at 7:30 or 8:00 A.M. Friday morning and organize into a caravan for the drive. The avowed purpose was to show support for the four signers at the hearing, but the group also meant to ensure that nothing happened to the Wards and Dowling on the road to Bethany.

Meanwhile, McFadin had called Baird on Wednesday and explained that the defense needed a continuance because he had a trial scheduled for July 10. Baird understood the problem with scheduling conflicts but said he could not agree to a continuance, because he was concerned that something might happen in Skidmore. McFadin said he had spoken to his client and instructed him not to go into Skidmore, so that would not be a problem. On that assurance, Baird finally acquiesced to the continuance, asking only that the hearing be set as soon as possible. That afternoon McFadin sent a letter to Judge Donelson requesting that the hearing be postponed until July 20, 1981. The judge granted the request.

McFadin called McElroy and told him not to go into Skidmore, because the people in town were riled up.

"Nobody can keep me out of anywhere," he replied. "I go where I want, when I want. I'm not afraid of anyone."

"Ken, use some common sense and stay out of there," said McFadin. "If you have to go, call me first."

39

On Friday, July 10, 1981, the sun rose early on the uneven horizon and streamed across the gently sloping bean fields and hedgerows. The white rays reflected off the Skidmore water tower and lit the tops of the tall elm and maple trees. A farmer arising at 5:30 could see the lack of moisture in the air, and knew there would be no clouds moving in before the day was over. Today would be like yesterday and the day before—hot and dry, with the south wind rising in late morning. The crops still looked healthy, but the sun had been beating hard and steadily for two weeks, and the roots were drying out in the parched soil. Most of the mud from the last rain had dried up and blown away; only a few traces remained on the streets. Even the clumps of grass in the cracks in the sidewalk seemed lifeless.

A few people had heard about the continuance, but they made little effort to spread the word, thinking that people might as well come in and talk about the problem and see what could be done. Pickups began arriving in Skidmore around 6:30, rumbling in from every direction and parking at the usual odd angles in front of the cafe and up the street toward the tavern. By 8:00, both sides of the main street were lined with trucks. Some of the men went inside the cafe for coffee, and others stood in clusters on the sidewalk and in the street. They had come from Graham and Maitland and Quitman, and almost everybody knew everybody else.

Rumors floated through the crowd that the hearing had been canceled. Finally, one farmer said authoritatively that the hearing had been continued to July 20, a full ten days away. A few men began drifting up the street toward their trucks, some went back inside the cafe, and others stayed where they were. Somebody mumbled that it wasn't any use with the courts and lawyers, and there was work to be done. Maybe they should go back to their farms and not worry about it until July 20. They had stuck their necks out and been sideswiped again, and what the hell could they do about it anyway?

Somebody else stepped forward and said, "Well, shoot, you know, everybody's here. Let's see if we can get together and figure out some way to protect these four guys."

Pete and his sons were there, along with Gary Dowling and the four Clement brothers and their father, which probably helped the group hold together. When someone suggested that everybody gather in the Legion Hall, there was no dissent. A few people got in their trucks and left, but most of the men headed up the hill, walking in twos and threes on the sidewalk and in the middle of the street, to the Legion Hall.

The men bunched up at the front door while a key was located and the door opened. The diffident mood outside the cafe had evaporated on the walk up the hill, and the frustration began to express itself.

"What the hell are we going to do now?"

"What's going to happen for the next ten days?"

The farmers talked first of protecting the four signers until July 20, but then somebody mentioned that McElroy was bound to find out about the meeting, and if he got paranoid, the whole town would be at risk.

Everyone began talking at once, and the din rose as more and more farmers came in. When the door finally shut, nearly sixty men were inside. Q Goslee had gone home after learning of the continuance, but he had decided to return to be with his buddies. He changed into his work clothes and arrived a few minutes late. His son Kermit, who had not heard about the meeting, noticed all the trucks and asked around to find out what was happening. He walked in a few minutes after Q. The Dowlings, the Clements, the Wards, the Sumys, the Kinneys, the Linvilles, and the Barretts—all the major families—were each represented by at least one member. Left out was Red Smith, who was stuck behind the bar at the tavern, as usual.

The gathering soon became rowdy as some men went over the past failures of the law, others talked about the caravan of McElroy trucks and the time the machine gun was hanging in his rear window, and a few suggested various other ways—some of them violent—of dealing with Ken McElroy. Finally, Pete Ward stepped forward and took the floor.

"No guns," he said forcefully. "We finally got him this time. He's going to be locked up, and let's don't do anything to jeopardize that." There was a murmur of agreement around the room, along with some grumbling. A few of the men scanned the crowd for unfamiliar faces and found none.

"No guns," Pete reiterated. "There can't be any guns. We've got to be real careful here and not do anything that would allow McElroy to come back and charge us with harassment and get his conviction thrown out." Pete looked around the room and met no challenges.

Bank president Ken Hurner, who had been in Omaha the night before, had planned to take a carload of farmers to Bethany in the caravan, but he was a little late getting to town. When he got out of his car, someone told him about the meeting in the Legion Hall. He walked in a few minutes after 8:30, and found the gathering completely disorganized. Some people were standing, others were sitting, and several were gesturing and talking at once. Pete Ward was trying to obtain order, telling people to be quiet and let one person talk at a time. Mayor Steve Peter was there, but he couldn't handle the crowd of upset farmers. When Ward saw Hurner, he turned to him and said, "Here's the banker, what do you think we ought to do?"

"I thought we were going to Bethany," said Hurner.

"It's been postponed," Pete responded. "What do you think we should do for the next ten days?"

"Let's get hold of David Baird and get some legal advice on what we might be able to do. Maybe he can come over and talk to us."

The concrete suggestion, the voice of reason, seemed to calm the crowd somewhat. Hurner walked across the street to the bank and phoned Baird. He told him the situation and asked him to come over. Baird refused to come and Hurner got the impression that the prosecutor didn't even want to talk about McElroy for fear that McFadin would come back into court and file a motion, and the case would be thrown out. Baird felt he could not attend the meeting because if anything happened afterward, he might be severely compromised in any ensuing prosecutions. Baird suggested they might want to hire a private attorney for some legal advice.

Hurner returned to the Legion Hall and reported his conversation with Baird. Some people grumbled and complained about Baird, and others tried to resurrect the idea of barring McElroy from town, calling for a special meeting of the town council. Q thought hiring a private attorney was a good suggestion, so he slapped a $50 bill down on the table. Other bills immediately followed and within a few minutes more than $500 lay on the table.

Hurner went back to the bank and called an attorney in Maryville. The attorney said he had to be in court at 10 A.M., but if four or five of them came over to his office around 11, he would discuss the problem with them. "No more than four or five," he repeated. He added that the town could not pass an ordinance against Ken McElroy.

By the time Hurner returned to the meeting, the men were talking about organizing a posse to patrol the town streets and the country roads to keep track of McElroy. The idea caught on: They wouldn't be looking for McElroy or going after him; they would simply be keeping track of him, trying to know where he was at all times. In years past there had been a Nodaway rural posse, and men had been deputized to patrol the back roads, looking mainly for hog and cattle thieves. Why not bring the posse back? More money hit the table as men talked about buying radios and gas for the trucks on patrol.

"Don't you think we should be deputized to do this?" someone shouted.

"Yeah," came another voice. "Let's get the sheriff over here and find out legally what we can do, and what we can't do. You know, how far is too far."

Ward and Hurner agreed that any posse had to be run legally, so getting Estes over to advise them made sense. Hurner left again and called the sheriff's office in Maryville. A woman answered the phone, and when Hurner said who he was and what he was calling about, she told him she didn't know where Estes was. Hurner explained patiently that the court hearing to revoke McElroy's bond had been postponed, that people were having a meeting, and that they were getting real upset.

"It's getting a little warm here in Skidmore," Hurner said. "You better tell the sheriff to get here as fast as he can, or this place is likely to fly apart."

Twenty minutes later, exactly enough time to drive from Maryville to Skidmore, Sheriff Estes walked through the door of the Legion Hall. The crowd turned to him, and questions flew from all sides.

"What can we legally do to protect ourselves?"

"How are these four guys going to make it through the next ten days?"

"How in the hell can we stop McElroy?"

After stressing that there should be no guns, Estes talked about forming something akin to a neighborhood-watch committee. A network of individuals in town and on the country roads would use radios to contact each other if McElroy showed up at someone's place, and they would come to their neighbor's assistance. They wouldn't do anything more than he did, just drive around and stay with him. If he created a disturbance, they would call the police.

"What if, when we're doing that, he sees us and realizes there are a couple of trucks around, and he steps out with a shotgun or a rifle? When could someone pull the trigger and not get hung for it?"

"Any time someone has drawn a gun and has it pointed at you," said Estes, "you've got a total right to blow him away."

"What if we shoot him some night when he's out stealing hogs on the back roads?"

"If that happens, it happens," Estes replied, only half in jest. "As long as I don't know anything about it." Later Estes said, "If he pulls down on you and you shoot him, I'd say it'd be the funniest case of suicide I'd ever seen."

Someone in the back remembered the earlier question and asked, "Can we be deputized? That's how it was done with the rural posse."

One farmer volunteered, and then another and a third and a fourth.

"That's not a bad idea," Estes responded. "But I'd have to go to the county commissioners and get their approval." He promised to try that afternoon. "But you boys be careful roaming the back roads at night looking for McElroy, or you'll get yourselves killed."

Everybody agreed that monitoring McElroy's movements was a good idea, but they still had some details to hammer out. One problem was that McElroy would listen in on their radio transmissions. Somebody suggested that if McElroy came to town and started driving around Pete Ward's house, Pete could get on the radio and say, "Let's go and have a beer," and that would mean "McElroy's here; I need help."

At 9:30, as Ken was filling his stock tank with water so the kids could go swimming, his sister Dorothy drove up.

"There's a meeting in town," she said, "and the streets are lined with pickups."

McElroy wasn't surprised—he had heard about the meeting the day before. He went inside and called McFadin's office, but the secretary said McFadin wasn't in yet. McElroy hung up the phone, turned to Trena, and said, "Let's go."

Trena had a bad feeling about going to town and tried to talk him out of it, but McElroy was adamant. "Let's go," he repeated.

To those who knew Ken, everything about his behavior that morning was strange. Usually, he cleaned up and changed clothes before he went to town. This morning he left just as he was. For the first time since the judge had prohibited him from carrying a gun, he went to town without a back-up truck and rifle. Tammy said she wanted to go in a second truck, but McElroy said no. Trena was to ride in the Silverado with him, and that was all.

In Trena's view, Ken had always been able to tell when things were going wrong for him, yet today he was walking right into obvious danger, unarmed and totally unprotected.

The Silverado stopped first at the small house down the road where Tim and Mabel lived. Mabel had diabetes and severe respiratory problems, and she was hooked up to an oxygen tank most of the time. She had been getting better, but just this morning Tim had had to take her back to the hospital in Maryville. Now he stood outside tending to the dogs.

"They're having a meeting about me in town, and I guess I better go see what it's all about," Ken told his brother. To Trena, Tim didn't seem particularly concerned.

When the Silverado passed the Methodist church on the right and came into view of the business section of the main street, Ken and Trena saw plenty of vehicles but no people. No kids were playing around the old railroad station, no farmers were standing around in front of the cafe, and no women were chatting on the post office steps with the morning mail in their hands. The town was deserted. Pickups stuck out at all angles on both sides of the street, and the only empty slot was right in front of the tavern. When Trena saw the single space, her sense of foreboding increased, and she tried to talk Ken out of stopping.

"It's all right," he replied nonchalantly.

The big Silverado swung left and slipped easily into the space. Ken and Trena got out, leaving the windows up, and walked into the tavern. The place was empty except for Red Smith behind the bar, a woman and her baby sitting at a table, and a couple of kids playing a video game. Ken stood at the north end of the bar, near the door, and ordered a Budweiser, a pack of Camels, and some Rolaids. Trena stood beside him and ordered a Pepsi.

The men in the Legion Hall were discussing the details of their plan to keep track of McElroy when Frankie Aldrich slipped in the front door, walked over to Pete Ward, and began whispering in Pete's ear. Frankie had pumped gas at the Sumy station for eight years. Before that, he had pumped gas across the street at Birt Johnson's for twenty years. This morning, Frankie had been alone at the station while the owners attended the meeting. Standing in the doorway at the station, he had watched the Silverado pull into town and park in front of the D & G. After Ken and Trena had gone into the tavern, Frankie had hurried across the street to the Legion Hall.

Pete Ward listened intently to Frankie, then turned to the crowd and said, "Well, McElroy's down at the pool hall right now."

Silence filled the room, and everyone froze.

Then somebody said, "Let's go and have a beer."

Steve Peter felt that they had no choice. They had just reached an agreement to watch McElroy, and now he had driven into town. If they did anything other than go down to the tavern and watch him, not a man there could have looked another in the eye. Ken McElroy would have run the biggest bluff in his life, and the town would have been his.

Men began shuffling out the door of the Legion Hall, talking casually as they left. No one seemed to be in a hurry to start down the hill. More than one man was wondering, *Is this a smart thing to*

*do? Are we going down there looking for trouble? Is he going to
remember each one of our faces when it's over?*

Outside the Legion Hall, eight or nine men split off from the
main body and, instead of heading down the hill, crossed the street
to the corner in front of Sumy's gas station, where they would have
an unobstructed view of whatever happened.

Some people recall Sheriff Estes standing by the door when
Frankie came in. They said he walked out with the rest of the men,
but as they headed down the hill, he got into his 1978 Mercury and
left town, swinging a block north to avoid the Silverado and the
men filing down the street. Others swear that Estes left the hall five
or ten minutes before Frankie arrived. (In either version, several
lawmen later shook their heads over Estes' leaving town when fifty
frustrated men were gathered to decide what to do about Ken
McElroy.)

As the men headed down the hill, it was clear to Steve Peter that
they had agreed to watch McElroy and try to keep track of him for
the next ten days, and nothing more. But he also sensed that something violent was bound to happen, if not in the next hour, then in
the next day, or the day after that.

When Ken Hurner left the meeting, he walked directly across
the street and returned to work. As he entered the bank, he felt
good; they had a plan, a solution to their problem. The sheriff was
going to seek approval to deputize the men into a rural posse. But
Hurner sensed that the plan might not work, that somebody could
end up getting killed. McElroy would be roaming the gravel roads
one night, and he would pass somebody's checkpoint, and that
person would get scared or nervous about what McElroy was going
to do, or McElroy would see him and stop and challenge him;
things would go haywire, and someone would get shot.

Red Smith had come to work a little early that day because a
beer delivery was due around 9:30 A.M. After the delivery man had
come and gone, Red cleaned up the bar, straightened the tables,
and prepared for the day. When Ken and Trena came in a little
after 10, Red served them, then came out from behind the bar and
joined the kids playing the video game by the front door.

Minutes later, Del Clement walked in the door and said, "You
better get behind the bar. There's going to be a bunch in here."

Red flipped on the air conditioner and went behind the bar. A few seconds later, the door swung open and two or three men came in and walked to the center of the bar. Soon, the place was full of men, most of them standing at the bar ordering pop or beer. Several of them, Red knew, had never been in the tavern before in their lives. Red moved in circles from the cooler to the bar, trying to keep track of the money. Most of the men took their beer to the tables or stood along the wall, talking and joking as if everything were normal. A few men stood near the bar, staring openly at McElroy, making sure that he got the message. Pete Ward, at the far end of the bar, glared unflinchingly at his adversary. McElroy acted as he usually did, staring at someone for a second or two, smoking a cigarette, drinking his beer, turning occasionally to say a few words in a low voice to Trena.

Steve Peter was one of the last ones in the door, and he noticed that many of the men seemed to be looking away from McElroy. When Gary Walker came in, the only empty spot at the bar was the stool right next to McElroy. Gary had half intended to tell McElroy to "get off our ass," but as he ambled over to the stool, he "ran out of guts." From the tension in the room, he almost expected some sort of confrontation then and there. He was nervous as hell. He ordered a beer, and McElroy turned to him and said casually, "Boy, this place is really filling up in here."

"Yeah," said Gary. "It sure is."

"Maybe they're going to have a crap game," said McElroy.

"Yeah, could be."

"Say, are you the guy who sells trailers?" asked McElroy.

"Yeah, it's me."

"Do you still have the blue trailer for sale?"

"No, I sold that one."

A few weeks earlier, McElroy had told Gary that one day he would come into Skidmore and start shooting and see how many people he could take with him when he went down. Now Gary felt that McElroy was marking him, letting him know he would be remembered when the time came.

As brief as the conversation was, the encounter became the main event in the crowded room. The talk died down as people turned to catch a glimpse of Gary and McElroy and perhaps to pick up a word or two. Some people found it strange that Gary was being friendly with McElroy. To Gary, the explanation was simple: he ended up in a conversation with McElroy because the stool next to him happened to be the only space at the bar.

As Trena looked around the tavern, she saw fifty or sixty men, many of whom she recognized. There were Sumys, Kenneys, Barretts, Browns, and three of the Clement brothers—Royce, Scott, and Del. She watched as Del and Red passed out cups of beer to the men; they seemed to be giving it away free, as if they were celebrating something. Everybody was talking, but only one man talked to Ken. Although no one said anything to her, and she didn't hear any threats or see any weapons, she was frightened. Ken had drunk about half of his beer when Trena heard the Silverado's horn honk.

She looked at Ken, but he didn't say anything. Finally, he said, "Well, we'd better go."

He ordered a six-pack of beer to go, paid with a $5 bill, put the Rolaids and the Camels in the sack with the beer, and stood up.

Outside, a nine-year-old girl with light brown hair and a pretty smile had escaped the watchful eye of her grandmother and was dawdling in the drive between the tavern and the rear of the grocery store. The girl heard the rear door of the tavern close and looked over to see a young man with a rifle in his hands. When he saw her, he stopped, then told her she better go on home. She went home and told her grandmother about the man with the gun, and her grandmother admonished her not to tell anyone else.

Inside the tavern, McElroy turned and walked toward the front door, holding the paper sack in his right hand. As he and Trena reached the door, a few men began to stir.

"Get out of town and stay out of town."

"And don't come back, goddamn it!"

The comments didn't reach Trena's ears, and if Ken heard them, he didn't react.

Cheryl had not moved from her window at the B & B, and her heart began to pound when the screen door swung open and the bulky form of Ken McElroy appeared on the sidewalk. She watched intently as he walked to the driver's side of the Silverado and got in.

When Ken and Trena began moving toward the door, Steve Peter realized that he and the others would have to follow them out. A watch committee was supposed to watch, and wouldn't it look stupid if all the watchmen sat in the bar while McElroy roamed the streets. Chairs scraped and men moved toward the door. Steve was the fourth or fifth person out after Trena, and he walked over to the front fender of the vehicle next to the Silverado, on the side closest to Trena's door. Most of the other men flowed up the hill in the same direction. The men at Sumy's station stood silently and watched the others collect on the sidewalk to the west of the Silverado.

If you kick and torment a nice dog long enough, if you're mean enough to him, one day when he's cornered, he'll turn and fight. Perhaps that is what happened in Skidmore that morning. The men had acted rationally and logically in adopting a plan that committed them to play by the rules. But in fact, they had turned to fight. They turned, most likely, when word of the continuance came, and they headed for the Legion Hall instead of going home. Or perhaps when they heard McElroy had come to town and was in the tavern. If three men didn't know in their guts that the town had turned, they would never have gone for their guns.

At some point between the moment Frankie brought word that McElroy was in town and the moment that McElroy left the tavern, the three men moved off by themselves for a brief conversation. After learning the day before that the hearing had been postponed, they had talked about what might be done. They had agreed that with McElroy running around loose for another ten days, nobody would be safe. Sounds of idling pickup engines would be the sounds of fear, and men riding tractors with their rifles beside them would watch the roads for the Silverado and worry about what was happening at home. The time had come to kill or be killed.

Maybe he would pull a gun on them, and they could act in self-defense, but they couldn't count on that. Each had brought a weapon: One had a shotgun, another a .30-30, and the third a .22. They would wait until he came out of the tavern. Two of them would stand across the street by their trucks, and the third would wait in the drive behind the tavern and the store. The blood rushed to their heads, then spread out to their hands and feet, cooling them down in the late morning heat.

* * *

McElroy sat calmly in the Silverado, ignoring the group of men on the sidewalk to his right. He reached into the sack, pulled out the pack of Camels, tore it open, and extracted a cigarette. He stuck it in his mouth, but before lighting it, he started the engine. His yellow Bic lighter lay on the seat beside him, and he reached over to pick it up as he glanced at the men on the sidewalk. His motions were slow and deliberate.

When Trena got into the pickup, she noticed that men were still coming out of the tavern. Most of those inside, except Red Smith, came out. Many of them turned west up the hill, and several stood on the edge of the sidewalk and the street, between the Silverado and the car parked next to it. All the men were staring in their direction. She turned to Ken.

"What're they staring for?" she asked.

"I don't know," he replied.

Steve Peter and a few others moved closer to the rear of the Silverado on Trena's side. She noticed Peter's hands moving in the air. She rolled down the window to see if he wanted something, but no words were spoken. Then she saw a solitary figure walking toward her from the side or the front of the tavern. She recognized Del Clement in his jeans, cowboy hat, and cowboy boots. Because Del was the only person moving, she turned her head and watched him as he crossed the street behind her. He walked to the cab of a dark red Ford pickup parked up the street a little way. He opened the door, reached inside, and pulled out a .30-30. Then he walked to the back of the Ford, closer to the Silverado. She saw him pull the lever down, snap it back up, raise the rifle to his right shoulder, and sight down the barrel.

"They've got *guns!*" she cried.

Ken didn't move.

Trena watched as Del squeezed the trigger, then she heard the crack of the shot and the sound of the rear window blowing apart. She turned to look at Ken and saw a huge hole in his cheek and the shattered rear window. She turned back to look at Del and saw his finger pull the trigger again and heard the explosion of a second shot. She looked at Ken and saw that he had been hit a second time.

"Oh, God! Oh, God! Oh, God!" Trena screamed. "Please stop shooting him!"

Someone jerked her door open, and a man yelled, "Get down, or they'll shoot you, too." A big man pulled her out of the truck onto the ground, and then another man, whom she knew but didn't recognize, grabbed her and hustled her up the street to the bank. As she went up the sidewalk, still screaming, she looked up and saw two women watching from a window in the bank. A few men noticed the spreading wetness on the inner thighs of her jeans.

When Steve Peter heard the first shot, his eyes were pulled to the shattering glass in the driver's door. As Trena began screaming, and her door opened, Steve decided he had better get down and out of the line of fire. He squatted between the trucks, not moving while the shots continued. Looking south, away from the shooting, he saw he was in a direct line with the west edge of the pool hall, and he figured that that would be the quickest way to get somewhere other than where he was, so he took off in a crouching lope down the side of the building. He circled west and north back to his pickup, which was parked across the street from the Sumy station, and drove home to tell his wife.

A twelve-year-old boy, who had gone inside Sumy's gas station a few minutes earlier to get a bottle of pop, was standing by the water cooler when he heard the shots. He looked out the front window and saw a man standing at the west edge of the post office with a rifle to his shoulder, firing across the street in the direction of the tavern. The boy bolted from the gas station and raced through alleys and across yards to his home. When he told his parents what he had seen, his father told him not to tell anyone.

When Cheryl heard the crack of the rifle she saw the window shatter and McElroy's head bob down. An instant later, the second shot pushed his head further down, and she saw Trena open the door and jump out screaming. Blood and dirt streaked her arms and blouse. Jack Clement came over to where Trena was lying in the grass, picked her up, and rushed her toward the bank. (One law enforcement official would comment later that only a man with a father's faith in his son's marksmanship would walk into the line of fire like that.) Through the screen in the tavern door, Kermit saw Trena—looking like a frightened animal in search of a place to hide.

Most of the men standing around dropped down between the vehicles or took off up the hill in the direction of Sumy's gas station. The men already there stayed where they were, watching the scene unfold below. At the sound of the gunfire their eyes shifted a fraction to the left of the Silverado, and the shooters and their blazing guns came instantly into focus. The flash of the gray gunmetal, the smell of burned gunpowder, the sounds of splintering glass and a woman's screams of terror, would be forever seared in their memories.

After the men had followed McElroy and Trena out the front door, Red Smith caught up on collecting for the beer and pop and was chatting with Kermit at the south end of the bar. A few men had begun playing pool, and the talk was picking up a little when Red heard what he first thought were firecrackers going off.

"Get down," someone yelled. "Those are bullets flying!"

Red dived onto the floor behind the bar. He lay on the cement floor shaking, listening to the gunfire and praying that the bullets wouldn't start ripping into the tin building.

Kermit heard the first *boom!*, a pause, and then a second *boom!* He hit the floor beside Red, thinking that somebody had shot at McElroy and missed, and now McElroy was shooting back. *There might be a goddamn war starting and those high powers would blow right through the tin walls,* he thought. He heard three more shots: BOOM! . . . BOOM! . . . BOOM! . . . In his mind he saw the levers of the rifles being cocked and the rifles being leveled and re-aimed between shots. He figured the shooting lasted fifteen to twenty seconds.

Q was sitting at a table with several of his buddies when he heard the *blammy! blam! blam!* of the rifles. He dived under the pool table, where several others soon joined him.

When the shooting ended, the people in the bar stayed put for several minutes, unsure of what to do, but not wanting to be part of whatever was happening on the street.

"By God!" someone finally said after looking out the door, "it's over with now. He won't be bothering us no more."

A few men picked themselves up from the floor, wobbled to the bar, and ordered beers. Red, his hands shaking, got up and did his best to oblige.

The big Silverado engine was roaring, and somebody said, "Better shut it off."

"To hell with it," came the response. "Let it burn."

Q stood up, turned to his neighbor, and asked, "How long do you figure it will run like that?"

"Oh, maybe five or six minutes."

The heavy, dark head, its oily black hair slicked back, slammed down on the massive chest. The shock of the hit flowed down through the thick torso and the lower limbs until a booted foot rocked forward on the accelerator in a heavy thrust. The V-8 leapt into life and roared out in full-throated angry protest. The engine wound up until, at full bore, its howl crashed through the town and ripped the still air like the bellowing of a mortally wounded beast. The howl rose to a terrible shriek, and smoke began pouring forth from the guts of the beast in thick black clouds. The head sat unmoving, like a huge black stone, but the heart continued to pump, and blood spurted from the holes in the neck and face, splattering everything around a bright, shiny crimson. The observers backed away slowly, mesmerized by the violence of the final throes. The heat of the struggle radiated outward in searing waves, turning the street into a huge blast furnace.

Finally, the beast's vital organs began to pop and snap under the strain, and the observers could hear the sickening sound of guts tearing apart. In the crescendo of the shriek, its insides seized and locked together in a death grip of flesh and metal, and the horrible noise ceased. A final sigh escaped, and fluids gushed into the burning pavement with soft, gurgling sounds. Then silence filled the town.

Inside the tavern, a man at the bar said quietly, "I think I'm going out the back door and heading home." Others followed him out the back, and then a few wandered out the front door. By now, the streets were clear of pedestrians, and the last few pickups were pulling out. As the men passed the Silverado many looked inside. Kermit got in his car and drove home, then drove back into town a few minutes later and stared at McElroy still sitting in his truck.

Q walked out, glanced at McElroy sitting immobile in the Silverado, and got into his own truck and drove around the block. He ran into a friend, and they pulled their trucks alongside each other and talked quietly for a few minutes before heading home. By the time Q walked in his back door, he was badly shaken and feeling poorly.

Left alone in the tavern, Red began cleaning the tables and the bar, picking up half-empty bottles of beer and washing glasses. Finally, at about 11:15, almost an hour after the shooting, he called the sheriff's office to ask whether anyone had reported the killing. Someone had.

Red had absolutely no desire to go out the door and look in the Silverado. He was so rattled over the shooting and the fact that McElroy was still outside, only a few feet away, that he started drinking beer himself. He didn't set foot outside the tavern until 7:00 that evening.

When Ken Hurner returned to the bank after the meeting, he found a young couple in his office with a certificate of deposit. About six months earlier, an elderly man from Graham had come to the bank and said he had $20,000 that he wanted to put in a safe place and avoid probate. Hurner had advised the man to put the money in a joint tenancy account with his niece and nephew, who weren't close to him but were the only relatives he had left. This morning, the two of them had come to the bank at 9:15, announced that their uncle had died a couple of hours earlier, and said they wanted the $20,000. Irritated with their greed and lack of respect, Hurner had called the hospital and verified the death, then told the pair somewhat gruffly that he would cash the certificate.

He was in the process of writing the checks when he heard a series of explosions outside. At first, he thought one of the gravel trucks was backfiring as it descended the hill. Then two cashiers rushed through his office shouting, "Someone's been shot! Someone's been shot!"

Hurner looked out his window and saw Steve Peter and Trena McElroy on the ground, about five feet apart, between the Silverado and a car. The cashiers were standing at the back door of his office looking out. He pulled them back in and said, "If you're going to watch, watch from the window. You don't want anyone knowing that you're seeing what's going on out there."

A minute or two later, Jack Clement brought Trena in the front of the bank and motioned to the two cashiers. "This is Trena," he said. "She hasn't been hit. Take care of her."

Lois was just leaving the bank, when Trena appeared in the doorway. Seeing Lois startled Trena, and she tried to back up, but Jack Clement maneuvered her on in. As Trena screamed and sobbed, Lois thought sarcastically, *Well, Trena, I haven't seen you in a while.* Without saying a word, Lois returned to the store.

Still screaming, Trena fell into a chair and gripped its arms. Blood speckled her shirt and arms, and tiny slivers of broken glass glittered in her hair. Between sobs, she cried out, "They shot Ken! They shot Ken! They didn't have to do that!"

A brown-haired woman in her forties walked up to Trena and said adamantly, "Yes, they did. You didn't leave us any choice!"

Hurner walked into the main room and was approached by an excited customer, a man from Savannah.

"What's the matter with that girl? What's going on here?"

Hurner did not respond.

"What is wrong with that girl?" the man demanded. "Why is she screaming like that?"

"You don't want to know what's going on," said Hurner. "Just get into your pickup and drive south out of town."

"Why are you so unfriendly?" said the man.

"If you go around that corner and look, you might be in trouble," the bank president warned.

The man left, mumbling under his breath.

Looking over at Trena, Hurner saw the blood and glass and noticed that Trena's pants were wet at the crotch. A puddle had formed on the floor beneath her chair. The cashiers, whom Trena knew, came over and tried to take her into the bathroom to help clean her up. But she only screamed louder and grabbed the chair tighter. She had heard Jack Clement tell the women to "take care of her," and she was afraid to go anywhere with them. She kept screaming at the top of her lungs, until the cashiers thought they would go crazy. After about ten minutes, when they realized they couldn't do anything for her, Hurner decided to call Tim McElroy.

"Tim," Hurner said, "there's been an accident involving Ken down at the tavern. Trena's in the bank. You better come get her."

Five minutes later, Tim drove his truck up the hill, slowing only slightly as he passed the Silverado. Tim came into the bank, looked around, thanked Hurner for calling him, and took Trena by the arm. As they walked out, she was sobbing and trying to tell him what had happened.

"Let's go check on Ken," Tim said.

"No, no, he's dead," sobbed Trena. "Take me home, and you come back."

Without looking in the direction of the Silverado, they climbed into Tim's truck. The truck sped up this time as it passed the Silverado on the way out of town.

Hurner walked through his office and looked out the back door to see whether anyone had removed the body. McElroy was still there, in the same position, and nobody was near the Silverado. All the trucks that had been on the other side of the street were gone. He walked back through the bank and out the front of the grocery store, where he asked whether anyone had called the ambulance. Someone said it had been called, so Hurner went back to work.

Inside the store, Cheryl was trying to steady herself. For a few moments, the pain she felt in her body was worse than the fear she had felt when McElroy was alive. It was a deep, aching pain, as if poison had been released in her bones. She and Bo stepped out on the loading dock for a minute and looked at the bent figure in the truck. Neither spoke. Eventually, she went out the front and saw Tim leading Trena across the street to his pickup, holding her and talking quietly to her. Cheryl didn't feel the slightest twinge of sympathy for either of them; she smiled at the sight of Trena's soaked jeans. Cheryl went back into the store.

A few minutes later, deciding to move her truck and the Bowenkamps' station wagon from the scene, Cheryl went back outside. She would really look this time, she told herself. She walked slowly up to the riddled truck. The passenger door was hanging open. She paused, leaned in and took a nice, long look. She had never seen a dead person before, but the sight of McElroy's corpse didn't bother her at all. Blood was all over him— covering his face, spilling over his front, and flowing slowly down his back. Large green flies buzzed and snapped around him in the hot sun. On the seat lay Trena's purse and the paper sack with the six-pack of beer in it. After fifteen months of terror, he was sitting there looking like a big, dumb, dead ape. Cheryl felt better than she had in a long time.

Evelyn Carter, who lived on a farm with her husband, Junior, northwest of town, was standing in front of the B & B Grocery talking with a friend when she heard what sounded like a string of cherry bombs going off. She glanced across the street at the men standing in front of Sumy's station and noticed the tense expressions on their faces. A group of men came running up the hill, moving fairly fast for a bunch of farmers. Putting their expressions together with the sounds, she realized that rifles were firing and assumed that Ken McElroy was involved one way or another. The door to the grocery store opened, and a woman motioned her to come inside. Evelyn pulled away, thinking that the grocery store would be the worst place to be if McElroy were coming after the Bowenkamps again. She and her friend crossed the street to Birt Johnson's station, where several of the running farmers had gathered. They stood staring, like a collection of wooden soldiers, staring silently down the street.

"What happened?" she asked of nobody in particular, staring down the street herself now.

"McElroy got shot." Not "somebody shot McElroy," but "McElroy got shot."

She sighed with relief. The ordeal was over. After a few minutes, she crossed back over to the grocery store to do her shopping. She walked up and down the aisles, thinking about what had happened and forgetting what she had wanted to buy. Finally, she just stuffed an assortment of items in her basket. At the checkout counter, Lois seemed calm. She didn't say anything about the shooting, just rang up the items, bagged them, and went on about her business.

A little embarrassed, Evelyn decided to drive down the street, even though it wasn't on her way home, and see for herself. She had expected to find McElroy slumped over the wheel, but he was leaning back with his head hanging forward, as if he were taking a nap. Once past the Silverado, she sped up and hurried home to tell her husband and listen on the scanner for the ambulance and police calls.

40

One of the boys who had been hanging around the tavern before Bo was shot was still in bed when a friend came to the door and told him not to go to town, because McElroy had been shot. The boy dressed quickly, and walked over to the main street. When he passed the cafe, he saw people with their faces pressed against the window, looking up the street. They turned and watched him without expression or recognition as he walked by. Approaching the truck, he noticed blood dripping from a crack in the door, and a small puddle forming on the ground. McElroy was beginning to turn blue, and the boy could see one hole in his face and another in his neck. Blood was everywhere, even on the shards of glass that remained in the rear window. *Jesus Christ,* the boy thought, *he needed killing, but this was a helluva way to do it!*

Tom, one of the kids who stole for McElroy, was in Graham when he heard about the shooting. He drove to Skidmore, parked by Sumy's, and walked down to the Silverado. Looking in the blown-out driver's window, he saw Ken's head slumped on his chest and some of his teeth up on the dash. Tom felt bad, as if it were his father sitting there, dead. He wasn't really surprised. He knew the trouble Ken had been causing, but this was a rotten thing to do—shoot him from behind, then leave him in the street like a dog. Tom's stomach churned, sweat broke out on his forehead, and he decided to get the hell out of town as fast as he could.

* * *

Jerry T. worked the night shift at a factory in Maryville, and on occasion he partied by himself when he got off work. At 10:30 or so on the morning of July 10, after smoking some Missouri ditchweed, he chugged into Skidmore on his motorcycle to have a beer or two at the tavern. Seeing the familiar Silverado with a figure behind the wheel parked in front, he pulled in next to it. As he slapped the kickstand down with his heel and switched off the ignition key, he turned toward the truck, waved, and said, "Hi ya, Ken!"

Jerry's hand wasn't yet off the key before the bloody hole in McElroy's face came into focus through the shattered window. In an instant, the haze lifted completely, and he kicked up the kickstand and switched on the key. Without taking another look, he backed the cycle up a few feet, headed down the hill, and roared east out of town at full throttle. He didn't slow down until he reached the V turnoff, where he pulled over beneath the Punkin' Show sign. He closed his eyes for a second while the images rushed over him. *What the hell had happened back there? Where the hell was everybody?*

Karen Rowlett was in the kitchen baking cookies when the phone rang.

"You're not going to believe this," a friend said.

"What?"

"They just killed Ken McElroy."

At first Karen didn't believe it, but her thoughts soon turned to the possibility of retaliation by Trena or by McElroy's friends or relatives. She found her sons and brought them in the house, then called Larry, who had gone to work when he heard of the continuance, and told him.

"Ding dong, the witch is dead!" Larry hooted over the phone.

David Dunbar had also planned to go to Bethany for the hearing that morning, but when he received a phone call around 6:30 saying that the hearing had been canceled, he decided, like Rowlett, to go to work on the pipeline instead. When a friend called him at work with the news that McElroy had been shot, he let out a loud whoop and danced a little jig.

* * *

The sun slipped a few degrees higher in the sky as Ken McElroy sat alone in the Silverado. In its ascent, the thin yellow disk of early morning had gradually turned to a shimmering white orb, so hot that it seemed to have parched the blue out of the surrounding sky. Now, as the hour approached midday, a red halo sparkled around its edges.

At the end of McElroy's heavily muscled arm, his hand still gripped the Bic lighter. His heart had stopped pumping, and the blood around the holes was beginning to thicken. In the heat from the roof and the pavement below, his heavy body was hardening, and its fluids were congealing.

The killers had to dispose of their weapons. According to one credible version, three or four men gathered at a farm west of town within an hour of the shooting, took the murder weapons out back to the barn, smashed the stocks off with a sledgehammer, and threw them into a stove. One of the men then fired up a blow torch and cut each barrel into fifteen or twenty pieces. The men divided up the pieces and threw half of them in wells seventy or eighty feet deep on farms west of town, and the other half in equally deep wells on farms south of town.

Deputy Sheriff Jim Kish had never had as much sympathy for the people of Skidmore as some of the other cops had. In his view, McElroy was nothing more than a bully, and the problem had developed because the town let him get away with everything he did for close to twenty years. If the townspeople had stood up to him when the trouble started, none of this would have happened. Instead, they would come into the sheriff's office to report McElroy's misdeeds, but they were nowhere around when the time came to sign a complaint. Kish knew that his boss, Danny Estes, was scared of McElroy, but to Kish, McElroy looked like just another pot-bellied man pushing fifty.

Kish was in the sheriff's office when the call came in around 11 A.M., about forty-five minutes after McElroy was shot.

"My name is Richard McFadin, and I have a call that my client has been shot."

"Who is your client?"

"Ken Rex McElroy."

"We haven't heard of it. We'll check into it and call you back." Kish turned to Danny Estes. "Danny, there is a report that McElroy has been shot."

"Bullshit," Estes responded.

An instant later, they heard the call for an ambulance on the scanner: There had been a shooting in Skidmore. Estes and Kish jumped in the Mercury and took off with lights flashing and siren howling, and arrived in town at 11:20, a few minutes before the ambulance. The streets were empty. Kish looked at the Silverado in amazement: the truck was full of holes, and broken glass was everywhere, as if a gang with guns had gone crazy and turned the vehicle into a shooting gallery. He could see the figure inside, and he wondered if McElroy might still be alive and armed.

By then, a few people had materialized to witness the law in action. One of them was Cheryl Brown. She laughed to herself when Kish pulled a shotgun out of the car and went creeping across the street and along the side of the truck with the shotgun on his hip, as if he were in a movie. McElroy was long past hurting anyone, but leave it to the cops who were afraid of him when he was alive, to go charging around in the streets with their guns now that he was dead.

Pressing his back against the side of the cab, Kish reached around inside, felt McElroy's neck for a pulse, and knew instantly that he was dead. At that moment, two men walked by with glasses of iced tea in their hands and said loudly enough for Kish to hear, "I wonder who that is inside the truck. Do you know?" "No, I don't, but he sure looks deader than hell, don't he?"

Kish opened the door, and blood spilled out on the dirty pavement like thick, red glue. *Christ,* he thought, looking at the pool, *there's no way the man could possibly be alive.* Down the front of McElroy's shirt, in the scarlet spill, were pieces of bone and hair. His skin was turning blotchy, and rigor mortis was obviously setting in.

When Kish walked up to the truck, Estes strode over to the few men standing around. His face was red, and his arms were flapping, like an excited rooster.

"Goddamn it, people," he said. "You were just supposed to watch him, not blow him away!"

He saw one man in particular coming around the corner from

the bank and walked over to him. Still gesturing wildly, Estes yelled at him, "You son of a bitch, you set me up!"

"I don't know anything about it," the man said, almost apologetically, "I didn't do nothing."

Estes turned back to the small crowd that had gathered and paused for a moment, trying to collect himself. "You weren't supposed to blow him away, goddamn it!," he yelled, his voice rising on the last two words.

Steve Jackson was drinking coffee in the ambulance barn in the back of St. Francis Hospital when his beeper sounded. He and his partner grabbed their equipment, jumped into the ambulance, and contacted the operator. She told them their destination was Skidmore, where a man had been shot. Jackson normally worried when responding to gunshot cases: He never knew if what had happened was really over. He called the Maryville police, which was standard procedure when running a siren through town. They confirmed the shooting and said that officers were on the way, so Jackson hit the lights and siren and took off.

On the way, Jackson thought back to the night a year earlier when the grocer had been shot. He remembered the crowds of people standing around and the hostile, sullen atmosphere. Driving across the rolling hills now, he wondered if this shooting was related. He knew it was serious, because about halfway to Skidmore, Danny Estes, who was a cousin of his, got on the radio and yelled, "Hurry the fuck up! Get out here now!"

Picking up the pace, they were flying by the time they hit the east edge of town. They found the truck with the body parked on one side of the street and a crowd, maybe twenty or thirty people, standing on the other side. Not one of them was moving or talking; they just stood there and looked over at the truck, as if waiting for something else to happen. Usually, when the ambulance arrived, Jackson and his partner found people clustered around the victim, trying to help and discussing the details of what had happened. But not these folks. There might as well have been a radioactive zone around the truck. The man obviously hadn't been moved or tended to in any way. The only sound was Danny Estes, who was real hot, pacing up and down the street, swearing and cursing—"fuckin' son of a bitch, goddamn"—anything he could think of.

Jackson walked up to the truck and looked at the victim, then reached in and pressed his thumb against the carotid artery. He came up with nothing. Jackson leaned over and looked at the wound in the man's cheek. The hole was so big and clean that he could see through it to the pattern on the seat cushion behind him. The man's face and neck were already mottled with swatches of purple and white. The purple coloring would have appeared fifteen or twenty minutes after the heart stopped pumping, but Jackson couldn't tell how long ago that had happened. He checked the man's eyes and found them dilated and fixed. The dark blue pupils didn't respond when he shone a flashlight into them.

From the looks of the body, the man had been dead nearly an hour. Jackson's partner came over with the drug box and the heart monitor. He pulled the victim's bloody shirt up, slapped the pads on his chest, and turned the machine on. A straight line moved across the screen. He ran a strip of paper to document the absence of any electrical activity and turned the machine off.

Estes walked over and started yelling: "Do something! Do something, for Chrissakes!"

"Danny, there ain't nothing to do. The guy's dead."

"Fuckin' son of a bitch!" Estes yelled, then walked off.

About four steps away, he whirled and yelled, "Well get him the hell out of here then!"

Some of the people in the crowd mistook the heart monitors for heart stimulators, and they thought the medics were trying to start up McElroy's heart.

"Is he still alive?" someone asked softly.

"He's not alive, is he?"

The person standing next to Cheryl gave a small cry. "Oh no, he's still alive!"

If he's still alive, Cheryl thought, *they'll just have to shoot him again, or else he'll figure out everyone who was in the pool hall and come after them one by one.*

Up until that point, nobody in the crowd had made a move toward the Silverado or said a word to Jackson or his partner. But as they rolled the cart up to the side of the truck, a couple of older guys came across the street and offered to help.

Jackson turned to one of them and asked, "Who is this guy?"

The old man looked at Jackson as if he were stupid and said, "This here is Ken McElroy."

Everything fell into place.

They swung McElroy's legs out the door, grabbed him by the shoulders and belt, and rolled him onto the cart, almost dropping him at one point. After placing his arms alongside his body, they strapped him in, pulled the sheet up over his head, and loaded him into the ambulance.

After they had him in the ambulance, Cheryl decided to walk around to the back and check on him. She sighed with relief when she saw the sheet pulled all the way up over his head. She walked back to the small crowd and announced, "He's dead. The sheet's over his face."

"Thank God!" someone said.

Cheryl went back to the grocery store. Evelyn Sumy had left earlier, not feeling well, and she had asked Cheryl to call and let her know whether McElroy was dead or alive. Cheryl made the call and then went back to work.

The ambulance moved slowly down the hill, leaving the town to police cars, the Silverado, and a few bystanders. The boy who had seen Trena enter the bar with the M-1 stooped down by the tin shed next to the tavern and examined the bullet holes. He and a friend stuck straws in the holes, matching the angle of entry, and projected an imaginary line that went to the top of the old bank building next to Sumy's. The boys ran over to the building, clambered up the back to the roof, crouched where the shooter would have crouched, and looked down at the straws poking out of the two holes. They searched excitedly for shell casings but found none. They did find some dents that could have been caused by someone kneeling on the tin roof.

In the bank, the customers talked about the killing. "Isn't it terrible what happened?" one said to the next in line. "It really was about time. The town didn't have much of a choice, did it?" a second said to the teller.

Hurner had another concern: Rumor had it that some of McElroy's friends and family were bent on vengeance and were coming to town. Hurner went home for lunch and immediately flipped on his scanner and listened to the traffic.

At the McElroy farm, Tim had dialed the phone for Trena when she called some of Ken's sisters and Gene McFadin. McFadin suggested that, for her own protection, she leave immediately for the state patrol headquarters in St. Joseph. With Ken's sister Wilma driving, she arrived around 1 P.M. The first cop she saw inside was Sergeant Rhoades. She refused to talk to him alone, because she was convinced that either he or Estes had been behind the second gun. According to Trena, she and Wilma sat there for over two hours, virtually ignored by the cops, until finally they went up to the window and demanded attention.

Trena gave a full statement, positively identifying Del Clement as the killer. To observing officers, she appeared very calm, almost as if she were in shock. Sitting with a spray of blood on her blouse and jeans, she went over the details in a flat monotone. She refused to take a polygraph test.

The tow truck slipped its hooked tongue under the axle of the Silverado and cranked up its rear end. The six-pack of Budweiser rolled off the seat onto the floor, hissing. The few people in the street, including the cops, stopped and stared as the Silverado, pocked, shattered, and bloody, moved slowly down the street on its two front tires.

The only remnant of Ken McElroy was the pool of thick, purling blood on the dirty pavement. One of the cops finally suggested that they hose it down. About fifteen minutes later, the new fire engine emerged from its cocoon in the city hall building and headed up the hill. The engine pulled alongside the hydrant on the corner by Johnson's gas station at the top of the hill, and a couple of men hooked up the hose. The lead man walked the hose to within twenty feet of the pool of blood and turned the nozzle on. When the water hit, the pool momentarily resisted, its mass changing shape but holding to the main boundaries, and then the thin crust broke and the blood spilled out into the dust, the bright red from the middle forming the leading edge as it ran downhill. The pinkish water turned clear before it reached the bottom of the hill. By early afternoon, the sun had dried the cracked pavement, and only a faint outline of the stain was visible.

41

Although eight to ten rifle shots had been fired, only two bullets hit Ken McElroy. The first one, from the .30-30, shattered the rear window in the cab, penetrated his lower neck or base of his skull, and splattered blood onto the top of the seat. A fine red mist, what the cops call "high-speed blood," sprayed the roof of the cab and the slivers of glass in the rear window. The bullet continued through his mouth, tearing through his tongue, his teeth, and his gum, before exiting through his lower left cheek. The blast blew the unlit cigarette, along with chunks of teeth and flesh, onto the dashboard. The slug shattered the driver's window and continued on into the side of the small Quonset hut a few yards down the hill from the tavern. Another .30-30 slug followed a similar path, but missed McElroy.

The high-powered rifle fired at least two more shots, which tore into the side of the truck bed, hit the metal wall of the cab, and careened off harmlessly.

The second shot that hit McElroy came from the .22. Apparently fired from further up the hill, more toward the middle of the street, the shot passed through the rear window, probably knocking out additional glass, and penetrated the upper part of McElroy's skull. By the time it had passed through the bone, the bullet was tumbling wildly, chewing the brain into tiny bits and pieces. This bullet, the .22, was the actual cause of McElroy's death, although given the time he sat unattended, he would have bled to death from the larger slug.

The .22 also fired at least two other shots, both low, leaving distinctly smaller holes in the side of the pickup, close to the passenger side. Wild shots punched other holes in the Quonset hut and shattered its front window.

A third man, the one Estes would yell at later, stood in the street armed with a shotgun, but whether he even fired the weapon or not was the subject of dispute. The cops found no pellets, and no one recalled hearing the distinctive sound of a shotgun firing. Some people said privately that when the shooting started, the third man lost his nerve and froze. Others said that the shotgun came out only as a defensive measure, in case McElroy pulled a gun, and when the man saw that his gun was not needed, he simply returned it to his truck.

But substantial evidence suggested that the shotgun was fired. Two small unexplained wounds in the back of McElroy's neck would easily have been made by pellets. The spider web cracks in the front windshield looked exactly like those made by BBs. Most important, the metal around the window behind the driver's head had numerous round indentations that, according to the men who later did the bodywork on the truck, could only have been made by shotgun pellets. They pointed out that the cops had not removed the dashboard, which was the most likely place for the pellets to have fallen. Even if the shotgun were fired, however, it was not the cause of McElroy's death.

David Baird was in the clerk's office in the Nodaway County Courthouse on Friday morning when his secretary burst in, pulled him out into the hall, and told him that McElroy had been shot and killed in Skidmore. Baird called the sheriff's office, and they confirmed the shooting and the death, but said no names were being used on the air yet. A short while later, Estes came into Baird's office, shut the door, and told him what had happened.

The circumstances created serious problems: The sheriff with primary jurisdiction had been at a meeting only minutes before the shooting, and had advised the townspeople how to deal with the man who had just been killed; and the man who would be responsible for prosecuting the killer had only days before convicted the dead man of assault. The two men decided to turn the investigation over to the Northwest Missouri Investigative Squad (NOMIS), a standing task force of lawmen from the surrounding counties set up to deal with special or unique crimes. Baird and Estes set a press conference for 3 P.M. that afternoon.

Richard and Margaret Stratton were eating lunch at her mother's house in Maryville when their daughter Pam telephoned to say that McElroy had been killed. Stratton, who took the call, exclaimed, "You've got to be kidding me!" Margaret heaved a sigh of relief, then proclaimed enthusiastically, "July tenth should be made a national holiday!"

With Margaret driving, the Strattons left to run an errand, but when they came to the street leading to the Maryville police station, Stratton suddenly said to Margaret, "Turn here!" Several police, patrol, and sheriff's cars were parked in front of the station, and several officers were standing around.

"Pull over," Stratton directed. He leaned out the window and asked, "Is what I hear about Ken McElroy true?"

Several officers responded cheerfully, in a mood bordering on celebration.

"Yeah, they finally got him!"

"That son of a bitch is dead now!"

The responses struck Stratton as unprofessional.

Other people's words weren't enough. Stratton had to make it real, to see for himself. He told Margaret to drive to Price's Funeral Home.

Stratton walked into the office of the director, an old friend, and said, "Is there something you need to tell me about?"

"Yes," said the director. "I've got someone for you to see. Go ahead on in."

Stratton walked into the embalming room and stared at the huge form slabbed out on the porcelain table. *It's over,* he thought. *Ken McElroy's dead.* Staring at the still body, Stratton felt as if he had lost a part of his own life. A strange feeling came over him: *What am I going to do with my extra time now?*

Stratton worried about Skidmore, what the people there were feeling and thinking, and how they were handling the killing. He felt a sense of failure. *They were good people, the law had let them down, and now they were in real trouble.*

Instead of driving home to St. Joe, Margaret turned on V and headed for Skidmore. Stratton wanted to see the people, the scene, and try and visualize how it happened. He spoke to the locals standing around in front of Sumy's, and they seemed numb, as if they had just come down from a heavy shot of adrenaline. The most they could express was a sense of relief. "Well, he's gone now."

Stratton talked to the NOMIS investigators, and they were confident that they would find the killer or killers. "We'll get 'em sooner or later," one deputy said.

After half an hour, the Strattons left town. *Damn it,* Stratton thought, *I always knew McElroy would die by a gun, but I never figured it to happen this way.* He had expected to find one of McElroy's pickups in a ditch with the windshield blown out and his head shot full of holes. Apparently, Stratton hadn't realized how bad the situation had become. He tried to express to Margaret his mixed feelings of relief and sadness.

McElroy's body made a strange journey—first to the hospital, where he was formally pronounced dead, then to the Price Funeral Home in Maryville, where he was embalmed, and finally to the hospital in St. Joe for an autopsy. At the funeral home, he was laid out on his back on the embalming table and incisions were made to drain the remaining fluids from his body. Around the table, supposedly gathering evidence, stood a couple of Maryville cops, a few deputy sheriffs, and two state patrolmen. As an officer from the Maryville Police Department took pictures, the mood shifted back and forth between joviality and shock.

Patrolman Dan Boyer attributed the good feeling in the room to a shared sense of relief: There the awful son of a bitch was, dead on the table. Some of the men clowned for the cameras. When the photographer was taking a shot of McElroy's head, Boyer leaned into the picture and gave a little Groucho-style grin and wave. In other moments, Boyer was almost awestruck by the sight: The body was huge, like a hairless grizzly bear, with a massive chest, broad shoulders, a huge gut, and skinny legs. He seemed almost bigger than life, even when dead, and Boyer waited for the eyes to pop open any second.

"Jesus Christ, I can't believe he's really dead!" one officer exclaimed.

From the blood in the cab, Boyer had expected more visible damage to McElroy's face, but there was only one long tear in his jaw where the .30-30 had exited. Fluid was drizzling out of his penis, and Boyer figured that either McElroy had had sex just before he was killed, or the impact of the shells had slammed his system awful hard. Three men were needed to roll the corpse over onto his stomach so that the holes in the back of his head could be photographed. He was lying in that position, facedown, arms at his sides, when Boyer left to rejoin the investigation. Later, when the FBI came into the case, there were regrets and admonitions about the clowning photographs.

When Vicki Garner heard of the shooting, she immediately thought of Trena—how horrible it must have been for her when Ken was shot, how dreadful for her to witness her husband's murder. *They maybe could have done it,* she thought. *But it was wrong for them to do it with her in the truck.*

Vicki called the McElroy house, seeking to comfort Trena, but Tim said she was too upset to come to the phone. Vicki asked him to tell Trena that she felt sorry for her and cared for her. Tim said he would give her the message.

McElroy had prevented Sue McNeely, Trena's step-grandmother, from seeing Trena since he took her over in the early 1970s, and Mrs. McNeely had missed her. She had always been afraid of Ken, but the way the killing happened bothered her. She couldn't grieve for Ken, but she felt that he shouldn't have been shot down like a dog.

The wife of one of McElroy's friends had a similar feeling. She had listened to McElroy joke about harassing Bo, and she knew that he had done a lot of bad things, but she felt that he deserved a better death than to be shot in the back of the head like a stray dog in an alley. She knew that the people of Skidmore would feel guilty for a long time for having killed him that way.

Ray Ellis, whom McElroy had asked for help in bribing a juror, was watching television when a newscaster announced that a Skidmore farmer had been shot to death as he sat in his truck on the main street of town. Although the details were sketchy, Ray turned to his wife and said, "That's Ken they're talking about, he got shot!"

Ray felt bad. In the nearly twenty years he had known Ken, nobody had ever treated him better. Although he didn't like the way Ken behaved toward his wife, Ray still considered him a friend, a good friend. Ray felt no anger toward Skidmore. From what he knew, Ken had had that poor town so worked up, so excited and scared, that killing him was the only way out. No, Ray had no bad feelings for Skidmore, but he would always wonder about the two Ken McElroys—the one they had shot and the one he had hunted coons and traded dogs with.

When Charlie, the reformed troublemaker who had talked to Ken about his soul, learned that Ken had been killed, his heart felt hollow. *What a waste,* he thought; *if Ken had given himself to God, he would have shone bright as a witness, like Eldridge Cleaver or Charles Colson. Whatever Ken said when he went before the throne of God, he couldn't say that nobody loved him. Charlie loved him. Charlie had gone to Ken in love, when there was no gain in it for him, and he had driven twenty miles and used his own gasoline. Yes, Ken would have to admit to God that Charlie loved him.*

On the morning of July 10, the clerk of the court in Bethany had begun calling the jurors in the Bowenkamp case to warn them that McElroy or one of his representatives would be coming by to question them about what had gone on in the jury room. Although the clerk explained that they didn't have to answer the questions if they didn't want to, several jurors were upset by the call. Having learned the truth about McElroy, they didn't want anything to do with him or his people.

One juror was watching the evening news when the story of the killing came on. He saw the picture of the truck, the same one they had heard about at the trial, being towed away. The newscaster kept describing McElroy as a "farmer from Skidmore." The juror couldn't believe McElroy wasn't locked up. *We did our job,* the juror thought, *tried, convicted, and sentenced him, and here he never went to jail!*

Daryl Ratliff, the juror whom Ray Ellis was supposed to have tried to bribe, was also upset when he heard that the McElroy people were going to be around trying to get him to change his mind about the verdict. When he saw the news of the killing on TV, he became angry. The system had worked the way it was supposed to: McElroy had had a good lawyer, perhaps too good; Donelson had been a decent judge; the jury had done its job, listening to the evidence and applying the law as the judge had said, and had found McElroy guilty. So what was he doing out on the street when he was killed? Why wasn't he in jail? How come the judge let him out? What was the point of the jury spending two days trying and convicting McElroy if the judge set him free?

Ratliff was so upset that, at one point, he considered going to Skidmore and explaining to the people that it wasn't the jury's fault that McElroy had been turned loose on their streets, that the jurors had done what they could. The way he felt about it, if McElroy had done all that people said, then he deserved killing.

Kathleen Whitney, who had taught Trena McElroy, Debbie McElroy, Del Clement, Steve Peter, Cheryl Brown, Romaine Henry's kids, the Goslees, and others, had a hard time believing that anyone in Skidmore could actually shoot McElroy in cold blood. If it was true, then the law was responsible for turning a bunch of decent farmers into killers. She was doubtful that Del Clement could have done it; in her opinion, Del thought too much of his own skin, and she doubted he was that good a shot. As for McElroy's death, she felt that it couldn't have happened to a nicer person.

42

A reporter and a photographer from the *Maryville Forum* arrived in Skidmore around noon on the day of the killing, and a news team from Channel 2 in St. Joseph followed close behind. By 1 P.M. the reporters had left to file their stories, and the police had gone to Maryville to organize their investigation. The Silverado, the most visible evidence of the murder, had been towed away. The town was left to itself. Perhaps for a few hours, the community believed that its worst problem had been solved.

Like many people in shock who pick up their routines and go on with their lives as if nothing has happened, the farmers went home that afternoon and told their wives and children what had occurred—or at least some version of what had occurred—then climbed on their tractors and went to work in the fields, or drove their trucks to Maryville for inspections, or scattered fresh straw for the pigs, or began repairing fences. The clerks went back to work at the bank, Cheryl Brown checked groceries, and the Sumys pumped gas and changed tires. If everyone acted normal, maybe life would be normal. Maybe the cops and the press had everything they needed and wouldn't come back. Maybe the nightmare really was over.

Few believed it. They might not have known exactly what was in store for them, but at least those in town that morning knew that life in Skidmore would never be as before. Images slipped too easily into their minds, one after the other, with extraordinary clarity—

the shattered glass, the blood, the still figure with a hole in his neck, the Silverado hanging on the hook.

They also knew that the legal system, which had so utterly failed the town, would now try to find and punish the killers.

NOMIS established its headquarters in the basement of the Savings and Loan Building in Maryville, and by 2 P.M. on the day of the killing, more than twenty officers from five counties had gathered, under the supervision of Sergeant Robert Anderson of the highway patrol. Assignments were made, and officers fanned out to interview all of the people who had been at the meeting in town that morning. Four officers, including patrolman Boyer, were assigned to interview Del Clement. They found his wife, Lisa, at home. She didn't know where Del was, but his father, Jack, was asleep in one of the bedrooms. She tried unsuccessfully to rouse him, then told the cops they were welcome to try. They went to the bedroom and woke him up. Startled and angry at the sight of four cops in his bedroom, Jack Clement said that neither he nor Lisa would have anything to say to them, and he told them to get out.

Meanwhile, Del had apparently gone to a small town in Iowa to play in the Clement Brothers Band. When the cops finally found him and brought him to Maryville for interrogation, his position was simple. He pushed his straw cowboy hat back on his head, put his feet up on the desk, and said, "Boys, I wish I could say that I done it, because he sure had it coming, but I didn't. He stole our livestock, shot our horses, and raped our women." (Deputy Kish shook his head at the hierarchy of crimes in Del's mind.)

Dave McLain, a city cop in Maryville assigned to work with NOMIS, knew McElroy mainly as the gun-toting character who bullied Skidmore and got away with everything he did. Not until McLain got out into the countryside that afternoon and talked to the farmers did he come to understand how far McElroy had pushed the people of Skidmore. Most of them seemed calm at first, but as the questioning progressed, some became resentful that the officers were there at all. The good of the community had finally been served, they said, and they should all be left alone in peace. A few farmers got irritated, almost angry, with him, but most were polite and blunt: "I didn't see anything, and if I did, I wouldn't tell you." As a lawman, McLain became frustrated over his inability to develop any information. As a human being, he came to respect the people for their strength and the way they stood together. By the time the sun went down, he knew the cops were up against a stone wall.

For the community, the feeling of relief was muted by the fact that a murder had occurred in town, and by anxiety over what was coming next. Being interrogated as if they had done something wrong gave rise to anger—an ugly, unattractive anger, directed, at least on the surface, at the judges, cops, and lawyers for leaving the town with no alternative. A vague, undefined sense of shame also flickered around the community, perhaps because the killing had happened in the heart of town, or perhaps because McElroy had been shot in the back.

But the events of the day had a coalescing effect on the community, drawing it closer together. Before the month was out, Skidmore would develop a rock core and an impenetrable outer shield. Richard Stratton was right when he predicted that a lot of people would say they saw nothing, would say they knew nothing, and that attempts to open them up would only tighten the seal and bind them further to the common good.

Stratton was a permanent member of the NOMIS squad, but he and his sergeant agreed that because of his past dealings with McElroy, he shouldn't be involved in the investigation. The decision was probably for the best; Stratton had a few ideas on how to go about unraveling the truth were he to be assigned to the investigation. (Oddly, another patrolman stayed on the squad even though the man suspected of holding the shotgun was his third cousin.)

Patrolman Boyer sensed the wall that afternoon. He felt as though the minute the rifles had stopped blazing, an unspoken bond of incredible strength had formed among the people. What happened might not have been right, they apparently felt, but what had happened before wasn't right either, and by God, you could walk the streets of Skidmore now without fear. In interview after interview, Boyer heard the same story: "I heard a couple of shots, hit the ground, and didn't see nothing."

As Boyer thought about it that afternoon, he knew other feelings would surface as the memory of the fear faded and the threat lessened.

Deputy Sheriff Kish drove from the Price Funeral Home to St. Joe to witness the autopsy. At the funeral home, the employees had treated McElroy with care—undressing him, washing him, combing his hair, laying aside his personal effects (a watch, a knife, and comb)—almost as if he would wake up when they were finished.

The approach was different at St. Joe. The pathologist took a large knife and cut McElroy's scalp in a circular motion on top and then peeled it down over his face, exposing his skull. The pathologist next sawed a large hole in the top of the skull, removing the circular piece of bone, stuck his hand in and lifted out McElroy's brain. There was no steel plate. Dictating while he worked, the pathologist laid the brain on scales that reminded Kish of those used in supermarkets, and weighed it, as if it were a vegetable. Picking up the brain, he described the shape, size, and condition, mentioning the massive hemorrhaging and damage to the brain stem. Then he began slicing the brain like a cucumber, describing the bullet fragments he found as he went. Dumbstruck, Kish stared at McElroy's hollow skull with the hair hanging over his face. Then the pathologist set the brain aside, stuffed paper towels in the skull cavity, replaced the bone fragments, lifted the flap into place, and casually stitched up the skin. Kish felt strange staring at McElroy with the top of his head back on, his hair in place, looking as if he were merely asleep—his head filled with dreams rather than paper towels.

The pathologist put the knife on McElroy's shoulder and sliced through the tissue at an angle to the center of his chest, and then down to his pubic bone. When he bore down, the fat almost exploded, as if he had cut open an overripe watermelon. The smell was foul when he opened the chest and the stomach. He reached into the cavity and took out the organs, one by one. The heart. The liver. The kidneys. Weighing and slicing them, he described their condition and noted whether they contained any foreign objects. As he finished with each organ, he placed it on the table beside the brain. At the end he scooped up all the organs, including the brain, and stuffed them into the stomach cavity.

How degrading, thought Kish, *to have your body used as a garbage can.*

Although vague and incomplete, the autopsy report concluded that the bullet that killed McElroy entered his head about three inches above the right ear, leaving a wound less than an inch long and half an inch wide. The impact of the bullet caused multiple skull fractures in a starburst pattern before penetrating the right hemisphere of his brain and lodging in the cavity that held his pituitary gland. The bullet essentially obliterated the right side of his brain, and the shock waves slammed the brain up against the left side of his skull, causing similar destruction in the left hemisphere. The front half of his skull was fractured in several areas, leaving most of the pieces movable.

The shot in his neck left a wound an inch and a half high and less than a quarter of an inch long. This wound connected linearly with the exit wound slightly beyond the left corner of his mouth. The exit wound was two and a half inches high and nearly an inch wide in its midsection. Beginning at the base of his skull, the bullet tore an angled groove along his tongue before smashing into his left jaw near his mouth and exiting. All portions of the lower jaw were fractured. This wound involved no vital organs and was considered survivable.

There was some damage to the soft palate, which would have been out of the path of the second bullet, suggesting the possibility that a third bullet entered through a small, unexplained hole in his right jaw. The report also described two small wounds in the back of the neck below the base of the skull as being "consistent with gunshot wounds" but did not indicate whether any attempt was made to locate the bullet fragments or their paths.

PART
FIVE

PART

FIVE

43

The wind began sometime in the middle of the night, most likely in the early, dark hours of the new day, rising gently from the south in light, gusty breezes. The golden dreadlocks on the cornstalks rose and danced in the cool night air. Gradually the wind picked up, and the gusts blew longer and more forcefully, lifting particles of the dry soil in rising swirls.

The cafe was full by 6:30 Saturday morning. The screen door slammed, engines started and stopped, and chairs scraped, as the conversation rose and fell, shifting back and forth from the weather to the killing. The northern horizon was clear, but many lifetimes of experience told the farmers that the sky would soon change, perhaps by midmorning. The warm southern winds would collide with the cooler northern air, and the sky would grow darker, until the thunderheads rolled in and the shadows disappeared from the land.

"He sure had it coming," someone would say.

"It's safe to walk the streets around here now," another would add.

"Betcha there aren't any more hog thefts around here!"

Someone would recount how long the engine ran and describe how Estes had blown up when he realized what had happened. But the mechanics of the killing—the types of weapons, who was behind them, the bullets—never came up. The official story, the shield, was "I don't know who killed him, and I don't want to know."

Whenever the creaking door announced the arrival of a stranger —an insurance salesman from Mound City or a truck driver from Savannah—the place would fall silent instantly. Then someone would murmur about the weather, about how much moisture was predicted for the next twenty-four hours, and the rhythm would pick up again.

Q Goslee was sitting at his breakfast table that morning with the radio tuned, as usual, to station KMA in Shenandoah, Iowa. He heard Skidmore mentioned, then McElroy's name, and then the word vigilante and killing. He set his cup down and turned to stare at the radio. The tinny male voice was saying that the entire town had killed McElroy. Years later, reflecting back on the course of events, Q would shake his head and say, "That's where it all started, when they used the word vigilante."

A thousand eyes watched the gray clouds spreading slowly across the northern horizon. Black and white thunderheads stacked up in billowing layers, and by late afternoon, the air was heavy and sticky with moisture. The wind blew harder in uneven thrusts, and the farmers left their tractors and came in from the fields. Deciding against his usual afternoon trip to the cafe, Q stood on his porch, watching and waiting. There was no beginning drizzle this day. Instead, the water suddenly burst forth and drove to the ground in huge drops, pelting the fragile bean plants and throwing up tiny puffs of dry soil. The wind rattled the windows and then slackened. Soon, the wind stopped altogether, and the rain fell even harder. Q went inside, pleased. In a couple of hours, he would check his rain gauges.

David Baird knew that the investigation and prosecution of the killing would be a highly charged process, but he had not the slightest idea what was truly in store for him until Saturday morning when he picked up the *Kansas City Times* from his doorstep and saw the front page headline:

FARMER SHOT TO DEATH
IN APPARENT VIGILANTE ATTACK

The article, which would set off the ensuing media binge, began as follows:

In what appeared to be a vigilante killing, a crowd surrounded a man and his wife Friday as they sat in a pick-up in Skidmore, Mo., and someone shot the man with a high-powered rifle, officials said.

The victim was 45-year-old Kenneth Rex McElroy, a part-time Nodaway County farmer who lived south of Skidmore, a northwest Missouri town of 440 people.

The article gave no reason for describing the killing as an "apparent vigilante attack," except for statements that the crowd had surrounded the truck and the residents had distrusted and feared McElroy. The story contained the kind of minor inaccuracies that often plague first reports: McElroy was forty-seven, not forty-five; his name was Ken, not Kenneth; the crowd did not surround the truck but stood uphill to the west. The article also claimed inaccurately that McElroy had been sentenced and an appeal bond had been issued, that McElroy was well known for "brawling," and that McElroy had died in the ambulance on the way to town. The funniest quote, if anybody had been laughing, was the following: " 'I've got three kids and I'm not married, so I just ain't gonna say nothing,' said Lois Bowenkamp, the daughter of the man McElroy was convicted of shooting."

This erroneous and provocative story turned the incident from just another local killing into a national story—an Old West tale where a frontier town takes the law into its own hands. The appeal to the news media world-wide was irresistible, and within days, almost every major paper in the country would carry articles about the community that killed the "town bully." Reporters were assigned to the story by both wire services, all three networks, the *New York Times*, the *Minneapolis Tribune*, the *Miami Herald*, the *Chicago Tribune*, the *Omaha World Herald*, the *Los Angeles Times*, *Newsday*, *Der Spiegel*, the *London Daily News*, the *Stars and Stripes*, *Time*, *Newsweek*, and the British Broadcasting Corporation. *Rolling Stone* and *Playboy* magazines assigned articles, and "60 Minutes" gave the story to Morley Safer. The casual description of the event as an "apparent vigilante attack" caused the media to descend like locusts on Skidmore, and the lynch mob angle allowed them to write dramatic, but sometimes inaccurate, articles.

Local residents contributed to some of the hyperbole by saying things about McElroy that the media could turn into provocative quotes. The residents also assumed that the reporters were interested in the truth, but when they realized that the press was interested primarily in facts that supported the vigilante angle (that the *town* had decided to take the law into its own hands and kill McElroy), people shut up. The silence only made matters worse.

Within a few days of the killing, the town also realized that it would be denied the clear-cut moral high ground. Many stories set up the ethical dilemma: Was the killing a matter of good versus evil or evil versus evil? Was the town any better than the man it had killed?

The spectacular failure of the NOMIS investigation inflamed the media reaction. On Friday afternoon, when Baird announced that NOMIS would be handling the investigation, he also announced that the investigation would last only five days. The investigators worked through Friday night and met Saturday morning to compare notes and receive new assignments. Everybody had essentially come up with the same thing—nothing. The witnesses weren't talking, and the investigators had no physical evidence, such as bullets or identifiable shell casings, to work with.

On Monday, the *Kansas City Times* picked up the lack of cooperation and introduced the second angle, one which would guarantee that the story wouldn't die: a conspiracy of silence.

TOWN NOT COOPERATING
WITH PROBE OF APPARENT
VIGILANTE-STYLE KILLING

The article stated that law enforcement officials weren't sure they would ever be able to solve the crime, because the witnesses weren't cooperating. Residents knew who killed McElroy, but they just weren't talking because they "apparently think more of the person who pulled the trigger than they did of McElroy." In addition to the conspiracy to cover up for the killer or killers, the article added support for the theory that there had been a broad-based conspiracy to kill McElroy. In her first interview with the press, Trena told the *Times* that when she and Ken left the tavern and got into the truck, the crowd " 'got closer to the truck from beside my door and just stood there, staring. It seemed like they were waiting for something.' Mrs. McElroy said she saw a man 'across the street shoot at them.'

" 'It was a setup,' Mrs. McElroy said. 'They've been having meetings.' "

The *Times* article did not, however, mention the one fact that would have lent the most support to the conspiracy theory: a meeting that had been held in the Legion Hall only minutes before the shooting.

The *Times* article drew the battle lines. Trena accused the town of shooting her husband, and the townspeople replied (in several quotes) that McElroy got what he deserved and that no one was crying over him.

The article also previewed the dilemma in which the town would find itself: On the one hand, the people defended the killing as justified; on the other, they claimed it wasn't a vigilante action. While arguing vociferously that McElroy deserved to die and that there really was no other choice but to kill him, the residents denied having had anything to do with his death or knowing who did. They seemed to accept the moral responsibility for the act, while denying the actual responsibility for it.

In reality, no conspiracy of silence existed. The stone wall was a spontaneous, reflexive action, like a mother's instinctual protection of a child in danger. Many residents wished that the killing hadn't happened, and some were angry at the killers for having put them in the position of having to lie or defend the act to the outside world, but the community had no intention of giving up its errant sons.

The solidness of the wall awed some experienced law enforcement officers. "They aren't cooperating with us," said the NOMIS public information officer. "They just aren't interested in talking with us." By Sunday evening, the cops had investigated thirty-five leads and "thirty-five leads saw nothing and heard nothing." NOMIS had received more than 100 calls on its special phone line, but not one from a citizen of Skidmore.

The citizens had learned the basic rule of the criminal justice system: no witness, no case.

The NOMIS investigators went back out to the farms and pulled some individuals into the Savings and Loan Building in Maryville for questioning. Mayor Steve Peter was questioned twice, the second time in Maryville. Like most of those present, the mayor said he was looking at the truck when the shots rang out, and he immediately ducked between the vehicles; when he looked up, the guns were gone. He saw nothing.

"Do you know who killed him?" the cops would ask.

"No, and I don't want to know," farmer after farmer replied.

On Monday, the *Forum* reported that the *Times* had called the shooting a vigilante killing. Sheriff Estes denied the allegation, saying, "These people were everyday people . . . friends and neighbors who wanted to help each other."

The *Forum* also broke the story that a meeting had been held Friday morning just prior to the killing, and that Estes had attended the meeting. Estes denied that the participants had discussed taking action against McElroy.

" 'I was asked to come to the meeting,' he said. 'They wanted to know what they could do to protect themselves. Basically, the questions asked concerned whether they could be allowed to patrol each other's houses and farms.' "

Some residents began putting forth alternative theories of the killing. They were all ridiculous. Several women recounted seeing a "long black car" with two or three men inside wearing dark pin-stripe suits drive down the main street a few minutes before the killing. Others said they saw the men in suits in the cafe drinking coffee that very morning. One suggestion was that some of McElroy's mobster friends from Kansas City had rubbed him out. Some pointed the finger at McFadin, arguing that McElroy had come to know too much about his alleged dealings with the Kansas City mob. Others suggested simply that the killer was some hired gun retained by farmers or grain dealers from a neighboring county. This second line of defense—"he had it coming, but somebody else did it"—was no more effective than "he had it coming, but we don't know who did it."

By Wednesday, no progress had been made, although the squad had been beefed up to twenty-four officers. Many cops still believed they could crack the case. They found it simply inconceivable that, with forty or fifty witnesses, they couldn't get at least one person to talk.

" 'We don't know how long the investigation will take,' said Owens. 'It could break any minute or it could last several days.' "

There were two "breaks." By Friday evening, the cops suspected one particular farmer of being the man with the shotgun. Two officers found him working in the fields the next day, and they handcuffed him and took him to Maryville for interrogation. Tough questioning brought him close to tears, and during a break Deputy Kish took him aside. "Look," Kish said, "there's no jury in the county that's going to convict the shooters. Why don't you just get it off your chest and explain what happened? It won't go any further than this room."

"I feel real bad."

"Tell me."

"They did it."

Kish named two people and asked the man if they were the ones he meant.

"Yes, they did it."

Kish said he had heard that the man had been holding a shotgun during the killing, and the man didn't deny it. He agreed to talk on the record and to take a polygraph test. But by the time he was wired up, he had changed his mind.

"Boys," he said, "I better not do this."

The following day, one of the men who had been standing on the corner at Sumy's gas station crumbled. Tipped off that he was the nervous sort, two officers confronted him at his home and grilled him. When he caved, they took him to Maryville for questioning. He gave a three-page, notarized statement setting forth in detail what had happened that morning. His version substantially confirmed Trena's statement that Del Clement had been one of the killers. The officers took him to the prosecuting attorney's office, where the statement was reviewed and signed.

The next day, however, the man reappeared with an attorney—the same one representing Del Clement. The man said that he had been under stress and duress when he talked to the officers, and that the statement was not true. When asked why a witness needed a lawyer, the attorney replied, "Everybody is entitled to an attorney."

Trena and McFadin became increasingly angry over the law's failure to arrest the man she had identified as the killer. From the very first interview, she had named Del Clement, and she never wavered. "I saw him do it," she would say, "I saw him hit my husband." Her statement as to where Del had stood was completely consistent with the ballistics. She gave Del's name to the papers, but they wouldn't print it. On the Wednesday after the killing, she went on the attack. Through McFadin, Trena charged that NOMIS was "dragging its feet and was not trying to do anything about the murder. I don't see anything done yet." She claimed that the police "never did a thing with the information" she had given them.

In a radio interview, McFadin belittled the investigation by the NOMIS squad and threatened to file a wrongful-death suit and refer the matter to the U.S. attorney for a federal investigation. McFadin added that, in his opinion, the killing was a vigilante action.

Cameron Police Chief Hal Riddle responded that NOMIS had spent more than 1,000 hours investigating the killing, and that part of the problem was that the investigators couldn't find Trena for further questioning. "It appears," said Riddle, "that Mr. McFadin and Mrs. McElroy are more interested in giving information to the media than to NOMIS." In Riddle's opinion, "if you don't know what you are talking about, keep your mouth shut."

Even after Trena had joined McElroy in harassing the Bowenkamps and others in Skidmore, a few people had hesitated to condemn her. They had difficulty blaming her for failing to stand up to a man who had been able to intimidate farmers and judges and cops. Her defenders felt that she wasn't acting of her own free will. But the last thread of sympathy snapped when, after his death had left her a free woman, Trena stuck up for McElroy and attacked the town.

In an interview with the *Daily Forum*, she accused the townspeople of making up stories about Ken and said that police officers had harassed the McElroys. Sobbing, she said, "I hope they just remember that he never kneeled down to them. They'll never forget him, because there will never be none like him. He was the best." She insisted that "they were all in on it."

Trena had loved Ken McElroy. "He was a goodhearted person," she said. "He'd help anyone that needed to be helped. He was good to his kids and good to me." In response to questions about the bad deeds people had accused him of, Trena said, "They're making most of it up. He was just a man who would stand up for his rights."

Some of the townspeople lashed back at Trena, ridiculing her for peeing in her pants and for sobbing and weeping every time the television cameras turned her way. One resident, a woman, said bitterly, "You know, some people said he was a nice man, that he was nice to his children. Well, how nice is it to rape a fifteen-year-old girl?"

Teacher Kathleen Whitney found it sad and hard to believe that the gentle, naïve girl she had known was saying the things quoted in the newspaper. In Whitney's mind, Trena didn't have the wherewithal to do and say what she was doing and saying. Someone else must have been putting words in her mouth.

Ginger Clement, who had seen Trena quake at the sound of McElroy's car, was outraged to read an article in which Trena said that she had never been scared of Ken McElroy and that they had planned to be married all along. Ginger remembered the little girl who had been afraid to sleep alone in her room for fear that Ken McElroy would come in the middle of the night and kill her and take the baby away. This couldn't be Trena talking.

Seeing Trena on television sobbing and feeling sorry for herself and talking about what a good husband and father Ken had been, Margaret Stratton thought, *You were plenty tough when you were sitting in my driveway in your big car and looking in my garage windows.*

44

Juarez told his mother he wanted to say good-bye to his father. A psychologist recommended to Alice that she allow the boy to view the body or else he might have a hard time accepting his father's death. The body was available for viewing only by family members on specific request, so on Sunday morning Alice made the arrangements. She, Juarez, and the two older girls took their last look at Ken. He was dressed in dark blue pants and a white shirt, and his black hair was slicked back. His face, a pasty yellow color, was puffed up, and Alice could see the thin red lines where they had put his face back together, like pieces of a jigsaw puzzle.

Juarez grew more bitter by the day. He didn't cry or break down, except for occasional outbursts of anger at the people of Skidmore, particularly the sheriff, who he heard had been riding with the killers on the morning of the killing. His behavior—quiet, cold, defiant—continued to remind Alice of Ken.

Tonia was the most fragile, frequently slipping back into the scene at the farm, and Alice watched her closely. For a few months before the killing, Tonia had been going to a fundamentalist church with a friend and her parents, and she went with them the Sunday after her father's death. The congregation said a prayer for the soul of Ken McElroy, and that seemed to make Tonia feel better. But even then, Tonia envisioned her dad lying in the cold ground, in pain, feeling abandoned and alone. She knew he didn't think his kids or anyone else loved or cared about him, and that he felt terribly lonely. She told her mother she might be able to make her dad feel better if she were with him. In long talks, and with the help of some church members, Alice tried to convince her that her father wasn't feeling alone, that he wasn't in pain, and that he knew that his kids and his family still loved him. She would sit Tonia down on the couch and take her in her arms.

"All suffering," Alice would say gently, "ends at death."

The funeral for Ken Rex McElroy was held at 1:30 P.M. on Tuesday, July 14, at the Price Funeral Home in Maryville. Funeral director Bob Braham had met Ken and other members of the family a few years earlier, when Tony McElroy died. For funeral plans, Tim acted as the primary spokesman for the family, although Trena, who seemed shaken but calm, offered several suggestions. The McElroys made it clear they wanted a private service—no strangers or media anywhere near. Two McElroy males stood at the door of the funeral home to control admission to the service. Braham tried his best to keep the media away, but reporters and television cameras from St. Joe and Kansas City filled the mortuary's two parking lots and recorded the coffin being loaded into the hearse and the widow being helped into the back of a limousine.

Swirling through the community on Monday and Tuesday morning were rumors that McElroy's friends and relatives were coming for revenge, and that Trena might be hit herself by the townspeople. The Maryville Police Department put extra officers on duty and stationed them at various locations around the funeral home.

Vicki Garner had not heard from Trena, but she continued to wonder and worry about her friend. On the day of the funeral Vicki and a friend drove over and parked in the funeral home lot. She watched as Trena was helped from a car into the building, sobbing and almost unable to walk, so unstable that several times she nearly fell down. *Regardless of whatever had happened,* Vicki thought, *Trena obviously had loved Ken on the day he died.*

Twenty or thirty people attended the brief service, which lasted about ten minutes and included no eulogies or extended prayers. The Reverend Mike Smith of the Skidmore/Graham/Maitland Methodist Church presided. Smith had moved to Skidmore only a few months earlier, and he had driven out to the McElroy farm on Friday afternoon when he heard of the shooting. Two rifle shots had been fired in his direction before he could make his mission known. Smith told others that he performed the service because no one else would, and because he wanted the members of the family to know that someone cared about them. He claimed that people tried to run his car off the road, threw rocks through his window, and sent threatening letters, because of his assistance to the family. Tim Warren had asked him how he could, in good conscience, hold a funeral for someone who was going to hell.

"Well, I don't know whether he's going to hell," said Smith. "The more I hear about the man, he could have been mentally ill. I would think he had some emotional problems."

Smith earned the town's everlasting enmity for preaching that the killers should step forward—some residents would describe him as troubled himself—and he left the area before the year was out.

All of Ken's brothers and sisters who lived in the area attended the funeral. Alice came with her three children by Ken, and Sharon attended with her four daughters. Even Ronnie McNeely, Trena's stepfather, showed up and served as one of the pallbearers.

The procession turned left on the main street, which became Highway 71 heading south to St. Joe. According to one of McElroy's brothers-in-law, a police officer usually directed funeral traffic through the stop light leading onto the highway, but on that day one cop sat a block north and another a block south, and allowed the light changes to break up the funeral procession.

The road south from Maryville was a familiar one to Ken McElroy, a road he had used when he had been drinking at the Shady Lady and wanted to head for Savannah or Faucett or St. Joe. But it might have been more fitting if the procession had headed down through Fillmore on the back roads he had known so well from his years of hunting and thieving.

The family had been so adamant about keeping outsiders away from the service that Alice had not thought to notify any of Ken's friends in St. Joe. Afterward, several of them told her that they would have liked to come. She felt bad about it—Ken probably would have wanted some of his drinking pals and coon-hunting buddies there. With his family present, Ken McElroy was buried in Memorial Park Cemetery in St. Joe.

* * *

During the first three or four days following the funeral, Trena and McFadin gave several interviews promoting their vigilante theory that the *town* had decided to kill her husband—and defending McElroy as a decent man who was hounded for sticking up for his rights. At a news conference one week after the killing, McFadin announced that he had asked for a probe by the FBI because of the evidence of a conspiracy: "He [McElroy] said they were having meetings all over town and following him around. I just told him to be careful because I knew he could take care of himself, and I told him to stay out of Skidmore. I didn't think anybody was going to shoot him."

Trena denied that Ken McElroy had ever mistreated her. "I was not a victim. We loved each other very much. I've heard those stories, too, about how he threatened my stepdad with a shotgun and burned his house down to get them to let me marry him. It's all lies."

She also denied that he had ever stolen anything. "He was a farmer, and he bought and sold antiques for a living. He did have a lot of hogs most of the time, but every one of them was his. He never stole from anybody."

She defended his actions. "He had his right to return to Skidmore. He was born not far away and has lived there nearly all of his life. Why should anybody be able to tell him he can't come here?"

She feared for her life if she returned to Nodaway County. "I'm scared they'd shoot me, too. I think they tried the other day. I'm not going back to find out."

In response to a statement by Ken Hurner that the people of Skidmore didn't wish her any harm, she said, "They should have thought of that, and the kids, before they shot him."

Tammy McElroy defended her dad as a loving father. In an interview with the *Kansas City Times* on July 17, she said, "All my life they've blamed him for everything. He was the best father anyone can have. I worshipped the ground he walked on. He took care of his family and loved us all. I don't know how anyone could shoot him down in cold blood."

The *St. Joseph Gazette* reported Lois Bowenkamp as saying, "The Bible says that there should be an eye for an eye. Those who live by the sword die by the sword. Ken McElroy lived by the gun. And that's the way he died."

Some residents shifted the responsibility for the killing, saying, for example, "The courts are to blame. If they hadn't postponed the court hearing, this wouldn't have happened."

"If the courts would have done something, as late as Thursday, none of this would have happened. But he got just what he deserved. He had terrorized some good people long enough."

The citizens were, of course, building the case against themselves. Every time one of them said how much McElroy needed killing, they reinforced the perception that the town had organized his death. If the residents said nothing, they appeared to be conspiring to cover up for people who had murdered an innocent hog farmer; but if they defended the killing, they appeared to be admitting responsibility for it.

"We're not a bunch of vigilantes," one citizen was quoted as saying in the *Gazette*. "We're just a bunch of townspeople who are trying to protect what is rightfully ours. Why should we have to live in fear all the time?"

But if the townspeople were talking to the press about *why* McElroy was killed, they were saying nothing to the press—or anyone else—about *how* he was killed. One NOMIS investigator was quoted in the same article as saying, "It's like pulling teeth that aren't there." But he remained confident. "In a town of 440 or so people, sooner or later, someone's going to talk."

Paul Stewart had covered northwest Missouri for the *St. Joseph Gazette* for years. He had visited Skidmore several times and found it to be an average small farming community, where everyone knew everyone else, and a stranger's car was noticed before it reached the railroad tracks. A quiet, isolated community, Skidmore was known only for two things: the Punkin' Show and the Festival Band. He had covered the Punkin' Show several times, and the people of Skidmore had always been friendly and courteous to him. Like everyone else, they enjoyed reading their names in the paper. When the Festival Band first started, the members were long-haired hippies who lived together without being married. Area residents initially had difficulty accepting the band, but when the leader, Britt Small, and a few of the other members joined the volunteer fire department and the American Legion, the town opened up to them. Much to its credit, in Stewart's opinion.

He and another *Gazette* reporter drove to Skidmore the afternoon of July 10, 1981. The place was crawling with lawmen—sheriffs, patrolmen, city cops, and miscellaneous officers from five counties. Stewart and his colleague took different sides of the street and began canvassing the residents. Although a few people were willing to talk about McElroy, no one would talk about what had happened to him. They would not verify the slightest fact—whether six or sixty people were in the tavern, what time of day the killing had occurred, or when the ambulance came. After a few doors were slammed in their faces, the reporters went into the post office. They could hear people chatting in the back room, but when the reporters knocked and said who they were, the voices stopped, and no one came out.

Stewart approached an old-timer who was sitting on the bench in front of the Legion Hall and had probably been sitting there every day for the past fifteen years. But when Stewart asked the man if he had been sitting there that morning, he said, "No."

As the months wore on, Stewart watched the bitterness of the residents grow. Even years afterward, when he would come to cover the Punkin' Show, people either refused to talk or gave very limited replies to queries about McElroy or the killing. They understood and deeply resented the fact that Skidmore would always be known as the place where the mob killed the town bully.

Stewart was startled by the extent of the townspeople's dislike for Trena. They seemed to be holding her responsible for everything that had gone on. Stewart found her public performances amusing. Lawyer McFadin was the director, and when a certain question was asked, she seemed to break into tears right on cue. At the various court appearances, beginning with the coroner's jury, McFadin and Trena would drive up in a big car and park on the south side of the courthouse. The reporters standing around would spot Trena and run over to her. McFadin would stop once or twice on his way to the courthouse door, talking to Trena and posing her in different positions for the television cameras.

The various press accounts had Trena giving different versions of events. An early story quoted her as saying that the crowd had gathered on the driver's side, while a later story had her placing the crowd on her side of the truck. One account had her saying that when they got to town, Ken went to the grocery store and bought Rolaids. In one article, she said she didn't know how many shots were fired; in another, she claimed to have heard four shots; and in a third, she said that the first shot had killed him and that he had been hit three or four times.

In a press conference on Friday, July 17, one week after the killing, Trena gave the following account:

"A man in the crowd told me to stay in the truck, that they wanted to shoot me, too. . . . Someone else pulled me out, I went to the ground and begged 'em to stop shooting."

The widow, according to the Associated Press report, said there was an eerie quiet when she and her husband went to Skidmore that morning.

"It seemed so strange," she said at the Kansas City gathering, "there were vehicles lining the street, but no people anywhere. We walked into the tavern and it was empty. Then all of a sudden it just filled with people. They were giving everybody beers, but nobody paid for them."

Over the weekend, the national media attention grew. The *New York Times* started off its piece as follows:

> Kenneth Rex McElroy was the bully of Nodaway County until an angry crowd confronted him last week and someone put a bullet in his brain.
>
> Now only the police and a few editorial writers seem to want to know who killed the man who wanted what few friends he had to call him Ken Rex. Many of the 440 inhabitants of this little farm town in northwest Missouri know who did it, but they are not talking.

The *Times'* article also referred to McElroy as a "part-time farmer who held various jobs between here [Skidmore] and St. Joseph."

The prize for concocting facts for the sake of drama went to a London newspaper for an article published July 18. Describing McElroy as "the swaggering bully of Nodaway County" who "beat up ranchers and punched it out in barroom brawls and rode rough-shod over anyone who stood in his way," the article said that "60 silent, vengeful citizens grouped around him." McElroy "grinned at the crowd," and as he was "climbing into the truck, a single shot rang out. According to the medical report, McElroy was dead before he hit the ground." The article claimed that the town meeting was held a week earlier at the school hall and was attended by Sheriff Russ Johnson and David Owens, who "had only hazy recollections of what transpired." After the shooting, the crowd "faded into the night, ignoring pleas to call an ambulance and leaving the showdown scene to the weeping widow and Deputy Sheriff Russ Johnson."

Meanwhile, time was running out for the NOMIS investigation. The original five-day charter had been extended another five days and would expire on Sunday the nineteenth if not renewed. The investigators met at nine o'clock that morning to review the situation and reach a consensus. They soon realized that there was no reason to continue: No progress had been made and none seemed likely. The case depended on eyewitness testimony, but the people who saw the killing weren't talking. The investigators had tried most of the techniques they knew, including pairing sympathetic and hard-nosed interviewers in good-cop/bad-cop routines, using different cops to interview people at different times, and talking to witnesses at their farms and then bringing them into headquarters. Nothing had worked. As Sergeant Rhoades explained to the press, there had been ninety leads and ninety dead ends. The investigators had nowhere to go. So NOMIS disbanded and turned its files over to Sheriff Estes for any further investigation. At this point, according to Deputy Sheriff Kish, Estes said privately that there would be no further investigation of the killing.

But the FBI had already stepped in. A few days before NOMIS disbanded, the U.S. attorney for the western district of Missouri had received a letter from McFadin on behalf of Trena requesting the FBI to investigate the killing. Federal law made it a crime to conspire to deprive someone of his or her civil rights under color of law, and McFadin's theory was that the sheriff and mayor and perhaps other officials had conspired to kill McElroy, thereby depriving him of his civil rights. The government decided to conduct a limited investigation to determine whether Ken McElroy's civil rights had been violated. Because of "intense media attention," the FBI investigation was to be expedited. The inquiry was initially limited to a review of documents and reports compiled by local officials, but eventually the effort expanded into a full field investigation.

When people in Skidmore read about the FBI's decision to become involved in the case, their reactions ranged from incredulity to indignation. The local cops were one thing, but the FBI? The federal government, which had ignored the community's pleas for help, was coming in to determine whether *McElroy's* civil rights had been violated? Where was its concern for civil rights when McElroy was terrorizing decent, law-abiding citizens? Behind the anger, however, lay fear: The FBI and federal crimes were serious business. Would the community hold together? If anybody talked, there would be a prosecution and a trial, and the cops and the press would be all over Skidmore for months, maybe years, to come.

The tavern had become the focal point for reporters and television crews. They stood outside on the sidewalk seeking interviews from anyone who walked by, and they crowded up to the bar, asking questions of the bartender or whoever was sitting there. The farmers heard French and German and Brooklynese spoken. A few locals forcibly ejected members of one network-television crew from the tavern for persisting in asking questions after being told several times that no one wanted to talk to them.

Lois and Bo were prime targets for anyone armed with a camera or a pad and pencil, and Cheryl began standing guard at the front of the store to protect them from the press. More than once, she physically barred the way to the back of the store, where Lois and Bo now spent most of their time. Once, when a cameraman slipped by her and she caught him talking to Bo at the meat counter, she threatened to break his camera.

45

Prosecutor David Baird, after four months on the job, found himself on the front line. When NOMIS disbanded, he became the spokesman for the investigation, possibly because of the allegation that Estes had conspired to kill McElroy, or possibly because Estes had done a poor job of handling the press for NOMIS in a murder case in St. Joe a few years earlier. In any event, Baird was articulate and low-key. As he dealt with reporters from small- and big-time papers alike, he appeared modest yet confident, issuing statements that revealed nothing but provided enough information for an article. His performance was that of a seasoned politician and was crucial for maintaining an atmosphere of normalcy and order.

When the Hyatt Regency collapsed in Kansas City shortly after the killing, Baird figured that interest in the McElroy case might diminish somewhat. Instead, reporters covering the Hyatt story drove up to Maryville for a quick run at the "vigilante killing of the town bully."

Week after week, pink phone messages from reporters around the world stacked up on Baird's desk, and reporters lined up at his door looking for a quote. To the unending questions, he usually responded, "There have been no arrests, and no arrests are imminent." But his easygoing nature, his obvious sincerity, and his intelligence precluded any thought that the prosecutor was stonewalling the press.

Baird faced an interesting prosecutorial dilemma. As a public official, he was well aware of the public sentiment that McElroy had got nothing more than what he deserved. Having participated in prosecuting McElroy for shooting Bo Bowenkamp and Romaine Henry, Baird knew that the victim was hardly an innocent hog farmer. As a lawyer and prosecutor with an oath to uphold, however, Baird could not let any personal feelings influence his judgment. He had read Trena's statement, and she had clearly, consistently, and without hesitation named Del Clement as the man who had pulled the trigger. Murder indictments had been brought and won on a lot less than one eyewitness. And McFadin was telling the press that Baird could and should indict Del Clement on the basis of Trena's statement. Yet, Baird had to consider the other thirty or forty eyewitnesses, any one of whom could corroborate or contradict Trena's story. If Del Clement went on trial now and was found not guilty, he couldn't be tried again, even if the other witnesses identified him in the future. Should the prosecutor file charges in such a tenuous situation?

Perhaps Baird would not have to make the decision. In a county the size of Nodaway, Missouri law required that a coroner's jury be impaneled whenever a death occurred under suspicious circumstances. The coroner's jury must first determine whether the death occurred in an unlawful manner, and then name, if possible, the person or persons responsible for the death. If the coroner's jury named someone, the law required that the person be arrested immediately and that an indictment be filed. If the jury named no one, the decision would be back in Baird's lap.

The coroner's jury met to consider the death of Ken Rex McElroy at 1 P.M. on Tuesday, July 21, eleven days after the killing. Convinced that the jury would name Del Clement as the killer on the basis of Trena's testimony, Baird had instructed his secretary the day before to prepare an arrest warrant and an indictment bearing Clement's name.

Baird had told the reporters that an arrest would be made immediately if the jury named the killer, and the courtroom was filled with representatives of the wire services and several major dailies, as well as the local news media. An FBI agent was also in attendance.

Deputy Kish testified first, and he described the scene he had observed as he drove into town and found McElroy in the brown and beige Silverado. Kish described the autopsy, and pointed out that the pathologist had said there were two bullet wounds and possibly four. Using photographs, Kish pointed to the wound in the top of the skull as the one that had killed McElroy.

Bartender Red Smith was the next witness. He said he was tending bar when McElroy and his wife came in. Ken ordered a beer, then fifty to sixty people came in, most of whom Red knew. A few minutes later, Ken bought a six-pack, then he and Trena left, followed by twenty-five to thirty people. A few minutes later, Red heard what he thought were firecrackers going off. When he realized that they were bullets, he hit the floor behind the bar. There was a big boom, a pause, and then a string of explosions, one at a time—BANG, BANG, BANG, BANG. When the shooting stopped, he stood up, still shaking, and served beer to several guys standing at the bar. He didn't go outside, nor did he call the law. He figured someone else would.

The next three witnesses demonstrated to the press what the investigators had been up against. Farmer Harold Kenney said that only about forty people came into the bar, and that only twelve people followed Ken and Trena outside. Kenney had followed them out, then headed west up the street without looking at Ken or the pickup. Upon hearing the shots—one big one followed by many little ones, coming from the north (across the street)—Kenney dropped to the ground between the Silverado and another pickup. He didn't look up to see who was shooting. Everyone was running up the street, and he joined them. When he finally glanced toward the Silverado, he saw that the driver's window was shattered and that the engine was steaming. Looking up the street, he noticed Jack Clement up at the door of the bank with McElroy's wife. Kenney saw no guns.

Mayor Steve Peter took the stand and testified, "I left the bar right behind McElroy. I was twelve to fifteen feet from his truck when the shooting began. I saw a side window break out, I guess from a bullet, but I didn't know if it hit him. I dropped to the sidewalk and heard maybe four shots in all." Steve couldn't tell where the shots were coming from, and he didn't see anyone with a gun.

Postmaster Jim Hartman testified he heard the shots and, after the shooting stopped, looked out the window and saw people across the street looking in his direction. The passenger door of the Silverado was hanging open, the glass in the back was shattered, and the engine was steaming and roaring. Hartman said the first shots came from the southeast and the others from west of the post office. He saw no one with a gun.

The final witness was Trena. She spoke in a soft, almost falsetto, voice, breaking down into sobs and wiping tears from her eyes as she went through her story. (Several locals described it as a great performance.) She said that fifty people followed her and Ken out of the tavern, and many of them came over to the passenger side of the Silverado. She saw some movement in the crowd, and then Del Clement emerged from the back of the crowd and walked across the street. She kept her eyes on him as he crossed the street, reached inside a maroon pickup, pulled out a rifle, and walked to the back of the truck on the driver's side. He aimed the gun, and when she turned to tell Ken, the window shattered, and the hole appeared in Ken's neck. She turned back, saw Del still holding the gun to his shoulder, and heard the second shot ring out.

"I seen him shoot my husband. I seen him do it. He hit my husband. I know it was him."

There were six witnesses, and the hearing lasted forty-seven minutes. The jury retired to deliberate and returned in twenty-seven minutes with the verdict: Ken Rex McElroy had died from a felony committed by a "person or persons unknown."

Reached by the *Kansas City Times,* Barbara Clement said that her son Del was serving as master of ceremonies at a rodeo and was not available for comment. She discounted Trena's identification of Del, saying, "That doesn't mean a damn thing. The family isn't worried about her statement, because it simply isn't true." When the *Times* reached Del later, he called Trena "a liar."

Much of the press held Skidmore responsible for the failure of the coroner's jury to name a killer. Editorial writers saw the outcome as proof that the townspeople were a gang of vigilantes. High prose flowed on the inevitable results of such premeditated, lawless behavior. On July 23, the *Columbia Daily Tribune* opined that "Skidmore offers the closest thing to frontier justice that you're likely to see anywhere today." Finding the failure of any of the townspeople to identify the killer as "preposterous," the paper asked if there weren't "somebody in that throng who thinks it is wrong for a citizen to be gunned down in the street," and called Estes a "kept sheriff." Predicting that the "selective justice" would backfire, the paper called for a grand jury to discover those responsible for McElroy's "public execution."

The *Joplin Globe* based its reaction on the assumption that fear, anger, and frustration had provoked someone in the crowd of sixty persons to commit murder:

> It is one thing for an individual to strike out in anger or fear, and quite another for a group of townspeople to conspire to kill someone because they perceive the criminal justice system as ineffective in dealing with him.
>
> Vigilante action is tragic in its brutal violence. It also indicates a breakdown in the system itself. Unfortunately, what is dispensed by such white-sheet, night-rider mentality seldom is justice. Vigilantes who see themselves as judge, jury and executioner have no place in a society governed by laws.

In the face of such condemnation, the community flinched and withdrew even further into bitterness and resentment. A cancer had been cut out of the body, but the wound hadn't been closed properly. Now infection had set in, and nobody could do anything about it.

The national press continued to report that the *town* had taken the law into its own hands. The reporters ignored Prosecutor David Baird's statement that he had no evidence of a conspiracy or a vigilante action.

Producers and writers in faraway places responded to the image. "It seems like an Old West drama," said Peggy Noonan, a CBS producer with Dan Rather's office. "When a local populace takes the law into its own hands, it raises so many questions, like is the town justified?" Jules Loh, a national columnist for the Associated Press, admitted to the *Forum* that the attraction was the "notion of a vigilante act, whether it was or not." Mr. Loh labeled McElroy as "Attila the Hun—the terror of the county."

On Sunday, August 2, the AP story by Jules Loh was carried in newspapers across the country. With its publication, the media machine cranked into high gear. "McElroy Struck Fear into the Residents," cried the *Forum;* "Brute of Nodaway County: Chilling Remembrances," said the *Kansas City Star;* "Skidmore Put End to Bully's Scare Tactics," announced the *Nevada Herald;* "Skidmore Residents Feel New Terror Grip Town After Shooting," headlined the *St. Joseph Gazette*. It was good stuff, and there was an insatiable desire for it.

Loh repeated the fiction that when McElroy was a boy, he had fallen off a hay wagon and had a steel plate implanted in his head. "Some wondered if that was what made him so mean." Loh compared McElroy to Jesse James, "who also met his maker just south of here." Loh claimed that McElroy had been acquitted in the Romaine Henry shooting because the witnesses had had faulty memories. The townspeople, according to Loh, referred to the killing as "the incident."

Surprised by the failure of the coroner's jury to name Del Clement, Baird now had to decide on his next move. In considering whether to file criminal charges, Baird normally reviewed the admissible evidence to determine whether it would be sufficient to establish the guilt of the proposed defendant beyond a reasonable doubt. In this instance, he could easily file the charges on the basis of Trena's testimony and the absence of any contradictory evidence. But one thing gave him serious pause: Twelve jurors from the same pool of people who had heard the same evidence he would introduce at a subsequent trial had decided not to name Del Clement. Moreover, the coroner's jury had to determine only that there was "reason to believe" that a person committed the crime, whereas a trial jury has to find guilt "beyond a reasonable doubt." If Baird couldn't establish "reason to believe" that Del Clement had committed the crime, what were the chances of his establishing it "beyond a reasonable doubt"? The most prudent course, in Baird's judgment, was to present the evidence to a grand jury, and let the jurors decide. A grand jury would have to find "probable cause" to believe that Del Clement had committed the crime, a lesser standard than "beyond a reasonable doubt." If twelve people couldn't find probable cause, then there was no basis on which to file the charge.

A few days earlier, Baird had in fact formally requested that Judge Wilson impanel a state grand jury to hear the matter. He was awaiting the judge's response.

"The McElroys have feelings, too," was the reaction of some residents to the plight of the nine or ten McElroy brothers and sisters and their numerous children and grandchildren who lived in the area. Everyone thought well of Mabel and most had liked old Tony to one degree or another, or had at least tolerated him. Ken's brothers and sisters were farmers, nurses, clerks, or housewives and were considered to be a pretty decent bunch, with one or two exceptions. Few of Ken's siblings stuck up for him while he was alive.

Although the residents in Skidmore wanted the McElroys to know that no one was holding Ken's sins against the whole clan, the people weren't surprised when the family closed ranks.

Within a few days of the killing, the McElroys came one by one into the Skidmore bank and withdrew their money. Most of them simply closed their accounts, saying little if anything, but they insisted on having Sherril Hurner wait on them. Trena had told them that the other two cashiers had mistreated her and tried to take her into the back room, and none of the family wanted to deal with them.

Harold Hoyt, one of Ken's brothers-in-law, who farmed west of Quitman, came into the bank and gave a long, bitter speech, saying that the people of Skidmore were jerks for what they had done to Ken, that Skidmore was a bad place, and that the people there were all rotten. The bank employees said nothing, letting him rage until he finished. Hoyt, who was married to Ken's sister Pauline, also wrote a letter to the *Forum,* published on August 16, in which he described the killing as a cold-blooded murder by someone afraid to face McElroy. He condemned the people of Skidmore for feeling no remorse and complained about the failure of many friends to call or visit or send cards. Hoyt described seeing the hurt in his wife's eyes when a truck backfired three times and someone yelled, "Ken McElroy must be in town." He said somebody in Skidmore was selling T-shirts that said on the front, "Who shot KR?" and on the back, "Who cares?"

Tim was probably the most popular McElroy around. A decent, soft-spoken man, he was renowned for his athletic ability and the way he could follow his dogs through the timber. To many in the town, Tim had always seemed somewhat embarrassed by Ken's activities and had tried to disassociate himself from Ken. A month or so before the shooting, Kermit Goslee told Tim that if things kept up the way they were going, something was likely to happen to Ken. Tim shook his head, saying that he didn't understand why Ken did those things, and that he knew what could happen.

But Tim's feelings changed after the killing. "There's no use telling the inside story," he said to a reporter. "Nobody will believe it. He and I, that's how it was. The other kids were married and gone. He and I looked after each other. I was attached to him."

Tim gave a bitter version of the killing day in the same article. "Someone had told Ken he was going to be shot. That was a couple of weeks before it happened. He had even told his kids, told them to make plans about where they would go to if something happened to him.

"The first thing I knew, the banker called me and said, 'Can you come to town? There's been an accident and Trena needs a ride home.' So I said, 'Sure.' When I drove into town, I saw his truck up on the hill by the bar. When I got closer I saw the windows were shot out and his head was bowed down. He had always told me that if something happened to him in his truck, not to go near the vehicle, so I didn't. I went straight to the bank, where Trena was just crying her eyes out. Nobody stopped to help her. The bank was full of people. And everybody was going about their business like nothing had happened. Now that's cold-hearted, wouldn't you say? Just going about their business, making deposits and withdrawals. If that ain't heartless, what is? There he is, dead."

A published statement by Scott Clement, one of Del's younger brothers, answered Tim: "Want to know why nobody checked and nobody called? It was because everybody was willing to let him stay like that. That was how we felt about him."

Another friend of McElroy received a note in the mail and gave it to the sheriff, claiming that it proved the existence of "some kind of vigilante group." The note read:

This is the only warning you will get. Our bellies are full of your kind. Ken did not pay any attention to leave the county when told to. Get out of this territory while you can. You have been warned. We don't want any thieves or rustlers or trouble-makers.

Rumor had it that McElroy's oldest son, Jerome, was on his way out from California with a bunch of motorcycle buddies to avenge his father's death. Jerome did, in fact, plan to come for the funeral, and he did say a few things about what he was going to do when he got to town. But Tim and one of Jerome's aunts got hold of him and talked him out of coming, saying things would be best if he stayed in California.

Several letters supportive of Ken appeared in the *Forum*. One woman in St. Joe wrote that Ken was a very nice person who had done lots of things for her family and many others. She maintained that the people saying bad things about him were doing it only as a way to get rid of guilty feelings. "Ken McElroy was one of the best men I have known."

Although Alice would later make peace with the killing and, in her mind at least, with the people of Skidmore, now she was antagonistic and belligerent. She wrote a letter to the *St. Joseph Gazette* stating that the real reason McElroy was hassled so much was that the ladies and wives of the big shots in the area liked his looks more than their husbands'. She claimed that the townspeople were determined to kill her and McElroy's children.

But how do I tell [his children] that they can't see their grandma because the same people who murdered their father want to see them dead, too, simply because they are his children?

Ken was simply fighting for his constitutional rights and the rights of his children when he was ruthlessly murdered.

I'll face those people and fight for our God-given rights and constitutional right to go where we want, and if we don't return alive, well, all I can say is that we have made our peace with God and are ready to face His judgment.

Can the people of Skidmore honestly say the same? I think not, because they can't lie to Him.

46

On Monday, July 20, Judge Monty Wilson received Baird's request to impanel a grand jury. Wilson's response enshrined for all time his reputation for vacillation and weakness. First, he said he was considering the request and would make a decision when he returned from a convention that Thursday or Friday. On Friday, after the coroner's jury had announced its decision not to name the killers, Wilson disqualified himself from making the decision to call the grand jury. He had mailed a notice of his disqualification to the Missouri Supreme Court and had requested that they appoint another judge to determine the matter. Wilson gave no reason for his disqualification, but to the community of Skidmore, there was no mystery: Wilson had been terrified of McElroy during his life and was still terrified of him even after he was planted six feet in the ground forty miles away.

On Monday, July 27, the Missouri Supreme Court appointed Circuit Judge Conley from Columbia, Missouri, to hear Baird's request. On Tuesday, Judge Conley granted the request and ordered the impaneling of the grand jury for the following Saturday. The promptness of his action was noted by the *Forum*, which pointed out derisively that "Wilson spent about a week deciding to disqualify himself." But the grand jury would not meet to begin taking evidence until August 11, and then it would consider other matters in addition to the killing. Almost two months would pass before the jury would reach a decision on whether to indict someone for the killing of Ken McElroy.

It was a long two months for the community. The grand jury met in secret, issued subpoenas, and put witnesses under oath, which meant that the witnesses could be prosecuted for perjury. This would be a true test of the strength of the bond of silence; telling the local deputy on your front porch that you dropped to the ground when you heard the shots and never saw anyone with a gun was one thing, but saying it in front of a grand jury after having sworn an oath in God's name was quite another.

Meanwhile, in a statement to the *Forum,* Trena announced that she was offering a $5,000 reward for "anyone supplying information to authorities which leads to the arrest and conviction of the person(s) responsible for the murder of Ken Rex McElroy." The only catch was that Trena didn't have the money. The reward would be paid only from the proceeds of the sale of Trena's movie rights. McFadin explained that several producers had contacted Trena about the purchase of her rights.

In Skidmore the announcement of the reward brought a big chuckle. Although five thousand dollars was a lot of money, there wasn't a farmer in Nodaway County who would put his rear end on the line for money that wasn't even there.

Of slightly more concern to the community was Baird's invitation to the public to submit information to the grand jury and the listing in the *Forum* of a post office box number for that purpose. Baird explained that if the grand jury found probable cause to believe that a specific person had committed the murder, an arrest warrant would be issued immediately by the judge. Baird said that he would submit the lab reports, the autopsy report, the ballistics report, and extensive oral testimony to the grand jury. The unspoken message seemed to be that if one witness backed Trena's story, an indictment would be issued.

The Punkin' Show was held on August 8, 9, and 10, the weekend before the grand jury convened. An extra deputy sheriff and two plainclothesmen were on hand in case of trouble. The reporters from St. Joe and Kansas City came, but not to cover the beauty contests or the talent show or the tractor pull or the parade; they wanted to talk about the killing and find out how people were feeling about it. Some residents were so annoyed that they told a couple of reporters to get out of town.

Festival played two nights in a row at the Punkin' Show. For years, the band had played at the show for free, and band members had worked on committees and helped design the sound system for the stage. But the band had been losing too much money recently, and members decided they would have to start charging for the concerts in the future. This didn't sit well with a few townspeople, who were already disgruntled that someone had passed a hat to help the band buy a piece of land. Band members noticed bad vibrations—trucks sometimes passed too close to them as they walked in the road, their waves were not always returned, and a few people made nasty comments about them.

After the shooting, Festival members felt their relations with the town grow particularly cool. The townspeople seemed negative and defensive. On stage at the Punkin' Show, Britt Small tried to break the ice with humor, describing Skidmore as a "small town of 440 people, well actually only 439 now."

No one laughed.

"People, we don't have to crumble in the face of the media," he said, hoping to rally the audience. "We can hang together; we can stand tall. There's no reason why we have to let this get the best of us."

He got no response.

The grand jury met for the first time on August 11 but did not turn to the killing until Thursday, August 20. The press kept the story alive because McElroy's death was the only news other than hog prices, predictions for the fall harvest and garden club meetings. After every headline—"Jury Work Begins," "Grand Jury Slated to Meet Again Thursday," "Grand Jury Reconvenes; McElroy Probe Started"—two sentences would be devoted to a new fact or two, followed by two columns rehashing the entire sequence of events. The articles continued to describe the crowd as surrounding the truck.

The grand jury subpoenas went out, and the recipients were eager to know who else was on the list. Those who had been outside the tavern at the time of the killing, but claimed not to have seen anything, were particularly nervous. They talked some about what was going to happen, but the discussions were generally superficial.

The first day, eight residents testified. Trena testified on Friday. She arrived with Alice Wood, Juarez, and McFadin, who was in a three-piece suit, briefcase in hand, to face a throng of reporters and cameras on the courthouse steps. Never far from Trena's side, McFadin was photographed and quoted extensively. Lest there be any doubt, he said that he "hadn't accepted a dime" from Trena and didn't intend to.

At a press conference after her testimony, Trena stated that she didn't think anyone would talk, for fear of being killed. "I think if anyone would come forward with any information they would have to get out of town or be in constant danger. I think the whole town would do as they did to my husband."

Trena's claims of grand jury bias got a slight boost when a newspaper revealed that one of the jurors was married to Del Clement's wife's great-uncle.

In August and September, Skidmore continued to draw attention from the national media. Staff from "60 Minutes" showed up to begin researching their story, and a free-lance writer doing the *Playboy* article came to town. He wrote a melodramatic piece entitled "High Noon in Skidmore," which angered the community by stating that the townspeople had hunted McElroy down like a coon and by portraying the town as a hick backwash.

People magazine published its article on September 14. It began: "Anyone looking for Ken Rex McElroy could usually find him at the D & G Tavern in Skidmore." McFadin gave his usual quotes about the immorality of the people taking the law into their own hands, but this time he proclaimed, "The whole county is guilty."

Newsday published its piece, entitled "A Town Bully Meets His Match," which described his vehicle (the shiny Silverado) as a "battered pickup" and McElroy as a "hulking 230-pound farmer." The article said that several "stony faced citizens surrounded him in the bar" and "stared him down in a wordless sidewalk confrontation." *Newsday* described the town as a "close knit, hardworking group of farmers" who, among other things, "appreciate good beer."

47

The first two weeks of September were hot, a scorching continuation of August. The growing season for corn was coming to an end, and the green stalks and leaves were gradually turning yellow, from the bottoms up and the tips in. The cobs, encircled with rows of plump kernels, peeked out of their husks, and began to point out and gradually downward, as the moisture left the plant and the stalk withered. In a few weeks, the leaves and stalks would shade from yellow to burnt orange, then to a rusty brown.

The bean plants expired more subtly. About a foot and a half tall, and covered with dark green leaves, the plants spread across the fields, hiding the soil beneath a solid green carpet. The carpet faded unevenly, and the fields became a huge impressionistic canvas: deep emerald fading into lighter, more delicate green shades, and small splotches of bright yellow emerging beside the palest hues.

Judge Donelson had not yet finished with the community of Skidmore. Reporters had been hounding Baird for information on the Bowenkamp trial, and he had referred them, logically, to the official court records in Bethany. Judge Donelson, upset by the reporters (the one from *Playboy* in particular) crawling all over his domain, and perhaps concerned about what they might find, decided to close the files to the public.

Under Missouri law, criminal files were closed in cases where the defendant was arrested but not charged, or where the defendant was charged but the case was later dismissed, or where the defendant was found not guilty. The rationale for the law was that the legal system should not maintain records of alleged misconduct of which a defendant was not convicted.

In this case, of course, McElroy had been charged, tried, and found guilty of a crime. But Donelson, relying on the technical status of the case, devised a way to twist the statute so that he could close the files. Because the motion for a new trial had not yet been filed or heard, and because no judgment had been entered by the court, McElroy technically had not yet been convicted. Since the case was thus still alive, it could be dismissed, and if it was dismissed, Donelson could argue that the records were sealed by statute. His only problem was that under Missouri law, the judge couldn't dismiss the case. But, at least arguably, the prosecutor could. Donelson telephoned David Baird and said that he wanted Baird to dismiss the case. Baird clearly understood that Donelson was seeking the dismissal in order to close the files. Although Baird was skeptical of his legal authority to dismiss a case after a jury verdict had been rendered, he bowed to the judge and filed a motion with the court reciting the facts of McElroy's death and dismissing the case. Now, when someone sought the files, Donelson could point to Baird's dismissal and say the law declared the files to be closed. Even if Donelson's action perverted the intent of the statute, a journalist's only recourse would be to file a lawsuit—in Donelson's court—to open the files. When that suit failed, the journalist could appeal the decision to the state supreme court.

Over the radio, almost incidentally, the townspeople learned that the case had been dismissed and the records closed. They were not particularly upset about the records, but to learn that the case against McElroy had been thrown out was galling. The judge had denied them their only victory against Ken McElroy; now in the eyes of the law, McElroy was not guilty of second-degree assault for shooting Bo Bowenkamp.

A vote of eight of the twelve members of the grand jury was required for an indictment to issue. Such a result was never very likely. The jurors knew all about Ken McElroy, and, in their view, if anybody was responsible for his being killed, the law was. Although Trena had identified Del Clement as the killer, no one else had backed her up, and she was as bad as Ken had been. Nobody was going to stand trial solely on the basis of what *she* said. Even if someone else had corroborated Trena's identification, if someone had cracked under pressure, an indictment would have been hard to come by. The man had got what he deserved.

On September 25, the final day of the grand jury session, Baird called a press conference to announce that the grand jury would issue no indictments in the McElroy case. He distributed a news release explaining that the grand jury had heard forty-five witnesses in more than eight days of testimony and had not found probable cause to return an indictment. Somewhat defensively, he stated that he had withheld no evidence from the grand jury.

Baird's announcement brought the press running back to town. The longer nobody was charged in the killing, the more newsworthy the story became. McFadin took the lead for the family, saying that Mrs. McElroy was "disappointed," but then she never expected the grand jury to indict anyone. Not only should Trena's identification of Del Clement have been adequate for an indictment, he said, but he had also turned over to authorities the names of other people who claimed to have seen the shooting.

Baird defended the grand jury, saying that they had worked hard and could consider only the evidence that was presented to them. And in a statement that endeared him to the community, he criticized the press, saying, "I think the major misconception has been the idea that it was some sort of vigilante killing—a killing by a town, so to speak. The point of view many papers have taken from the very beginning is the vigilante-type killing. That is one area where we've disagreed. The idea that it was a vigilante killing makes a nice story, but I simply feel there is no evidence to confirm that."

The grand jury action not only let Baird and the killers off the hook, at least temporarily, but the failure to indict also marked Skidmore as the town that killed the town bully. Editorial writers condemned the jury's action as a continuation of the conspiracy of silence—as if the entire town had gone into the jury room and denied seeing anything and was, therefore, guilty of a vigilante action. Headlines that followed referred to "vigilante justice" and to the "public execution" that had occurred in Skidmore.

The *St. Joseph Gazette* led off with a statement that it "didn't seem possible" that a grand jury could investigate the killing for two months and not indict anyone. The paper compared the shooting of Ken McElroy to the burning of Ray Gunn in 1931, and opined that "Missouri must not get the reputation of a state where murder is tolerated."

A Kansas City paper compared the killing with the assassination of Anwar Sadat and called it a "planned execution" that threatened the "destruction of the system of government we have fought for 200 years to maintain." Saying that "the bullet that killed McElroy was a direct hit at the basis of democracy," the paper called on someone in Skidmore to step forward and point the finger.

For the people of Skidmore, the most devastating editorial appeared on September 28 in the *Maryville Forum*. Attacking the *St. Joseph Gazette* because it criticized the grand jury for failing to do its job, the *Forum* said that the real problem was not the grand jury, which could act only on the evidence before it, but the townspeople who saw the killing and lied in front of the grand jury. After praising Baird for handling the matter so well, the editorial concluded, "For now any condemnation of the grand jury should be edged out by a chilling fear: citizens who take the law into their own hands are to be dreaded much more than the McElroys of the world."

No harsher judgment could possibly have been delivered: The town was worse than Ken McElroy. What they had done to him was worse than what he had done to them.

The community's only solace was that at least now, the crazy circus was surely over. There would be no more strange cars prowling the town, no more television cameras in the tavern, and no more cops out in the fields serving subpoenas. The grand jury didn't indict anyone, so the story was finished, and the people could get back to farming and living their private lives. Perhaps the healing could begin.

Not long afterward, in a Kansas City shoe store, Q Goslee was talking with a salesman from Lawrence.

"Skidmore?" said the salesman, scratching his head. "Isn't that where you shoot 'em out in the street?"

Later, on a vacation to the West Coast, Q registered at a motel in a tiny town in Oregon.

"Say," said the clerk, "isn't that where you killed the bully?"

"Yeah, that's where it happened."

"From what I read he sure had it coming. He must have been a helluva ornery guy."

Q said nothing.

"Why did he carry on so long without the courts or the law taking care of him?"

"A lot of us wondered the same thing."

When Kenny Weston, an alderman, wore his Punkin' Show hat to a fair in Shenandoah, Iowa, a man approached him, saying, "You're from Skidmore, huh? Isn't that where you guys shot the bully? By God, from what I read, he sure had it coming."

The approval of their countrymen only made matters worse. Most people in Skidmore didn't enjoy being looked on as vigilantes, whether the man deserved to be killed or not.

48

By the first week of October, the fields of corn were russet armies of stiff, dried stalks. The once upright cobs now hung almost straight down, their golden silks a dirty brown, their brittle leaves rasping and rattling in the autumn winds.

The bean fields were now spectacular arrays of bright yellows and oranges. The greens had vanished, and the early patches of orange had faded to rust. Soon the leaves would begin to fall. In the timber bordering the fields, the trees and bushes shimmered red and gold and orange.

The evenings were cool, and a heavy fog sometimes crept in on the south wind. The vaporous mist draped the fields and collected in the troughs between the steep hills, making the roads dangerously slick.

For days, the mornings dawned gray and gloomy, the steady drizzle punctuated by bursts of rain. The fields stood wet and empty, abandoned to the clinging moisture.

Finally, the sun broke through, and its light illuminated the autumn leaves, many now in full color and beginning to fall. The hedge was still green, but the hackberry leaves radiated a light yellow, and the wild cherry was mixed with flaming reds and golds. Q sat on his porch and looked up at the translucent leaves on the tall linden tree, trying to predict which leaf would fall next.

Squirrels scampered down the trees and across the lawn, going about their business of burying walnuts for the winter. Q didn't believe, as some people did, that the squirrels would remember where they buried each walnut. He had seen the animals sniffing uncertainly across January snow, and he had seen the nuts they had missed, or forgotten, shoot up as saplings in the spring.

Down the Valley Road, in the middle of the second curve, the two-story house stood empty and quiet. The windows were nailed shut, the yapping dogs and their cages were gone, and the weeds were beginning to grow in the drive where the pickups once stood. A hundred yards away, in the small house, eighty-four-year-old Mabel McElroy still lived with her youngest son, Tim. The once-sturdy body which had borne and raised fourteen kids and toiled in the harvest fields had grown frail and weak. Mabel had come home from the hospital a few days after Ken's death, but her diabetes was worsening, and her respiratory system was failing. She spent most of her days sitting in a chair hooked up to an oxygen machine, with vials of medicine on the table next to her. Tim had told her that Ken had been shot and killed, but he spared her the details of how and why. She seemed to accept the news without wanting to know more. On some days, her mind slipped, and she would sit by the window looking for him.

"Where's Ken?" she would ask. "He hasn't been to see me in several days." Turning away from the window, she would say, "He should be home soon."

The morning after the first day of sunshine, a few combines clambered into the fields and began stripping the stalks of their fat cobs. The debate in the cafe that morning was fierce, one side arguing that it was time to get going and get 'er done, and the other side insisting that the corn wasn't dried down enough to avoid penalties at the elevator. If the moisture was above 16 percent, the farmer would be docked so many cents per bushel. Around midday, a few big stock trucks hauled the corn to the elevator in Maitland, and the chits given to the drivers indicated penalties. The combines shut down.

After two days of sun, when the air was dry and crisp and the corn was an even yellowish brown, the combines fired up again. Like ravenous creatures, the cumbersome machines lurched noisily into the fields. The glass cabs sat atop the tall wheels like huge eyes, staring out over the long, tapered metal spokes, as they guided the corn stalks into the grinding teeth. Up and down the rows the combines roamed, awkwardly but steadily, until finally they stopped beside a truck, and a long metal tube swung out and disgorged the corn in huge yellow heaps.

In the morning, the blacktops and gravel roads were crowded with the metal creatures moving to new fields of forage. Their shiny-spiked heads were a foot or two wider than a single lane and would rip open an oncoming car at the level of the headlights. Trucks ahead and behind the creatures signaled with flashing lights, warning other vehicles to slow down and move over.

The October push to get the crops out of the ground was as powerful as the April push to get the seed in. Seven days a week, as soon as the dew had evaporated, Kirby Goslee started the red behemoth rolling down the rows, and ran it on into the night until the moisture made the stalks too rubbery to snap. A happy man, he worked to the point of exhaustion, interrupted only by the arrival of the pickup from home with coffee and sandwiches.

In town, the streets were clogged with stock trucks and huge semis hauling grain to St. Joe. Weary men covered with dust and grease piled into the cafe for lunch. Conversation centered on bushels per acre and dollars per bushel—how much would actually end up in their pockets?

There was little talk of Ken McElroy or the shooting. He was dead and buried, the way he should be, and there was really nothing more to say.

At the little house on Valley Road, Ken's mother was troubled. During a visit from Alice Wood, Mabel began talking about Ken's soul. She knew Ken had sinned in his lifetime, and she also knew that he had never been able to admit that he had done anything wrong. If he couldn't admit to God that he had sinned, he wouldn't be able to ask for forgiveness, and if he couldn't ask for forgiveness, he would surely spend eternity in hell. Mabel grabbed Alice's hand and pleaded, "Surely Ken will be able to ask for forgiveness in the end, won't he?"

Skidmore held its fall smorgasbord to raise money for the next year's Punkin' Show. Sunday dinner was held in the basement cafeteria of the schoolhouse, and long tables, set end to end, were covered with the dishes women cooked and brought for the feast:

vegetable casseroles, broccoli, noodles, beans and bacon, Jell-O salads, mashed potatoes, fresh breads and muffins, and enormous platters of chicken and ham. At the end of the tables sat banana, raisin cream, apple, pumpkin, peach, and cherry pies, and at least four varieties of cheesecake. Pumpkins lined up around the room were judged for the biggest, smallest, oddest, and best dressed.

Q and Kirby stood quietly on the porch of the Goslee farmhouse, their hands in their pockets, their shoulders slightly hunched, and looked east over the fields of corn and beans. They had been working on the combine in the yard—Kirby using a wrench on one of the big gears and Q observing and making suggestions—when the sky opened suddenly, and sheets of rain drove them to shelter. Of the four boys, Kirby was the most like his father—stubborn, generous, funny, and insatiably curious about human nature. As they stood on the porch, he seemed even more his father's son. Both men were tall, with broad shoulders, thick arms, and pale blue eyes. The pot bellies protruding from their large frames were nearly the same size. Neither had much of a rear end, and their pants hung low in the back.

The sky overhead and to the east was swollen a heavy bluish black. Behind the house, to the west, the autumn sun broke through the clouds, and clusters of light rays slanted almost horizontally across the fields, burnishing the landscape a pale gold. The chill fall wind whipped the rain about and under the eaves of the porch, and at the same moment, in the same motion, both men zipped up their red jackets. After a few minutes, the rain slowed, and a bright, opalescent rainbow appeared in the eastern sky, one end off in the fields and the other just behind Q's equipment shed. Q waited for his son to comment. "I've never been at the end of a rainbow before," Kirby said finally. "The pot must be just beyond the shed."

Under the arch of the first rainbow, a second one appeared, further east, smaller and fainter, but fully arrayed in brilliant hues. Q pointed up to the eastern sky, over the horizon. "Geese," he said, "heading south for the winter." Thousands of Canada geese were rising from the fields in a dramatic flurry. The upward spiral of birds gradually swung southward, forming a graceful arc that undulated in the middle as it continued to rise. The scattered spears of light from the west picked out the birds, and the black sky sparkled with tiny flashes of silvery turquoise. As the tail of the crescent rose from the fields, the head leveled out and made a final southward adjustment, disappearing into the darkness between the arches of the two rainbows.

"It's quite a sight," Kirby said softly. The rain had stopped completely, and the air was sharp.

Q nodded, then mumbled, "Well, I guess we can get back to work." The two men descended the steps and ambled easily out to the combine, their gaits identical except for a little hobble in the older man's step.

In November, Mabel's frail body finally gave out, and she was laid to rest. Sons, daughters, grandsons, granddaughters, nephews, and nieces came from all around for her funeral. Because the family had been offended by a remark the owner of the Price Funeral Home had made in the *Kansas City Times* about Ken's death, the service for Mabel was held in another funeral parlor in Maryville. Juarez, who had been staying at the small house helping to care for Mabel, had not yet recovered from seeing his father's puffy, yellowed face, and could not bring himself to attend his grandmother's funeral. *It's too bad,* thought Alice. *The pain is gone from her face, and she looks like she's finally at peace.*

Harvest was over by mid-December. The ground began to freeze, the snow began to fall, and the light faded by five in the afternoon. The grain had been either sold or stored, and the machinery put away in the sheds. The emotional letdown was severe —the intensity of twelve- to sixteen-hour days had dissipated. The farmer might sleep a little later and take a nap after dinner, but it was hard to relax. For a few weeks, he would ask himself if farming was worth all the trouble, if it really made any sense to work so hard for so little.

49

As the weeks and months passed, Ken McElroy continued to hold sway over the community of Skidmore. If a stranger brought up the subject, even innocuously, a resident was likely to snap, "McElroy's dead, and that's the way it should be. Let's leave him buried." However much the community hoped that the memories and the feelings would fade with time, the events of 1981 merely sank deeper into the collective psyche, only to come flooding to the surface at the slightest provocation.

Eventually, the subject of McElroy became all but taboo among the townspeople themselves. In the cafe, in the tavern, in the fertilizer store, no one talked about what had happened that July morning—not even about the safe parts. Perhaps talking about the nightmare had helped to keep it alive; perhaps if people turned their attention away from the killing, it would lose its power over their lives. Besides, no one knew who was going to be called to testify under oath as to what he had seen or heard. The murder charge was hanging over the community, the killers were in their midst, and nobody could tell what the next twist in the road might bring. The easiest thing to do was to hear nothing, to say nothing, and to go about your business of farming or pumping gas or serving beer.

In a sense, the town was cheated of its moment of relief after the long struggle. The people needed a chance to run up and down the main street jumping and shooting firecrackers and yelling that McElroy was gone, that the good guys had finally won. Celebrating might also have helped purge the anxiety over the fact that McElroy had been one of them. Denied even the briefest moment of euphoria, the community was denied that cathartic effect.

As it was, the bonds of silence, never articulated, never sworn to, drew even tighter in response to the grand juries, the subpoenas, and the press. Regardless of the price to be paid, the community would not give up the guilty.

A Maryville businessman who had grown up, gone to school, drank beer, and chased women with several of the men who had been on the street when McElroy was shot spent five or six hours drinking with them at a Maryville bar a month after the shooting. When he casually asked what the hell had really happened that day, they looked at him as if he were from the FBI and said, "We don't know anything." The harder he pushed, the stonier they got.

Although Ken McElroy was indeed gone, he could not be forgotten. Like a large stone falling into still water, his life and death kept rippling out and touching everyone and everything, seeming to lose no force along the way.

One immediate effect of McElroy's death was a steep decline in the number of hog and cattle thefts in Nodaway County. According to the records of the county extension agent, such thefts began decreasing in August 1981, the month after McElroy's death. Of course, some of the decrease may well have been due to the jailing of his friend Larry.

On December 15, 1981, Larry went on trial on charges stemming from the night he had driven a trailer full of hogs home on a rimless wheel. Without McElroy's largess, Larry could not afford to hire a private attorney, and his public defender apparently did not mount a spirited defense. The primary witnesses against him were the rat who had set him up and the cops who had found the trailer and the pigs. Larry had four prior convictions—three assaults and one rape, which had been reduced to contributing to the delinquency of a minor. At the time of the trial, he also had two pending charges for second-degree assault and brandishing a weapon in a rude and angry manner on July 10, 1981. For the hog theft, Larry was sentenced to six years in prison. On December 29, two weeks after his trial, he went to jail. He eventually pleaded guilty to the weapons charge and received an additional sixty-day sentence.

* * *

Festival, which had recently settled into its new farm near Skidmore, was touring the West and Midwest after the release of a tape entitled "Just Another Band from Skidmore." As part of their performance, the band had always done a humorous routine about Skidmore, the tiny, out-of-the-way town in Missouri, but now members of the audience began interrupting the routine, yelling, "Who shot McElroy?" It happened everywhere—at state fairs, conventions, and night clubs; in Fargo, Indianapolis, and even Las Vegas. At first, the band made a joke out of it. Each member would raise a hand, smile broadly, and yell out, "I did!" After a while, they dropped the routine because the audiences wouldn't let go of it. Finally, the band members stopped mentioning Skidmore altogether.

The FBI's initial investigation was very limited; the agents reviewed the evidence collected by the local authorities and waited to see how the state grand jury turned out. In March 1982, when it was clear that nothing further was going to be done on the local level, the FBI launched a major investigation. In April, they sent a team of ten agents into the field under the supervision of an attorney from the Justice Department in Washington, D.C. The agents interviewed more than a hundred witnesses—questioning many of them several times—and issued sixty subpoenas to appear in front of the federal grand jury in Kansas City.

The townspeople knew that the FBI was involved in the case, but the federal invasion of the community caught most people by surprise. Although the agents' sudden appearance made everyone nervous, it sparked a lot of laughter, as well: The federal cops from the big city came dressed as farmers, wearing overalls, scuffed-up boots, seed-dealer hats, and wrinkled work shirts. With their soft hands and pale complexions, they were the funniest-looking farmers to float in and out of Mom's Cafe in quite a while.

A young bachelor farmer had just gotten out of bed at 5:30 one morning when he saw a light green four-door Ford LTD pull into his driveway. He knew right away who the men inside were. One of the passengers, about 6 feet 3 inches and muscular, wore a straw hat, a work shirt, and jeans; the other one wore bib overalls and a cap. They were much too clean looking to be farmers. When they flashed their badges and said, "FBI," the farmer invited them in.

They sat at the breakfast table and began to chat amiably, asking how the farming was going, what the women around Maryville were like, whether there was any action, and so on. Then they shifted to the murder.

"Somebody told us you know who shot him," said the tall agent. "That you been running around shooting your mouth off about who did it."

"I wasn't even in town that morning," said the farmer. "I was here loading oats. I didn't see a thing."

"We know that, but we think you know who did it."

When the farmer continued to profess his ignorance, the agents switched the conversation back to women and places to go and the spring weather for a while. Then the tall agent stood up, leaned over, pounded the table, and stuck his finger in the farmer's face, saying, "We know you know who did it. Tell us or you'll never get us out of here!"

As the farmer repeated his denials, the pattern—pleasantries followed by accusations—continued. Because the farmer was known to be good friends with one of the primary suspects, the agents were convinced he was lying to protect the killers. One agent rattled off the names of the three suspects and said, "We know you know it was them."

"I don't know anything," said the farmer, "and I don't want to know anything."

"What?" said the agent. "In a small town this size, you expect us to believe nobody told you who did it?"

"Right," said the farmer. "That's how you can get in lots of trouble—if you know."

Finally, in order to give them something, the farmer told the agents about two cars that had sped down the gravel road by his farm on the morning in question. "I knew something was up that morning because around 10:30 a couple of cars came tearing down the gravel road about ninety miles per hour."

The agents demanded to know who was in the cars, but the farmer said that he didn't know, that he hadn't seen. He didn't tell the agents that one of the cars had stopped at his drive.

"They just shot McElroy!" the driver had said, after pulling to a halt in a cloud of dust.

"What?"

"Yeah, they shot McElroy." The man had been pale and shaking. "We're in trouble now; we don't know what's going to happen."

The agents finally left at about 9:30, after additional accusations and finger-wagging failed to produce results.

About two weeks later, when the farmer was on his tractor disking the fields, he saw the green Ford pull up by the fence. He motioned the agents to the gate, drove the tractor over, and turned it off. This time, they were interested in only one thing—who was in the cars speeding down the road.

"I don't know," the farmer said. "I really don't remember."

The agents stayed nearly two hours and kept pumping him. Toward the end, they threatened to put handcuffs on him right there in the field and take him to Maryville.

"We just want to know who was in the cars."

Finally, he gave them the name of a neighbor who had been in one of the cars, and they left. But not before handing him a piece of paper that summoned him to appear before a federal grand jury in Kansas City the following week.

Trena, her three children, and Sharon's girls had moved down to Faucett to stay with Alice. Everyone seemed to need each other, and both women thought the kids would benefit from being together.

After the funeral, Alice took charge of cleaning out the house, collecting the papers, and dealing with the Silverado. A week or so after the killing, as she was driving up to the farm to deliver some papers to Tim, a pickup with three men inside had pulled over in front of her, forcing her to the edge of the road.

One of the men got out and came over to her, saying, "Don't you think it's a little dangerous to be driving around here in a McElroy truck?"

Alice picked up her shotgun from the passenger seat, pointed it out the window, and asked, "Don't you think it's a little dangerous to be threatening someone with a gun in their hands?"

"I just wanted to warn you," he said, stepping back a pace or two.

"I'll take care of myself," she said. "Don't you worry. And I'll do what I want to do and go where I want to go. If you or anybody else tries to stop me, you'll have to shoot me."

Alice would mellow as time passed, but at the moment she had more problems than she could handle. The kids were having difficulty adjusting to their father's death, and the reporters were hounding her constantly. She tried to explain how Ken really was —that he had a good side, too—but she stopped when she realized they didn't want to hear anything positive about him.

Her frustration peaked when photographers and reporters from *People* magazine came and spent the entire day at the house. While Alice was talking in the living room, the photographers were taking pictures of the two boys in their bedroom where a shotgun that Ken had given to Juarez hung on the wall. One of the photographers took the gun down, handed it to Juarez, and shot pictures of him aiming it in the air. Then they persuaded Alice and the kids to go to the cemetery, so the kids could be photographed next to their father's grave. Alice finally called a halt to the interview when the photographer suggested taking flowers from an adjoining grave and putting them on Ken's grave for the picture.

After the *People* interview, Alice stopped talking to reporters. She would go downtown for the day or hide out at a neighbor's house.

Not long after the shooting, after Alice's name and address had been in the paper, her three children were in the yard playing when two men in a Jeep drove by and fired a rifle twice in the direction of the house. Juarez ran inside and got a rifle and shot back, but the Jeep was down the road by then. Although Alice called the police, no action was taken.

Shortly thereafter, the landlady told Alice she and her children would have to leave. With a real estate agent, they looked and found another house in Faucett and talked about renovating it. Two days later, the agent called and explained that Alice couldn't have the house because some of the neighbors in the area didn't want her and her kids around.

Juarez and Tammy were angry and bitter about their father's killing, and they didn't seem to be getting better. Against the advice of his mother and the coach, Juarez had gone ahead and pitched the baseball game his dad had planned to attend; his team lost. Alice explained to him that whoever shot Ken would pay for it throughout eternity, but Juarez didn't want to wait for eternity. Alice continued to see strains in him that reminded her of Ken— the way he withdrew in the face of pain, his anger ready to spill out —and she felt frightened for him. Ken, Jr., did not try to hide his pain. Others wouldn't let him forget who he was: The mother of one of his friends called Alice one day and said that upon learning that Ken, Jr., was a McElroy, her husband had insisted that the two kids not play together. Bluntly, the woman explained that little Ken was not to have anything to do with her son. The St. Joe cops had also picked up both Ken, Jr., and Juarez and hassled them on what Alice felt were bogus charges.

Tonia, after the shock had worn off, seemed to be adjusting better than her brothers, perhaps because she had friends and was active in church.

Sensing that the kids would *never* get away from the McElroy name in St. Joe, Alice began thinking seriously of moving.

After a few weeks with Alice, Trena moved to a small town in the Ozarks only a couple of miles from where her parents had moved when they fled Ken McElroy some eight years earlier. Initially, Sharon's three daughters lived with Trena and her children. After a few weeks, Tammy went back to the farm to help Tim care for Mabel, then Debbie went to live with Sharon in a small town not far from St. Joe. Finally, Tina went to visit Debbie and Sharon for Christmas and didn't come back.

Trena still lived with the vague fear that something bad was yet to come, that the violence wasn't over. She focused on her children, trying to settle them into a new life in the small community. When other kids on the school bus made cracks about their father, Trena put a stop to it with phone calls to their mothers.

In the beginning, Reno, the youngest, would ask every day or so, "Where's Daddy?" And Trena would tell him, "Daddy's in heaven, baby."

She enrolled in training to become a nurse's aide and waited for time to make things better.

Vicki thought about Trena a lot and wondered how she was doing. She sent Trena a birthday card on her twenty-fifth birthday, January 27, 1982, in care of lawyer McFadin's office in Kansas City. The card came back marked "address unknown." *McFadin's got her isolated,* Vicki thought. *There's not much more I can do.* (In fact, McFadin, along with everybody else, had lost track of Trena for a while.) Later, Vicki saw Trena's grandmother and asked about her. *Well,* Vicki thought afterward, *Trena knows where to find me if she wants to.*

"60 Minutes" aired its show on January 24, 1982. As in many things surrounding the killing, the town's reaction was ambivalent. Skidmore came off fairly well, although Morley Safer described it as "a town that had never seen better days." While saying that McElroy was a bad character and that the townspeople probably had no choice, the program pondered the complex ethical questions involved in taking a life outside the law. Dunbar's interview was chopped up in a way that made him appear to be a chicken. The highlight of the program was a scene showing Lois and Bo Bowenkamp, Tim Warren, and Romaine Henry sitting at a dining room table. (Steve Peter declined to be interviewed.) Lois, in her deliberate biting style, proclaimed that everyone in town was resting better now that McElroy was gone. Safer asked them in turn if they would identify the killer if they knew who he was; each one said no. In a high-pitched voice, the rotund Reverend Warren quoted the Old Testament, saying, "Whosoever sheddeth man's blood, by man shall his blood be shed."

The program made the town's agony a national topic. Skidmore was portrayed as something of a victim-hero—a victim for its long suffering, and a hero for finally blowing the bastard away. (There were always those who would ask, "What took them so long?") The community didn't want to be a hero any more than it wanted to be a victim—such a label assumed that it was a vigilante act, that the *town* deliberately decided to take the man's life, and that wasn't true. Protecting the killer afterward was one thing—what would giving him up solve? But accepting responsibility for the killing—as if the community had agreed to it beforehand—was another.

In the wake of the "60 Minutes" show, Mayor Steve Peter received stacks of letters from viewers offering support to the people of Skidmore.

Dear Sir:

I want to tell you how much I respect your town for what they did to protect their citizens from the "bully."

I wish some of the people who live there could come to Little Rock and help us with our "system."

I know it's *all* tragic, but I think you all are really what America is made of.

Thank you.

Dear Sir:

You and the citizens of Skidmore hang in there! The overwhelming majority of the people of America are behind you in the belief that the citizens of Skidmore have a right to safety and peace from the bastard who terrorized them for far too long.

Now the crooked lawyers, stupid, weak judges and his ignorant, trashy wife want to bleat about his rights: where were they when that filthy SOB was violating the rights of innocent people?

Sincerely,

Several letter writers offered to come to Skidmore and serve as the town sheriff; one even enclosed a picture of himself, stripped to the waist and holding an automatic rifle. Mayor Peter didn't answer any of the letters, the majority of which were from Florida and southern California.

50

As the federal subpoenas papered the Missouri countryside that spring, the old anxieties returned. This time, however, the farmers would be in Kansas City, in the federal courthouse, on the turf of the people who were trying to get to the bottom of the killing. And this time the recipients of the documents discussed a coordinated strategy. Someone suggested that they take the Fifth Amendment —simply refuse to answer any question on the grounds of self-incrimination. There would be no talking to the media, whose behavior the men could not predict.

The farmer who had been threatened with arrest in the fields spoke fervently to the Justice Department attorney, trying to persuade her to release him from the subpoena. "What the hell do I know?" he said. "I wasn't even in town that morning! I'm a farmer. I've got work to do." But she insisted that he honor the subpoena. To avoid driving to Kansas City, the farmer rode with friends. He spent the day waiting with the other witnesses in a small room. He was the last to be called, later in the afternoon. When he walked into the hearing room and saw twenty-three people sitting in four tiers, all higher than his head, he felt dizzy. He couldn't look in one direction and see them all. No one said a thing, they just sat and stared down at him. For a second, he thought he might pass out. He focused on the stenographer, a good looker who took down every move he made—he'd raise his hand to his mouth and cough, and she'd tap away on her little machine. When the questioning began, he nervously took the Fifth as they had agreed. He was scared as hell, but the prosecutor let him go after the fourth or fifth question. When he went outside, he discovered that he had been the only one who had refused to answer questions; the others had decided that taking the Fifth would make them look as if they had something to hide, which had been his reaction when he had first heard the suggestion!

Neither the FBI nor the grand jury developed evidence to support the theory that either Sheriff Estes or Mayor Peter had conspired to murder McElroy, but the investigation turned up three eyewitnesses to the killing—enough, in the government's view, to warrant an indictment of the actual killer or killers under state law. On September 2, 1982, United States Attorney Robert Ulrich held a press conference to announce that there was insufficient evidence to conclude that McElroy's civil rights had been violated under color of law, but that "substantial new evidence" would be forwarded to the county prosecutor for his consideration in filing murder charges. The federal attorneys were certain that they had put together a solid murder case for Baird.

In developing the case, however, the government lawyers had granted immunity from prosecution to two of the three witnesses. When one changed his story before the grand jury, the lawyers considered bringing perjury charges. They were also eager to file obstruction-of-justice charges against a woman for allegedly tampering with witnesses before the grand jury. (None of these charges was brought.)

A few weeks before the press conference, Ulrich had asked for a meeting with Baird. In the presence of an FBI agent and a representative of the state attorney general's office, Ulrich explained that there was no evidence of a conspiracy under the federal statutes, but that he had two eyewitnesses (one had recanted) who had identified the shooter and provided details of the entire crime. He could not release the statements at that point because, under the law, he needed the court's permission to release grand jury material to local law enforcement officials. Ulrich, who wanted to be able to tell the grand jury that murder charges would be filed in state court, asked Baird for assurances that he would file charges based on the statements. Baird declined, saying he could not make such a promise without seeing the statements and interviewing the witnesses. The two attorneys discussed preparing the paper work to seek the court's permission to transmit the grand jury material to Baird.

Del Clement and one of the eyewitnesses filed suit in the federal district court to prevent the transfer of the grand jury material to the Nodaway prosecutor. The judge denied the motion, and an appeal to the circuit court of appeals was denied on the grounds that by then the material had already been transferred.

After he formally received the material from Ulrich, Baird issued a statement saying he would decide on a course of action after he had fully reviewed the documents and interviewed the witnesses. One witness was the man who had given a statement within forty-eight hours of the killing, only to recant it the next day. The man had told the federal investigators that he witnessed the murder, but when Baird interviewed him again, he claimed to have seen nothing on the morning of July 10, 1981. Four different stories by the same witness—certainly not someone to base a prosecution on.

Reading the other witness's statement, Baird thought her identification of the killer seemed vague. When he reinterviewed her, she backed off completely. She admitted to having been in the area of the shooting, but said that she hadn't seen what had happened and simply could not identify the shooter. The FBI, she said, had leaned on her pretty hard, then taken her words and stretched them. Another pillar too weak to support a prosecution.

On November 11, 1982, Baird announced that the federal grand jury material did not contain "substantial new evidence" and that, therefore, no charges would be forthcoming. The case would remain open, of course, and he would review any new evidence that came to his attention. The feds were chagrined, and a few were angry.

Surely, thought the people of Skidmore, now the ordeal was over. Although the state had no statute of limitations on murder, the fact that the coroner's jury, the state grand jury, the federal grand jury, and the final prosecutorial review all had come up with nothing should be enough to convince those in the legal system that nobody in Skidmore was going to crack.

Meanwhile, the family harmony among the McElroy clan had disintegrated. Alice and Trena, the two women who had stuck together through all the trials during Ken's life and the various proceedings after his death, had severed their relationship. Alice, who had married Jim, remembered Ken saying he would give the old Chevy pickup to Juarez. According to Alice, Trena initially agreed to give the Chevy to Juarez, but later she changed her mind. Alice also thought the money Trena received for the photographs of Ken in *People* magazine was "blood money." One day about ten months after the killing, Trena called and said she had met a new man, and he didn't want her to have anything to do with the McElroys or people associated with them. Trena wouldn't be coming up to see Alice or her kids anymore, and Alice shouldn't come down or call. The four older girls got the same message from Trena's mother, Treva.

In the fall of 1982, fire swept the farmhouse on Valley Road where Ken McElroy had lived. Neighbors said they saw lightning strike the building in the middle of the night, but Tim said he didn't see anything from the small house down by the road. By morning, only a stone foundation, ashes, and a few outbuildings remained. There was no investigation because Sheriff Estes received no complaint, and as a matter of policy, he only investigated matters when somebody complained. The people in town speculated that one of the McElroys had probably burned the house to get rid of all the sightseers who had been poking around and taking pictures. The McElroys denied it, but they didn't seem too upset that the old house was gone.

Toward the end of 1982, the townspeople's fear of criminal proceedings abated, and the media coverage dropped off. With no developments to report, journalists contented themselves with updates every July 10.

On April 2, 1984, Trena married Howard J., a curly-haired roofer in his forties who had lived in the little town most of his life and had two children from a previous marriage.

But a rumor persisted that McFadin and Trena had married. Some people swore that they had even seen the announcement in one of the Kansas City papers. McFadin denied the story in a newspaper article, saying that he was already married and that "the rumors were probably started by someone wanting to cause me some aggravation." Nonetheless the idea of McElroy's widow and his lawyer consorting after his death had too much appeal to die easily.

51

On July 9, 1984, one day before the three-year statute of limitations would have expired, Trena filed lawsuits in state and federal courts against the city of Skidmore, Nodaway County, Danny Estes, Steve Peter, and Del Clement for the death of her husband. In federal court, she alleged that the defendants had knowingly violated Ken McElroy's civil rights under color of law. She sought $5 million in damages.

In state court she charged the defendants with the wrongful death of her husband and an assault upon herself. In this suit, she sought $6 million, including $2 million for loss of support, services, and companionship; $3 million in punitive damages because of the reckless and wanton nature of the acts; and $1 million for her own pain and suffering.

In both suits she alleged that the residents of Skidmore and Nodaway County held a meeting for the specific purpose of determining how to get rid of her husband; that Estes and Peter failed to do anything to stop the assault on her husband; and that Del Clement shot her husband in the head with a high-powered rifle and killed him.

The suits blindsided the community. The residents had thought their only worry was whether the criminal justice system was finished with them; the idea that Trena would sue them for killing her husband had never occurred to most of them. Whatever healing had taken place was instantly undone. Media veterans now, they knew the press would be back in full force—peering in every nook and cranny of the town, shoving microphones in people's faces, then misquoting them or taunting them when they said nothing. The tavern would fill with TV cameras, and curious strangers would inhibit normal discourse in the cafe. The farmers would be traipsing to courtrooms so lawyer McFadin could turn them upside down and inside out when they should be out in the fields on their tractors or combines.

The defendants' lawyers drafted answers to Trena's complaints and filed motions to dismiss the suits. In the state court, Monty Wilson disqualified himself from hearing the case. Naturally. Skidmore undertook to pay the cost of Mayor Steve Peter's legal defense, and the insurance company's lawyers represented the county and Sheriff Estes.

In February 1985, the defendants took Trena's deposition. Her testimony was a disaster; she was unsure of basic information, hesitated on simple matters, was wrong on others, and contradicted herself from one answer to the next. The one fact about which she never wavered, however, was the identification of Del Clement as her husband's killer. She claimed that she had lied under oath about the rape, arson, and molestation charges against McElroy, but insisted that she was telling the truth now. She would not be a good witness if the case came to trial.

Trena's deposition was kept in the clerk's office in Skidmore for anyone who wanted to stop in and read it. Those who read it had a good chuckle—she seemed not to have known what she was saying most of the time.

Sometime after her deposition, Trena decided she didn't want to proceed with her lawsuits. The turmoil would prevent her and her children from putting the killing behind them and getting on with their lives, which was what she wanted. She instructed McFadin to drop the lawsuits. He resisted mightily, arguing that he had a solid case, and that they stood a good chance of winning if they went to trial. Even without going to trial, he explained, their chances of a substantial settlement increased as they got closer to trial, which was still a long way off. He stressed the amount of money that would be available for Ken's children and the likelihood that the publicity and the trial would result in the prosecution of his killer. Despite all of McFadin's many persuasive skills, Trena was adamant in her demand that he drop the lawsuits. But she finally agreed to let him try to obtain an out-of-court settlement.

Most residents learned of the settlement as they had learned of the lawsuit, through the media. On September 5, 1985, the *Forum* announced that the suit had been settled but that, under the agreement, the parties could not release the terms. Townspeople had little trouble finding out the terms, however. Trena received a total of $17,500 from the defendants. Nodaway County paid $12,500, Del Clement paid $3,000, and the town of Skidmore paid $2,000.

The reasons for settling the claims were obvious: The amount paid was less than the legal fees for defending the suit would have been; witnesses would not have to testify yet again (some had done so three times already); the defendants would not have to face the possibility of losing; and the settlement would put the whole thing behind the community once and for all.

Although the townspeople understood the rationale, a good many were livid. You didn't pay money to get out of something unless you were guilty, they reasoned, and the settlement would be seen as an admission that the town had conspired to kill McElroy —and it hadn't. To many, the cost of the lawyers would have been worth it to ensure that Trena didn't get a damn penny. The sentiment ran so high that some people talked about impeaching the entire city council. Even today, finding a council member who recalls arguing in favor of the settlement is difficult.

As time passed, however, a new sentiment gradually took root: "Well, $17,500 wasn't too bad a price to pay to get rid of the bastard, was it?"

52

The theme of the 1985 Punkin' Show was "Farmers Feed the World." Co-chairman Cheryl Brown worked nonstop for weeks preparing for the three-day celebration. On Friday afternoon in a field next to the school, hundreds of people sat on the grass or on the tailgates of pickups and drank beer in the hot sun as they watched tractors pull a heavy iron sled over a dirt strip. Two women took admission for the first forty-five minutes, then quit and left with their beer to join the others. Evelyn Carter sold hamburgers and hot dogs at the Methodist church booth, while Del Clement served as the announcer for the tractor pull, calling out, "Next up!" and noting the distance pulled by each contestant. The table in front of him was bright with trophies.

A storm blew in, but the tractors kept pulling until the rain arrived and the electrical equipment had to be unplugged. The evening's events were moved to the cafeteria in the school basement. Then the electricity failed and the contest to choose Mr. and Miss Punkin' had to be held by flashlight. Finally, generators were located and hooked up, and the beauty pageant was held in an uncertain, wavering light. In the tavern, the customers drank by kerosene lamps.

Around eight o'clock, the storm ended. The sky cleared in the west, revealing a blue horizon streaked with fiery pinks and oranges. Overhead the sky loomed a billowing black, and silver lightning bolts streaked across the darkness.

The township garage had been decorated with colorful balloons and streamers for the dance. No alcohol could be sold, so people came with their own whiskey and beer. A popular country-rock group, Midnight Rain, was scheduled to play, but the electricity had not been restored. Emergency generators were brought in, but they made a terrible racket and the sound came and went. Around 11:30, the band gave up and went home. The hard core got down to serious drinking.

Early the next morning, the frog jumping contest was held in the little park uphill from the post office. Ten or fifteen young children had frogs of all shapes and sizes—mottled, wet frogs, fat brown frogs with bulging eyes, and little bitty green tree frogs—stuffed in jars and boxes. A circle eight-feet across and a smaller circle inside had been spray-painted on the grass. Two kids at a time put their frogs in the small circle and blew and hollered and slapped and stomped the ground behind their frogs to get them to jump to the outside circle. One freckled four-year-old girl got so mad when her big brown frog wouldn't move that she stomped on its head, then picked it up and threw it disgustedly into a shoebox.

The parade began at 10:30. The morning was beautiful—warm in the sun and cool in the shade, with a light breeze. Lining the streets were four or five hundred people—including lots of kids, lots of old people, and lots of clowns.

The procession came from the south and turned east onto Elm Street, heading downhill, a continuous stream of high school bands, Shriners' patrols with fat men driving tiny cars in small circles, beauty queens and attendants, seed dealers, members of the Skidmore Saddle Club, a wagon carrying a small girl dressed as a pumpkin, a Confederate soldier marching with a 109-year-old rifle, three fire trucks, Lions Club members sitting in a truck throwing candy to the children, a float supporting a huge globe made of papier-mâché and labeled "Farmers Feed The World," and various and sundry folks in cars and on horses. Guy Hamm, at ninety-eight the oldest farmer in town, was the grand marshal. He raised his hand slowly as he drove by, his gaunt face working a crinkly smile.

In front of Sumy's station sat a flatbed trailer holding a podium and chairs for the judges and luminaries. Behind the podium, dressed in stiff new blue jeans, a white cowboy shirt, a white straw cowboy hat, and polished cowboy boots, Greg Clement announced the parade, describing each participant and ad-libbing to the crowd. From a truck next to the speaker's platform, a video camera followed the procession as it passed in front of the post office and the tavern.

The Junior Queen Show was held that evening on the school grounds just east of the school building. From folding chairs and wobbly sets of wooden bleachers, two or three hundred spectators watched the contest unfold on a makeshift stage. The contestants were ten to thirteen years old, well-scrubbed pictures of flowering innocence. Wearing ribbons in their hair and colorful gowns with matching heels, the girls sat upright in chairs on the stage, hands in laps, looking prim and pretty, and smiling at their parents in the audience. Their hair sparkled in the bright lights.

In the final part of the contest, each girl walked to the podium and answered a question designed to demonstrate her poise and ability to think on her feet. The first girl was asked, "If you could be any animal in the world, what would it be, and why?"

The second finalist, a slender girl with shoulder-length chestnut hair, stood shyly in her sleeveless lavender gown before the podium.

"If you could change one thing in the world," she was asked, "what would it be, and why?"

She paused, looked out at the crowd and then down at her clasped hands, before saying, "There would be no more murders."

She looked up, her brown eyes clear and bright, her hair lifting gently in the evening breeze.

"Why?" the questioner prompted gently.

The answer slipped from the girl's lips, seeming to surprise even her with its clarity: "Because I have trouble sleeping at night."

Skidmore continues on its precarious economic path. Maurer's Hardware store closed a couple of years back because it could not compete with the discount stores in Maryville. Bo and Lois would like to sell the B & B Grocery, but so far there are no takers; chances are, they will simply close the store someday.

A few years after Bo was shot, the wounds in his neck became infected and had to be reopened. The doctor removed pieces of wadding that had lodged deep in his flesh. At seventy-eight, Bo has slowed some, and has occasional grouchy spells, but he still spends several hours every day cutting meat and grinding hamburger at the store. For Lois, "life goes on." She serves on the board of aldermen and works hard on community projects. While she has softened somewhat, she has not forgiven the criminal justice system for what happened to her family and the town.

The beautiful Methodist church with the stained glass windows was torn down last year. The walls were becoming unstable, and the congregation couldn't raise the money to repair the structure. The people built a simple one-story building in its place.

Del and Greg Clement sold the D & G Tavern in 1982. The couple who bought the bar renamed it the Robin's Nest, after the woman, but many people still refer to it as the D & G, or simply the pool hall. Although the tavern hosts occasional dances, with the music often provided by the Clement Brothers Band, the bar has never recovered its earlier place as a social center.

Cheryl Brown divorced her husband in July 1986 and moved

into Skidmore with her two daughters. She tended bar at the tavern until it closed for a few months when the new owners split up. Now she works at the Wal-Mart store in Maryville.

Sheriff Estes survived a challenge by Deputy Jim Kish in the 1984 Democratic primary, only to be defeated by David McClain in the general election. Estes now works as a city cop in Maryville.

Judge Monty Wilson was reelected circuit judge without opposition in 1982, but decided not to seek another term in 1988.

Q Goslee retired from farming in 1985, and now Kirby works the land under a sharing agreement with his parents. Margaret still serves as the Nodaway County probate clerk, and Kermit sells real estate and calls auctions in Maryville.

Red Smith quit bartending at the tavern not long after the killing and now works as a hand for a farmer west of town. Red seldom talks about McElroy or the killing, but, in the right mood, he will display the bullet that McElroy gave him from his pistol that afternoon in the tavern.

Richard Dean Stratton was promoted to sergeant in July 1982 and transferred to Bethany as the new zone commander. Every once in a while, his thoughts wander back to Ken McElroy and the murder. Still unsure of how it all came about, he wonders if there might not have been some way he could have headed it off.

David Baird was reelected prosecuting attorney without opposition in 1982 and 1986. Baird considers the killing an open case, and says that he would welcome any new evidence that could lead to a prosecution.

After five or six years of estrangement, Tim McElroy now gets along well with most of his neighbors, although he doesn't patronize the businesses in Skidmore. Regarding what happened to his brother, Tim feels "that was between him and the people of Skidmore."

Alice Wood separated from Jim and moved into an apartment in St. Joe with Juarez, Tonia, and Ken, Jr. Juarez married a St. Joe girl and had a son. The three of them lived with Alice until Juarez got a job as a construction worker. Ken, Jr., continued to have trouble in school; in Alice's view, the teachers had the attitude that since his dad was a troublemaker, he was one, too. Finally, Alice transferred him to another school.

Del Clement nearly died from injuries suffered one night when he was driving home from St. Joe and his pickup jumped a barrier on the interstate. The short, wiry, hot-tempered cowboy denies any involvement in the killing. "I was wrongly accused. That's all I have to say."

I sat with Trena and her husband, Howard, at a picnic table under tall cottonwood trees in a park on the edge of a small town in the Ozarks. The August air was hot and sticky, but the shade and a soft breeze made it barely comfortable. The woman across from me, dressed in a red blouse and dark slacks, seemed a little nervous. Her long blond hair had been cut short and it lay in waves close to her head, accentuating the roundness of her face. Her skin was soft and her complexion clear. Her striking gray-blue eyes were open and friendly.

At her request, we had met at a convenience store in this small town, not far from where she lived, and then driven to the park. I was late in arriving, having misjudged the narrow, hilly roads of southern Missouri, and feared that she might have left. I knew she had wanted to break the appointment the previous day. On the drive, I wondered whether I would find the abandoned child of the early years, the tough, hard woman of the McElroy years, or somebody totally different. McFadin had told me that she was still very loyal to Ken. She could break into tears at any minute, the lawyer had warned. From the beginning, I had felt she was perhaps the most fascinating, surely the most tragic, character in the story. Over the years, my feelings toward her had gone full circle, from sympathy and pity to distaste and distrust, several times.

Trena had not given any personal interviews in nearly five years, and at first she seemed shy, her answers tentative. Her voice was neither the shaky falsetto of the TV interviews and court testimony, nor the harsh monotone of Mrs. Ken McElroy. She spoke firmly, but gently, with the slightest lilt.

As we talked, she seemed to relax. Her stories of life with Ken McElroy seemed like distant memories, as if she were no longer connected to them. She told of the time the man came to the farm claiming he had been hired to kill Ken, and the time Ken went up to Pete Ward's porch to ask him about the affidavit. She described the day of the killing in great detail, noting her thoughts and emotions, and even drawing a diagram with the locations of everyone, including the killer.

"It's over for me," she said, looking me in the eye. "I don't really hurt anymore."

But she was still bitter, still certain that the entire community, including Sheriff Estes, was in on the killing. She believed their day would still come.

"I would never go back to Skidmore," she said. "People who would kill a man in broad daylight don't deserve to live. They would have shot him even if the kids were in the pickup. I could never live around people like that. It amazes me that Timmy can live among people that killed his brother."

She no longer sees Ken as the perfect human being. "He maybe shouldn't have done what he did, but they shouldn't have either."

When asked about her life today, Trena relaxed further and leaned forward on her elbows.

"I've changed," she said confidently. "I don't have to hold my head down to nobody anymore. I can look up at people and not have to worry about looking at the wrong person and getting in trouble over it."

She turned to her husband several times with affectionate looks or pats on the thigh. Thin, about average height, with slightly graying brown hair, Howard had a pleasant countenance. He was soft-spoken and genial.

"I've got a pretty good man right here," she said, smiling.

She still worries about her children. "They don't talk about Ken much anymore," she said softly. "Howard is real good to them, and they have a lot of love for him. They're starting to see him as their daddy. But once in a while, I can see one of them is hurting inside and not expressing it."

Her eyes filled with tears, and she looked away.

"When they grow up, what will they think of me? Will they think I didn't do enough to punish their father's killer?"

I asked her about the time she had pointed a shotgun at Kriss Goslee and Dave Dunbar in the drive outside the tavern. "Yes, I did it, but I never knew why. I was told to get the gun out and I did it. I always did as I was told." I thought of the incident when Trena and McElroy held guns on Beech Vogel, and McElroy explained to Beech that if his women didn't shoot when he said shoot, he would shoot them.

Trena explained that although her mother had always told her she had no idea where Trena's father was, Trena had heard in 1974 that he was still alive and had been paralyzed in a car accident. When Ken found out, he had taken her to the Social Security office in Kansas City to see if she had any money coming to her, but they couldn't track her father down.

She has had no contact with the McElroys since 1982. The price of her new life with Howard has been cutting all ties with her former one. Her life has always seemed to be separated into compartments.

Trena was full of questions. Had Alice married Jim? What did the farm look like? How was Timmy? Did Vicki get married? How many kids did she have? How was Juarez? (Ken had let him get away with too much, in her opinion.)

After three and a half hours, Howard turned sideways on the bench, a signal that he was ready to go.

She leaned forward slightly on the table. "I'm happy," she said. "The kids are happy. I love Howard.

"There's some things I could tell you, but I won't because of the kids. But, you know, I wish I had listened to Ginger and the others back then. It was a mistake to go back. I just had nowhere else to turn. If I had it to do over, he wouldn't be in my life."

She stood up, and the interview was over.

The south Missouri sun beat down on us as we walked back to our vehicles. She apologized for having given me mixed-up directions to the small town, and Howard described the quickest route to Kansas City.

"Have a nice trip back," Trena said. We shook hands, then she smiled and said good-bye. Howard was in the van waiting, and I watched for a moment as she walked away. After a few steps, she stopped and turned toward me. In the afternoon sunlight, her hair shone brightly above her red blouse.

"If you see Vicki," she said, "would you say hello to her for me?"

EPILOGUE
2006

Summer 2006

Twenty-five years have passed since Ken Rex McElroy was shot to death on the main street of Skidmore. No one has yet been charged with his murder. I often think that were it up to the citizens of Skidmore, McElroy would still be sitting slumped over the wheel in his Silverado in front of the D&G Tavern, his face jigsawed from the impact of the high-powered bullet. A reminder to all who passed that true justice is in the eye of the beholder.

I researched the story of the killing for three years in the mid-eighties. After *In Broad Daylight* was published in 1988, I returned to the town every couple of years. I had developed an odd sort of affection for the place and its citizens. I didn't believe the deep wound it suffered could heal without some sort of expiation, some act of contrition or acknowledgment, and yet I doubted it would ever happen. You never heard the word "murder" in reference to the incident, only "killing." Moral issues raised by the death were often answered with a single question: "What choice did we have?" As I drove the farm roads and knocked on doors, and approached strangers in bars and on their combines in the fields, notebook in hand, I didn't argue with them. I told the people who would give me a chance that I wasn't interested in the names of the killers. The better story was the "Why?"

of the whole thing. And so I never asked, straight out—Who killed Ken McElroy? Still, I listened to the whispering: There were three men—one, the primary shooter, fired first with a high-powered rifle; a second opened up with a .22; and a third brought out a shotgun, which was or wasn't fired. Or there were only two men, both with rifles.

It had been several years since my last visit when I drove into town in December 2005. I had come to spend time with the Goslees, the farm family who took me in, and other friends I had made during my years there. Driving into town on Highway V, under a canopy of tall maples and past small white houses, I felt again the stark isolation of the place. Skidmore was not on the road to anywhere.

I drifted down the hill, then pulled to a stop in front of a low brick building with a tin roof. It used to be Mom's Café; now it was Newton's Community Center. The building had been repainted and fixed up some, but the wide sidewalk in front of it was still cracked and broken. Up the street to the right was the tavern where McElroy had been sitting with his wife in the Silverado when he was shot. I thought back to my first day in town, over twenty years ago, when I had sat in my car here and tried to work up the courage to go in the café. The moment I entered, the voices of the farmers at the tables fell dead silent, as if somebody had switched off the sound system.

The town was dying. The high school had been torn down. The bank on the corner had closed a few years earlier. Across the street was the old post office, which now stood empty. The paint was peeling and a window was broken. By most accounts, the shooters had stood in front of or just a few feet west of the building. A cluster of 30.30 shells had been found by the curb in front of it. Newton's Corner, a gas station at the top of the hill, was also closed, and was fast falling into disrepair. I stopped in front of what used to be the B & B Grocery; it was shuttered, too, and had been for many years. On the dock in the back was where McElroy had shot Bo Bowenkamp in the neck with a shotgun, leaving him there to bleed to death. People now bought their groceries in Maryville.

The Legion Hall across the street, where the men had met the morning of the killing to talk about what to do with McElroy, was closed up and tattered and peeling. The wooden bench at the north end of it, where old-timers used to sit and watch the comings and goings of the town, was broken and crooked. There wasn't anybody in the streets now, I saw. The town was uptight about another grisly murder that had recently occurred in its midst. Last year, in a house a couple of blocks from where I stood, a stranger had strangled a young pregnant woman to death and cut open her womb and taken her baby. The mother's name was Bobbi Jo Stinnet: I remembered her as a little girl playing in the aisles of the grocery store, where her mother, Becky, worked as a clerk. Becky had found her daughter in a pool of blood. She said her stomach looked like it had "exploded." The media has descended on the town once again. Many of the articles recalled the shooting of Ken Rex McElroy. People were quoted as wondering if maybe there was some sort of a curse on Skidmore. The town was taking it badly, I knew. By pure chance, I had arrived in town the day before a memorial service for Bobbi Jo was to be held.

The town just wanted to be left alone, like it always had, I thought, as I drove east to the Goslee farmhouse. The problem with being left alone was that it provided fertile ground for the likes of McElroy to spring up from. McElroy, for his part, had been simply trying to right the wrongs that had been done him and his family by the rich farmers. He hadn't done too badly, when you looked at the hell his death had brought down on the town. McElroy would be 73 now, but I doubted he would have survived prison, which was where he was headed. One lawman, who had lots of dealings with McElroy, saw what happened that July day as a form of suicide by vigilante. McElroy knew they were holding a meeting in town about him, and he went in unarmed as a provocation. Personally, I had always thought it was his ultimate bluff. Maybe the only one he didn't pull off.

In the evening, I met a few friends at the Palms Bar in Maryville, the county seat. I had logged lots of hours in this place, listening to drunks talk and brag, and getting drunk myself. I used to write notes to myself in the bathroom about what was said—one night the discussion turned to the murder weapons and what had happened to them—and then stay up until dawn in my second-floor room of the farmhouse drunkenly typing up the notes.

The conversation in the bar turned to the upcoming twenty-five-year anniversary. One fellow, who was in the tavern when the shooting began, allowed as how he didn't think Del Clement—the person identified consistently by Trena as the man on the 30.30—had killed McElroy. He refused to say why. A local seed dealer had told me the same thing earlier in the day. According to him, Del had had a rifle in his hand when someone called out, "Shoot the sonofabitch!" When Del hesitated, another man took the rifle from his hands and fired. In all my years on this case, I had never heard a name other than Del's seriously mentioned as the primary shooter. I had never been interested in proving Del's guilt, partially because I had always thought Trena's statement spoke convincingly for itself. But what if Trena had been mistaken? Who had killed Ken McElroy?

I stopped into the prosecutor's office the next day. David Baird, who was three years out of law school when he successfully prosecuted McElroy for shooting the grocer, and who had also failed to indict anyone for McElroy's murder, was still in office. As amiable as ever, his hair a little thinner, he readily—and to my shock—agreed to my request to look into the investigative files on the McElroy killing. No one outside of law enforcement, as far as I knew, had ever seen the files. I was particularly anxious to read the statement of Frankie Aldridge, the witness who had, I had heard, identified the killer or killers within days of the shooting and later recanted. Baird sent me to the sheriff's office, where the official files were kept.

Sheriff Ben Espey had been in office for ten years. He had obtained some renown for his handling of the Bobbi Jo Stinnet case. The baby was found alive and well in the arms of a woman in a small town in Kansas less than twenty-four hours after the murder. When I asked to see the McElroy files, he glumly told me there weren't any. In his first day in office, he had looked for them, and they were nowhere to be found. At my request, Espey had the storage room searched, but no files were found.

The remembrance service for Bobbi Jo began at 7 p.m. in the park just west of the old post office on the main street. In the center of the park, candles had been placed around a brick memorial. Thirty or forty chairs had been lined up in front of a gazebo, which had been hung with Christmas tree lights. It was a bitterly cold night, barely 15 degrees above, and the wind pushed it well below zero.

The television satellite trucks, antennas poking up into the black winter sky, were lined up across the street. The print reporters circulated warily on the edge of the crowd, trolling for a useful comment. The hostility in town toward the media was palpable. In the tavern earlier, I had heard one fellow curse the media—he argued they should all be run out of town. Cheryl Huston (Brown), who, along with her friend Carla, had organized the event, had assigned several locals the sole task of keeping the media away from Becky when she arrived. This was part of the legacy of Ken McElroy, I knew. In 1981, his death had been labeled a vigilante murder, and now, twenty-five years later, the papers were wondering if there wasn't something still evil in the town. The gazebo sat not thirty yards from where the shooters had stood on that hot, bright morning.

Candles were passed among the crowd. I took one and cupped it for warmth. A small elderly lady pulled me aside and reminded me that I had had dinner at her house years ago. I asked her what she thought should happen to Bobbi Jo's killer. "She should be forgiven," the lady said kindly. "But she should die for what she did."

A brilliant rim of a full moon slipped over the top of the post office, just as a car pulled up to the curb. Two women stepped out, and were escorted to seats in the front row. The baby's birthday, I realized, would always be the day of her mother's death. The service was short. Carla asked the media to please leave the family alone, Cheryl recounted the terrible pain suffered by the family and the town from the killer's selfish act, and Sheriff Espey recounted in detail how the case had been solved. The crowd clapped loudly when he stepped down, as if to say, That was how the law was supposed to handle things—rather than how it had when it let McElroy run wild all those years.

The moon, high in the sky now, illuminated our ghostly walk across the street to the community center for a reception. I went in, and wandered over to the table where pictures of Bobbi Jo and the "miracle baby" stood. In one photo, the baby was wearing a sundress and hat, and she had an amused smile on her face, like "What's the big deal?" It was a big deal that she was alive at all. The killer had used a kitchen knife to cut her mother open, and the baby had suffered only a minor scratch on her head. I erased from my mind the image of a bloody-handed woman lifting a baby from the womb of its dead mother. It seemed more evil than anything McElroy had ever done.

The sheriff and his deputies stood on one side of the room; the few reporters that had braved the door hovered by the buffet table. I made my way over to Becky, who was small with long blond hair reaching the middle of her back, and who was surrounded by friends. I slipped through the cordon, and mumbled words of condolence. She said she remembered me well, and thanked me for coming. I went back outside into the cold.

I left town in the early morning a few days later. A thick, white fog lay over the land as I drove down the drive of the Goslee farmhouse. I paused on the main street for a few minutes waiting to see if it would lift. The heavy grayness collected in the troughs between the steep hills, and the roads were narrow and twisty and harbored several one-way bridges. I made a few notes in my book about what I'd learned: Trena had gotten divorced and remarried; one of McElroy's boys had ended up in jail for pulling a knife in a bar; Cheryl, diagnosed with PTSD, had been married and divorced three times; lawyer McFadin, ill with heart disease, diabetes, and neuropathy, was practicing law in Gallatin, a small town to the east; Pete Ward, one of the few men in town to stand up to McElroy, had died. Lots of people had died. The town itself was falling apart. In addition to everything else, an outsider had been buying up houses in town and using them as junkyards. There were a lot of riff-raff moving in because of depressed housing prices. Skidmore might hang on for a while, but it would never outlive its reputation as the town that shot the bully to death on its main street; and, now, the town where a young woman had been murdered and cut open for her baby.

The temperature had climbed to ten degrees above by the time I swung north out of town. The fog was lifting over the fields. Frost glazed the barbed wire and the tops of the fence posts. The wind had blown the snow into ridges on the edge of the field, and tall grasses sheathed in ice were bent over like ballet dancers. I passed the road leading to the Clement ranch. Skidmore would never give up the killers, I thought. It would mean all the suffering had been for nothing.

Murder—whether it's of a mother to get her baby, or a bully to end his reign of terror—is still murder. The fact that this murder, conducted almost in a public forum, hadn't been cracked in twenty-five years remained probably the most compelling fact about the crime. I had run into this wall around the killers in the eighties, and I had gone around it. But now doubt had been raised in my mind about the identity of the killers, and the investigative files were missing. I wanted to see what those witnesses on the street that day had told the officers; I wanted to see what Frankie Aldridge had said in his statement. And what about the second, and possibly third, shooters? Although the official files in the sheriff's office were missing, Baird had maintained copies of the NOMIS reports, which contained all the interviews. After much pushing and negotiation, he and Sheriff Espey agreed to turn them over to me. As I suspected, they contained a wealth of information about the murder, the murderers, and the witnesses.

In a statement to the police, given only a few hours after the killing, and with blood still on her arms and blouse, Trena unhesitatingly identified Del Clement as the shooter. She gave oral and written statements to officers in the State Patrol headquarters in St. Joe. She was clear beyond a shadow of a doubt that the man who had shot her husband was Clement. She knew that he worked as an auctioneer and owned the tavern with his brother. She could describe him physically, how he was dressed, the type of rifle he used, and the color of the truck he pulled the rifle from. Her story of what happened in the bar, and later as she and Ken left, matched up in most particulars with the statements of others present. She described what happened after she and Ken left the tavern.

> TRENA: Got in the truck and here they all came out all these people came out . . . We turned around and looked and there was Del Clement going across the street to his pickup
>
> POLICE: Who was? Del Clement?
>
> TRENA: Yea. And he got his gun out, it was either a 30-30 (?) or a .357 magnum, I don't know for sure which one it is, either one.
>
> POLICE: Or a 357 magnum
>
> TRENA: Yea. Lot of his are rifle type. And I turned around talked to Mac. They've got a gun out there when I said that the gun went off and I turned around to tell my husband what was going on and the whole town was around they shot three or four more times they kept on shooting and one guy come over there . . . cowboy hat said the trouble is, you'll get shot too . . .
>
> POLICE: Del Clement, he went over to his pick-up.
>
> TRENA: Yea. A red brand new pickup, it was just across the street just before the post office.
>
> POLICE: OK. It was by the Post Office, right?
>
> TRENA: Yea, right in front of the Post Office . . .
>
> POLICE: Did he come walking back towards your truck?

TRENA: No. He got it out of his truck and walked back toward the tailgate of his truck, then he started to shoot.

Trena stated that Clement was no more than 50 feet away when he fired. After the first shot, she looked at Ken and saw the hole in his cheek, and then looked back around. Clement just "kept on shooting," at least four times.

POLICE: Now you can say definitely that Del fired the first shot.

TRENA: Yea, I seen him do it. I seen him get that gun out there, that's how come I know what kind of gun it is, cause he had it up in the air. I thought he was just going to act like a fool and I told Ken they had a gun out there . . . The gun was lever action.

POLICE: Lever action, you can say that he definitely fired that first shot, is there any possibility

TRENA: He was still holding the gun after the first shot cause I turned around.

POLICE: He wasn't attempting to put it back in the truck?

TRENA: No

POLICE: He was still standing back of the pickup

TRENA: Yea . . . I don't know if it's his pickup or not but it is a brand new red pickup

POLICE: Deep red

TRENA: Yea.

After reading her statements, I wondered if Trena could distinguish Del from among the three other Clement brothers (Greg, Scott, and Royce). They were all about the same size and usually wore jeans, cowboy boots and cowboy hats. Maybe she had the brothers mixed up. Several facts indicated, however, that she definitely knew who Del was. She said in her statement that, while she and Ken were sitting at the bar, Red Smith, the bartender, was playing a video game across the room. When Del came in the tavern, he told Red to quit the game and come over behind the bar because they had business to attend to. Red told me, and is quoted in the book as saying, that he was playing a video game with some kids at the front door when Del came in and said, "You better be behind the bar. There's going to be a bunch in here." Trena, Del and Greg Clement all told police that Del went behind the bar to help Red serve drinks. No one placed either Greg, Scott or Royce behind the bar. I think Trena knew who Del Clement was.

Trena told police that Del walked to a brand-new red pickup in front of the post office. Del told police that he was driving a Pontiac, which he parked up the street from the post office. Del also told police another interesting fact: a man by the name of Gary Dowling was driving a "new red 81 GMC Searia (sp) 1/2 t 4 × 4 bright red P/U, it was parked in front of the post office on the n. side of the street." Trena made it clear she didn't know if the red truck was Del's or not, only that he took the rifle from it. Both Del and Trena said that the truck was bright, red and new, and parked in front of the post office.

Gary Dowling was a farmer who, at the time of the killing, lived on the same road west of town as Del Clement. He was one of the four men who had earlier signed the affidavit saying McElroy had brought a gun into the tavern in violation of a court order. On July 10 he was scheduled to testify to that effect in the hearing to revoke McElroy's bond, and McElroy knew that. According to Del Clement, Dowling was contacting people and asking them to come to the meeting in the Legion Hall the morning of the 10th to form a caravan to escort him and the other signers to Bethany, where the hearing was to be held. From the moment I hit town, I had heard Dowling's name as one of the possible shooters. I didn't mention him in the book because he had neither been identified publicly nor to me privately by an eyewitness to the shooting.

Frankie Aldridge, who worked at Sumy's gas station at the top of the hill, gave a statement saying that that he was at work when he heard a shot, saw Jack Clement walking Trena to the bank, and that was all he saw. The next day, however, he gave a different statement at NOMIS headquarters in Maryville. The statement says that the first shot was followed by a rapid series of explosions.

> Mr. Aldrige [sic] said that he then observed two men that he knows as Del Clement and Gary Dowling standing on the north side of the street across from the D & G bar and in the area of the post office. When Mr. Aldrich [sic] observed Del Clement and Gary Dowling they were both armed with what he thought were rifles and both men were aiming at Ken McElroy's truck. Mr. Aldrich stated that he then observed Clement get into a blue pontiac or buick and drive east on Highway 113 in a "big hurry." He also observed Gary Dowling get into a red pickup truck and drive east on Highway 113 in the same manner as Clement. Mr. Aldrich stated that he then saw Jack Clement helping Mrs. McElroy up the street and into the bank.

In a statement written out by a trooper and signed by Aldridge, Aldridge gave a little more detail:

> I heard a "boom" which I thought was an M-80 firecracker. It sounded like it came from the east. I looked up, east, and I saw Del Clement and Gary Dowling holding guns on the north side of HWY 113, Dell [sic] aiming the gun at the back of McElroy's truck. I saw Gary aiming his gun in the direction of McElroy's truck also. Gary was in the area just west of the post office next to his truck. Del was standing east of his blue pontiac or buick diesel in the area of the post office.

The next day, however, Aldridge reappeared at headquarters with an attorney—the same one that, strangely enough, represented Del Clement—and recanted his statement, saying he had given it under stress and duress.

The police took Dowling off the combine in the field, arrested and cuffed him and took him to Maryville. According to his statement, Dowling first said that when he left the tavern and started walking up the hill he heard shots fired and fell to the ground, covering his head for protection. He didn't see anyone with a weapon, before or after the shooting. Later, in a pre-polygraph interview, when the officer told Dowling they had information that he had a shotgun in his truck at the time of the shooting, Dowling admitted that upon hearing the shots fired he "crouched down to the left rear of his truck, opened the driver's door and removed a shotgun from the truck but upon doing this, the shots ceased and he placed the shotgun back into the cab of the truck, behind the seat." Dowling then told the officer that there were three males shooting and he knew who they were, but wouldn't say. Dowling refused to take the polygraph test.

Del Clement denied any role in the killing. In one statement, he said he was walking out of the tavern when he heard the shots and he lay down in the doorway until it was over. In another, he said he saw McElroy getting shot as he walked out of the tavern.

A state trooper involved in the investigation told me in the mid-eighties that he was absolutely convinced from everything he knew that the two shooters were Del Clement and Gary Dowling. In fact, he never heard any other names associated with the shooting. Another trooper, not involved in the investigation but very much aware of the situation, confirmed that the only names he had heard mentioned in law enforcement as the shooters were Del Clement and Gary Dowling. The only two driver's license photos contained in the NOMIS files were of Del Clement and Gary Dowling.

Months later, Aldridge repeated his identification of Del Clement as the shooter to FBI agents, but when Baird called him in for an interview he once again recanted the identification. A woman—probably one of the women in the bank—also gave a statement to the FBI, one which we can assume matched Aldridge's and Trena's identification of Del Clement. When Baird interviewed her, however, he found her statement to be so vague as to be of little or no value.

There remain lots of unanswered questions: Were there two or three shooters? If three, who was the third? Was a shotgun fired? How did Aldridge get turned around so quickly? (It's unlikely he went home that night and told someone that he had identified the killers to the police, so one can't help but wonder if someone in law enforcement leaked the word.) And how did he come to be represented by the attorney for Del Clement, the prime suspect from the very beginning? (According to one statement, the same attorney also represented another potential witness, the postmaster, who after initially agreeing to a polygraph, refused to take one, on advice of counsel). Who was the woman who identified the killer(s) to the FBI agents? What happened to the weapons?

The files clear up certain things about the shooting. Although there is some disagreement, the consensus of the men there that day seems to be that about sixty people walked from the Legion Hall and into the tavern. After the crowd followed McElroy and Trena from the bar, about eight to ten people remained, which means that roughly 50 people went out the door. Which also means that there were approximately 50 people who were in a position to see some or all of what happened.

Everyone agrees that when they left the building they turned west, or up the hill. (Except Del Clement, who said he walked east down the hill to the restaurant, which is odd because that would have put him in the line of fire). Most of the men apparently stopped either on the sidewalk or within one or two car spaces west of McElroy's truck, and stared at him. This would have put the men almost directly across the street from the post office. If the shooters were either directly in front of the post office, or just to the west of it, they would have been within 40 to 50 feet of the men on the sidewalk, at most. The witnesses in the street would have been even closer to the shooters. In other words, the shooters would have been only fifteen or so yards to the left, or west, of the witnesses, when the firing began. Maybe the witnesses didn't see the shooters take the guns from the vehicles, but certainly when the shots sounded fifteen yards to their left they would have glanced in that direction to determine the source and figure out how not to get hit. There were from five to eight shots fired, in succession. Even if they ducked during the shooting, they would have looked up when it stopped, if for no other reason than to make sure it was over. And most likely they would have seen the guns being put away.

The men at Sumy's station at the top of the hill, where Aldridge was standing, could not have missed the shooting. They would have been no more than 30 yards away from the red truck. If they were watching the scene, staring at McElroy's truck or the men gathered just up the hill from it, when the shooting started, which seems likely, they could barely have missed seeing the shooters a few degrees to the left.

One thing is clear—in spite of all the witnesses, there will be no prosecution unless and until at least one of the men comes forward and tells the story of the killing under oath.

Assuming that the NOMIS files are complete, one can argue that the investigation was not impressive. Despite the almost immediate identification of Del Clement by Trena, he was not interviewed until the following day. A search warrant was never sought for his house or vehicle. Neither was a search warrant sought or issued for Gary Dowling's house or vehicle. Pete Ward, one of the key players in the drama, was never interviewed. And neither were Scott or Royce Clement, who Trena placed inside the bar just prior to the shooting. It almost seems that the officers were so sure of the identity of the killers that when they ran into the stone wall—I didn't see anything, and if I did I wouldn't tell you—they simply hung it up. NOMIS disbanded ten days after the killing, and since then little appears to have been done at the local level to bring McElroy's killers to justice. The Patrol followed up a few leads in 1983, and occasional leads filter into the sheriff's office, but they don't amount to anything. No one has been out trying to solve the case for twenty years. One thing seems certain: not a person in town that day offered aid or assistance to McElroy as he lay dying in his truck. No one stopped by the truck to check his vital signs, and the ambulance that finally came to the scene an hour after the shooting was a result of a call from McElroy's lawyer to the sheriff's office.

All this, of course, leaves the underlying moral issue of the killing unresolved. I have never settled the matter for myself. As a lawyer and an advocate of the justice system, as a citizen of a country committed to the rule of law, I know it is a highly dangerous thing to excuse murder, no matter what the reason. Due process means only the state can decide when a man's behavior warrants his death. Another part of me is simply curious to know what actually happened on the street. If an eyewitness required a promise of eternal silence in exchange for telling me what went down that morning, I would give the promise, and live up to it.

My sympathy has always lain with the townspeople. When the law failed, two or three renegades decided to take care of the problem on their own, leaving the town forever cast as a bunch of vigilantes. Was it right to kill Ken Rex McElroy? If it was wrong, would it somehow even the moral scales to prosecute his killers? July 10 was a bad moment in time, when all seemed lost, when there seemed no choice. The killing was an impulsive act, brought on by ongoing, unrelenting fear. You might call it the battered town syndrome. It's not good to have it hanging out there, though, unresolved. The town can't get on its way.

As for the killers, I wonder what goes through their heads when they drive through town, past the spot where they stood with their rifles, past the spot where McElroy sat dead in his truck. I wonder if they feel a tiny thread of regret or guilt—lots of kids lost their father that morning, after all. Finally, I wonder if they worry. There is no statute of limitations on murder. Even now, it would take only one guy out of many to have a change of heart. A death bed confession, say, or a conversion to the faith of a God who viewed lying under oath as a serious sin.

At the remembrance service for Bobbi Jo, I asked two girls, age 6 and 8, if they knew of Ken McElroy. Oh, yes, they both said. I asked what they had heard.

"He was a bad guy, who bullied lots of people," the older of the two said.

"He was shot here in town," the younger one joined in. "Right over there." She pointed at the tavern.

"He had it coming," the older one said.

It's hard to argue with that, I thought.